Pétain

Also by Charles Williams

Adenauer: The Father of the New Germany
The Last Great Frenchman: A Life of General de Gaulle
Bradman: An Australian Hero

Pétain

How the Hero of France Became a Convicted Traitor and Changed the Course of History

Charles Williams

PÉTAIN

First published in 2005 by
PALGRAVE MACMILLAN™
175 Fifth Avenue, New York, N.Y. 10010 and
Houndmills, Basingstoke, Hampshire, England RG21 6XS
Companies and representatives throughout the world.

PALGRAVE MACMILLAN is the global academic imprint of the Palgrave Macmillan division of St. Martin's Press, LLC and of Palgrave Macmillan Ltd. Macmillan® is a registered trademark in the United States, United Kingdom and other countries. Palgrave is a registered trademark in the European Union and other countries.

ISBN 1–4039–7011–4

Library of Congress Cataloging-in-Publication Data

Williams, Charles, 1933–
    Pétain / by Charles Williams.
        p. cm.
    Includes bibliographical references and index.
    ISBN 1–4039–7011–4 (alk. paper)
     1. Pétain, Phillippe, 1856–1951. 2. Heads of state—France—Biography.
 3. Marshals—France—Biography. 4. France. Armâé—Biography. 5. France—History—
    20th century. 6. France—Politics and government—1940–1945. I. Title.

DC342.8.P4W55 2005
944.081'6'092—dc22
[B]   2005040550

A catalogue record for this book is available from the British Library.

Design by Newgen Imaging Systems (P) Ltd., Chennai, India.

First edition: October 2005

10 9 8 7 6 5 4 3 2 1

Printed in the United States of America.

*For Justin and Caroline,
Tim, Katharine, Peter,
Eleanor and Hannah*

Contents

List of Illustrations ix

Acknowledgments. x

Introduction: On the Wrong Side of History 1

One
    "The Son of My Sorrow". 5

Two
    Choosing the Saber Over the Book. 11

Three
    Saint-Cyr: Lessons in War 18

Four
    The Dreyfus Affair 28

Five
    Love, Retirement, and a New Beginning. 36

Six
    The Dogs of War. 43

Seven
    "The German is the Enemy". 54

Eight
    The Battle of Verdun. 63

Nine
    Hero of France and Commander-in-Chief 75

Ten
    Total War 89

Eleven
    Pétain, Architect of Victory. 98

Twelve
    Nini, the Wife Next Door. 108

Thirteen
    Saving the Spanish in Morocco. 116

Fourteen
    The Politics of Peace 123

Fifteen
    The Hollow Years 130

Sixteen
    The Unpopular Front 138

Seventeen
    Ambassador to Spain 147

Eighteen
    Defeat 155

Nineteen
    The Road to Vichy 164

Twenty
    The Royal "We" 172

Twenty-one
    The Germans, Darlan, and the Jewish Question 184

Twenty-two
    The Specter of Communism 195

Twenty-three
    The Trap 204

Twenty-four
    The Collapse of the House of Cards 211

Twenty-five
    Occupied France 220

Twenty-six
    Vichy: The Final Act 228

Twenty-seven
    Reluctant Flight 236

Twenty-eight
    The Marshal of France Defends His Honor 243

Twenty-nine
    Prison for Life 260

    Notes 272

    Bibliography 285

    Index 291

List of Illustrations

1. The young officer
2. With Joffre at Verdun (*Keystone*)
3. With Primo de Rivera, Tetuan, 1925
4. Decorated by King Alfonso XIII (*Keystone*)
5. Pétain (center) and de Gaulle (behind Pétain) in 1926 (*Giraudon/Bridgeman Art Library*)
6. The handshake at Montoire (with Ribbentrop in the background) (*Hulton Archive*)
7. Pétain and Darlan in Marseille, January 1941 (*Bettman/Corbis*)
8. Pétain and Darlan with Franco at Montpellier, February 1941 (*Keystone*)
9. With Göring in December 1941 (*Keystone*)
10. Leahy taking leave of Pétain, April 1942 (*Keystone*)
11. Paris, April 1944 (*Keystone*)
12. The trial: Isorni pleads (*AFP*)

*   *   *

Photosection appears between pages 146 and 147.

Acknowledgments

In the course of this endeavor I have benefited from the wise advice and detailed knowledge of so many that it is difficult to know how even to begin to acknowledge them properly. My main guides as the book has progressed have been Philip Bell and Nicholas Atkin, both with the greatest patience for my various stupidities as well as an acute perception of where I was wandering into dangerous historical territory. Martin Alexander has been kind enough to read my final draft and make lifesaving corrections. Christopher Arnander and Jane Nissen have read through the proofs with the greatest diligence. I owe them all more than I can say—debts that I am afraid I will never be able to repay—while accepting, as is appropriate, that any errors which have slipped through the fine mesh of their scholarly net are my responsibility and mine alone.

Others have helped on specific topics. Audrey Bonnery, Agnes Ooms and Jaime Alvarez have been indefatigable in research on my behalf, respectively in France, Germany and Spain. Mia Stewart-Wilson has been a brilliant researcher of pictures; Renata Propper has been kind enough to write a penetrating analysis of Pétain's handwriting; Matthew Buck has been wholly persuasive on the subject of the Pétain–de Grandmaison alleged disagreements in their lectures at the École de Guerre; Hugh Thomas has been full of information about Spain, and unsparing in the attention he has given to my questions; Martin Gilbert has given me the benefit of his great knowledge of Winston Churchill; Julian Jackson has been most helpful on the events of May 1940 and the Vichy period; Gerd Krumeich and Holger Afflerbach have contributed to my understanding of Germany in the First World War; Maurice Vaïsse has been most informative on French military history; Père Montagnes of the Couvent des Dominicains in Toulouse and Père Duval of the Couvent Saint Jacques have been most helpful on Pétain's education; and Richard Griffiths has followed up his earlier book with some generous suggestions to me. My thanks to all of them.

Others have helped me with vital pieces of information or by pointing to sources, or just friendly encouragement: Robert Boyce, Jean Crouzat, Philippe Denis, Piers Dixon, Alexei Filitov, Jonathan Haslam, Ken Morgan, Jacques Le Groignec, Denis Lesage, Gilles Nolleau, Felipe Propper, Hew Strachan. I must also record the unstinting and friendly help I have always received from the House of Lords library, in particular from David Jones, Shorayne Fairweather and Caroline Auty. Sarah Tyack and William Spencer at the National Archives in Kew have gone beyond the call of duty in assisting me to unearth hitherto ignored primary material, as have the staff of the Archives Nationales in Paris and the staff of the Service Historique des Armées de Terre at Vincennes. Finally, I thank Richard Beswick and Stephen Guise of Time Warner Books, Airié Stuart of Palgrave Macmillan, Andrew Wylie and Tracy Bohan of the Wylie Agency for their enthusiasm and efficiency in bringing the ship safely into port.

The book is dedicated to my step-family, Justin and Caroline and their children Tim, Katharine, Peter, Eleanor and Hannah, in the hope that their love of France will not be diminished by my efforts in French history. It goes without saying that none of this could have happened without the full-hearted and loving support of their mother and grandmother—in other words, my wife.

Introduction: On the Wrong Side of History

"Quoiqu'on puisse penser de Vichy c'est tout de même quelqu'un"

It is always a mistake to end up on the wrong side of history. History, as has often been remarked (not least by Adolf Hitler), is written by the winners. Winners, of course, tend to emphasize their own virtues and the wickedness of their opponents. Outright losers, on the other hand, are not allowed—or are in no position—to write history (nobody, for instance, has heard much from the Hittites defeated by Ramses the Great, from the Persians defeated by Alexander, or the Gauls defeated by Julius Caesar). But if, having lost the battles, the losers end up on the winning side of the war, the history they write inevitably attempts to mitigate their embarrassment at their initial defeat by fierce attacks on those they hold responsible. France is an illustration of the general rule. In the First World War, she was one of the winners, and history was written accordingly. Pétain, for instance, was a great figure in 1918—a Marshal of France and the "Victor of Verdun." In the Second World War, however, she was a loser—but a loser who ended on the winning side. Pétain was deemed to have borne the main responsibility for the collapse of 1940 and was duly condemned for treason. Again, history was written in a corresponding manner. His reputation thus went up and down, like a float, on the consecutive waves of French adulation in 1918 and French excoriation in 1945. Since the second wave came after the first, and since there was no third wave, his reputation has never recovered. He has ended up on the wrong side of history.

Pétain was born into a dysfunctional peasant family in the north of France in the early years of the second half of the nineteenth century. As a boy, he was lucky enough, after losing his mother, to be nurtured by a grandmother and two clerical uncles. For an intelligent peasant lad of the day there were only two careers which could lift him out of the drudgery of subsistence farming—the Church and the army. The Church soon lost its attraction, and the army was his choice. Coming as he did from a peasant background, he fitted uneasily into the officer class of the French Army which he aspired to join. In fact, throughout his life, although he was able to command obedience, respect and even devotion among his juniors in rank, he made no true, long-lasting male friends. Nor was he good at forming permanent relationships with women, though he was blessed with inordinately good looks—piercing blue eyes, blond hair, smooth and slightly babyish skin—and an apparently insatiable sex drive.

At the onset of the First World War Pétain, ambitious as he undoubtedly was, found himself at a dead end. He was due to retire in 1916 at the age of 60 and had set about finding a suitable place for his retirement. Circumstances intervened, and within four years he found himself, almost to his own surprise and certainly to the surprise of his more aristocratic colleagues, a Marshal of France and Commander in Chief of the French Army. In fact, there is little doubt that, had Pétain died in the 1920s, he would even now be celebrated as a great French military hero. France had borne the main brunt of the slaughter on the Western Front during the First World War and had come out as winners. Pétain, thanks to the defense of Verdun in 1916 and the reconstruction of the French Army after the mutinies of 1917, would quite rightly have been rewarded with all the honors France had to offer. Furthermore, had he been allowed to follow his plan in November 1918 to drive into Germany to pursue and destroy a defeated German army which had retreated in good order, he might even have occupied a higher place than the much lauded Marshal Foch.

In May 1940, however, France (and Britain, for that matter) suffered an overwhelming military defeat. Pétain, having witnessed the early stages of the defeat from his embassy in Spain, came to the conclusion that Britain would soon collapse and made his dispositions accordingly: an armistice would be followed by a peace treaty, and France would take its place in a Europe dominated by Germany. It was far from an isolated view. Indeed, there are few, even now, who do not recognize that in mid-1940 the odds were very firmly in favor of a German victory—sooner rather than later.

In the end, Germany lost the war in Europe. Yet the story of winners and losers was far from over. Charles de Gaulle, who had fought on the losing side in May, took off to London in June 1940 without any immediate prospect of success—and ended up on the winning side in 1945. Even so, he could hardly claim to have been victorious (although, of course, he would). In truth, the Second World War in Europe was won by the Soviets, the Americans and the British. Up until 1943 the contribution of Free France, or "Fighting France" as it was by then called, was negligible; and after that, it was no more than peripheral. Nonetheless, de Gaulle and his followers had the undying distinction of saving what remained of France's honor. But the shame of defeat still remained. To help wipe it out the official propaganda machine held the losers of May 1940 up to obloquy—conveniently forgetting that almost all of those who were most vocal, including de Gaulle, had been themselves in one way or another among those who had lost.

The attempt to wipe the slate clean was fully illustrated in Pétain's trial. As a judicial event it was little more than ridiculous. The main burden of complaint, and the one on which de Gaulle laid particular emphasis, was not what had happened at Vichy but that Pétain in person was responsible for the ignominious "capitulation" of 1940—in other words, responsible for France's shame. He was convicted of treason mainly on that count. The losers of 1940 had turned into winners—and had written an almost predictable script.

Vichy was never going to be easy to deal with in the postwar period. Of course, many—perhaps most—people in France claimed by then to have been members of the Resistance (even though their participation might previously have escaped everybody else's notice). But de Gaulle was contemptuous of the Resistance. In fact, one of his first acts was to disband it, telling its leaders to go back home and do a proper job. Moreover, both Pétain and de Gaulle—de Gaulle was, after all, Pétain's protégé in the 1920s—shared most of the opinions of the French military of the time. Both were suspicious of politicians, fervently nationalist and even more strongly anticommunist. Nobody can say what de Gaulle would have made of the National Revolution, but President Roosevelt, for one, certainly thought that de Gaulle was authoritarian almost to the point of fascism. De Gaulle thought that the whole development of Vichy was easily traced to Pétain's fundamental mistake, the signature of the Armistice in 1940. The fate of the Jews—the dreadful conditions of deportation; the horrors of the holding camps at Compiègne and Drancy; the dreadful roundups in Unoccupied France, which followed the Paris roundup that has gone down in history as the infamous "Vel d'Hiv," let alone the final horror of the death camps—seemed at the time of Pétain's trial to be of little concern. Nor was there much mention of the persecution of Freemasons, the brutal sadism of the Milice and the feebleness of "collaboration." In all these matters Pétain might legitimately have been held to be either complicit, through the turning of a blind eye, or directly responsible; but they were, for a long time, hardly mentioned. In fact, it took many years after the end of the war and much wringing of hands before historians, let alone politicians, were prepared even to look beneath the stone under which the corpse of Vichy had been buried.

Pétain spent his last years in prison until his death in 1951. But campaigns to reverse his conviction continued, and were to continue, as he himself had instructed his lawyers, "even after his death." For more than 30 years his supporters demanded his reburial in Douaumont at Verdun. Committees were formed to defend his memory. In 1973 his remains were dug up from his grave on the Île d'Yeu off the west coast of France and shipped to the mainland for reburial, only to be discovered in a garage in a Paris suburb—and shipped back again. Moreover, surprising as it may seem, successive French presidents, starting with Charles de Gaulle in 1968 and ending with Jacques Chirac in 1998—and most notably, President François Mitterrand—arranged for flowers to be placed on Pétain's grave on each anniversary of the Armistice of November 1918.

"Pétainisme," such as it is or ever was, is by now dying. Young people in France hardly recognize the name itself. Vichy has become a regional center for tourism in the Auvergne. The Île d'Yeu is now a favored resort for intrepid surfboarders. The battlefield of Verdun is no more than a vast area of unsightly bumps in the ground. The past, as well as its lessons, is being put out of mind. None of that, of course, is necessarily a bad thing. The past can sometimes be too painful. But the past can never be truly forgotten; and Pétain was, and is, part of France's past, not least because he was, above all, a patriot. He was a fine general—not great, since he did not have the genius for surprise of a Napoleon, but fine enough to stand high among the mediocrities around him in the First World War. To be sure, like many ambitious generals before and since, he was bewildered by the world of politics. Blunders and misjudgments became daily characteristics. He was lax, to say the least, in standing out against the persecution of Jews and Freemasons and the brutal excesses of his subordinates. History has recorded all that in detail. But he loved his country and had a touching faith in what de Gaulle was to call the eternal France. Inadequate he may have been for the task for which he thought himself qualified, but he was not, and had never been, a traitor. In that particular at least, and perhaps—dare it be said?—generally, Clio, the maverick muse of History, has not played it entirely fair.

"The Son of My Sorrow"

"Il en est ainsi de notre passé. C'est peine perdue que nous cherchions à l'évoquer, tous les efforts de notre intelligence sont inutiles."

It was raining. It was also, for April, unseasonably cold. At the Swiss frontier station of Vallorbe, the checkpoint lights had been turned on earlier than usual, and a larger than usual contingent of Swiss frontier guards had moved in, along with a few journalists. There was to be an important event that evening. A special train had arrived in the late afternoon with some distinguished passengers, who even then were resting in the modest railway station waiting room. Word also had it that more than 100 armed police and soldiers were mustered on the French side.

There was, indeed, to be an important event. On 26 April 1945, at 7:27 P.M., Marshal Philippe Pétain crossed into France for the last time. As his car reached the checkpoint a platoon of Swiss soldiers presented arms—his due as a Marshal of France. Waiting for him on the French side was General Pierre Koenig, the former Free French general but by then governor of Paris, whose task it was to escort the Marshal to Paris to stand trial. Once out of his car Pétain, again as a Marshal of France, saluted the French soldiers. Some moved to present arms in their turn, others just shuffled about uncomfortably. Koenig stood to attention. Pétain held out his hand, but Koenig remained fixed at attention, merely inclined his head—according to one newspaper report, "in deference to an old man"—and refused the proffered hand.[1]

The warrant for Pétain's arrest was then read out. The charges were "plotting against the internal security of the state" and "collusion with the enemy."[2] Pétain identified himself, stated that he was in his ninetieth year, signed the form acknowledging his arrest and returned to his car. The car was escorted under heavy guard for the eight kilometers to the railway station at Les Hôpitaux-Neufs, where he boarded another special train, this time for Paris, in which a coach had been set aside for him and his wife. Apart from the reading of the warrant, nothing of consequence had been said.

When the train arrived at Pontarlier just before ten o'clock, a crowd besieged Pétain's coach. There were shouts of "traitor" and "hang him," and some in the crowd spat at his window. It was a complete—and, to Pétain, unexpected—contrast to the scenes which had greeted him a year earlier, on that precise date, when he had visited Paris. Indeed, Pétain would have been less than human if he did not at that moment recall the adulatory crowds of compatriots such as these whom he had used to address as his "children." He would also have been less than human if he had not reflected that his return to France to face his accusers was at his own insistence. He had, after all, refused the offer of a secure and peaceful home in Switzerland. The conviction that he had saved France in the hour of her greatest danger had overcome his inherited peasant caution. What had not been obvious to him, although it was obvious to everyone else, was that the political tide had turned so decisively against him that he was, without any doubt, returning to a sentence of death.

It was, perhaps, naïve; but it was not dishonorable. There was also an element of self-importance, the belief that his rank would allow him special treatment, and even that he might successfully negotiate with his former protégé, Charles de Gaulle; but self-importance and pride had long been a feature of his life. He had always prided himself on what he supposed to be an almost mystical relationship with the people of France. It came, he said, from his own peasant ancestry and upbringing. In speech after speech he had extolled the virtues of the peasant: thrift, honesty, hard work, loyalty to country and to God; needless to say, his picture of the peasant became progressively more idealized as he grew older. What he revealed only when the mask slipped was that his own peasant childhood had not been quite the idyll he was accustomed to describe. As a matter of fact, he had been only too content to leave his family and his birthplace as soon as he could, and, apart from fleeting visits, never to return.

Pétain's childhood was typical of the time and the place. He was born at Cauchy-à-la-Tour, a village of some 400 inhabitants in the Department of Pas-de-Calais, at 10 P.M. in the evening of 24 April 1856 to his mother, Clotilde Pétain, née Legrand. Omer-Venant Pétain, the baby's father, was particularly glad that it was a boy. Until then he had only managed three daughters. For a family whose life depended on working the land, a son was a gift of providence; daughters were considered no more than a burden.

The new baby was duly baptized as Henri Philippe Bénoni Omer Pétain at the little church in Cauchy, so small it had previously been under the care of the vicar of the neighboring parish, Auchel. He was given the names of his maternal uncles, his grandfather and his father. An oddity to modern ears is the name of his Pétain grandfather—Bénoni. Biblical names were, of course, not uncommon, but this one, although not unknown in the district, was unusual elsewhere. The name had originally been taken from a passage in the Book of Genesis. Rachel, Jacob's second wife, gave birth to a son as she lay dying. Before she died she gave him his name, Bénoni, "the son of my sorrow." Jacob, more prosaically, called him Benjamin. But it had gained some sort of mystic meaning among the French peasants of Pétain's neighborhood. Some said that in its meaning it reflected a nostalgia for the *ancien régime*, others that it signified no more than the normal pain of childbirth.

There is no suggestion (however interesting it might be in the light of subsequent events) that the name indicated any Jewish blood in the Pétain family veins. Originally of Flemish stock—the name itself is a French version of *Piet-heim* (Peter's home)—the Pétains had settled in Cauchy at the end of the seventeenth century. They had married and intermarried, bred copiously, worked the land for their subsistence, and had, above all, lived by the maxims of the Catholic Church. As marriages took place, land was transferred by way of dowry; and as deaths took place the same land was divided up or transferred back again by way of inheritance between the larger peasant freeholders in Cauchy: the Tahons, the Legrands, the Lefebvres, the Carons, the Pétains and the Cossarts.

Peasant families of high standing called themselves *cultivateurs* as opposed to *paysans*. They were literate, and, from time to time, adventurous. Omer-Venant Pétain, for instance, had decided in the late 1840s to escape from peasantry to participate in the excitements of the wave of industrial inventions which were a feature of the time. Indeed, he had even tried his luck in Paris. There he had for a time been apprenticed to Louis Daguerre on the then-new invention of the daguerreotype, and had written to his parents in 1846 of his enthusiasm ("The person who showed me was earning by himself more than 100 francs a day") and about his ambitions to set up shop on his own account—while requesting 50 francs to tide him over.[3] The revolutionary days of 1848, however, put an end to all such thoughts, and Omer-Venant had returned swiftly to the family farm.

His brother Cyrille also had ambitions. Cyrille decided that the Army was an attractive proposition, and signed up for 15 years of service. It was not a sensible decision. After a posting to Algeria, Cyrille was assigned to the Crimea. He deserted.

However embarrassing Cyrille's career, it illustrates that one of the traditional ways to escape from the drudgery of peasant life was to enroll in the army. This was particularly true in the Pas-de-Calais (the old province of Artois), where memories of unremitting warfare were part of the folk inheritance. The history of the place is scarred by stories of battles. Ever since the arrival of the Romans, the territory had been fought over. Romans, Franks, Normans and English had all, at one time or another, laid their claim. All around are the sites of ancient battles: Crécy, Azincourt, Lens, Cassel, Ramillies, Mons-en-Pévèle, Bouvines, Fontenoy.

It is not difficult to see why there was such constant military mayhem in Artois and the adjoining provinces of Flanders and Picardy. They were obvious targets for incursions from England; they lie at the western end of the extensive plain of northern France and thus are open to attacks from the east; and, not least, the northern border of the provinces lie exposed to attacks from the lowlands of the Rhine delta.

Peasants had to be continuously on their guard. The English were particularly feared—the Duke of Marlborough's soldiers had been unforgiving. Moreover, if life was dangerous, there was little compensation to be gained from either a fertile soil or a beautiful environment. The soil is chalky and the landscape can only be described as dull. There is one peak of more than 200 meters near the town of Saint-Omer, but even that seems curiously out of place. Nor, apart from the constant coming and going of armies, has the area attracted much attention. For tourists, it seems always to be on the way to somewhere else.

In the middle of the nineteenth century, outside the major towns of Arras, Béthune and Saint-Omer, the countryside around was largely populated by peasants, each family with a smallholding which provided them with the basics of life. The coalmines of the prolific basin south of Lille were then only gradually extending eastwards. Certainly, when they arrived, a new and different population encroached onto what had until then been peasant territory. There was little love lost between the two. The miners were paid by the day, their wages some four times the average daily wage for an agricultural laborer; they spent their money in the local bistro; they were rough and their children undisciplined; and worst of all, they showed no inclination to go to church. But they brought money, and with the mines and the money came roads and railways, and a new generation of subsidiary industries.

Nevertheless, for the Cauchy of the 1850s that process was only just beginning. Cauchy was still little more than an agglomeration of family farms in a largely subsistence economy. As Karl Marx put it in his study of French rural sociology, "The great mass of the French nation is made up of a simple addition of units bearing the same name, just as a sack filled with potatoes forms a sack of potatoes."[4]

The Pétain family farm was one such unit. By the time of Pétain's birth, the family smallholding consisted of some ten hectares. There were two horses, five or six cows, a few pigs and a scattering of chickens. The farmhouse had over the decades been added to and was a house of some substance. In fact, the house still stands, by the side of the main road from Arras to Thérouanne. The wall facing the road was divided by an archway which led from the road to the courtyard behind. To the left of the archway were the living quarters, one large kitchen off which lay two little rooms and a small dairy. Pétains of all generations, together with their animals, lived in close—and presumably at times suffocating—proximity to one another.

By the peasant standards of southern France they were relatively prosperous. But relatively prosperous though it might be, the Pétain farm was nevertheless far from comfortable. There was no indoor sanitation; the kitchen was communal; and apart from the central fire there was no heating. Nor was there much light. The house had only a few narrow and primitive windows, and in the long winter evenings there was only the light provided by poor quality tallow candles. Summer was bearable, since the animals could be put out of doors and the days were long. When the autumn rains came, rainwater leaked into the house, and since there was no internal drainage there was no method of drying the floors. The stench must have been dreadful. Since water was too precious to allow for baths—or even for cleaning teeth—clothes became dirtier, and more pungent, as the weeks progressed. Food, too, was monotonous. Life was, indeed, hard. In Cauchy in 1859, for example, nine out of fourteen babies died in infancy.

As for social life, there was not much of it. To quote only one account, "there are no friends in the countryside; only relatives or neighbors."[5] The women gathered around the communal washing place and the men in whatever establishment was available to provide a cheap glass of beer or cider. The market, too, was part of social life. There was also the communal assembly, at which the great and the good of Cauchy would deliberate about local problems. They were elected by the male universal suffrage which had been revived (for males over 25 only) in 1848; but it always seemed that the same names were returned. Above all, however, there was the Church, and the Pétains, as good Catholics, attended without fail.

On 1 October 1857, three weeks after the birth of her short-lived fourth daughter, Pétain's mother, Clotilde, died. For Omer-Venant it was a triple blow; he had lost a wife, a mother to his children and a fellow worker on the farm. He looked for another wife. At the age of 42, upright, good-looking and even-tempered, and with what passed for a substantial property, he was certainly an attractive proposition; and soon he was engaged to Reine Vincent, from the nearby village of Aumettes. They were married on 7 April 1859.

It was not long before there was a problem. Reine produced three children in quick succession. Seven children on the farm were far too many for one person to look after, particularly when she had to work on the farm as well. It was only normal to ask relatives to help. It was equally normal—and at the time not at all unusual—for the children of the first marriage to be the ones to be parked with their nearest relatives. The young Pétain, by then age five or six, was lodged, together with his sisters Marie-Françoise and Adélaïde, with their neighboring grandparents.

In later life, Pétain complained that his stepmother had forced him out of his childhood home, and that the only motherly love he had known had come from his grandmother. The complaint was certainly an exaggeration. For a start, his stepmother referred to him as "my son" rather than as "my stepson."[6] Far from being the Wicked Stepmother of legend she was by all accounts a kindly soul, and anxious to ensure a good upbringing for all her husband's children. Nor, by comparison, was grandmother Françoise particularly demonstrative in her affection. Her fierce blue eyes, a physical characteristic which she had passed on to her grandson, betrayed an almost fanatical sense of religiosity.

Clotilde's brother, Abbé Jean-Baptiste Legrand, lived in a comfortable two-story house at Bomy. Although the journey to Bomy took several hours, the boy took every opportunity to visit his uncle and his elder sister, who had been lodged there. Abbé Legrand also took the boy's education in hand. Under Legrand's tuition, the boy's reading widened in scope and his devotion to the Catholic Church was—needless to say—heavily reinforced.

There was, however, another, and quite different, source of information—this time from a wider world than that of a parish priest. Pétain's great-uncle, Clotilde's mother's brother, Abbé Philippe-Michel Lefebvre, had led a more varied, even at times exotic, career. After studying science and philosophy he had entered the seminary at Hinnin, and was about to be ordained deacon when the seminary itself was suppressed under the Revolution. He was then called up into the army, fought at Jemappes in 1792 under General Dumouriez and in Italy, under Napoleon, in 1794. A subsequent—and quieter—career in the priesthood led finally to retirement at the presbytery at Bomy, where he was happy to regale anybody who would listen with anecdotes of his life as a soldier in both the Revolutionary and Napoleonic armies.

One such, of course, was the young Pétain. But the old Abbé's influence on his young great nephew should not be exaggerated. The young boy, like any young boy, would certainly have listened to his great uncle, but since Lefebvre died in 1866, just before Pétain's tenth birthday, it would be an exaggeration to maintain, as some have done, that it was in listening to stories of heroic military exploits that Pétain decided on a military career. As a matter of fact, his uncle was a much greater influence, and Pétain resolved to follow the well-trodden path of the priesthood.

Matters were so arranged between Abbé Legrand and his former pupil, Abbé Graux, that in October 1867 the ten-year-old Pétain embarked on the first stage of his formal education, at the school of which Graux was the director—the Collège Saint-Bertin at Saint-Omer. Childhood and the peasant family were left behind; adolescence, with all its difficulties, lay ahead.

Choosing the Saber
Over the Book

*"Vous ne vous doutez pas de la sombre atmosphère où nous sommes grandis
dans une France humiliée et meurtrie . . . élevés pour une revanche sanglante,
fatale et peut-être inutile."*

The emotions of a ten-year-old boy leaving home for his first boarding school
can easily be imagined—a mix of shyness and sheer terror. That the young
Pétain would be spending almost all his time with a wholly new set of hitherto
unknown companions in a strange environment must have been particularly
daunting. It must therefore have been with a wildly beating heart that the new
pupil, Philippe Pétain, stood in front of the huge gates of the Collège Saint-Bertin
in the first week of October 1867.

In fact, it can hardly be said that the town of Saint-Omer in the mid-
nineteenth century was a place of great excitement. What it did have, however,
was an aura of holiness. It was not simply that many of the priests of Artois had
been educated there, nor that the town boasted two saints. It was as though
through the whole town there pervaded a lingering smell of incense and almost
monastic quietness. It was in these surroundings that the young Pétain was to
grow up—surroundings, to be sure, carefully selected by his uncle to encourage
the boy's ecclesiastical ambitions.

Dull it may have been, but Saint-Omer had had its fair share of history. It was overrun by the English in 1337 and 1339, and after its annexation by France in 1677 was again besieged—this time by the Duke of Marlborough and Prince Eugen—in 1711. As local legend has it, a heroine by the name of Jacqueline Robins came to the rescue by sailing down the river Aa with a boatload of arms and provisions for the defenders. Unlikely as it may appear today, the heroine, if she ever existed, is revered in Saint-Omer as a local Joan of Arc.

The gaunt red-brick building of the Collège Saint-Bertin is not, by most standards, an attractive building. The architect, a M. Lejeune, had hitherto confined his attentions to the design of railway stations. It is hardly surprising that the building is known—with more than a trace of mockery—as the "gare du nord." The design replicates, almost to a brick, the design of the London railway station of St. Pancras. Work started in 1850, but during the whole of Pétain's stay there, between 1867 and 1874, workmen were going in and out, hammering and sawing and sculpting away.

It was to this gloomy establishment that the ten-year-old Pétain arrived in a peasant cart drawn by his family's two horses. There is little doubt that, even after the maneuvering of his uncle Legrand to get him accepted, he could only have gone with the encouragement of a legacy from his recently dead great-uncle, Abbé Lefebvre. It was, after all, a boarding school, and the boys had to wear a special uniform—a frock coat with tails with a row of buttons in front and a peaked cap—all of which cost money.

Pétain's arrival at his new school marked his first—and decisive—separation from his peasant family and friends. To be sure, he retained the close friendship of one of the Occre boys—Cauchy neighbors—but the other boys were almost entirely from middle-class families. None of this is surprising. At the time only about one in fifty pupils at all secondary schools were sons of unskilled workers. Moreover, bourgeois families preferred to keep their sons away from the state run *collèges*, which were regarded by the higher ranks of society as demeaning. As for peasant families, it was not everybody who could benefit from a great uncle's legacy to pay the many extras (the boarding and tuition being provided free by the Church).

For the first time in his life, the young Pétain met boys from quite a different class; and though he seems to have taken to them, nonetheless, Pétain's new life with the sons of the bourgeoisie was far from easy. In the dormitories there was no heating; pupils shivered throughout the long nights of the winter. Even the water froze from time to time in the washbasins. Furthermore, it was reported that "the only equality is won with the fist."[1] Bullying was commonplace, and Pétain was no doubt bullied in the way that a peasant boy could expect to be.

There was little escape. The pupils were at Saint-Bertin for nearly 11 months out of 12, from early October until the second week of August of the following year. At Saint-Bertin, religious zeal even required the boys to stay at school for Christmas Day and curtailed the New Year and Easter holidays to no more than three days each.

The working day was equally rigorous. It started early, at 5 A.M. From 5:30 to 6:15 there was a period of prayer, followed by 35 minutes of study before the daily Mass at 6:50. Only after Mass were the pupils allowed their breakfast. The afternoon was taken up with classes, with short recreational breaks, followed by a short lecture on a spiritual subject, prayers, supper at 7:30 P.M. and bed at 8 P.M.

The long day was made worse by the teaching methods. Classes were largely devoted to an exposition of the matter in hand by the priest, with minimal contribution from the pupils. Study consisted of written work, frequently of an essay or translation by the pupil, in or from Latin or Greek, on an improbable topic—such as an imagined conversation between two characters from Roman or Greek mythology or history.

Discipline, of course, was strict. For instance, reading was closely controlled. Pupils were only allowed to read improving literature, such as the lives of the saints or, as a concession, the right-wing Catholic newspapers—*L'Univers, Le Monde* or *L'Union*. Any attempt to smuggle in subversive material was punished. Corporal punishment, however, was forbidden, and for all the strictness there was no resemblance to English schools of the period—which seemed to give a license to schoolmasters tantamount to official sadism.

Although Pétain arrived at Saint-Bertin in 1867, it was not until 1870 that he began the five-year course of studies in the French language which was designed to take "with honor the examination for voluntary enlistment and other examinations unconnected with the teaching of ancient languages" (in other words, the *baccalauréat*).[2] Up until then it had been a question of learning Latin and Greek grammar, of getting by heart long texts from the classics and, of course, pursuing the unremitting study of the teachings of the Catholic faith.

Pétain's scholastic record was not altogether bad. Indeed, in later life he claimed to have been proud of it. On the other hand, it was far from good. In his first year class, known as the *septième*, he won a (second) prize for "good sense." In the next year, the *sixième*, he could only manage third place in "Greek themes," "History and Geography" and "Arithmetic." It was not until he reached the *deuxième* in the school year 1872–1873 that he made any particular impact: first prize in English and Geometry and second prize in Greek translation and music.

It was to his religious studies that Pétain seems to have had the greatest commitment. It was not just a question of particular diligence in attendance at the morning Mass or the evening Rosary. These were compulsory anyway. Nor was it simple obedience to the declaration of the Emperor Napoleon III that by spreading education he was winning "to religion, morals and comfort" the large section of the population "that barely knew the precepts of Christ."[3] In fact, he went out of his way in his piety. In 1873, for instance, at the age of 17, he was an active member of the Society of Saint-Vincent-de-Paul, whose purpose was to alleviate the sufferings of the poor—presumably by offering them scraps of the already inadequate food of Saint-Bertin.

He went even further. In February 1874 he was received into the Congregation of the Virgin, dedicated to the veneration of Our Lady. He participated, as was customary, in the processions through the town on appointed days, and was no doubt diligent in times set aside for special prayer. All in all, it was a particularly pious adolescence, and there is every reason to suppose that Pétain's respect for the Church hierarchy and the rhythms of its worship were ingrained—whatever his later religious beliefs—during this time.

Yet Saint-Bertin was not only concerned with religion; even before 1870, there was something of a military flavor as well. It was not just the uniform, which made the boys look like young soldiers "or municipal guards."[4] There was a good deal of marching up and down in recreation periods, no doubt to encourage respect for military virtues. Nevertheless, the tone changed quickly in 1870. About halfway into Pétain's career at Saint-Bertin, France blundered into what was at best an absurd and, in the outcome, catastrophic war with Prussia.

The whole complicated story has been recited many times. But the simple truth is that, after the victories of the 1850s over Russia and Austria, there was a general belief in France that she was militarily invincible. It followed that any slight was taken by the French political right as a pretext for military action; and the attempt by Prussia to put a Hohenzollern on the throne of Spain, followed by some brusque treatment of the French ambassador in Berlin, was certainly slight enough.

Few in France had taken the growing military power of Prussia at all seriously. Admittedly, the Prussian victory over the Austrians at Königgrätz in 1866 had sparked off a process of reform of the French army. But the reforms were far from complete by 1870. It was still the general opinion of Paris society that the Prussians were "dim-witted, beer-drinking, pipe-smoking peasants, led by inexperienced officers good only at military theory."[5]

Popular enthusiasm in Paris for the war—apart from the political left—was unbounded. It was widely assumed that the French army would merely stroll across the north German plain until it reached Berlin. At that point Prussia would sue for peace, the price for which would be the cession of the Rhineland to France. The reality, when it came, was something of a shock. By the middle of August 1870 the bulk of the French regular army had been pushed back to the fortress of Metz, where it was trapped. In early September a second army, mostly reservists of one sort or another, under the direct command of a painfully ill Louis Napoleon, was surrounded at Sedan. "*Nous sommes dans un pot de chambre,*" noted General Auguste Ducrot, "*et nous y serons emmerdés.*"[6] His prediction was borne out: 130,000 men, including the emperor, surrendered. The German advance on Paris was swift, and by mid-September the capital was surrounded. Finally, Metz itself capitulated on 29 October.

Events then took on a bewildering pace. A new republic was declared; a Government of National Defense was formed; there was a resurgence of fighting spirit, symbolized by the escape from Paris of the minister of the interior,

Léon Gambetta, in a balloon. But however successful Gambetta might have been in rallying the remaining French Army at the Loire, it was not long before the position in the north was desperate. It seemed only a matter of time before the Germans marched into Saint-Omer.

The effect at Saint-Bertin was electric. Students were encouraged by their tutors to train to become soldiers in the defense of their country. Particularly enthusiastic was a Father Jérôme Ducroos, under whose supervision the older students paraded up and down in the courtyard of the vast building with wooden "rifles." The students engaged happily in this charade, and none more so than Pétain. By early 1871, he had become a leader in these events, apparently by self-appointment. "I made myself captain," he reported in later life, "with the tacit agreement of my soldiers."[7]

This was all very well. But, in truth, it was little more than adolescent whistling in the wind. More seriously, there is some anecdotal evidence that the students of Saint-Bertin were marshaled to help in the field hospitals behind the front line. If that is true, the students were perilously close to the real action. In fact, as they might have found out, the rearguard action was being conducted with great skill. The general in charge of the northern front was General Louis Léon Faidherbe. The result was that the confrontation between the French and German armies in the north became a succession of skirmishes until "the French and Germans withdrew north and south like exhausted boxers to their corners at the end of an inconclusive round."[8] Saint-Omer was safe, and the efforts of the Fathers of Saint-Bertin and their pupils could, at least temporarily, be suspended.

But Paris was in uproar. By the end of October 1870 the city had become uncomfortably detached from the rest of France and, Paris being Paris, near the point of insurrection. In March 1871, a detachment of troops tried to recover some guns which had been paid for by public subscription and spirited away. They were met by a crowd of men, women and children who blocked their path. There was a mélée. A general was shot and killed; troops broke ranks; the authorities quickly moved out of Paris to the safety of Versailles. In bloodshed and confusion, the Paris Commune was born.

The Commune was dominated by the same spirit as had flourished in the working-class districts in eastern Paris at the time of the Revolution. It was half idealistic—but half revengeful, too, against those whom they thought had betrayed them. Among those were the priests of the Catholic Church. The Communards closed church schools, threw out the nuns who had been working in the hospitals, ransacked parish churches and arrested the Archbishop of Paris. In late March, some 24 priests were rounded up and shot.

Nevertheless, the conservative priests were to have their day. In April 1871 the French government, after agreeing to a peace with the invading Germans, instructed the army to lay siege to Paris. After five weeks, the government troops broke through the defenses of the Communards. There followed the worst bloodshed seen in Europe since the French Revolution. Between the 20th and 28th of May, possibly as many as 10,000 men and women were summarily shot and another 20,000 arrested (most of whom were sentenced to deportation after a cursory trial).

The impact of the events of 1870–1871 on the adolescent Pétain can only be guessed at. But two conclusions are sure. First, he and the other boys at Saint-Bertin became conscious of the movement for "revenge" against Prussia. Moreover, the young man came to know and admire the officers of the Light Infantry battalion which was stationed at Saint-Omer at the time. The second conclusion is that, under the influence of his ultramontane mentors, Pétain was conditioned to detest all that the Communards stood for. Hatred of the Communards became, in the course of time, hatred of communists (or "Bolshevists" as he was to call them), which lasted until his dying day.

The immediate upshot was that Pétain decided against the priesthood as his future career and chose the army instead. At this point Pétain had a piece of good luck. In 1873 a decree was promulgated by the government of the new republic which abolished the advantage (apparently "100 points") hitherto enjoyed in the competition for entry to the military academy of Saint-Cyr by those candidates who had passed their *baccalauréat* (the final examination in the secondary school system).[9] The result was that a student who was only a year or two away from his *baccalauréat* and who intended to apply for Saint-Cyr was able not to bother to take the examination. Pétain, instead of attending Saint-Bertin for what would have been his last year, simply left.

The decision was approved by his uncle Legrand, who furthermore gave it as his opinion that if the young Pétain was to go into the army he should go in as an officer. (His stepmother, on the other hand, considered that it would be cheaper for him to go in as an ordinary soldier.) At a family conclave in 1875 the Abbé's view carried the day. So it was that Pétain prepared for his next step, a move to the Collège Albert-le-Grand at Arcueil, run by Dominican monks. The long shadow of the Catholic Church was still to loom over the young man even as he prepared himself for war.

In fact, Arcueil proved something of a surprise. This was no gloomy monastic establishment. The monks turn out to have been enthusiastic sportsmen. The college itself had been founded in 1863 by a Father Captier, and its motto demonstrated the good father's intentions: *citius, altius, fortius*. It was no accident that this was also to become the motto of the Olympic Games of 1896. The fathers were determined that their charges should follow the principle of sporting excellence. This, they thought, combined with proper religious teaching, gave the best results in the chosen vocation, which was to prepare their pupils for the examination for entry to the great schools of the Navale, the Ecole Spéciale Miltaire de Saint-Cyr, the Ecole Polytechnique and the Centrale.

After the events of 1871, the management of the school had been taken over by the vicar-general of the Dominican teaching order, Monsignor Laurent

Lecuyer. In his opening address after the murder of his predecessor (by the Communards), Monsignor Lecuyer was forthright. "For the generation we are raising," he proclaimed, "the future is revenge: revenge against the foreigner . . . revenge also against the revolutionary spirit which surprised us."[10] The message could hardly have been clearer, and reinforced the signals Pétain had received at Saint-Bertin: revenge against the foreigner and revenge against those who pursued violent revolution at home.

Pétain was a diligent student at Arcueil. He learned the sports specified by his Dominican teachers, becoming, in particular, a proficient horseman. He is also said to have been a robust leader of his colleagues in the parades they held. All in all, it was a confident young man who, in 1876, took the Saint-Cyr examination at the military college in Nancy. But in the event he only just scraped through. Of the 412 who were accepted by Saint-Cyr in that year, Pétain came no higher than 403rd in merit.

But at least he had not fallen at the first hurdle, and his uncle and the rest of his family could be proud of him. He was about to embark on a career as an officer in what he still considered, as did others, to be the greatest army in Europe. In his view, there was no greater honor than that. For a lad from Cauchy, it was almost beyond his dreams.

Saint-Cyr: Lessons in War

"Froid. Gagne à être connu, n'est peut-être pas encore complètement fait, sera un bon officier."

On the morning of Wednesday, 25 October 1876, Officer Cadet Designate Pétain presented himself at the doors of the École Spéciale Militaire of Saint-Cyr. There is no doubt that it was an immensely proud moment. The young man had emerged from his peasant family background, had survived adolescence in Saint-Bertin and Arcueil, and had reached the gate through which lay a career as an officer in the Army of the Republic.

Pétain would as a matter of course have expected to be treated with social disdain. But both the social and intellectual composition of intakes to Saint-Cyr had changed markedly in the decade prior to Pétain's arrival. Indeed, even before then, the dominance of the sons of the aristocracy, which had been a marked feature of Saint-Cyr after the Restoration in 1815, had diminished. Sons of serving officers or of minor civil servants—most of them intellectually superior to their aristocratic contemporaries—had begun to appear on the list of entrants. But the major change had come with the Falloux Law of 1850. Schools run by the Catholic Church, such as Saint-Bertin and Albert-le-Grand, had been enabled to specialize, if they so wanted, in the preparation of pupils for military careers. The Jesuits had been particularly successful in this endeavor—to the point that there were political rumblings about the religious, and therefore supposedly anti-Republican, nature of the new officer class.

Originally a school to educate the daughters of impoverished nobility funded by Madame de Maintenon, mistress of Louis XIV, the building in Versailles was taken over during the First Empire and turned into a military academy to replace a much more modest officer training unit at Fontainebleau. In subsequent years and decades it was added to extensively, and by the mid-1870s the dormitories could accommodate over eight hundred cadets. The new academy flourished, both academically and in prestige, in the first half of the nineteenth century; but by the time of the Franco-Prussian War signs of decadence were in clear evidence. The behavior of cadets outside the school became a matter of public scandal. It was not just a question of cadets visiting the local bordellos and contracting unpleasant diseases. There were riots, and behavior that by any standards was outrageous.

By the time of Pétain's arrival stricter discipline had been enforced. Noncommissioned officers were posted on the Paris trains, as well as in the dormitories. Civilian teachers who were unable to keep order were replaced by military officers. Punishments were reported to cadets' subsequent regimental postings. In 1876, just prior to his arrival, cadets were dispatched to learn discipline by participation in the annual autumn maneuvers.

Pétain was a most handsome young man. At Arcueil he had cultivated a rather plaintive adolescent wisp of a beard; but that had now disappeared in favor of a military moustache shaped, as was the custom in the army, in the form of a saber. His hair had, at Arcueil, been parted on the left, with a hint of adolescent vanity in its wave; at Saint-Cyr it was now parted in the middle, and brushed smartly down on either side. As his registration for military service at the *mairie* (town hall) of Béthune reports, he had "blond hair, blue-grey eyes, a wide forehead, and an oval face," and that his height was a modest "1.74 meters."[1] This attractive young man seems, in spite of his social origins, to have adapted without too much difficulty to the life of a *"fine galette"* (those who ranked toward the bottom of the class but were all the more admired for that). To be sure, the required dress was somewhat odd. The uniform at the time consisted of breeches, a frock coat with the flat *"galette"* (epaulette) on the shoulder and a képi. The distinctive mark of the lowly newcomer was that the peak of his képi had to lie uncomfortably flat against his forehead. In compensation, the new intakes were graciously allowed to share in the communal pleasures of their seniors. There was a large room with a piano and a billiard table available to all; and there were, of course, the same opportunities to show off in swaggering strolls in the streets of Versailles.

For Pétain there were some pleasures which had to be denied. He had, after all, to take good care of his money, since he had little of it—a small allowance from his uncle Legrand and perhaps an even smaller supplement from the family farm at Cauchy. But the one pleasure that he denied himself without difficulty was participation in the expensive feasts or drinking bouts of the better-off cadets. The simplicity of living which had been his peasant heritage stayed with him—at least until his success in his career allowed at least a measure of relaxation.

For a cadet from Pétain's background, the curriculum was not unduly harsh. Although 5 A.M. was the wake-up time, he was used to that. Later on, the regime was somewhat relaxed, but cadets still did not see their first meal until 9:30 A.M., and then only for a quick 15-minute breakfast. Moreover, lunch at 12:30 was for only ten minutes. In between, following the curriculum of 1872—designed, it was said, to "prepare for the hour of *revanche*"—the cadets were required to study military tactics and capabilities, to practice riding, shooting, fencing, boxing, gymnastics, swimming and, last but by no means least, dancing—an important attribute of the peacetime officer, and one at which Pétain showed himself to be particularly adept (though how it aided the "*revanche*" is unclear).

Pétain gradually moved up the ladder of promotion within his intake. He made a great friend of one of the cadets senior to him, Alphonse Guide. Guide's origins were in the south—in Antibes. His parents were Provençal bourgeois, with means enough to keep their son in a reasonable, but not unduly luxurious, style of life. He and Pétain forged the kind of friendship which was typical of young men of their age and background. They walked together in the streets of Versailles and even, on days off, took the train to Paris—like any other day-trippers—to see the sights. It was only on their holidays that the two friends separated, Guide to return to his home in the south and Pétain to the rectory at Bomy—with occasional visits to his family at Cauchy and occasional escapades, mostly shooting rabbits, with his old friends from the Collège Saint-Bertin.

By the time Pétain had completed his first year at Saint-Cyr, he seems to have adapted to its particular culture. The ceremony which transformed the Officer Cadets Designate into Officer Cadets apparently held no terrors. To others it had been intimidating. Known as the "baptism" of the intake, it resembled an elaborate and grotesque religious service. There was a great deal of shouting and singing of idiotic songs dedicated to the "*noble galette*." At the high point of the ceremony, the juniors knelt in front of the Tricolor and their seniors, and, in the solemnity of the moment, found their intake "baptized."

Petain's intake was duly baptized, the name chosen being "Plewna." Plevna, was, and is, a small town on the banks of a barely significant tributary of the river Vid in what is now Bulgaria. The reason it was very much in the news at the time was that it was the scene of one of the greatest defensive military engagements of the nineteenth century. The choice of the name, and the fact that the engagement would have received special study by the intake which bore it, is of at least some interest in the light of Pétain's own subsequent views of the importance of defensive war strategies.

The defense of Plevna by the Turkish commander Osman Pasha lasted from mid-July 1877 until Osman's final capitulation in mid-December. Three Russian assaults were repelled by the Turks with heavy casualties on both sides. Frustrated by the failure of all their efforts, the Russians called on General Todleben, the defender of Sevastopol in the Crimean War, who laid siege to the town. As supplies ran out Osman Pasha requested permission from Constantinople to withdraw, but was refused. A Turkish sortie on the nights of 9–10 December failed. Osman Pasha surrendered soon afterwards.

The lesson was certainly not lost on the cadets of Saint-Cyr. It was simply that mere defense is not enough. On either of the three occasions when he had defeated the Russians, Osman could, have broken out onto the offensive. His failure to do so led to his eventual defeat. Plevna thus became a symbol of defense to the—ultimately unsuccessful—end.

The Plewna *"promotion,"* to use the French word, came to its day of stardom on 13 September 1878. At their passing-out parade, the cadets, soon to be junior officers in the Army of the Republic, knelt on one knee in front of the Tricolor and solemnly swore to live and die for their country. It was a splendid occasion, attended by the parents and relatives of the cadets who were about to receive their commission. Some cadets, of course, had no surviving relatives; others had relatives who did not come. Such was the case with Cadet Pétain. None of his family attended the ceremony.

On the same day, the Ministry of War published the list of successful candidates in the *Journal Officiel*. Of the 386 considered worthy of their commission, Pétain was ranked—by merit—number 229. The peasant boy had performed better than his entry score might have led him to expect, and he could therefore hold his head up high as a newly commissioned officer.

"I would have been perfectly happy in this School," Petain wrote in later life, "if they had not required us to master the finer points of theory."[2] In other words, if it had not been for the more cerebral parts of the curriculum, he would have found himself at home there. As it turned out, his result was not good enough for him to have his pick of regiments in which to serve. As a good horseman, he might at first have hoped to go into the cavalry, but all available positions were occupied by those who came higher than him on the roll. The infantry was therefore his only option.

He could have chosen to join the infantry in the colonies. Some of his colleagues did so, and achieved an initial rate of promotion faster than those who had chosen to remain in metropolitan France. Moreover, colonial officers gained valuable experience in real warfare denied to their domestic brothers (and, as a result, learned to look down on them). But Pétain chose, presumably on the simple grounds that he did not want to leave France, to opt for the domestic infantry. This being so, his ranking at Saint-Cyr was good enough for him to have the pick of domestic infantry regiments. Apparently under the influence of his friend Guide, Pétain's choice lighted on the 24th Light Infantry Battalion, stationed at the time on garrison duty not far from Guide's home at the little Mediterranean port of Villefranche-sur-Mer.

It was with pride and a suitably light heart—and a somewhat romantic idea of soldiering—that he took up his post as "*sous-lieutenant*" (second lieutenant) at his new home in his battalion.

His pride was to some extent justified. The prestige of the Army, even after the catastrophe of the Franco-Prussian War, remained high. It was generally regarded as the guardian and symbol of the nation. Moreover, it was in the process of re-equipment, with modern artillery and rifles, and a series of impressive fortifications on the eastern frontier. The idea of "revenge" for the defeat of 1870 was to many, not just in the army, an inspiration. War memorials, particularly the black-veiled statue of "Strasbourg" in the Place de la Concorde in Paris, became the sites of emotional ceremonies. With these ideas in mind, the young *sous-lieutenant* could take up his post at Villefranche, guarding the French frontier with Italy, with enthusiasm.

In fact, it turned out that there was really not very much for a junior officer to do. There was no great call to arms. Furthermore, the longer-serving officers of the 24th Battalion regarded the newcomer from Saint-Cyr with suspicion and, since most were former noncommissioned officers, with ill-disguised jealousy. Besides, Pétain had by that time developed a caustic wit which was not at all appreciated by his seniors—or, as it happened, by the fiery southerners he accosted on his walks in neighboring Marseille. Moreover, the pay was poor, the company indifferent, and the battalion was struggling with the reputation of garrison life as seen from the outside, as one of "threadbare boredom, drink, debt, duels, pox and suicide."[3]

Nevertheless, Pétain enjoyed his four years in Villefranche, and looked back at them with nostalgia. There were, of course, moments when he was doubtful about the whole business: the discipline was harsh, the tasks of a *sous-lieutenant* were in many respects menial, and the life for a young man was, compared with Saint-Cyr, in many respects monotonous.

But there were three things which made life for Pétain in the 24th Battalion not just bearable but enjoyable. The first was that his commanding officer, Colonel Cazé, understood the frustrations of the young man. It so happened that within the light infantry certain battalions had been chosen to specialize in mountain warfare and the 24th was one of those selected. Cazé in turn chose Pétain to lead the training. Here was, after all, an athletic young man who seemed to have no difficulty in getting on with his inferiors in rank. Pétain in his turn felt himself to be in his element. "We climbed the mountains together," he wrote later, "helping each other without regard to rank. Living together for several months each year made it easy to discover men's inmost thoughts."[4] Clearly, he was already discovering his own particular talent for military command.

Second, life was made more bearable by the rise, after 1870, in the social standing of junior officers. They were still badly paid, but they were no longer shunned in local society. By the time Pétain arrived in Villefranche junior officers were accepted—indeed, if they were young, good-looking and intelligent, they made a welcome change from the young men of the bourgeoisie who had previously been the staple fare of the social circuit.

Third, Pétain had his friend Alphonse Guide as companion, and Guide provided the entry to the bourgeois society of the Côte d'Azur; Pétain provided the looks and the charm. They went swimming together—Pétain recalled swimming across the port of Villefranche and back. They went gambling together at Monte Carlo—strictly not allowed to officers but Pétain, at least, disguised himself in civilian clothes for the purpose. But, above all, they chased women.

It so happened that the terrain was favorable for their purpose. The starchy rectitude of the Second Empire had given way to the greater freedom of the Third Republic. Women no longer shied away from open awareness of the facts of life or from reading the romantic—and, at times, near-pornographic—novels of the day. Dissatisfied wives felt able to engage in extramarital affairs; and there were few more ready to oblige them than the handsome young garrison officers. Indeed, in some regiments officers were specifically permitted to form such attachments, in order to avoid their constant attendance at the local brothels. There is, for instance, a photograph of Pétain dressed as a jockey at a fancy-dress ball in Menton in 1881. Oddly enough, it was on that occasion—that Pétain met his future wife. Berthe-Alphonsine-Eugénie Hardon, known generally as "Nini," was four-and-a-half years old. At the time she appeared dressed as a flower girl to dance with the other children in the afternoon. The "jockey" was due to dance in the evening with the grown-ups. Somehow the two met. Her father was a successful civil engineer, involved in the construction of the Panama Canal. Her mother was exceptionally beautiful, her beauty enhanced by the pallor of tuberculosis.

Introductions to the family followed, and Pétain thereafter frequently visited their home in Menton. There is no particular reason to believe that the visits were anything other than innocent. But Pétain's reputation was well known to the family. "In those far-off days," Nini was later to recall, "*sous-lieutenant* Pétain courted many pretty ladies . . . people often talked, with a smile, of his conquests."[5] In the light of this, it is perhaps not too fanciful to assume that Pétain's real target was the mother rather than the daughter, and in dandling the daughter on his knee he was pursuing a well-known technique—the way to a mother's heart through a demonstration of affection for her child.

No doubt one or two tears were shed when he announced in December 1883 that he was to be posted to a rather more stern environment—the 3rd Battalion of light infantry in the garrison town of Besançon. Besançon proved to be quite different to Villefranche-sur-Mer. "Not particularly jolly" was Pétain's own verdict.[6] It is easy to sympathize. Lying at the end of the Jura mountain chain in the middle of eastern France, the city, although it still boasts an attractive center within its original site of the meandering horseshoe of the river Doubs, carries even now an air of dissatisfied gloom. Historically, the territory had been fought over many times, but the worst moment in the city's life had come with the Franco-Prussian War. In the Frankfurt peace treaty which formally ended the war, France only just managed to keep Besançon.

Those wounds, like all wartime wounds, took a long time to heal. Not least among the scars was the unwelcome arrival in the Franche-Comté, and its capital Besançon—their migration sanctioned by the Frankfurt Treaty—of a number of Alsatian Jews, among them a family by the name of Dreyfus. Moreover, perched on the eastern frontier of France, the city suffered an industrial decline, only alleviated by the founding of a watch industry by refugees from Switzerland. In the last quarter of the nineteenth century it was overtaken by Dijon in terms of both population and wealth. The railway passed it by: The Paris–Geneva route, thanks to Besançon's refusal, was snapped up by Pontarlier to the south. All in all, it was a city in decline at the gates of which Pétain, now a full lieutenant by virtue of seniority, arrived in January 1883.

Besançon was much more serious a garrison town than Villefranche, facing, as it did, any future German threat. There is little doubt that Petain found Besançon boring. There was a society of sorts—the theater, receptions, the occasional ball or wedding celebration—where a young lieutenant might meet an engaging lady or even an entertaining civilian male friend who would turn out to be a good drinking companion. There was always the possibility of a visit to a brothel or, more likely for an officer, a quick excursion with a young secretary who wished to supplement her income.

But the army was becoming more strident in its disapproval of its lieutenants either contracting venereal disease or fathering illegitimate children on the ladies of the garrison towns. Pétain decided, in mid-1883, that it was time for him to get married. He was, after all, in his late twenties. He had sown, and perhaps more than sown, his wild oats. It was time, in the hallowed phrase, to "settle down."

This proved to be more difficult to achieve than he might have imagined. His first choice of bride was almost predictable. She was a girl from his home country of Artois, and also a distant cousin from the well-to-do peasant community around Cauchy, by the name of Célina Brassart. But the lady in question did not find the prospect enticing. For a start, she was nine years older than Pétain and dedicated to holy and good works. The handsome lieutenant was thus unceremoniously turned down by his pious cousin.

But he was not discouraged. Next his eye lighted on one of the girls he had met on the social circuit: Antoinette Bertholin. Unfortunately, M. Bertholin's enquiries showed that there was little future for the lieutenant other than a long and frustrating slow march toward eventual obscure retirement. They would continue to remain friends, Bertholin assured Pétain, but he did not think that the lieutenant was the husband which he would wish for his daughter.

Pétain, still undeterred, was prepared for one more shot. This time the target was Angéline Vuillaume, the daughter of the Besançon manager of the Société Générale, one of the most powerful banks in the region. Again, his initial approach to Vuillaume was well received; and, again, enquiries were made by the prospective father-in-law. Presumably, Vuillaume asked the opinion of the same people who had given their opinion to Berthelin, since the answer was the same: a very polite refusal of the daughter's hand.

For the time and place—the last quarter of the nineteenth century in provincial France—such a series of marital rebuffs for an officer of at least reasonable standing was, to say the least, unusual. For Pétain it was more than a blow. He could not understand why the bourgeoisie of Besançon would not take him to its heart. They, on their side, understood quite clearly that Pétain was by origin a peasant, and that he could not possibly have the connections which would allow him anything other than a humdrum career in the army.

On 5 May 1888, Pétain learned that his father, Omer-Venant, had died. Although relations between father and son had not been particularly good ever since the father's second marriage, the death of the second parent is, however benign the circumstances, a matter of distress. Whatever emotional turmoil there was became very much more intense a few weeks after his father's death. Invited to a ball in the house of M. Léon Regad, the owner of the Forges de Quingey and one of the richest men in the province of Franche-Comté, Pétain met, and danced with "a girl of a rare beauty."[7] It was immediate, and apparently reciprocal, love. By the end of the evening the couple had exchanged sighs and promises—and had even agreed, well beyond the social conventions of the time, to address each other by their Christian names, "Marie-Louise" and "Philippe."

The following morning, Pétain asked his commanding officer, Captain Louis Ernest Maud'huy, to approach the parents on his behalf to request the hand of their daughter Marie-Louise in marriage. This de Maud'huy did. But, much to the distress of Marie-Louise and Philippe, there followed the usual investigation of the prospective bridegroom's fortune and prospects with which Pétain was wearily familiar. The result was the same as on previous occasions: there was to be no wedding. Nevertheless, thanks to the entreaties of the daughter, the parents offered Pétain a compromise. If, they said, he would abandon his military career, resign from the army, and join the family firm in Besançon, then they would give their consent to the marriage.

Faced with this dilemma, he concluded that there was only one thing to do. He sought advice from his uncle, Abbé Legrand. In the end, the uncle's decision was clear: forget the lady and stick to your career. Pétain, after much hesitation, agreed, but did not dare to tell Marie-Louise, who had asked her parents to prepare for another ball to celebrate her engagement. But nothing happened. The charming lieutenant did not send so much as a word. There was only a message from Captain Maud'huy. The ball was cancelled.

Pétain's last failure to marry led him in a different direction. To be sure, he continued the flirtations and seductions which were a feature of garrison life. But there entered into his life at that point a more serious note, which was to echo down the years almost to his death more than 60 years later. Abbé Legrand had reminded him of the oath which he had taken at Saint-Cyr "to serve France." Like a monk, the officer was to give himself to his country—without let or hindrance. That oath taken and reaffirmed, the army was to become forever the officer's family, and the service of France and her people his destiny. It was a hard view, but Pétain seems to have accepted it. Of course, the oath did not prevent philandering. It did not even prevent marriage. What it prevented was a marriage whose condition was the abandonment of the fundamental belief that the graduate from Saint-Cyr had acquired a mystical relationship with his country. It therefore comes as no surprise to find Pétain himself describing his years at Besançon as "decisive for my career."[8]

With this emotional baggage now on his back, he devoted himself to his study for the entrance examination for the École de Guerre. The examination duly passed, on 1 November 1888 he returned to Paris and, along with 39 other officers from the infantry, entered the gaunt building of his new college. Lieutenant Pétain was now formally classified as a "high flier," with a career on the general staff lying before him.

It was at the École de Guerre that the professional Pétain started to flourish after the personal difficulties of Besançon. The military doctrines which were taught at the college still dated from the Napoleonic era—it was not until the Germans published their accounts of the Franco-Prussian War in the early 1890s that the curriculum was brought up to date—and there was little scope for discussion. But in some ways this suited Pétain's by now apparent ambition. His paper on the defense of northern France against a possible attack through Belgium, for instance, apparently put forward ideas for defensive warfare which were certainly not Napoleonic. He also played his full part in other activities. In May 1889 he scored a mark of 16 out of 20 in a field exercise. In June there was a week's course with an artillery battery, firing live ammunition, at Nîmes. On his return to Paris in July, he was again marked 16 out of 20 for map-reading and 17 out of 20 for infantry training.

High marks continued into his second year at the École de Guerre. It was noted that he had "a voice of command—clear and firm."[9] So it went on: always good marks, reports of an officer who was "serious," "reflective," "willing" and so on. There was also the frequent qualification: "cold," "cold character," "cold aspect" and "difficult to understand." Pétain was quite clearly no longer the sparkling young officer of Villefranche-sur-Mer; he was an older, perhaps sadder and more bruised, middle-ranking infantry officer. To be sure, women were still on his agenda, but there is no mention of any serious liaison, let alone any suggestion of marriage.

On 7 July 1890 he was promoted to the rank of captain—yet again only on the basis of seniority—and was sent as a staff officer to XV Army Corps at their Headquarters in Marseille. There "I spent three years bound to the most monotonous office job, doing my best to carry out the duty of staff writer for which,

I confess, I had no inclination."[10] To cap it all, Pétain was a victim of a mild version of typhoid fever—a common occurrence in the Marseille of the day—which put him in the hospital for two months. At the end of 1893 he moved again—army regulations required former pupils of the École de Guerre to alternate between staff appointments and field commands. This time it was to the command of a company of the 29th Light Infantry Battalion, then stationed at Vincennes, a short distance to the east of Paris.

Pétain was by then nearing 40. At this time he seemed to have developed some characteristics which would normally be associated with disappointed bachelorhood. For instance, he was happy to claim that he had finally abandoned the religious faith of his childhood (attendance at Mass being confined to the requirements of social and military convention); he took, in a fit of personal vanity, to riding on a white horse and, at Vincennes, to reviewing his company on it; above all, he became much more querulous toward his army superiors. Nor had he any of the normal means of solace of bachelorhood. His reading was no more than army texts; his musical ear did not reach further than an army band or the tunes from an operetta; and the visual arts were a closed book. But the study of the history, the doctrine and the governing regulations of the French Army, became daily reading. The peasant mind developed into an acute analytical instrument.

This was the rather different Pétain who was posted back to Paris in July 1895 to the staff of the military governor of Paris. Here, he was at the center of events; and, as it happened, events were unusually exciting. It had only been six months earlier that Captain Alfred Dreyfus had been stripped of his badges of rank, and his sword broken in front of him, in a humiliating public ceremony. His alleged crime was treason. But the evidence against him, the nature of his conviction, and his sentence to a life on Devil's Island were even then being widely challenged. The whole affair was throwing the army into turmoil and provoking civil disputes almost to the point of civil war. The ambitious Captain Pétain was to be at the center of it all—in the eye, as it were, of the hurricane.

The Dreyfus Affair

". . . et pourtant je refusai de me rendre pour ne rien devoir à l'un des agents les plus en vue de l'affaire Dreyfus."

"Cold, even icy, this beautiful blond man, his head already almost totally bald, attracted both men and women by the power of his blue eyes."[1] The Pétain of the early 1900s was a man who was glacial in his relations with his fellow officers but who exercised an apparently irresistible attraction for women. The photographs of Pétain at the time, few as they are, show the face and physique typical of a military man of the day—upright in posture, authoritative in the frown and direct look, heavy eyebrows, classically molded moustache, and a well-formed chin. The only oddities in the head are the premature baldness—normally obscured in photographs by his képi—and the protuberant, but rather small, ears. There is also in the carriage more than a hint of personal vanity.

To the modern eye it is not a particularly attractive image. Pétain had, until his promotion to the general staff, moved from garrison town to garrison town, when not in barracks or in the field, living in a hotel or in furnished rooms, taking with him, on each transfer, his personal effects and his limited collection of books. He had no doubt left behind him, on each occasion, a number of broken hearts. Almost certainly, too, there had been a number of unwanted results of his liaisons: a girl assistant at a toy shop in Besançon, for instance, seems to have become an unintentional mother. There were, almost certainly, others; but Pétain was careful enough to escape the consequences, or at least callous enough not to bother about them.

Once Pétain joined the general staff his lifestyle—though not his habits—to some extent changed out of necessity. After all, the life of a staff officer was very different from that of a field officer. Apart from the fact that he worked in an office and only visited maneuvers in the comfort of a car or, at worst, on a horse (the field officer was expected to muck in with his men), the staff officer was a member of the army's elite. In fact, such was the self-regard of the general staff that it can reasonably be said that they were largely responsible for the refusal of the army to admit to a mistake over the Dreyfus affair.

The main events of the Dreyfus affair are well known. Dreyfus was an artillery officer attached to the general staff when, in September 1894, a list of French military documents had been found by a cleaning lady doing daily duty sifting through the contents of a wastebasket in the German embassy in Paris. The counter-espionage service of the Army, the "Statistical Section," mounted an inquiry and concluded that there was a German spy in the Ministry of War in the rue Saint Dominique. Since Dreyfus was not only not a permanent member of the general staff but was also an Alsatian Jew, it became immediately obvious to the "Statistical Section" that he was the culprit.

Dreyfus was duly tried in a secret court-martial, found guilty and, because he failed to do the honorable thing and commit suicide, received his dreadful sentence—to be publicly stripped of his rank and sent to Devil's Island for life. At the time when Pétain took up his office in the Military Government of Paris in mid-1895, Dreyfus's case was only being pursued by his brother Matthieu Dreyfus. But by the time Pétain left, in the autumn of 1898, the row had escalated. Not only had a vigorous campaign proclaiming Dreyfus's innocence been mounted by Georges Clemenceau, then proprietor of the newspaper *Aurore*; not only had the vice-president of the Senate, Auguste Scheurer-Kestner, taken on the job of lobbying influential politicians on Dreyfus's behalf; not only had the author Emile Zola launched a vitriolic attack on General Mercier, the minister of war at the time of Dreyfus's arrest (in an open letter entitled *J'accuse*); but, most important of all, the "Statistical Section," by then headed by Colonel Georges Picquart, had become convinced that they had picked the wrong man. The true culprit, it appeared, was another staff officer, Major Ferdinand Esterhazy.

In early 1898, Esterhazy was tried but, to the disgust of many, he was acquitted. (It subsequently turned out that the evidence which led to his acquittal had been forged by yet another officer of the general staff, who, when exposed, committed suicide.) Zola was also tried and quickly condemned. At that point, Pétain, in September 1898, was posted to the 8th Light Infantry Battalion stationed in Amiens. From then on he was no longer at the centre of events.

To this day there remains the delicate question of whether Pétain believed in Dreyfus's guilt. He must have had a view. But it is reasonable to suppose that he was pulled in two opposite directions. The first would have been toward suspicion of the Dreyfus verdict. The office of the military governor of Paris in the Place Vendôme was not large, and those who worked there were naturally loyal to their senior officer. A staff captain would certainly have picked up all the rumors which were running around at the time. There was, furthermore, an inbuilt rivalry between the Military Government of Paris and the Ministry of War. Each was suspicious of the other's machinations. The attack on Dreyfus had come from the ministry, and this in itself would lead to suspicion in the Place Vendôme. But by far the most important pointer of all was that General Félix Saussier, Pétain's immediate superior as military governor—and vice-chairman of the Conseil Supérieur de la Guerre, a job which carried with it the command of the French Army in the event of war—had enough doubts about Dreyfus's guilt to sign the warrant for Esterhazy's trial. In the jargon of the day, Saussier was a "Dreyfusard."

On the other hand, the Catholic hierarchy, led by the archbishop of Paris, formed a solid front against Dreyfus. The question, it was said from many pulpits, was not whether a wretched individual was guilty or innocent; it was whether the Jews and the Protestants were or were not the masters of the country. The "anti-Dreyfusard" writer Maurice Barrès even managed to convey the impression that what was at stake was the integrity of the nation. Furthermore, only a fortnight after signing a warrant for Esterhazy's arrest and trial, Saussier retired— to be replaced by General Emile Zurlinden, who immediately backpedaled on Saussier's position.

All that, in turn, would have led Pétain in the opposite direction. Although he had lost whatever remained of his childhood faith, he was always very respectful of clerics and clerical opinion. He was also loyal to the army and to the general staff. Moreover, although the French peasant was perhaps less vociferous in anti-Semitism than the *bourgeoisie*, there was no doubt that the army and the Catholic Church were deeply anti-Semitic, and there is no evidence that Pétain was any different from his military colleagues.

But there was the matter of Saussier. If Pétain's military superior—and a respected general—had doubts about the whole procedure, would that not be persuasive? In fact, there is no means of even guessing at the answer to the question, since there is no contemporary evidence of Pétain's opinions on the affair, and his later comments are, to say the least, delphic. All that can be said with certainty is that after Saussier's retirement he continued to work with, and as aide-de-camp was trusted by, General Zurlinden, who was certainly not prepared to fight Dreyfus's cause (and was even implicated in the general staff's efforts to smear Dreyfus further). But it might also be reasonable to speculate that Pétain was reluctant to openly take sides. In other words, whatever his feelings, it was a time for him to keep his head down.

Petain's posting to Amiens in 1898 came at a time when the Dreyfus furor was at its height; it was clearly a good moment to be out of Paris. In that he was perhaps fortunate. But there was also something better than avoiding the storm. In 1900 he made a further step in his slow progress up the ladder of rank. His promotion to major after ten years as a captain meant he could take command of a battalion instead of languishing as a quasi-permanent company commander. But it was not just the promotion which was cause for satisfaction. He had been noticed by no less a figure than General Guillaume Bonnal, who reported Pétain as "a remarkable captain . . . top flight."[2]

By the time he became a battalion commander Pétain was quite clearly a considerable figure in the military world. He had matured from the youthful and somewhat cavalier *sous-lieutenant* into a responsible and thoughtful staff and field officer. He had read much military history and was developing his own views on strategy and tactics. His stay in Paris had allowed him to make influential contacts in the higher reaches of the general staff, contacts which were certainly to prove useful in the future.

Those, however, were not the only features of his stay in Paris from 1895 to 1898. There were, of course, the liaisons enabled by his new status as a staff officer in the military government. Of course, there was no question of him storming the heights of the aristocracy. Nor was he interested in the substrata of Parisian life. But it was the upper-middle class—the *haute bourgeoisie*—which he found attractive. There is, for instance, an account of the seduction of the 18-year-old daughter of the mayor of Provins in 1898. But, in particular, his eyes had become fixed on one of the daughters of the *haute bourgeoisie*, none other than the little girl he had dandled on his knee all those years ago in Menton— Nini Hardon.

Nini had grown into a tall and comely young lady in her early twenties. Her mother had died in early 1898, her father had married again, and she was living with her grandmother, father and stepmother in a pleasant apartment in the reasonably fashionable rue Cambon. How Pétain and Nini met again is not clear. But meet they did, and Pétain's mind wandered again toward marriage. After all, Nini was attractive, had no apparent suitor and—of some importance to the middle-ranking officer—would bring with her a substantial dowry.

Two things prevented Pétain from pursuing this new idea. The first was the illness of his uncle Legrand which led to his death in 1899. If anybody had set the young peasant boy on his road to advancement it was Abbé Legrand. Pétain was present at his uncle's deathbed, and at his funeral behaved with all the dignity and restrained emotion that the occasion demanded. His true father had been Omer; but his spiritual father had been Abbé Legrand.

The second problem was his posting to Amiens; it was hard in those days to be a pressing suitor at a more than 100-kilometer distance. Besides, Nini's stepmother would certainly wish to have her say in the matter, and Pétain had hardly met her, let alone paid her the attention which would be the necessary part of his wooing of her stepdaughter. So for the moment, Pétain had to be content with the ladies of Amiens.

No sooner had he been promoted to the rank of major than he was given the command of the 133rd Regiment of infantry, then stationed at Belley, another garrison town near Aix-les-Bains in south-eastern France. It was to be the shortest of all his postings, since he was almost immediately assigned to the Rifle School at Châlons at the instigation of his former teacher at the École de Guerre, General Millet, by then the most senior general in the infantry. The assignment, as it happened, was not a success. Current theory required that riflemen should simply saturate the battlefield with indiscriminate fire. Pétain, himself no mean marksman, thought differently. Quite apart from his contempt for his superiors (he later wrote that he found at Châlons "a school of mutual admiration"),[3] he believed in accuracy of fire above all.

Although at the time this seemed radical, this view was already gaining ground in the Ministry of War. There is evidence to show that Pétain was not producing a novel theory but acting as an instrument for those in Paris who argued for change. Nevertheless, Pétain's lectures on the matter profoundly irritated the commander of the Rifle School, Colonel Vonderscherr. Eventually Pétain was invited to resign. In February 1901, he took command of the 5th Regiment of infantry, then stationed in the barracks of Latour-Maubourg. Then in autumn 1901 he was invited to become assistant professor of infantry tactics at the École de Guerre. The appointment was certainly prestigious, but it was entirely due to General Bonnal, who had by then become the school's director. Pétain's immediate superior, also was a figure from his past—the same Maud'huy who had acted so unsuccessfully as Pétain's intermediary in his attempts at marriage at Besançon.

Little is known about Pétain's teaching during his two year period from 1901 to 1903 at the École de Guerre. But it appears that even then there was a clear division of opinion on infantry tactics among the teaching staff. There were those who still taught the Napoleonic guiding principle—throwing maximum force against the enemy—and there were those who held that not even a large force could withstand well-directed and accurate fire. Pétain took the latter view, and was presumably duly put out when a draft regulation in 1902 came down firmly in favor of the former.

The teaching of infantry tactics was not the only thing on Pétain's mind. On his return to Paris in late 1901 he had decided to renew his pursuit of Nini. Accordingly, he made an approach to her stepmother and grandmother, but it comes as something of a surprise to learn that Pétain omitted to mention his project to Nini herself. Moreover, neither Nini's grandmother nor her stepmother thought it worth consulting her.

The grandmother and the stepmother decided that the difference in their ages made a marriage between the two out of the question. Nini was still not told. "If he had told me," she said many years after, "I would probably have married him on the spot in spite of my family."[4] Pétain's reaction to this latest rebuff is not the least surprising feature of the whole affair. Instead of retreating in dudgeon, he took Nini aside and advised her to get married—to somebody else. This she promptly did. The upshot was that Pétain's curious tactics in romance lost him some 20 years of married life.

There were other matters afoot which were to profoundly affect his future. In the middle of his period at the École de Guerre the political climate changed dramatically. The Dreyfus Affair had all the time been rumbling on. In June 1899 the coalition of the moderate right which had run France for most of the decade collapsed, to be replaced by a left-leaning anticlerical coalition. The new government brought such pressure on the army's high command that Dreyfus had been brought back the following month from Devil's Island—an emaciated ruin of a man—and tried again in secret. The court found him guilty again but cited "extenuating circumstances" in giving him a shorter sentence. The general staff was still trying to shore up its now dubious position. Indeed, one officer was heard to remark "I am convinced of Dreyfus's innocence but . . . I would convict him again for the honor of the army."[5]

Needless to say, the verdict and such a fatuous justification commanded the headlines of the world. The row was such that the government was obliged to offer Dreyfus a pardon, which, although still protesting innocence, he accepted. (In fact, it was not until 1906, at a hearing in the appeals court, that Dreyfus was acquitted and that there was a somewhat grudging official admission that the whole thing had been a most regrettable miscarriage of justice.)

The overall result of the affair, and, in particular, of the fierce anti-Dreyfus and antigovernment offensive mounted by the hierarchy, was that in the national elections of May 1902 the Catholic Church became almost the sole issue. The left wing won a majority in the National Assembly of just over 80 seats. The new government was headed by the fiercely anticlerical Emile Combes, a somewhat eccentric elderly country doctor who was at the time carrying on a fond correspondence with an aristocratic nun, Princess Bibesco. Moreover, it was noted that Combes's council of ministers was composed entirely of Freemasons.

Pétain's reaction to this new government needs little imagination. French Freemasonry had long been the enemy of the Church, and Pétain, for all his avowed loss of faith, maintained his respect for the priesthood. Distrust of Freemasons was ingrained, and distrust of politicians quickly followed. This distrust was exacerbated by the new government, which was quick to run its colors up the anticlerical mast. Soldiers were dispatched to close down convents, three in Brittany and one in Tarascon. To use the army against the Church was, in the view of most officers—including Pétain—wholly unacceptable. If that was the way the masonic government were going to behave, then the sooner they were turned out the better.

At that point the Vatican intervened, with a volley of encyclicals directed at the newly elected French government. As might be expected, a protracted row ensued, which ended only with the repeal of the Napoleonic Concordat between Church and State in 1905. In the interim period, however, the government pressed forward with its program, one feature of which was a proposal to "republicanize" the Army.

The chief promoter of this campaign was the new minister for war, General Louis André. It turned out that the real meaning of "republicanization" was a purge from the army of all officers with Catholic sympathies. Key positions in the ministry, the general staff and the military schools were filled with André's trusties. The main target for removal was any officer who was known to be a practicing Catholic.

It was around this time—the date is uncertain—that Pétain was sent for by the minister's private secretary, Alexandre Percin, who had been impressed by his grasp of infantry tactics, to be offered the command of the Rifle School at Châlons. It was an odd move by Percin, since the school, as Pétain pointed out, was usually under the command of a lieutenant-colonel, not of a major such as himself. The objection was brushed aside. He would be promoted immediately. "This would place me," Pétain wrote later, "in a very advantageous position for future promotions."[6] In spite of this, Pétain turned the job down.

The reasons for Petain's refusal are far from clear. It was certainly damaging to his own interests. In fact, he had to wait another four years for promotion to lieutenant-colonel, which effectively barred him from further promotion before his retirement date, due in 1916 when he reached the age of 60. He himself claimed that he did not wish to be indebted to one of the main protagonists in the Dreyfus affair; but that explanation should perhaps be treated with caution. A more plausible reason for Pétain's refusal is that he did not wish to get too close to the group of Freemasons who were by then running the army.

Pétain returned to Paris in March 1904—yet again as a teacher of infantry tactics at the École de Guerre. His lectures—whatever their controversial content—were clearly of too much value to be dispensed with. He had returned to the capital, to a job which he enjoyed and at which he was becoming more and more confident and competent. But in November of that year there were revelations about André and Percin's conduct of affairs that threw relations between the army and the republic into turmoil.

The policy of the Ministry of War since 1902 was to promote those officers who were considered reliable and "in this way to block the road to the students of the Jesuits."[7] To discover who was reliable and who was not, Percin had relied on a network of Freemasons of the Grand Orient to assemble a store of cards, or *fiches*—some 20,000 in all—each one recording for a particular officer information about his religious beliefs, his wife's beliefs, where his children went to school, and so on.

On 4 November 1904, the deputy for Neuilly, a former army officer, revealed to an astonished National Assembly the extent of Percin's machinations—and of André's ultimate responsibility. The ensuing debate was suitably rowdy. André, after putting up a feeble defense, was saved by the fact that a nationalist deputy punched him on the nose. This was enough to gain the sympathy of the majority. But André recognized that he had lost all authority and, one month later, he resigned. That was far from the end of the affair. Duels between officers and masons were widespread. Officers who reported on their colleagues were often forced to change regiments. All in all, during 1905 the talk in the army was of little else.

The affair, which became known as the "*Affaire des Fiches*," gradually died down, but there were permanent scars. For instance, it now appeared certain to those seeking promotion that it was no longer a matter of how good you were; it was a matter of whom you knew in the rue Saint Dominique. They were clearly right. The 1906 promotion lists, for example, were drawn up by a captain on the war minister's staff, a young friend of his who happened to be a diplomat and the diplomat's girlfriend—who apparently went by the name of Blanche—over lunch at Maxim's. By any standards, the whole thing had become very odd.

There is little doubt that among the 20,000 or so *fiches* there was one on Pétain, although it has not come to light. The mere existence of a *fiche* would have been unpleasant; for Pétain the situation was even worse. He did not count many influential politicians among his acquaintance. His prospects for promotion, under the new dispensation, were correspondingly diminished. Furthermore, although he had grown out of the faith of his childhood, he retained his respect for the cloth, and was therefore instinctively on the side of Catholic officers against Freemasonry. The events of the "*Affaire des Fiches*" only served to reinforce that ingrained view.

Yet if his political acquaintance was limited, Pétain's military acquaintance was expanding fast. His lectures were attracting attention. He was by now an expert not only on infantry tactics but on military history as well. He was also an impressive lecturer. On the days when he was lecturing the large semicircular hall in the school filled rapidly. Indeed, so many senior officers from the general staff crowded in that there was little room left for the students. But Pétain was listened to in silence, such was the interest in what he had to say. His delivery, too, was arresting: cold, impassive, without gestures or rhetorical flourishes.

The message was simple and direct. *Le feu tue*. Firepower kills. It was accurate firepower which made movement possible. Artillery and infantry had to work together. "Offensive?," he said. "Of course, on condition that gunfire which was powerful and destructive enough had opened the way."[8] These precepts were delivered in the clipped voice which earned him the nickname of "Précis-le-Sec." But they were far from popular with many of his superiors on the general staff. The prevailing view was that artillery could operate on its own, and that the cavalry would provide the momentum for attack—as it had in the days of Napoleon.

Pétain's lectures were enough to earn him, as he himself put it, "a bad press at the Ministry."[9] The result was that in 1906 he was posted not, as he had hoped, to a battalion of the eastern army but to the 118th Regiment of infantry at Quimper in Brittany. It was not at all to his liking. Petain's long apprenticeship seemed to be leading to nothing; his promotion up the ranks had been desperately slow. True, he had over the years broadened his intellectual horizons, but this was no compensation for the lack of a settled family life or a truly successful career. Retirement was only 11 years away. Life in a peacetime army was hardly a good preparation for what in all likelihood would be a lonely old age. The best he could do, as he wrote to a nephew in December 1907, was to "find the means, by working a great deal, not to be bored."[10] It is hardly a message of unalloyed joy.

Love, Retirement, and a New Beginning

"Vraiment le petit écolier de Saint-Bertin ne s'attendait pas à faire une si belle carrière."

Pétain was rescued from his Quimper exile in April 1908. A newly appointed commandant of the École de Guerre, General Joseph Maunoury, had met Pétain some years earlier (personal endorsements were a prerequisite for appointments in those days) and invited him back as a full professor. From 1908 to 1911, therefore, Pétain was able to expand on his views on infantry tactics without running the risk of his superior's disapproval. Furthermore, he had the active support of Percin—by then promoted to the rank of general. Percin had been heavily involved in fixing the case against Dreyfus. But Pétain's later expressed distrust of Percin seems to have vanished like the morning mist after Dreyfus's final acquittal in 1908, and Pétain's refusal of promotion as commandant of the École de Tir seems also to have been conveniently forgotten.

Back in Paris, Petain renewed acquaintances—and formed many more. He was in touch again with Nini, whose marriage, in spite of the birth of a son, was not altogether happy. He moved up the social ladder—the Marquis Louis de Chasseloup-Laubat was one of those who introduced him to what passed for the proper society of the day. His old partner in the hunt for female company, Alphonse Guide, was a frequent companion for lunch or dinner. Pétain started to relish his food, and became something of a gourmet, although still not much of a connoisseur of wine.

Intellectually, too, his horizons were expanding. For instance, the philosopher Henri Bergson was the flavor of the intellectual day, and Pétain apparently read and mastered his views to the extent that he was able "to conduct a detailed conversation on Bergson and his works."[1] In itself, this was no mean feat. Bergson was far from an easy read, and his ideas were difficult to grasp. Many—better educated than Pétain—professed themselves defeated. (In a series of lectures at the Collège de France, published in 1907 in his book *L'Évolution Créatrice*, Bergson asserted the primacy of the freedom of the human spirit— *l'élan vital*, which inspired all life. The idea, whatever it signified in practical application, was little short of revolutionary for the time, and for those brought up in the careful discipline of the Catholic Church and of the French Army, not far short of blasphemous.) Even at a late stage in his life, Pétain was starting to educate himself in matters of high philosophical moment—many of them wholly unrelated to his military career.

Pétain's lectures at the École de Guerre now took on an air of theatricality. As in earlier days, the large semicircular auditorium was crowded with senior officers who had just come in to listen and, further back, row upon row of student junior officers. In one sense, it was as it had been before. But there were some important differences. His earlier modesty had now disappeared. As a full professor, he was confident in his delivery. Furthermore, the argument had moved forward. By 1910 there was no longer much debate about infantry tactics. In one form or another all the tactical theorists accepted that infantry, properly supported by artillery, should look to the offensive. Moreover, the experience of the British in the Boer War, for instance, together with a clear appreciation of modern weaponry, had led to the view that the infantry front would have to be dispersed to avoid the menace of the machine gun and the modern rifle. But if artillery could be brought to bear in sufficient quantity to destroy small arms emplacements in support of an infantry attack, all would be well. The importance of firepower, artillery support for infantry and a dispersed infantry front were no longer in dispute.

If Pétain's lectures had little to offer which was not part of the consensus of the time, they were nonetheless rigorous in their analysis and in their presentation. He concentrated on three basic themes. The first was an analysis of the role of the infantry in the Napoleonic Wars and the changes in weaponry which had ensued. The second theme was the analysis of the Franco-Prussian War of 1870–1871. The potential of the Chassepot rifle introduced in 1866 had, he argued, largely been misunderstood by the generals. The tactical implications of the fact that the Chassepot was accurate to a meter at 400 meters had simply passed them by. Pétain was also critical of the Instruction of 1867 which claimed that "with the new weapons the advantage lies with the defensive." "Only the offensive," Pétain held, "could lead to victory."[2] Pétain was quite clear that there had to be an offensive if ground was to be won and the battle successfully brought to an end; but the enemy had to be severely damaged first.

The third theme was built around a study of the various infantry regulations which had appeared between 1875 and 1902. The point was, he insisted again and again, that the modern rifle, properly handled, could inflict such damage that it was foolhardy to rush into an offensive without having prepared the ground with firepower. The Boer War, for instance, was a clear example of how the accurate use of the modern rifle in the hands of skilled marksmen could stop a traditional heavy infantry advance in its tracks.

If nothing else, Pétain's lectures of 1908–1911 show how far the peasant boy of the Artois had come in terms of his intellect and of his personality. The analysis is rigorous. The form is precise and effective. The rogue lecturer of earlier years had become the impressive spokesman for the consensus on infantry tactics—and was regarded by this time as a repository of the wisdom of the day.

Nevertheless, another debate was engaged in late 1910 about the strategic deployment, and the shape, of armies in the field—in other words, what was known in French as "*la grande tactique*."[3] The view set out in a decree of 28 May 1895 containing regulations on the deployment of armies in the field stated that in the initial phase of a battle, an advance guard of infantry and artillery would reconnoiter enemy positions in force. It would penetrate the enemy's defense, stop an enemy attack and start the inevitable process of wearing him down. At a suitable moment the main body of the army would engage in battle. The whole operation would be phased and maximum force would only be applied gradually. This doctrine was based on Napoleonic principles and was proclaimed as the last word on the matter in a book, *De la Conduite de la Guerre*, written by one Colonel Ferdinand Foch in 1896 on his appointment as the new director of the École de Guerre.

An opposite view was put by a relative newcomer—Lieutenant-Colonel Louis de Grandmaison—in two lectures at the École de Guerre in late 1910. He criticized the 1895 regulations on the grounds that the system they advocated—the phased introduction of maximum force—was too slow, allowed successively deployed waves of support attack to be challenged successfully at any given point, and was still—for the historical reasons on which the regulations were based—too fearful of defeat. "There is no other means," Grandmaison declared, "than immediate and total attack."[4] He went on to argue that the proper system was to pack the front line with as many divisions as possible and advance on a broad and extended front. Reconnaissance was no doubt important, but what was more important was to attack on such a wide front that the enemy would either be outflanked or would open up points of weakness which could be exploited.

De Grandmaison's language was, admittedly, intemperate. He did not, however, use the expression "*offensif à l'outrance*" (offensive to the end) as has been claimed. Instead, he used the expression "*offensif sans arrière pensée*" (offensive without second thoughts).[5] But his central message was clear. It was no good trying to mount an attack half-heartedly—while trying to anticipate enemy moves or, worse still, trying to make preparations for possible defeat.

Much has been made of the supposed clash of opinion between the followers of Pétain and the followers of de Grandmaison. In fact, there was no such clash. Apart from the timing, Pétain's supporters—notably Debeney and Maud'huy—supported de Grandmaison without reservation. The reason is simple—a matter of, in the colloquialism, "apples and oranges." De Grandmaison was dealing with the deployment of whole armies and Pétain was dealing with infantry tactics in localized battles. Both of them favored the "offensive." Moreover, the de Grandmaison view—armies deployed in such breadth and weight as to be able to find the weaknesses of their opponents, either by turning their flank or by piercing the center if it was weakened by moves to protect their flank—was reflected in the new field service regulations of 1913–1914.

Pétain's professorship at the École de Guerre came to an end in June 1911. He was due for another posting in the field. By then he had moved up a rank to full colonel, with, as it happened, an enthusiastic recommendation from Foch. He was posted to command the battalion of the 33rd Regiment of infantry, then stationed in Arras. It is difficult to avoid the suspicion that he was regarded as something of an irritant, and that senior officers believed that the sooner he was away from Paris the better. In fact, although he did not particularly like the posting, Pétain took it as a compliment that those who were posted to guard France's northern front were the elite of the French Army of the day. It was regarded as the most vulnerable front by the Ministry of War, and word had it—whether rightly or not—that the most able commanders were posted there.

Pétain had taken a further step in his private life. Before he left Paris he renewed his friendship with Nini. It had turned out that her marriage had been going badly, to the point where she had apparently engaged in a series of extramarital affairs. The temptation was too much for Pétain, who was never one to decline such an obvious opportunity. The battalion commander of Arras regularly deserted his command to travel to Paris for an assignation with Nini—having set up a small pied-à-terre for the purpose.

The new command brought its own difficulties. According to available reports, discipline in the 33rd had become very slack. The long years of peacetime boredom had taken their toll. Soldiers of all ranks did not even bother to come back from leave on their due date.

Pétain wrote to the families of defaulting soldiers demanding a greater degree of patriotism, and he was not slow to punish those who persisted in ill discipline. By the middle of 1912, the regiment was being held up as an example to others. Pétain was helped in his efforts by a shift in the political wind. The trauma of the Dreyfus era had worn off and the climate of opinion was no longer pacifist. Patriotism was back on the agenda. It was even possible for a Radical deputy to say in 1911, "When the guns begin to speak it is best that the politicians keep quiet."[6]

No doubt encouraged by the new mood, Pétain became even more diligent in his efforts. But the sailing was not to be smooth. During 1912 there were two forced breaks. Early in the year he was sent, along with General Léon Durand, to reconnoiter the defenses in the area around Namur in Belgium. The suspicion, perfectly justified in the event, was that if war came Germany would not hesitate to violate Belgian neutrality. As it happened, it did not take the two officers much time to realize that the Belgian defenses were wholly inadequate. This was duly reported to the Ministry of War. Pétain's Belgian task was thus shorter than he had expected. But there was to be a second break—to run a course on infantry tactics at the cavalry school in Saumur on the river Loire. But Pétain much preferred to continue the work of pulling his battalion into shape.

It was to this by then well-disciplined unit that a tall young officer, fresh out of Saint-Cyr, was posted in October 1912. The new *sous-lieutenant* Charles de Gaulle was pleased to be posted to Arras, and particularly to the 33rd. Apart from the attraction of his own background in the north of France, he much admired his new commanding officer. Pétain's lectures at the École de Guerre were still remembered, and de Gaulle admired both his stand against prevailing orthodoxy and his disrespect for the generally accepted conventions of the army. Pétain, in turn, took to de Gaulle. Thus did the strange and ambiguous relationship between the two, which was to be such a feature of both their lives, start in the failing light of a northern French autumn.

By all accounts, Pétain led his battalion well in the annual autumn maneuvers. They were, in truth, a curious affair. They involved virtually the whole French Army, strung out in large formations across various plains in metropolitan France. In all cases the procedure was the same. Umpires would blow whistles and wave flags to indicate that this or that battalion or company or platoon had been blown up or wiped out—or whatever fate the umpires decreed. This done, and the maneuvers completed, everybody went home, satisfied that all was well in the world.

These maneuvers were, as a matter of course, observed by other parties. Indeed, they were invited so to do. The autumn maneuvers of 1913 included many representatives of foreign governments. The French high command thought it better for the maneuvers to be held well away from the German frontier to be less irritating to the German government. This was done, and the maneuvers were deemed to have been a great success. There had been, unfortunately, one casualty—the German military attaché, whose car had run off the road while he was on his way to observe events. Nevertheless, the Kaiser felt able to write to the French president to say how pleased he was that the whole exercise had gone so well. (It was, as a matter of fact, only a few hours later that he told the King of the Belgians that he was tired of the French and determined to finish them off "by a necessary and inevitable war.")[7]

There was another curious incident, in which Pétain displayed what can only be described as flagrant insubordination. At one point in maneuvers the

33rd was ordered to storm a hill and capture the village on its summit. They set off with flags flying and a band leading them. It was quite obviously absurd, but the hill was duly stormed, the village duly captured, and the umpires declared that there had been no casualties on the French side, while the enemy had been successfully eliminated to a man.

Pétain was unable to contain himself. When his divisional commander asked him to give his opinion on the exercise, Pétain turned to his men and pronounced in a loud voice that he was "sure that intention of General Le Gallet, in order to impress it on your minds, a catalogue of all the mistakes that a modern army should not make."[8] General Le Gallet's reaction has not been recorded.

By this time Pétain had become convinced that further promotion was out of the question. He had made too many enemies by his early lectures, his sarcasm and his disrespect for senior officers. In short, his career was finished. By way of confirmation, word had it in the Ministry of War that he would never be promoted to the substantive rank of *général de brigade* (Brigadier-General). On 24 April 1914, therefore, Pétain was still a colonel when he left the 33rd in Arras to take command of the 4th Infantry Brigade. Such a posting was not unusual. Typically, a brigade was commanded by a colonel. Pétain's brigade, however, was not an obviously cohesive force. It was spread widely across northern France. The 110th Infantry Regiment was stationed just outside Dunkirk, and the 8th Infantry Regiment was spread between Saint-Omer, Calais and Boulogne-sur-Mer. Of all the choices he could make among those battalion headquarters, Pétain chose to make his own brigade headquarters in Saint-Omer— the city of the two saints which he had known in his childhood. By then he had come to the conclusion that this was to be his last posting. In short, his military career, which had followed a pattern typical of a peacetime officer of some (but not outstanding) distinction, was coming to a gentle end.

There was one consolation, if that is the right word. His relationship with Nini, after a bad break in April 1913, had been restored. Nini had apparently become tired of their secret trysts. Making love in a small pied-à-terre with a gentleman who had quickly to leave her to return to his duties—and to the affection of other ladies—was apparently no longer to her taste. It seemed as though the relationship was at its end. But a few months later, Pétain had a nasty fall from his horse, which needed a quick operation on his knee. He used the opportunity— a frequent male ploy—to write to Nini asking for sympathy, and perhaps more. "I had given you all my love," he wrote, "all my devotion, all my life. I shall never recover from this."[9] It was, of course, not wholly true. He had been philandering with the ladies of Arras all the time. But it seems that Nini fell for it. Once out of hospital, Pétain wrote again suggesting a meeting. Nini agreed. The result was predictable. "With what intoxication," he wrote afterwards, "my lips took your kisses in total forgetfulness of everything which separates us."[10]

Not all was sweetness and light. Nini accused Pétain of being obsessed with sex. She wanted something more spiritual—this time it was her turn to use a well-established female ploy. Pétain tried to wriggle his way out of this charge—uncomfortably near to the mark as it was. "If I did not love you physically it would not be love," he wrote, "since love takes over the entire physical and intellectual being."[11] It was a good try, but for those who were familiar with Pétain's philandering it rang false. Nonsense or not, Nini seems to have been satisfied, and by the time Pétain left Arras for Saint-Omer in April 1914 the visits to the pied-à-terre in Paris had been resumed.

The parade in Saint-Omer on Bastille Day 1914 was meant to be Pétain's farewell to the army. He thought it fitting that he should make his final display in the city of his childhood. Not only that, but he had found, through a local *notaire*, a small house just outside Saint-Omer to which he planned to retire.

There was, however, to be a hitch in his plans. On 28 June 1914, just over two weeks before Pétain's final parade, Archduke Franz Ferdinand, the heir to the empire of Austro-Hungary, was assassinated at Sarajevo. Europe suddenly found itself hurtling toward war. The world was about to change—and to change for good. Pétain's plans for retirement moved quickly off his agenda. There was a job to be done; and, in practice, there was no alternative for him but to stay in the army and help to do it.

There is little doubt that, had the Pétain story ended there, it would rate no more than a short footnote in the history of the French Army—yet another military career spent without seeing a shot fired in anger. He would probably not have married Nini, for whom marriage to a colonel and retirement in the country would have had limited attraction. But in the middle of 1914 he was rather pleased with himself. He thought that his career had been a great success, given his peasant background.

What neither he nor anybody else could have expected was that his career was about to be much more spectacular and infinitely more successful. At the age of 58 he was on the point of retiring as a colonel. At the age of 62 he was to be still in active service as a Marshal of France.

The Dogs of War

"Ce fut . . . vraiment la première journée 'cruelle' de la guerre"

To the general public, the outbreak of war in early August 1914 came as something of a surprise. True, there had been intense diplomatic activity in the weeks following the assassination of Archduke Franz Ferdinand, but diplomacy in those days was conducted by a select group, speaking to each other in the most elegant French, whose deliberations were not usually disclosed to the outside world. The press, whether in London, Paris or Berlin, was hardly bothered. The assassination in Paris on 31 July of the French Socialist leader Jean Jaurès, for instance, created a much more interesting storm.

The summer was exceptionally fine. The Kaiser set off for his customary three-week cruise in the Norwegian fjords; the president of France, Raymond Poincaré, embarked on a state visit to Russia before, in his turn, taking his holiday; and the beaches all over Europe were filling up. And Pétain, in his last flourish in Saint-Omer, gave no sign that he was aware that he would be at war within three weeks.

By the last week in July, however, the atmosphere had changed. Austria had sent an ultimatum to Serbia on 23 July, demanding the immediate arrest of Serbian officials believed to be implicated in the crime and demanding that Austro-Hungarian prosecutors should sit alongside the Serbian authorities both in the investigations and in any subsequent trials. The Austrian ultimatum was noticeably fierce; and it was at that point that the diplomats went into overdrive. Notes sped all around Europe counseling caution, advising the Serbs to accept the terms of the Austrian ultimatum, warning all concerned about the dangers, and proposing meetings of all parties. It was to no avail. On 28 July, Austria formally declared war on Serbia, sparking off in Russia (Serbia's traditional friends) at first partial and then total mobilization. Germany, in its turn, issued a series of ultimata—to Russia, to France, and, lastly, to Belgium, demanding free access through her territory for operations against France. Britain, too, issued an ultimatum. But by then, whatever its merits, the war of the ultimatum was over. Everybody mobilized.

Both Germany and France rightly assumed that mobilization would lead inexorably to armed conflict. From one assumption followed another. It had become clear to German strategists that it was no use massing troops on France's eastern frontier. The rail connections from the Rhine bridges were too difficult, and furthermore, the French frontier was too well fortified. In particular, the rail connections from Cologne, which was a central point of assembly, were much easier if the movement of troops was directed toward the immediate west—in other words, toward Belgium.

The use of Belgian territory was therefore necessary for the execution of the German war plan. In its original version, which came to be named after its author, Graf Alfred von Schlieffen, it required a mass movement of German cavalry and infantry through Belgium and down into France. This concentration of military power would allow German armies to move southward to the west of Paris and subsequently turn eastward to envelop the French army which lay along France's eastern frontier; which, after the inevitable French surrender, would conclude the war. The war, it was estimated, would be over in 40 days.

It remained to be seen how well it would work out in practice. In fact, even after all the years developing the Schlieffen plan, there were still those who had their doubts. Field-Marshal Helmuth von Moltke, the commander-in-chief of the German armed forces which would have to execute it, thought the plan would not work if the enemy massed enough troops and military hardware to defy the German assault through Belgium. The German frontier, and Alsace and Lorraine, could not just be ignored. Thus, even before any action, it was clear that the mice were nibbling at the plan itself.

The French, too, had a plan—Plan XVII. This was also supposed to lead to a quick end to the war. By ensuring a speedy and efficient mobilization—the lessons of the chaotic 1870 mobilization had been carefully studied—a dashing French offensive would rush through Alsace and Lorraine and into Germany, cross the Rhine and not stop before it arrived at the gates of Berlin. In fact, Plan XVII, in its final form, was little more than a plan for the mobilization of large units. It was certainly not an operational plan for the use of those units. Nevertheless, such was the belief of the French military establishment in the virtue of an immediate offensive to the east that it was difficult to know what was to be done with troops except march into the lost provinces of Alsace and Lorraine. Moreover, the plan was firmly based on the assumption that the Germans would not violate Belgian neutrality for fear of bringing Britain, one of its guarantors, into the war. Finally, the textbook methods of attack were to be rigorously followed: The artillery would destroy the enemy's fire-power, allowing the cavalry to charge freely and the infantry to occupy the ground. Unfortunately, in practice there was no reasonable method of communication between the three arms and the artillery barrage was uncoordinated and ineffective.

In the event, neither plan was successful. The German thrust through Belgium was unexpectedly held up, first by the resistance of the forts at the entry point of Liège and then by some further stout defense by the small Belgian army. In its turn, the French mobilization was indeed efficient, but the subsequent attack eastward was met by such resolute German artillery and machine-gun fire that it was halted after gruesomely heavy French casualties.

By then, French Commander-in-Chief General Joseph Joffre had ordered Plan XVII to be quickly modified to allow troops to be moved up into Belgium to block the German attack. In doing so, they were to link up with the British Expeditionary Force (BEF), dispatched to Belgium under the command of Field-Marshal Sir John French. The BEF was, even at the moment Joffre changed the plan, disembarking at the Channel ports. Thus Plan XVII was consigned to the wastebasket and Plan XVII(b) emerged.

The area of Belgium to be defended was the triangle of the southern Belgian plain bordered by the river Sambre to the north and the river Meuse to the east. This, it was thought, would not only be enough to halt the German advance but also provide a springboard for a counterattack eastward. But, whatever the assumptions behind Plan XVII (b), it was clear that French strategy had fundamentally changed. Those who had thought that there would an immediate breakthrough to the east (even to the gates of Berlin) suddenly found themselves confronted with the idea that French soil had to be defended. The north now had to be defended; and the force which was chosen for the role, the order went on, was the French 5th Army; and one of the 5th Army's units was the 4th Infantry Brigade, commanded by Colonel Pétain.

The French generals whose job was to implement Plan XVII(b) were something of a motley crew. Joffre himself was a bull of a man, heavily overweight as a result of his fondness for good food, but nevertheless of great intelligence and clarity of vision. By training first a railway engineer, and then a gunner in the artillery, he was perhaps short on imagination, but he was long on courage. He also had a formidable ability to bring his subordinates into line, either by his refusal to panic or by the use of his temper—which, when unleashed, was ferocious. His main characteristic was imperturbability. Indeed, his placidity was such that at times his subordinates were left baffled. For instance, there were occasions when Joffre would turn up at a headquarters, listen to what he was told by staff officers urging one course or another, and then leave again without saying a word. It was, by any standards, unnerving.

General Charles Lanrezac, the commander of the 5th Army which had formed the left flank of Joffre's initial order of battle and which was now to move into Belgium, was a quite different matter; and, needless to say, the two men did not get on. They had little in common beyond corpulence. It was said that Lanrezac had some mulatto blood in him—his dark and flabby face was said to show it—but he had inherited the title of "marquis" which, apparently, he never used. When he was teaching at the École de Guerre—inspirationally, according to accounts—his nickname was "*le voyou*" ("the hooligan") because of his habit of shouting at his pupils. Although he was certainly able, he was rude and morose. He was also irrevocably opposed to everything British, and since part of his job was to link up with the BEF, this was to prove disastrous. Nor was his contempt confined to the British; the Belgians were just as bad in his view.

General Louis Franchet d'Esperey, on the other hand, the commander of the 1st Army Corps under Lanrezac, was a character from a quite different mold. Nicknamed "Desperate Frankie" by the British, he was short and squat like a brick. Even his face seemed to be made up of right angles. His preferred method of command was to shout instructions in a high-pitched voice. There was no question of asking for advice or of permitting any questions. As it happened, however, Franchet d'Esperey had his courteous side, and, furthermore, was anglophile. In sending telegrams to the British he signed them punctiliously "Franchet d'Esperey KCVO," in recognition of the British knighthood he had received in April 1914.

It was this mixed bunch that Pétain had to deal with as a subordinate commander in the field. He liked and admired Joffre. In the days to come, when communications between Lanrezac and Sir John French virtually broke down, he would absorb at least some of the former's intense dislike of the British. As for Franchet d'Esperey, he was so far from Pétain's peasant background that a meeting of minds was, to put it mildly, not easy, and was only to come later on in the war.

Thus it was that Pétain found himself, on 5 August, ordered to assemble his brigade and to move, with the utmost dispatch, some 200 kilometers to the southeast to the town of Hirson on the Belgian frontier, there to join up with rest of the 1st Army Corps. It was far from an easy task. To be sure, he was confident in the spirit of his troops—the "*gars du nord*,"[1] "the lads from the North," as he called them, using the patois of his peasant childhood (which he did when talking to his soldiers—to crucial effect later on in the war). But garrison duty was no serious introduction to the real thing. Moreover, the brigade had only a nucleus of regular soldiers, the remainder being conscripts, or recently discharged or recalled reservists. It is little wonder that Pétain, when he received the orders to move on what was to be a perilous journey, complained that he had had no time to pull his brigade into shape. Moreover, he must have recognized that he himself had no experience of the fearful nature of warfare and little idea of what it was to become in the future.

The 4th Brigade set out on a forced march eastward to join the rest of the 1st Army Corps, and the rest of the 5th Army, on its journey into Belgium. It was a long, hard struggle, particularly for the reservists, who had been civilians only a week earlier. Not only were they in the middle of a blistering heat wave, but they were carrying, in addition to their rifle, a pack and gear that weighed some 22 kilograms. Moreover, they were required to wear the traditional uniform of the infantry of the line—red trousers and a blue open jacket made of wool. The Grande Armée of Napoleon had worn it, and it would strengthen morale, so it was said, for modern soldiers to show themselves as the descendants of the Emperor's formidable military machine. The German infantry, of course, wore field grey; and the British, after the experience of the Boer War, wore khaki. By the time they reached Hirson, Pétain's troops were dead tired. But there was to be no rest. On 10 August, the 1st Army Corps was ordered to march north and east to take up positions guarding the west bank of the river Meuse. This they did—shadowed, as it happened, all the way by a German spotter plane. There were many stragglers and some men collapsed from the heat. It was said that noncommissioned officers had to use sticks to get their men off the ground. Nevertheless, on the evening of 12 August they reached their positions. The 4th Brigade itself arrived at Revin, threw off their clothes and equipment and settled down to sleep. But even then they were not given any time to rest. That night, the 1st Army Corps was given further instructions—to move northward to occupy the area east of Philippeville, and in particular to secure the bridge at Dinant; yet again, they rose to their blistered feet and marched.

It was at six o'clock in the morning of 13 August that the first detachments of the advance guard of 1st Army Corps arrived in front of Dinant bridge. Just as they sat down to rest, the German artillery and machine guns, strategically located on the citadel on the other side of the river, opened up. The point platoon tried to rush the bridge. Almost immediately the platoon commander, Lieutenant de Gaulle, was hit in the knee, and only escaped with difficulty. He left his platoon sergeant on the bridge—dead, along with several of his platoon. As he crawled away, de Gaulle noted "the dull thud of bullets entering the bodies of the dead and the wounded which lay there."[2] It was de Gaulle's introduction to real warfare. Pétain's introduction was not long in coming.

The 4th Infantry Brigade was not far away. Their march had been severely hampered by the flood of refugees trying to escape the German advance. The Belgian farmers had no idea of their destination; it was simply a time to move. For a day or two the weather had broken, leaving the roads a sea of mud. It then cleared again, and left the roads a desert of dust. Indeed, at one point Pétain had found himself giving orders for road repairs so that the soldiers could make their way past the refugees going in the opposite direction. In a diary of the journey, he noted the warmth of the reception given to the French troops, and took evident pleasure in describing the women of the homes where he was billeted.

On 15 August they finally arrived in front of the Meuse bridges of Yvoir, Houx and Anhée which they had been ordered to protect. Here, in whatever state they were, they were to prepare for battle.

It was on that day that Pétain saw his first action. In fact, as so often in war, the whole thing was due to a mistake. There had been an unauthorized salvo from an overenthusiastic French artillery battery at Dinant. The Germans had responded, and the commander of the 1st Infantry Division, General Deligny, had to move his troops in haste to deal with a possible follow-up German attack. This duly happened. The German retaliation was swift and effective. In the ensuing exchange, General Deligny himself was wounded when a shell burst in front of him. Furthermore, some 100 soldiers of various ranks were subsequently registered as killed, nearly 600 were wounded, but no fewer than 500 simply "disappeared"—presumably blown to pieces by German shells. It is little wonder that Pétain wished to withdraw his brigade, and to order them to construct all the defenses they could in the way of trenches and barbed wire. To say the least, it was not a happy baptism of fire.

Pétain wrote as much to Nini, whose divorce had become final in March 1914 and who, according to the harassed colonel, had been pursuing him ever since. True, he had been something of a willing victim, but war had brought a different tone. "We had a bloody engagement," he wrote, "on the 15th. A great battle is coming; I go to it without regret and without fear, since I have made the sacrifice of my life; the physical sufferings which may be inflicted on me are little compared with the moral tortures undergone because of you."[3] In other words, he was inviting her to let him get on with his war.

The German strategy had become clear. The German 1st Army, under General Alexander von Kluck, was to strike westwards to Brussels and then turn left to make for the French frontier. The 2nd Army, under General Karl von Bülow, was also to move westwards, past Namur, follow the line of the river Sambre to the southwest and, turning left to guard von Kluck's right flank, join him in the race to the frontier. The 3rd Army, under General Baron Max von Hausen, was to cross the Meuse at several points between Dinant and Namur, and then head southwards, guarding von Bülow's left flank.

But there was a weakness. As his army moved westward, von Bülow's left flank would be exposed. Joffre saw an opportunity. Accordingly, he ordered Lanrezac to attack von Bülow on the Sambre at Charleroi. The BEF would advance to protect his left flank. At the same time, Franchet d'Esperey's 1st Army Corps was to hold or destroy the Meuse bridges to prevent von Hausen from attacking Lanrezac's right flank. With any luck, von Bülow's army would by that time be crippled, leaving von Kluck isolated and vulnerable to attack from both Lanrezac and the BEF on his left. The plan was clear, decisive, and, on paper, excellent. On 21 August 1914, therefore, the Battle of Charleroi began.

Needless to say, it did not go according to plan. Obviously in ignorance of the French dispositions, units of von Bülow's army succeeded in crossing the Sambre. Lanrezac ordered Franchet d'Esperey immediately to leave his position on the Meuse and engage them. But that left his flank—and the Meuse crossings—unprotected, allowing von Hausen in his turn to cross the Meuse in their rear.

On 23 August Franchet d'Esperey changed direction yet again, ordering Pétain to cover his flank as he tried to push von Hausen back across the river. The battle was hard, and much blood was shed—but to no apparent effect. By the evening of 23 August, Lanrezac had realized that he risked being attacked on both flanks at once and possibly encircled. The Battle of Charleroi had undoubtedly been lost. This being so, there was only one possible conclusion. Lanrezac promptly ordered a general retreat. The instruction was firm: "With the aim of evacuating as soon as possible an area where the deployment of the offensive capability of our troops and the co-ordination of efforts are difficult, the general commanding the Army has decided to resume the retreat" (*reprendre la marche rétrograde*).[4] First Army Corps was to form the rearguard for the 5th Army; and 4th Brigade was to form the rearguard of 1st Army Corps. The British, apparently, could do what they wanted—which, in the end, was the retreat from Mons.

Bitterly, Pétain seized on the expression "*reprendre la rétrograde.*" What it really meant was defeat. Depressingly, the excursion of the 4th Brigade into Belgium had lasted only 11 days, and his troops were tired and disheveled. The reserve forces had amply revealed how badly trained they were. All in all, their first action had shown that the French troops were no match for the Germans. Pétain, in his own mind, tried to shift the responsibility onto the government. He was starting on the long road, familiar to military men and a recurrent theme in his future, of blaming civilian politicians. But the truth was that French troops, badly trained, badly led and badly equipped, were once again called on to defend French territory.

For Pétain, the news was not all bad. On his arrival at the little town of Iviers, he learned that he was to be promoted to the rank of brigadier general, and that he might soon be given the command of a division. Moreover, on 28 August there was a halt to the retreat. Joffre had planned another counterattack, to block the German advance in order to allow the assembly of a newly constituted 6th Army under General Michel Maunoury, whose task it would be, if the retreat continued, to defend Paris. Joffre ordered Lanrezac to attack von Bülow's 2nd Army by crossing the river Oise and heading west for St. Quentin. At first light on 29 August, therefore, units of Lanrezac's army duly crossed the river, took the Germans by surprise, and managed to advance some four kilometers toward St. Quentin. The Germans soon regrouped, however, and by midday had retaken the lost ground and were even beginning to attack Lanrezac's northern units.

Lanrezac quickly perceived the danger, and ordered Franchet d'Esperey to counterattack to the north with vigor. Franchet d'Esperey, who had been waiting impatiently all day, needed no further encouragement. Divisional commanders were goaded into action. They and their troops were clearly more frightened of their general than they were of the Germans ahead. "The little square man with the bullet head, whose gestures were like cracking whips, as violent as dynamite," was terrifying in his energy. But he was also respected, "and liked, too, for men love a real leader."[5]

Franchet d'Esperey, on horseback and surrounded by mounted staff officers, gave the order for general attack in the direction of the town of Guise. The bands started playing, the colors were unfurled, bayonets were fixed and the 1st Army Corps went on a brisk offensive. Franchet d'Esperey placed himself at the head of one of the leading brigades. "As he rode by, he spotted a sad, stern-faced officer with a drooping moustache the color of pepper and salt standing with the small staff of [his] brigade . . . and called out to him as he rode by 'What do you think of this maneuver, *Monsieur le Professeur à l'École de Guerre?*' "[6] The officer was, indeed, Colonel Pétain.

Pétain's 4th Brigade, which up until then had been held in reserve, was ordered into the attack late in the evening. He moved his troops forward in open order, to take advantage of any features of the ground which could give shelter from enemy fire. But time was short. To be sure, a farm was captured; but by that time it was difficult to see much apart from the burning farmhouse. There were dead men lying on the open field; the wounded were screaming in the near darkness. That apart, there was a danger that his troops, unused to nighttime fighting, would lose their way. In fact, much of the night was spent in finding out where they all were and regrouping them for a further assault in the morning. All in all, it had been a dreadful introduction to the horror of war.

Nevertheless, Franchet d'Esperey had led a successful action. French soldiers had shown the enemy what they were capable of. But it did not lead to much. On the morning of 30 August, 4th Brigade found itself isolated. Lanrezac had sent orders that the general retreat should be resumed. As it happened, he was right; there was, once more, the danger of encirclement. Depressing as it was, in the moment of their first success the French were moving backwards again. But the Battle of Guise had been won. It was the French Army's first victory of the war, and stopped the German advance in its tracks.

Pétain's brigade had played only a limited part in the Battle of Guise, but Pétain himself had by then earned the reputation of being a competent, disciplined, if somewhat undistinguished officer. At least he had not failed, and, in the midst of so much failure, that in itself was merit. It was certainly this that allowed him to survive the purge of senior officers undertaken by Joffre in the late summer and autumn of 1914.

The purge was understandably brutal. Apart from the prevailing incompetence, the average age of a general in July 1914 was just over 64 years. Many generals had been appointed under André's efforts at "republicanizing" the army. Moreover, a number of retired generals had been called back with the mobilization of the reservists. Certainly, there was much weeding to do. By 6 September, three army commanders (including Lanrezac, who was replaced by his erstwhile subordinate Franchet d'Esperey) had been sacked, along with scores of corps and divisional commanders and 14 brigadiers. Dozens more went by November. In January 1915 all but 7 of the 48 commanders of peacetime infantry divisions had been dismissed or moved. Pétain was a clear beneficiary of Joffre's purge. On 3 September he took command of the 6th Infantry Division, part of the 3rd Army Corps of the 5th Army. When he arrived, however, he found his new division in a sad state. The soldiers were "like skeletons . . . They turned their exhausted eyes toward the as yet unknown commander and seemed to implore him to give them some respite from the long catalogue of their miseries."[7] Pétain brought his units into close order, so that their commanders were able to exercise more efficient oversight; he was severe in punishing laziness and negligence—not to mention sporadic looting; but he was equally ready with a word of encouragement to his troops.

Yet the orders were still to retreat. By the time Pétain took command, at the village of Fismes, they were deep into French territory only 30 kilometers from the city of Reims. It was not until the evening of 5 September that there was a break. In six days they had retreated over 80 kilometers, in difficult terrain and in constant fear of enemy ambush. It was now time to stand and fight.

By then the Schlieffen plan had been abandoned by the Germans. "Without pause or preparation, [Moltke] was shifting the conceptual base of the German advance from envelopment to breakthrough."[8] Von Kluck was, understandably, confused. Already ahead of von Bülow, convinced that he had a clear run to attack the French 5th Army, he decided to ignore the order to protect von Bülow's flank and simply march on. On 3 September units of his army crossed the Marne.

All this was carefully observed, through intercepted signals and by spotter aircraft, by Joffre and the military governor of Paris, General Joseph Galliéni. It seemed to both of them that von Kluck, on his new course, was dangerously exposing his right flank to an attack by Maunoury's 6th Army, whose job hitherto had been to sit tight and defend Paris. Furthermore, a gap was opening up between his advance and the slower von Bülow, which could be exploited by the BEF. This, in turn, would allow Franchet d'Esperey's 5th Army to mount a frontal assault on von Kluck's left wing. The 9th Army under General Foch could then attack the unprotected von Bülow. Joffre and his staff drew up their plan carefully. The stage was thus set for the first Battle of the Marne.

On 5 September, Joffre appealed to Sir John French to accept his plan. Fortunately, the sour relations with the BEF had vastly improved since the dismissal of Lanrezac. Sir John agreed. The British would march.

At 6:30 P.M. on that evening Franchet d'Esperey issued his orders to his corps and divisional commanders. The battle, he told his generals, would last several days, and corps commanders were instructed not to commit all their infantry at the outset. These orders were reflected in Pétain's orders to his division—but Pétain added the provision that the infantry should not leave their positions for the advance until the artillery had done its work to his satisfaction.

The following morning the French artillery laid down a heavy barrage on the German lines, and in the afternoon the infantry moved forward. Almost immediately they came under equally intense artillery attack—and started to waver. One of Pétain's brigades lost 600 men in two hours to capture one farm.

It looked as though the attack would stall, at least in his sector, until Pétain himself, in an extraordinary display of bravado, rode up to his front line and, seemingly oblivious to the shells raining around him, took personal control of the forward troops. It says a great deal about the state of morale of his troops that Pétain had to resort to such desperate measures.

As Pétain had calculated, the 6th Division rallied to its commander. By nightfall, the German 6th Brandenburg facing them had been driven back over two kilometers and had abandoned the strategically important village of Monceau-les-Provins. A brigade from the neighboring 18th Army Corps was able to move through and secure the village. At that point, it was clear that there would be little more action that day. As the sun set, Pétain turned to his staff officers and said, "The sun is going to bed; we will do the same."[9] With that, he turned his horse around and trotted back to his headquarters.

The German line had been broken, and during the next few days Pétain's main task was to advance northward harrying the retreating enemy as it went. They marched nearly 90 kilometers in six days. The feat must go down as one of the most remarkable achievements in military warfare. An army which three weeks before had looked irretrievably beaten had roused itself, defeated its enemy and pursued him right up to the bounds of physical endurance.

It was along the line of the Aisne canal that the German retreat was called to a halt. On the evening of 13 September Pétain ordered an attack across the canal in the direction of the village of Brimont. For the first time for many days the French met determined German resistance. The attack floundered with heavy casualties. As it turned out, this was to be the pattern over the next few weeks. The German defensive positions were so strong, and their artillery so powerful, that they could not be shifted. A series of French attacks failed dismally. Nevertheless, it was essential to maintain the rhythm of these attacks to keep the German troops pinned down. On 1 October, Joffre ordered aerial reconnaissance to see whether it was worth having another shot. The answer came back that it might be. A further major French offensive was announced for 12 October, but few thought that it had much chance of success. Certainly Pétain was gloomy about its prospects, and only ordered one battalion of infantry, supported by artillery, to take part. He was not far off the mark. The offensive was a failure.

Pétain by then had become pessimistic about this form of warfare. On 16 October, he wrote to his corps commander, General Hache. The whole picture, he said, had changed. The campaign now resembled siege warfare. It was no good wasting human lives in futile assaults. The whole concept of war needed to be thought through again. In the future, it would be heavy artillery which would determine the course of a battle. The French 75 mm light artillery was all very well when used in support of infantry movements, but it was no good in static trench warfare. Others, for instance generals Édouard de Castelnau and Auguste Dubail, commanders respectively of the 2nd and 1st Armies along the eastern frontier, were coming to the same conclusion. Nonetheless, it was to be some time before the general staff would be brought round.

But Pétain and his division had performed well in the Battle of the Marne, and recognition was not long in coming. On 16 October 1914 he was appointed officer of the Légion d'Honneur—the citation records that he was "remarkable in his bravery, his calm when under fire, and in the example that he sets to his men."[10] Moreover, on 20 October he was ordered to report to General Foch, by then commander of the armies of the north. He was to be given the command of 33rd Army Corps, whose headquarters were at Aubigny near Arras. His immediate superior, as commander of the 10th Army, was his old friend General Maud'huy. Thus in a matter of under three months of war, Pétain had achieved a rate of promotion unthinkable in the previous 40 years of peace.

The appointment, although again due to Joffre's purge, was perfectly sensible. Pétain knew the country well. It was, after all, his home, and before the war he had conducted maneuvers with his battalion on the Lorette plateau and on Vimy Ridge. Be that as it may, he hardly had time to settle in before he was called on to repel a ferocious German attack aimed at Arras itself. By the time he took up his command, German units were within three kilometers of the city. The situation was desperate. Pétain had to respond immediately, which he did. The German attack was halted, but French casualties were very severe. Pétain was not slow to draw the lesson.

The German attack had not been an isolated occurrence. In fact, it was to set the pattern of the next few weeks, in what became known as the Battle of Artois. The Germans would attack, and initially gain ground. The French would resist, and then counterattack to regain the lost ground. From time to time, the position would be reversed. The French would attack and gain ground, which the Germans would recover in their counterattack. Both sides suffered horrendous casualties.

It was obvious to Pétain, if not to others, that new tactical thinking was required. Seeing the number of French casualties in these attacks and counterattacks, Pétain adopted a much more subtle approach. In defense, camouflage became all-important, as were centers of resistance in built-up areas. Trenches were dug deeper and machine guns more carefully hidden. Above all, a second line of defense was constituted, on which a German attack would break if it managed to pierce the first line. Counterattacks were only permissible when the enemy had been weakened by his own attacks. Random and meaningless offensive movements were no longer on the Pétain agenda.

As it turned out, the tactic was successful. By the end of October it had become clear that the Battle of Artois had ground to a stalemate. To be sure, Arras had been saved, but the French troops were far too exhausted, and morale was far too low, to allow any major offensive in the foreseeable future. The German troops, too, were exhausted, and started to wonder what they were doing so far away from home. The conclusion was unavoidable. It was time to dig in.

"The German is the Enemy"

"Adieu 1914 et vive 1915 qui sera l'année de la victoire"

"I got to know Pétain well when he commanded the 33rd [Army] Corps on the deadly Lorette Ridge, today covered by a forest of wooden crosses. In those early days of the War it buttressed the Vimy Ridge near the junction with the British Army, where my duties as a liaison officer with the French often led me. From almost daily visits to this sector, careful examination of the tactical methods employed by Pétain, his use of fire power, the combination of artillery and infantry power, his disciplinary practices which were both firm and stern, the ingenuity with which he set up small factories and workshops to provide him with some of the weapons and objects his men needed but could not obtain from army sources, I soon realised that there was much to be learned from him which could be of benefit to our own army."

Thus Lieutenant (acting Captain) Edward Louis Spears, the official liaison between the British and the French army headquarters in the autumn of 1914. "I presently found out," Spears went on, "and wondered at my discovery, that General Pétain had a marked sense of humor deeply concealed under his frozen exterior, like *edelweiss* beneath a snowdrift, as unexpected as a spring of fresh water in the desert."[1]

Spears had accompanied the BEF after the Battle of the Marne to their new station at the northernmost end of the Allied front line at the same time as Pétain had taken command of the 33rd Army Corps. The move, requested earnestly by Joffre, had proved to be right. After the Marne, both armies had tried to maneuver round their opponents on their northern flank. Sometimes called the "Race to the Sea," the operation consisted of attacks by both sides where generals perceived that the enemy line ended. It was not finished until both sides had completed their front. It was the BEF's task to seal off the northern section, which they did after the bloody first Battle of Ypres. The line of trenches by the end of 1914 stretched without a break from the Belgian coast to the Swiss frontier.

Spears was bilingual in French and English. However, he was neither one thing nor the other. The son of a raffish commission agent, probably of German origin, and of Irish stock on his mother's side, he had had a signally unhappy childhood, and then grown into an unruly and frequently violent adolescent. But he was ambitious; and his chief ambition was to rise so far socially as to be accepted as a true member of the English aristocracy. Spears joined the British Army through the Irish militia at the age of sixteen in 1903 and was gazetted into the Royal Irish Hussars in 1906. At the end of the war, still intent on establishing his English credentials, he moved seemingly effortlessly into the House of Commons as a Conservative MP. Yet he could never quite slough off his origins. For all his life Spears was to be an outsider, and as such, he took to Pétain. Their paths crossed repeatedly during the war, the interwar period, and, most notably, in June 1940. Spears's undoubted charm was spread widely. Maud'huy, too, enjoyed his company. Indeed, on one occasion Maud'huy persuaded Spears to accompany him and three of his corps commanders (of whom one was Pétain) on a visit to the ruined city of Arras. (Spears thought the idea "really stupidly dangerous.")[2]

If Pétain's adoption of this strange half-French, half-Irish hussar showed the "outsider" aspect of his character, his friendship for two officers in his command, Bernard Serrigny and Emile Fayolle showed the other—the army as a surrogate extended family. Serrigny, doting but self-important, had been known to Pétain as a junior officer in the 8th Infantry Battalion. Fayolle, on the other hand, was an older acquaintance: a fellow member of the "Plewna" year at Saint-Cyr, he had been on Pétain's staff at the École de Guerre, and was now one of Pétain's divisional generals. Yet there was a divide. There was, after all, a difference in rank—of which Pétain was always punctiliously aware. Both Serrigny and Fayolle were admirers rather than friends of equality, although Serrigny's admiration, which comes out very clearly in his diaries, is much more devoted than that of Fayolle, who from time to time in his own diaries had some harsh opinions of his friendly superior officer.

When Pétain was given command of the 33rd Army Corps it was understood that he would follow the instructions of his army commander, Maud'huy, to take the offensive wherever possible. But Pétain knew perfectly well that to follow Maud'huy's instructions successfully he had to restore the battered morale of his newly inherited troops. During the days of inaction after the hectic defense of Arras, his soldiers had become bored. They even started to ask themselves awkward questions about why they were there. In short, they had to be found something to do. Pétain's solution in the dreary autumn of 1914 was to allow them to go on leave to Amiens, and even to make contact with what Serrigny chastely described as "female elements."[3] But most important, he went out to meet his troops on the ground. He visited each of his three divisions, talked to the brigade and battalion commanders, went down into the trenches, and at one point even told the machine gunners in a trench where their line of fire should be. He noted the poor state of their equipment and clothing and hectored the army's quartermasters for more supplies. He noted carefully the shortage of ammunition and complained bitterly about it to Maud'huy.

All this served to alleviate what Serrigny described as the "depressing monotony" of the front.[4] There were other unofficial diversions for the troops that became unthinkable later in the war. On 12 November 1914, for instance, a hare ran into the 100 meters of no man's land which separated the trenches of the 10th Army Corps from the enemy. Immediately, fire from both sides was concentrated not on the enemy but on the hare. To general surprise, the hare was hit and killed. But at that point there arose a difficult problem: To whom did the unfortunate hare belong? The problem was solved by German soldiers shouting that they would rather have tobacco than the hare. A delicate negotiation followed. In the end, the exchange rate was fixed: four packets of tobacco for the hare. The deal done, a French soldier went out, deposited the tobacco and collected the hare; whereupon a German soldier came out and collected the tobacco. After that, the two sides started shooting at one another again.

On Pétain's front, the two lines of trenches were particularly close, and there was a spring between the two in no man's land. Each morning a cow emerged from the German trenches to drink at the spring and to graze. The cow made a convenient conduit for messages between the two lines—messages which were tied to the cow's tail. On the same day that the hare met its fate further down the line, the cow was bringing a message from the Germans to the French: the French were to get their water from the spring at 10 A.M. and the Germans at 11 A.M. The French sent back a message—via the cow—that they accepted the arrangement. It was rigorously adhered to.

When he finally heard what the troops were up to, Pétain put a stop to it. "The German," ran his order of 14 December 1914, "is the enemy under whatever pretext he presents himself, and the first duty of every soldier is to shoot at him as soon as he shows himself."[5] Improving morale was one thing; slackness in discipline was another. Indeed, Pétain was enough of a martinet to have no compunction about enforcing military discipline. Fayolle noted that Pétain's dealing with self-inflicted wounds was particularly fierce. On one occasion he was prepared to have 25 men who had shot themselves in the hand or the foot taken out and executed by firing squad; on reflection, he commuted the sentence. He ordered that the offenders should be tied up and left in no man's land near the German trenches for a night.

Even before and through Christmas 1914 serious hostilities, however bizarre the interruptions, were unremitting. Joffre and his staff assessed the strategic situation. It was intolerable, they concluded, that French territory should be occupied by an enemy. Moreover, the territory which was occupied contained the heart of the French coal and steel industry and much of its manufacturing base. War could not be fought without the tools with which to fight. The French army must therefore continue to take the offensive. It only remained to decide where on the front the breakthrough should come.

The most promising areas for attack were the Artois—and, in particular, the German salient in the chalklands of the Somme around Arras—and the Champagne. It was therefore in Artois that the 10th Army was ordered to attack.

The plan was carefully prepared by Pétain on Maud'huy's instructions. The phasing of the battle was worked out in detail, and Pétain made sure that there was proper coordination between artillery and infantry. On 17 December, the first wave went over the top. On the 18th the 33rd Corps went into action. A German trench was taken; then a line of German trenches. A point platoon was held up by heavy machine-gun fire from its flank. The attack was redirected toward the village of Carency. But it was to no avail. Progress was minimal and casualties heavy. The only relief was that on the following day the battlefield was enveloped in thick fog. The weather did not clear up until the 27th. Yet again the men were ordered forward, on the same line of attack. Yet again losses were heavy—the 226th Infantry Battalion lost 19 officers and 800 men in the first assault—and the ground was atrocious. Advancing troops found themselves at times up to the waist in water in the shell holes, and mud jammed their rifles. The attack was brave but fruitless. It seemed fortunate that in the night of the 28th–29th there was a storm so intense that trenches and galleries started to fill up with water. Further action was pointless. The 10th Army withdrew to lick its wounds.

1914 thus came to a bitter end. The French Army had sustained losses on a dreadful scale: more than 160,000 killed, wounded, missing or taken prisoner in August; more than 200,000 in September; over 80,000 in October, 70,000 in November and more in December. Yet there was little public weeping, except among the families of those concerned, at this hemorrhage of French youth. It seemed that the bulk of the army, of peasant stock, had developed a peasant stoicism, even fatalism, about death or mutilation. Pétain seems to have shared this mood. He is recorded as worrying about the extent of the loss of manpower, but much more as a damaging effect on the war effort than as a pitiful waste of young human life.

Nor, it seemed, was Joffre much concerned. On 15 January 1915 he wrote to his army commanders that "there was not enough vigor in attack and not enough stubbornness in defense." Moreover, he went on, "the present war has by no means weakened the principles which are the basis of our offensive doctrine."[6] There was, he ordered, to be another offensive in Artois as soon as possible. But given the dreadful weather, all the planning was directed toward the spring.

The overall plan for the 1915 spring offensive was worked out in meetings at northern army group headquarters at Chantilly in March, and approved by Joffre on the 24th. General Victor d'Urbal—another contemporary of Pétain's at Saint-Cyr—who had replaced Maud'huy as commander of the 10th Army (to Pétain's evident disgust, since he was hoping for the job), fleshed it out on 6 April. The attack was to be launched by the 10th Army on a front of 6.5 kilometers. The target was the row of low hills which blocked any French breakthrough into the northern plain and whose main feature was the ridge of Vimy. In this attack, the five army corps were to move forward together in line, 33rd Army Corps taking the central role.

Pétain settled down with his staff to map out not just a battle plan but a program of training exercises at division and brigade level. He toured the trenches, visiting every front line battalion, talking to officers, engineers and, above all, the artillery. Each battery was required to fire one shot in Pétain's presence to satisfy him that they were properly aimed. His army corps was further reinforced by the arrival of three more artillery batteries and a Moroccan division. It was not by any means what Pétain had wanted, but it was all he could get.

On 6 May Pétain was able to write to d'Urbal that "the preparatory works for the attack are complete."[7] But there was an unpleasant prelude. On 22 April the Germans had launched the first gas attack against the Algerian divisions defending the Ypres salient. It was deadly. Troops fled coughing and screaming as they turned blue in the face. The neighboring Canadians were instructed to shoot them down for fleeing in the face of the enemy. Thus, an extra dimension of fear touched the men who were about to embark on the spring offensive. On that day perished once for all the idea that war was a gentlemanly pursuit.

Throughout 6, 7 and 8 May it rained, only clearing late on in the evening of the 8th. At first light on 9 May 1915, the French guns opened up. The barrage was massive and well directed. Between 9 and 10 A.M. the infantry moved forward in wave after wave, running as fast as they could across the muddy fields, leaving the comparative safety of the trenches to face a hail of small arms fire on open ground. As it happened, the preliminary artillery barrage had done its work, and the German resistance was less robust than expected. With the Moroccan Division in the van, the French troops surged forward. Within an hour the German line had been broken and the Vimy Ridge occupied.

The Moroccans, supported by the 77th Infantry Division, achieved a startling success. Not only had they taken Vimy Ridge ahead of schedule, but their forward units had penetrated as far as the villages of Petit-Vimy, Givenchy and Souchez. By midday they were on eastern slopes of the ridge. They could see the town of Lens lying undefended in front of them. Moreover, in achieving all this they had captured two German artillery batteries, dozens of machine guns and between 1,200 and 1,500 prisoners. By mid-afternoon there was no doubt about it. Reconnaissance aircraft reported German troops fleeing in all directions. Not only was the German line broken but discipline seemed to have been cast to the winds.

But German reserve regiments were moving up to close the breach in the line, and it was plain that the French attacks on the rest of the front were going badly. By nightfall on 9 May both forward divisions of the 33rd Corps had reported heavy losses—and the supporting artillery had almost run out of ammunition.

But it had been a good day's work—the best for the French since the Marne. On the following day, Joffre sent a message to Pétain, raising him to the rank of Commander of the Légion d'Honneur and urging him to continue the attack. At last, it seemed to Joffre, the long-awaited breakthrough had been achieved. Foch, too, was enthusiastic—and d'Urbal could hardly be contained.

Pétain, however, knew perfectly well that the enthusiasm was misplaced. Neither on his left nor his right had the French made any progress. German reserves, unlike the French reserves, had been moved up quickly. His troops were exhausted, and their formations badly depleted by casualties. They were in a pocket, in danger of attack from three sides simultaneously. Around 7 P.M. they had faced a German counterattack—repulsed only with greater loss of life. That done, they had dug in for the night.

On the morning of 10 May d'Urbal sent another message to Pétain. "This is the decisive day," he wrote, "The 33rd Army Corps will have the honor of landing the great blow."[8] Pétain then did his best. He ordered a further attack, following d'Urbal's instruction to take the village of Souchez on his northern flank. But the German machine guns did their work. Both the Moroccan Division and the 77th suffered dreadful casualties without making any progress.

Pétain sent a long report to d'Urbal drawing the lessons to be learned from the attacks of the previous three days. He pointed out that the "breakthrough" was only possible when an assault was meticulously planned, launched on a broad front and in open country. Improvised attacks on fortified positions were doomed to failure. Pétain's complaints remained unheard. He was ordered to continue his attacks, which he did on 13, 14 and 16 May, again without success. By then, D'Urbal was obviously becoming impatient. When Pétain protested about the lack of ammunition d'Urbal told him sharply to make sure that there were, for instance, enough homemade grenades to deter the enemy. "I demand a fresh attack on 29 May," he wrote; "33rd Corps must be ready like the others to meet this date."[9] The familiar *tu* of 9 May had given way to the more distant *vous*. In short, tempers had become frayed to the breaking point.

It was not until late June that Joffre finally threw in the towel. By then, the 10th Army had lost well over 100,000 men. All the ground which had been gained had been lost to enemy counterattack. Whatever the initial tactical success, the whole thing had been an expensive strategic failure. Joffre's placidity deserted him; he was profoundly and obviously depressed, reduced to tears.

By that time, Pétain was well out of it. On 22 June 1915 he had been appointed commander of the 2nd Army, which held an extended line north of Châlons-sur-Marne in the Champagne. His promotion had been quick—and remarkable. In less than a year, Pétain had risen from field commander of a brigade to strategic commander of a full army—by any standards, as Joffre remarked, an exceptionally rapid rise. Yet Pétain by then had come to differ fundamentally with the optimists over the conduct of the war. "The present war," he wrote, "has taken on the character of a war of attrition. There is no longer a decisive battle as there used to be. Success will in the end belong to the side which will have the last man."[10] He was, however, rather more circumspect in a letter to Foch written a month earlier. Indeed, it was Pétain's boasting about his achievement of 9 May which seems to have persuaded Joffre that he was the right person to be promoted to the command of a full army.

On 22 June Pétain arrived at his new headquarters in the little town of Souilly. A shock awaited him. Such was Joffre's concern for the element of surprise that he had ordered de Castlenau, commander of the Center Army Group, to announce the disbandment of the 2nd Army and the transfer of their positions to the British. Furthermore, he should give out that elements of the disbanded army were being posted to Italy and the Dardanelles. This was essential, he considered, since Pétain's reputation had gone before him and once the Germans got wind of the fact that Pétain was in the area they would know precisely when and where the next attack would be. Pétain therefore arrived to find his supposedly new headquarters redesignated as the headquarters of the 9th Army. He was not to be General Commander of the 2nd Army but Deputy Commander— to de Castelnau—of the Center Army Group. The 2nd Army in turn was redesignated as "the Pétain Group" and did not recover its proper title until 17 September. It was all very confusing.

By the time Pétain arrived at Souilly Joffre had almost reached a decision to launch an offensive across the whole front of the Center Army Group to break the German front by the power and surprise of the assault. The final decision was made in mid-July. In announcing this to de Castelnau on 25 July, Joffre gave instructions that the methods employed on 9 May in the Artois should be used in the planning of the offensive: careful preparation, meticulous orders to both the artillery and the infantry and, above all, surprise.

Indeed, so impressed was Joffre by this element of surprise that he devised an elaborate camouflage for Pétain himself. On 13 September Joffre instructed Pétain to spend some days in Nancy, putting himself about and openly declaring that there would be an offensive in the east. To top it all, a dummy army headquarters was constructed at Bayon, facing the frontier with Alsace. He was only to return, almost incognito, on the 20th.

Whether these maneuvers confused the German High Command or not is, to say the least, uncertain. At all events, another great offensive, the second major action of the French army in 1915, was set to begin on 25 September. The main attack was to be in the Champagne, but planned to coincide with a lesser French offensive in the Artois and a British attack to the north at the village of Loos. The 2nd Army, commanded by Pétain, and the 4th Army, commanded by General Fernand de Langle de Cary, attacked along a front of some 35 kilometers with 17 divisions, a further 15 being held in reserve. The pattern was by now familiar. At first light 1,000 guns launched their barrage on the German first line. Gas attack followed—then the waves of infantry. It had rained the previous night, which made the gas attack ineffective, but the sun shone in the morning— carefully picking out the French infantry as they emerged from the cloud of gun smoke and dust. Some regiments even went so far as to advance in the old style, with flags flying and bugles sounding. Others, which had learnt the lessons of previous engagements, were more cautious.

Although the German High Command suspected that an attack was imminent, the actual date was unknown, and the French, as Joffre had wanted, achieved at least a measure of surprise. The 14th Army Corps, at the center of Pétain's line, in two hours overran the first German trenches opposite them and moved forward a further kilometer and a half. The 11th Army Corps pushed even further. By nightfall on 25 September it seemed that the French were heading for a great victory. Pétain gave orders for the offensive to continue. Perhaps, de Castelnau thought, the "breakthrough" might be achieved at last.

But the following day there was no progress. The French infantry had run up against the German second line, which the artillery had been unable to reach and where, consequently, the wire was intact. Continued attacks only resulted in men stumbling into barbed wire, presenting easy targets to the German machine guns. Yet there was still a glimmer of hope. De Langle de Cary had succeeded in advancing some two kilometers on his front. De Castelnau ordered Pétain to support him by further attacks at Tahure. This he did, and further ground—the hill above the village—was captured.

Yet again there was to be disappointment. De Langle de Cary reported that he had failed to overrun the German second line and was held up. Pétain considered that in that case continued attacks by the 2nd Army would inevitably fail. It was time, he suggested to de Castelnau, to consolidate his positions and to prepare carefully an attack at a later date. De Castelnau agreed. But time was running short. The Germans were bringing up reserves. On 6 October, the French tried again; but yet again they made no progress. Both armies were held up—and then subjected to fierce counterattack. For the rest of October there was only sporadic fighting, as each side tried to consolidate their positions and remove the salients which the offensive earlier in the month had left behind. But on 30 and 31 October, German gas attacks practically wiped out 12 companies, and the subsequent infantry assault dislodged the French from the hill above Tahure.

At that point all attacks were called off. The overall result, the French generals concluded, was minimal. The German positions remained intact. The cost in human life had been horrific: the total casualties of the 2nd and 4th armies from 25 September to 31 October were officially estimated at "191,797 men"[11]— probably a gross underestimate.

Pétain, for his part, concluded that the battle showed the difficulty of taking the enemy second line—usually placed on a reverse slope and so invisible to ground attackers until they breasted the summit of the hill—without preparation at least as thorough as that for the original attack. Yet shortage of artillery ammunition would at present make that impossible. The answer, he considered, was a tactic of limited strikes at the enemy front line. Once that had been overrun, the attackers should retreat. But if there was to be a more general attack it should be on the basis that "the breakthrough is not an end in itself, but the means of arriving at an engagement in open country."[12] In all, 1915 was the bloodiest year of the war for the French Army. The total number of casualties for the year came to nearly 1.5 million men. Even Joffre realized that casualties at that rate were not sustainable. There were simply not enough men of military age in France. Not that Joffre himself was particularly popular in Paris. His promotion in early December to the new post of Commander-in-Chief of the French Armies was more an attempt to enhance the status of France in the campaign for a joint Franco-British command than a sign of confidence in his leadership.

But Joffre was still there, and although he did not agree with Pétain's conclusions about the offensive in the Champagne, he valued Pétain as a source of new ideas. Perhaps the idea of the "breakthrough" had perished in the mud of the battlefields, but Joffre would not give up. The lessons of 1915 had to be learned. More artillery, more troops and more training were needed.

Joffre set about this program with his usual energy. Once the exhausted troops had been stood down for the winter, he asked Pétain to direct the training of four army corps of reservists who were to be employed in the spring offensive for 1916. Pétain agreed. The posting was duly announced just after Christmas. Pétain's headquarters for this exercise were to be at Noailles, just outside Paris. Pétain, of course, knew Noailles well. He had been stationed there before the war. The surroundings were peaceful; he could ride in the forest as before; and he could even make trips into Paris. Waiting for him on his trips to Paris was the ever-devoted Nini. That particular wheel, it seemed, was about to come full circle.

EIGHT

The Battle of Verdun

"The fall of each one of your soldiers was a stab in the heart of his general, and the impassive expression under which you hide your feelings masked constant and unremitting grief."

The best part of a century has gone by since the Battle of Verdun of 1916. With the passage of time, the living experience of those dreadful ten months has to a large extent been drowned in the quicksand of historical analysis. But those months left indelible, nightmare memories for the survivors, and left families up and down the length and breadth of France in grief for their sons who were lost. Indeed, it is not too much to say that if there is one single battle which defined the Great War for France, it is Verdun.

Those same dreadful months, however, also saw the birth of a legend. Individual memories of the hideous slaughter faded as the collective heroism was honored. In time, too, legend developed into myth. Verdun was, the myth-makers asserted, a war within a war. Whatever happened elsewhere, Verdun stood for all that was French, noble and courageous, the true revelation of the Gallic spirit. As it happened, no one was a greater beneficiary of that particular myth than Philippe Pétain.

The city of Verdun stands astride the river Meuse as it gently wends its way northwards through the surrounding hills. The countryside around is still scarred with the remains of battle, but for the casual visitor the landscape beyond the site of the battle could easily be taken as one of gentle and almost nostalgic tranquility. History, however, tells us otherwise. Like so much of eastern France, the quiet fields are, inch-deep below the surface, soaked in the blood of war. (In fact, Verdun's bloody history goes back as far as the Roman Empire.) In September 1870 the Prussians invaded, laying siege to the city and bombarding it on three fearsome occasions. Returned to France under the Treaty of Frankfurt in 1871, the city then found itself once more at the centre of French military attention. What had been a small fortress built by Louis XIV's architect Vauban became the hinge of a great line of powerful forts designed to rule out for ever a future German invasion.

The new line was built by the sapper general Séré de Rivière, on plans laid down by the Ministry of War in Paris—temptingly leaving a gap through which German armies could march only, so went the plan, to be encircled and destroyed by French counterattack. It was at Verdun that the line of forts was at its strongest. Verdun thus became the linchpin of the whole massive line. Around the city there were sixteen major and some twenty smaller constructions in a protective ring fifty kilometers in perimeter. The names of those forts echo down the years—Douaumont, Vaux, Souville, Moulainville, Tavannes, Belrupt, Rozellier, Houdainville—like some melancholy roll-call. Even today, the sight of their ruins is a gloomy reminder of the tragedy they witnessed.

The stabilization of the Western Front in the autumn of 1914 left Verdun tactically vulnerable. The forts on the eastern, or right, bank of the Meuse had been enough to deter a further German advance there, while the movement of the French 1st Army to defend the western, or left, bank had secured a front some 20 kilometers to the west of the city. A salient was formed, digging into the German front. It was only toward the end of 1915 that German planners, fearing a Franco-British assault to the northwest along the line of the river Somme, thought about attacking Verdun.

All salients are weak points in a front. The German planners took the view that the best chance of success lay in an assault at the top of the salient, along the front due north of the city. The assault would be concentrated on the most direct route to the city along the right bank.

In fact, in spite of all that has been written about Verdun—and is still being written—the German intentions remain obscure. At the end of the war, Graf Erich von Falkenhayn, who had replaced Moltke as German commander-in-chief after the Marne, published in his memoirs the text of a draft memorandum written, he claimed, in December 1915. The memorandum purports to set out in detail the strategy of a static battle around a place which, for reasons of prestige, the French would be bound to defend to the last man. "If they do so," the memorandum goes on, "the forces of France will bleed to death."[1]

Whether the memorandum ever existed at all in December 1915 is now a matter of doubt. What is not in doubt, however, is that it was the Kaiser himself who approved the assault on Verdun in mid-December 1915 and who, after the success of the first assault, went himself to the frontline in order to view—through a heavily protected periscope—the fall of the city. Furthermore, one of

Falkenhayn's most trusted generals, Schmidt von Knobelsdorf, who had been appointed to keep an eye on the Crown Prince Wilhelm—the heir to the Kaiser's throne and the commander of the German 5th Army which was to lead the assault—not only gave the news to the Crown Prince himself but, as the Crown Prince's chief of staff, drafted the orders to the Army "to capture the fortress of Verdun." In the normal run of things, those orders must have been approved by Falkenhayn, in spite of his previous directive to the 5th Army, which only mentioned "an offensive in the direction of Verdun."[2]

But there had been strategic confusion at the start. Crown Prince Rupprecht of Bavaria—in his own right a general of distinction—wrote in his diary the comment that Graf Erich von Falkenhayn "was not clear what he really wanted . . . and was waiting for a stroke of luck that would lead to a favorable solution. He wanted a decision in the spring, while declaring a breakthrough impossible, but how else should the change from the war of position to the war of movement be achieved?"[3] That was probably the truth of it; in other words, it was a question of "either" or perhaps "or."[4] Knowing the fickle nature of his master, Falkenhayn was hedging all his bets.

From this uncertain start the German tactical buildup during January 1916 was efficient and massive. Engineers built ten new railway lines across the marshy Plain of Woevre to the east of the city. Some 1,200 guns were brought up, ranging from the huge 380 mm Krupp naval guns down to the 77 mm field pieces, which were to continue their battle for supremacy with the French 75s. Two and a half million shells, it is said, were delivered in more than a thousand trainloads. The Crown Prince's army was reinforced to the point where it boasted 72 battalions—some 400,000 men, the best trained and most experienced in the German Army. To ensure surprise, the German sappers burrowed into the earth to build large concrete *Stollen* (dugouts) in which the infantry could be concealed up until the moment of assault. Finally, no fewer than 168 aircraft were assembled, not just for reconnaissance but, for the first time ever, in support of a ground attack.

Opposite them the French defenses were notably weak. On Joffre's orders, in 1914–1915 the forts had been largely denuded of guns, which were transferred to other parts of the front. At the time there had been sense in this. Joffre was a gunner. He knew all about the inferiority of the French artillery, particularly in heavy pieces of over 75 mm caliber. (In fact, the heavy guns were not just taken from Verdun. Forts at Toul and Epinal were stripped as well.) Moreover, enthusiasm for a defensive line of forts had gone out of fashion. Since the front had been quiet for a number of months the French trenches had been badly maintained, and the third line was almost nonexistent. As it happened, this was pointed out by one of the many deputies in the National Assembly who had signed up for service and who, much to Joffre's displeasure, reported what he saw directly to his fellow politicians in Paris. As the leaks of the German movements became more frequent and more threatening, a battalion of engineers was sent to shore up some of the trench work, but beyond that little was done. Joffre's mind, and that of his staff, remained concentrated on preparations for the spring offensive on the Somme.

Pétain's mind, on the other hand, was elsewhere. Nini had by that time returned to the charge. She had read of his promotion to three-star general in the newspapers and had written to congratulate him. At first, all went well, and in January there were assignations at the Buffet-Hôtel at the Gare du Nord where Pétain arrived on his train from Beauvais. But Pétain was jealous. It appears that after her divorce Nini had been rather freer with her favors than was appropriate in his view. Pétain insisted that he was too proud to accept anything other than monopoly rights. In order to make his feelings perfectly clear, he added a postscript to his letter to her of 11 February 1916 in tone much more like the one he used with fellow officers or politicians. "Your writing paper," the brutal postscript went, "has the same smell as the suffocating gas used by the Germans. It reeks of chlorine."[5] Nini's reaction to this onslaught does her credit. She was not in the least deterred, and apparently gave her difficult general without delay the assurances he required. The path after that ran more smoothly. Nini was summoned to further assignations; Pétain's letters became more enthusiastic.

On the morning of 21 February, the first shots were fired in the Battle of Verdun. As overnight snow turned to early frost, the German heavy guns opened up. Their noise could be heard 200 kilometers away. After three hours, their bombardment was supplemented by the medium and light artillery, attacking directly the French positions on the Meuse right bank. Within minutes the air had been turned grey with smoke, snow, earth and splinters of trees thrown into the air. If men were caught in the open they were torn apart. "A great pile of earth," ran one account, "round, shaped like a pyramid with a hole gouged out all round. Sticking out of it, symmetrically, to a distance of about 40 centimeters, were legs, arms, hands and heads like the bloody cogs of some monstrous capstan."[6]

But worse was to come. Just as dusk was falling, patrols of German storm troopers broke from their trenches, not in the customary waves but in small groups—zigzagging, crouching, running and then pausing, all to avoid the defensive fire. As though that were not difficult enough for the French defenders, dazed after a day of ferocious artillery assault, the attackers brought with them a terrible new weapon—the flamethrower. In the first attack, French defenders were burnt to death as they stood. Others simply ran away in desperate fear.

There was, to be sure, much courageous resistance. At the Bois des Caures, the German attack was held up for a crucial 24 hours. But whatever the courage shown by the French troops the advantage always lay with the enemy. By the evening of 24 February the Germans had made their breakthrough. The way to Verdun was open.

The reaction to these events was mixed. Joffre still seemed unconcerned; but that was his customary reaction to any crisis. Castelnau, his deputy, was much more worried. With Joffre's agreement—and, as always, together with his nephew, who doubled as his personal father-confessor—he rushed to Verdun on the evening of 24 February. At breakfast time the following day they reached the city. Castelnau quickly went on a visit to the troops, such as they were, on the front line. He returned to the regional headquarters, only to find chaos and panic. To stiffen everybody's backs, Castelnau immediately issued an order that the defense of the Meuse had to be made on the right bank "cost what it may."[7] Any idea, then or in the future, of a tactical retreat from the right bank to narrow the salient and preserve the integrity of the Meuse left bank—whatever a future commander might think—was thus ruled out.

At the same time, however, Castelnau urged Joffre to appoint Pétain, a general known to be prepared to countenance tactical retreats, to the overall command of French forces at Verdun. Even on the French side, there was strategic confusion.

Joffre agreed that Pétain should be summoned to Chantilly. However, there was a snag. Only half an hour after Castelnau's call to Joffre, Pétain had told Serrigny that he was going off—again—from Noailles to Paris, and would not return before lunch the following day. Since there was nothing particularly pressing, Pétain did not tell Serrigny where he would be that night. In fact, it was his latest assignation with Nini for the evening—and night—of Thursday 24 February. It was hardly to be a night of languid and amorous calm. At around 10 o'clock that evening at Noailles, while Serrigny was playing a quiet hand of bridge in the officers' quarters, a telegram from Joffre was brought in. "General Pétain," it read, "should present himself at GQG Friday at 8 A.M. to be received by the Commander-in-Chief."[8] At that point, there was in the officers' quarters a degree of panic. It was clear that this was a matter of urgency. But where was the general himself? Serrigny set off for Paris to find him, guessing—from previous experience—where he would be, and duly arrived at the Hôtel Terminus in the small hours of the morning of 25 February. At first, the owner of the hotel denied hotly that Pétain was in her hotel, but soon retracted when Serrigny told her that it was a matter of "the safety of the country." Serrigny then ran up to the room which she had pointed to, recognized a general's yellow boots sitting alongside two "charming little, wholly feminine, 'molière' shoes,"[9] and knocked loudly on the door. Sure enough, Pétain emerged—in his nightshirt. A quick conference ensued. Pétain, once apprised of the situation, told Serrigny to find a bed somewhere in the hotel. They would leave together at seven o'clock that morning. This done, Pétain returned to Nini, told her that he was going to Verdun—whereupon she burst into tears—spent an apparently passionate remainder of the night with her, and left her, by all accounts somewhat drained, in the early morning.

Pétain and Serrigny arrived at Chantilly on time at 8 A.M. on 25 February. They found panic everywhere. It was said that the Germans had taken 20,000 to 25,000 prisoners, that they had captured 800 guns, that Verdun was about to fall. A few minutes later Pétain was ushered in to Joffre's office. "Well, Pétain,"

Joffre said at once, "you know things are not going badly at all."[10] He went on to say that Castelnau was on the spot with full powers to change the Verdun regional command. Pétain's 2nd Army, at present in reserve, should be made ready to shore up the defense of the city. Pétain himself should go forthwith to Bar-le-Duc, prepared to assume immediate command.

Joffre's summons had not been unexpected, however inconvenient its timing. Pétain knew that he was the only senior general without a current active command, and that his army had been resting for three months since the abortive Champagne offensive. It made sense for Joffre to give him this command. There was, in truth, no one else.

Eventually, he arrived at Châlons in the early afternoon—to find General Gouraud (apparently another of Nini's former lovers) with a message from Castelnau telling them to make as quickly as possible for the château of Dugny, the headquarters of General Herr, the commander of the Fortified Region of Verdun. Gouraud, however, persuaded Pétain and his party to stay to lunch at Châlons. "Since we had been without food since the early morning," Serrigny sighed, "and since love and other emotions generally serve to sharpen the appetite, the invitation of the Commander of the 4th Army was accepted with gratitude."[11] Although the lunch was reasonably jovial—there was apparently much shared reminiscence of Nini, which Pétain gave no sign of resenting—Serrigny noticed that Pétain had developed a tic in his right eye. It was, he noted, a sure sign of worry.

It took four frustrating hours to reach Dugny. Once there, they found "a madhouse."[12] Indeed, the news could hardly have been worse. The great fort at Douaumont had fallen without a shot being fired. Although they had been held up by initial fierce French resistance, the Germans had advanced eight kilometers—into open ground, and only four kilometers from the last line of defense in front of the city itself.

Castelnau insisted that Pétain take command at midnight. Pétain wanted to wait. Most of his staff, he pointed out, would not arrive until the following day. Castelnau would not budge. Finally, Pétain agreed, but as a parting shot he said to Serrigny, in a voice loud enough to be heard by others, "in that case we will set ourselves up at Souilly where I hope we shall find a little bit more calm."[13] On the following morning, Pétain woke with a high temperature and a bad cough. A doctor was summoned—and diagnosed double pneumonia. There was immediate and understandable consternation. News of Pétain's arrival had leaked out to the troops. His reputation as a careful commander had run before him. If he were now to die or be incapacitated the blow to the army's morale would be disastrous. Pétain therefore spent the next five days confined to his bedroom, issuing orders nonetheless to his staff officers, who in turn conveyed them to the soldiers in the field.

However hard the task, the tactical appraisal of the situation shows Pétain at his analytical best. He very quickly saw that there had to be a line of defense which must be held at all costs. He even got up from his bed to draw a line with a piece of charcoal on a map to instruct his generals precisely where their respective positions were to be. There were, he also ordered, to be three lines: a forward line, designed to blunt an enemy offensive but not to be held at all costs; a principal "line of resistance," to be held come what may; and a third line, which would serve as a base from which counterattacks would be launched. Second, he realized that since the Crown Prince had only attacked on the Meuse right bank, the field of battle was narrow. It was therefore all the more important that the French heavy artillery should be concentrated under central command, to be deployed and targeted at a moment's notice. Third, he recognized that the army at Verdun would be slowly strangled if there were no quick solution to the problem of reinforcements and supplies of food and ammunition.

It was here that Pétain had a piece of luck. There was only one road—of inferior quality—leading from Bar-le-Duc into the Verdun salient. It so happened that a member of Pétain's staff, a Major Richard, had been in civil life an engineer in the maintenance of bridges and roads. He turned out to be something of a genius. Pétain faced him with the problem of how to convert this inferior road into a road capable of carrying traffic the like of which it had never seen. It was not, Pétain explained, just for reinforcements and provisions. Whole battalions, even brigades, had been decimated. It was no good just putting new troops into the line. The units themselves lost the collective will to fight. There was, he said, to be a system of constant replacement—he called it the "millwheel" after the primitive mechanism for irrigation: a chain of buckets attached to a wheel, dipped into a river, brought up, emptied and sent down again. Whole units would be taken out of the line and replaced by new units. They, in their turn, would in the course of time be replaced by the old units, suitably refreshed.

Major Richard was up to the task. He discovered that the road could be reinforced and widened to take two lanes of traffic by constantly digging out the limestone shale which lay on both sides of the road, shoveling the pebbles on to the surface of the road, and relying on the lorry traffic to act as a steamroller to bed it down. Richard's idea worked. Eight thousand territories were put to work with shovels, working in shifts day and night. More than a million tons of pebbles were shoveled onto the road. Some 3,500 daily trucks acted as steamrollers—one passing by every 25 seconds.

By the first week of March it seemed that the "line of resistance" had held. The Kaiser had gone home, disappointed once more by the failure of his son and heir to take Verdun. In a mood of optimism, Poincaré and Joffre visited the headquarters at Souilly to urge Pétain to take the offensive. Poincaré and Joffre might be optimistic, but Pétain knew that the position was far from stable. Crown Prince Wilhelm had other thoughts in mind. On 6 March he attacked on the left bank this time on a broad front. The French first line was quickly overrun but the "line of resistance," along the ridges of Mort Homme and Hill 304 down to the hamlet of Avocourt, was not breached. Moreover, for the first time the German losses were as heavy as the French.

Day after day the pattern of battle was the same. At the beginning of an attack there was a crushing German bombardment. This was followed by patrols running out from their trenches to find gaps in the French lines, followed by a full infantry charge across the broken ground. There was then a confused mêlée, with soldiers hiding randomly in shell holes and fighting in groups at close contact with grenades. Once the German advance was seen to falter the French in turn launched a heavy artillery barrage and then counterattacked. For the most part, the ground which had been captured by the Germans in the morning was recaptured by the French in the afternoon.

It is hardly surprising that morale on both sides was by the end of March beginning to crack. There were, for instance, reports of German soldiers refusing to charge, and of French soldiers surrendering too easily. Nevertheless, by the end of March the German pressure was starting to tell. Gradually their front moved closer to the city. The little hamlets, or what was left of them, fell one by one: Malancourt, Haucourt, Bethincourt.

It was getting close. On 9 April the Germans launched yet another offensive, this time on both the left and right banks. Mort Homme was taken after desperately heavy fighting. The "line of resistance" was broken. Pétain felt it necessary to issue an order to his troops to bolster their morale: "*Courage! On les aura!*" (Courage! We'll have them!)[14]

Fortunately, the French guns on Hill 304 had exacted such a heavy price that successive French counterattacks during the following ten days finally won Mort Homme back. All the initial German gains made in the early April offensive were lost again in a fortnight. Mercifully, on 22 April it started to pour rain. Carnage was, for the moment, suspended, and on 26 April Pétain, in the moment of calm, was able to celebrate—if that is the right word—his birthday.

By then, there was no doubt that the "millwheel" was working as planned. A constant supply of reinforcements and munitions had been assured. Although the rations for the troops were meager, at least they got through. Water, too, was no longer a problem, thanks to the ingenuity of the French engineers in laying pipes. Living conditions were still miserable, but by the end of April it seemed at last as though the German assault had finally been blunted and held.

For Pétain, this was a mixed blessing. While the position was critical he had Joffre's confidence. But he was starting to get on Joffre's nerves with his unceasing demands for troop reinforcements. By the end of April some 40 French divisions—nearly half the entire French Army—had been on the "millwheel" through the fire of Verdun. Yet Joffre was still concentrating on what he thought would be the decisive battle of the Western Front, on the Somme. Moreover, Pétain was still in no mood to launch a sustained counteroffensive. Joffre thought he was just being overcautious.

Pétain was also starting to get some unpleasantly (for Joffre) favorable press limelight. When he was first posted to Verdun, the press searched in vain for a suitable photograph. None existed. It was not that Pétain had been particularly reluctant; he was simply not a public figure. By the end of March, however, the press had taken an intense interest in this hitherto unknown general who was apparently performing such heroic feats at Verdun. Reverential articles—complete with illustrations—started to appear in the Paris press. This annoyed not just Joffre but the politicians in Paris, who tended to feel that the function of generals was to get on with the job and not to hog the limelight which was properly theirs. Poincaré had his own personal annoyance. During March and April he paid several visits in his special train to Verdun. He thought that it would be good for morale—and certainly not bad for his own public image. On those occasions Pétain would be invited to dinner. The invitations were unwelcome, but he could not refuse. He therefore made it his business to be as rude as possible.

Pétain was nevertheless fighting a successful defensive engagement at Verdun. Even in early March there were rumors that he would soon take over the command of the Center Army Group. But for the moment that idea had been put aside. It was resurrected by no less a figure than the Prime Minister Aristide Briand. His suggestion was that de Langle de Cary's command should be put in abeyance, for Pétain to take it up once he had finished the job at Verdun. That was not enough for Joffre. He wanted Pétain out of Verdun. In fact, he had in mind to promote General Robert Nivelle, one of Pétain's Army Corps commanders, to Pétain's job.

Nivelle was almost all that Pétain was not. For a start, he was adept at dealing with politicians. He was good-looking, cultured, sure of himself, silver-tongued and charming. He was also fluent in English, thanks to his mother, which endeared him to the British. Moreover, as an officer, although he subsequently chose the artillery for a career, he retained all the spirit of his alma mater, the cavalry school at Saumur. Again unlike Pétain, he was stiff and overbearing to the infantry soldiers he commanded—and refused to look at the casualty lists. Like Foch, he believed that battles could be won by the sheer force of morale and will power. Poincaré found him irresistible.

Nivelle's closest ally was one of his generals, Charles Mangin. Mangin—not to put too fine a point on it—was a thug. He had spent most of his career in Africa, and as long ago as 1898 he had been on the expedition to Fashoda, and had worked his way up through the colonial army. He was competent, brave and exceptionally aggressive. "Reckless of all lives and of none more than his own," Winston Churchill was to write of him, "charging at the head of his troops . . . Mangin beaten or triumphant, Mangin the Hero or Mangin the Butcher as he was alternately regarded, became on the anvil of Verdun the fiercest warrior figure of France."[15] On the day he arrived at Verdun, he had immediately flung himself into battle—with startling success.

On 19 April 1916, Castelnau telephoned Pétain from headquarters, the Grand Quartier Général (GQG) at Chantilly. De Langle de Cary was definitely going to retire at the end of the month, and Pétain was to replace him. Pétain's 2nd Army was to be commanded by Nivelle but under the overall command of Pétain as commander of the Center Army Group. Underlying the promotion, of course, was Joffre's intention that the day-to-day conduct of the battle of Verdun would be left to Nivelle. Pétain left Souilly feeling that he had been sacked.

For Pétain it was an uncomfortable situation. Formally, he was still responsible for the 2nd Army at Verdun along with the three other armies in his group. But Nivelle, as the general commanding the 2nd Army, pulled all the immediate strings. To add to the discomfort, Pétain himself reported to Joffre. He was thus caught in the middle. Both Joffre and Nivelle were in favor of an immediate and decisive counterattack at Verdun, while Pétain thought that the time was not yet ripe. Moreover, Joffre's eyes were still fixed on the Somme, where he expected the final breakthrough to be made. Pétain's eyes were still fixed on Verdun.

The result of these changes was that the "millwheel" was halted on Joffre's own instruction. The 2nd Army was told to get on with the battle by themselves. But this was much easier said than done, as Nivelle soon found out. On 3 May, the Germans took Hill 304—the first breach of Pétain's "line of resistance." On 8 May, a huge explosion inside the fort at Douaumont convinced Mangin that the fort itself was there for the taking, and on 13 May he launched his attack. But after ten days of slaughter the Germans fended it off. Moreover, by the end of May the German attack on the left bank had been successful to the point where the whole of Mort Homme had fallen.

From that platform, on 1 June the Crown Prince launched his own offensive—the largest in scale since the initial assault of late February. On 7 June Fort Vaux, the second most important strategic point after Douaumont, surrendered. The way was then open to Fort Souville and to the city of Verdun itself. Nivelle, in desperation, immediately called for reinforcements. Pétain supported him—and made daily visits to Souilly to keep in touch with a situation which was obviously becoming ever-more dangerous. He telephoned Joffre to tell him bluntly that "the situation at Verdun is very serious; unless there are immediate reinforcements I shall be obliged to evacuate the right bank."[16] It was, of course, bluff; but it worked. Joffre immediately ordered a further four divisions to Verdun. Even if the Somme was to be deprived, Joffre knew that it would be a military and political catastrophe if Verdun fell.

By 23 June 1916, the Battle of Verdun had reached its climax. The Germans had failed to break through to Verdun itself. Fort Souville had held. A gas attack with the new, more deadly, phosgene gas had created panic, but the French had a new gas mask and their field artillery—the 75s—was destroying the German assault troops as though they were rabbits running out of a cornfield. And then, on 24 June, a rumble was heard, like distant thunder, to the northwest. The British guns had started their massive barrage on the Somme. At that point, both sides knew that Verdun was saved.

The battle itself, of course, dragged on—through the autumn of 1916 and into the winter. But the French grew in confidence as German morale collapsed.

Falkenhayn was sacked. Crack German regiments were withdrawn for redeployment on the Somme. Pétain himself even found time to spend a weekend with Nini in Châlons. The new German commander in chief, Field Marshal Paul von Hindenburg, ordered all German attacks to cease. By mid-September Nini was permanently settled in Châlons, and Pétain was fighting off her allegations that he had been too heavily involved with a nurse in one of the Verdun hospitals—which, of course, he had been. In other words, life—at least to some extent—was returning to normal.

The French counteroffensive started on 19 October. It had been carefully planned by Nivelle and Mangin, and was decisive. By mid-December the battle was to all intents and purposes won. Nivelle rightly claimed the victory, and on the strength of it was appointed commander-in-chief in December 1916—in succession to Joffre, who had lost his job after the failure of the Somme offensive. As for Pétain, he was understandably aggrieved at Nivelle's promotion over his head, but more important in the story of his life was the effect of those dreadful months.

There is no doubt that Verdun was decisive in changing his view of casualties. Up until then he had been—almost intellectually—cautious in the expenditure of human lives on the grounds that the military effectiveness of the units in his command would be diminished if he was too profligate with the lives of the soldiers. Verdun changed all that. Pétain himself summed it up. "Indeed my heart bled," runs his account of the battle,

> when I saw our young twenty-year-old men going under fire at Verdun, knowing as I did that with the impressionability of their age they would quickly lose the enthusiasm aroused by their first battle and sink into the apathy of suffering, perhaps even into discouragement, in the face of such a task as was theirs . . . Huddled into uncomfortable trucks, or bowed under the weight of their packs when they marched on foot, they encouraged each other with songs and banter to appear indifferent. But the discouragement with which they returned!—either singly, maimed or wounded, or in the ranks of their companies thinned by their losses. Their eyes stared into space as if transfixed by a vision of terror. In their gait and their attitudes they betrayed utter exhaustion. Horrible memories made them quail. When I questioned them, they scarcely answered, and the jeering tones of the old *poilus* awakened no spark of response in them.[17]

The experience without a doubt marked him for life. Nonetheless, he was too much a product of Saint-Cyr to be mawkish. "Fortunately," he told a writer on a visit to Souilly, "I have a chilling mask."[18] As it happened, both the compassion of Verdun and the mask were to be in evidence in the year to follow.

In truth, there was no "Victor of Verdun." The whole gruesome episode did not allow for a victor. There were, of course, many heroes on both sides, and, if any group can be singled out, it should be the *poilus*, the rank and file of the French infantry. But even with them Verdun had taken its toll. As it happened, in the extremity of the hell of battle there were those who started to wonder whether the whole game, in crude terms, was worth the candle. Indeed, many of them were soon to make their views felt. "Victory" at Verdun was little compensation for the suffering of those ten months. Nonetheless, Pétain emerged at the end of it—even though he had spent no more than two months out of ten in direct command of the battle—as the figure who would be seen as the emblem of the French spirit which had kept the ordinary soldiers fighting. The mythology, powerful as it was, carried Pétain through even to the end of his life. If there was in reality no "Victor of Verdun," this did not prevent Pétain from being awarded the title. In fact, it was to stay with him—even in 1940 and after—both as a prop for his own ambition and, more important, as a mythic symbol of France's will to victory.

Hero of France and Commander-in-Chief

"On ne m'appelle que dans les catastrophes."

"Pétain believes he is a great man; he says seriously that the Republic is afraid of him."[1] Thus Pétain's fellow general, Fayolle, in January 1917. There was, in fact, some justification for Fayolle's otherwise rather caustic opinion. Pétain's reputation at Verdun had placed him firmly on the domestic—and, indeed, international—political map. Even the British press had taken notice, and he had been awarded in June 1916 the Grand Cross of the Order of Saint Michael and Saint George. Moreover, there was a good deal of coming and going between Paris and Pétain's headquarters at Châlons—some of it more welcome than others. Clemenceau, for instance, was, unlike Poincaré, always welcome. In fact, when he arrived on 7 January to tell Pétain that the Briand government was losing support and had limited life expectancy, Fayolle thought that the two were plotting something.

There were visits, too, from foreigners—American journalists, Italian generals, Spanish war correspondents, Belgian and Dutch liaison officers, and so on—who were interested in making contact with this new military phenomenon. Pétain was pleased, although he grumbled to Nini that they "take my house for a hotel."[2] The Paris press was another matter. He had certainly enjoyed the attention, but, as 1917 went on, what looked like a honeymoon at Verdun changed into divorce over the coverage of the mutinies of the summer.

Nini herself, much to Pétain's only too clearly expressed regret, had left her nursing post in Châlons (whatever in truth it might have been). She had not been well and disliked the cold winter. She was certainly not used to the temperatures of minus 10 degrees Celsius which Pétain regularly recorded during January, and preferred to remove herself to the south of France with her son, Pierre. Pétain clearly missed her. At one point he even proposed to take a week off to spend with her in the warm south, but, in the event, this admittedly improbable project came to nothing. He also took care to behave himself, writing to her that he had been "very good" since she had left.[3] He was, of course, tempted. Serrigny's daughter Chantal, by all accounts an attractive young lady, paid a visit of several days to Châlons with a friend. Pétain immediately whisked them both off on a tour of Reims. (Serrigny was much relieved when they returned, apparently without incident.) But if Châlons was relatively quiet, much was going on elsewhere. Joffre had planned an offensive for the spring of 1917, but it was modest compared with the new plan of his successor Nivelle. Nivelle's strategy was to hit the bulge in the German front line which had resulted from the Allied advances on the Somme. The British, the strategy went, were to attack the northern flank of the German salient at Arras and the French were to attack the southern flank at Soissons. After the German armies on both flanks had been broken, a joint Allied reserve force would smash through the middle—and thereby end the whole war in a few days.

Pétain did not share Nivelle's heroic optimism. The main French attack, he noted, would almost immediately run into the heavy defenses and difficult terrain of the Chemin des Dames, a rugged and wooded ridge parallel to the River Aisne. The French artillery would be unable to get close enough to hit the German second line. Pétain's alternative suggestion was to direct an attack toward the north-east with more limited ambitions. Nivelle's response was to tell General Fayolle openly that Pétain "was not offensive enough."[4] He removed the 5th Army from Pétain's command, and put the main French attack under the command of General Alfred Micheler—leaving Pétain with only a minor role.

In early January 1917 the Allied leaders (British Prime Minister David Lloyd George, Briand and Italian Premier Giovanni Borelli) met in Rome to discuss plans for the year. They agreed that there should be a joint Franco-British offensive on the Western Front, but they could not see how to avoid another Somme—which would be, for obvious political reasons, wholly unacceptable. But on his way back to England Lloyd George stopped in Paris, where he had a hurried conversation at the Gare du Nord with Nivelle, who was invited to London to explain his plan in detail. In London on 15 January Nivelle said that he planned to amass enough artillery to break all the German lines at once—rather than concentrating only on one line at a time. That would be followed by a creeping barrage, behind which the infantry would advance, carefully avoiding any strong enemy positions which might slow them down. The whole thing would be over with minimal casualties in a matter of hours. The British generals were doubtful. What had worked on a small scale at Verdun, they thought, would not necessarily work on a larger stage. Lloyd George, however, not only overruled them but insisted that the British forces under Field Marshal Sir Douglas Haig be placed under Nivelle's command. Haig took this badly, and complained to King George V over the prime minister's head.

Whatever the intrinsic merits of Nivelle's strategy, the one crucial component for its success was the element of surprise. This was signally lacking. In his efforts to raise the fighting spirit of his troops, Nivelle allowed details of his plan to be circulated widely, and to lower ranks. Needless to say, at an early stage they fell into the hands of the German High Command. The German response was, in tactical terms, quite (there is no other word) brilliant. On 9 February, Operation "Alberich" was launched, named after the devious and wicked dwarf in Wagner's *Ring of the Nibelung*. The plan was to retreat to a line which would smooth out the bulge, in other words to eliminate the salient. Not only was this line to be well fortified, but the territory which was to be vacated was to be rendered virtually uninhabitable. Bridges and roads were mined; booby traps were laid; all trees were cut down and the wood burned; houses were systematically blown up; dead animals lay everywhere, gorged on by rats—which grew to a truly terrifying size. There was almost nothing left for the French to occupy other than a burnt-out and barren desert.

Nivelle refused to accept the obvious logic of the event: if there was no salient there was no salient to attack. The whole basis of his strategy had been removed from under him. But Nivelle defiantly insisted that the attack was on. It would be directed at the southern end of the German line—the Hindenburg Line as it was called, after the German commander-in-chief—and the connecting Chemin des Dames.

By that time, politicians in Paris had started to worry. The Briand government, as Clemenceau predicted to Pétain, had on 19 March given way to a government headed by the 80-year-old Alexandre Ribot. His council of ministers included the Radical Socialist Louis Malvy, generally regarded as the creature of the most prominent pacifist of the day, and a former Premier, Joseph Caillaux. But from Pétain's point of view there was one significant appointment: the new minister of war was to be Paul Painlevé.

Painlevé was far from being a professional or even a skilled politician. At an early stage in his life he had attained some considerable distinction as a mathematician. It was perhaps something of a surprise to him that he found himself, at the age of 53, projected into the position of minister of war. He was short in stature, with a "square head and face built around a nose rather like a turned up thumb,"[5] and a voice that sounded, as was remarked at the time, like a strangulated contralto. He was not an obvious person to confront the great generals of the French Army.

But he was a Pétain supporter. He had met Pétain in the spring of 1916 when he filled the post of minister of inventions. As such, he had become interested in the development of the tank as an instrument to break the deadlock of the trenches. He had visited Pétain at Souilly and found a ready interlocutor. In fact, Painlevé seems to have been the one politician to whom Pétain was not insufferably rude. Painlevé, as the new minister of war, wished to consult Pétain about Nivelle's plans. It comes as no surprise that Pétain told Painlevé that in his view they were nonsensical. He recognized Nivelle's point that the war must be won in 1917 because the French Army could not hold out for another year, but he argued that a series of limited offensive operations would sustain morale without risking the whole army on what was, after all, one throw of a rather doubtful dice. Painlevé reported all this to the new Premier Alexandre Ribot, who passed it on to President, Alexandre Poincaré.

On 3 April Nivelle was summoned to Paris to explain to ministers how he responded to the objections of Pétain and others. He was, understandably, furious. His subordinates had, in his view, used their connections with politicians to undermine their superior general. In a speech brimming with confidence he assured Painlevé and his ministerial colleagues that this was not to be another Somme, that he had a perfectly clear and workable plan which would lead to a "breakthrough" in 48 hours. In spite of Nivelle's rhetorical success, Painlevé still persisted. At a meeting of French ministers on 5 April he explained his objections. He introduced another factor to an already difficult equation: that the United States was about to declare war on Germany. The whole balance of forces would thereby be changed, not only because of American industrial strength but, much more important, because the reserve of manpower which America could mobilize. There seemed to be no reason, he argued, why French manpower should be wasted on a doubtful offensive when American reinforcements were not far away.

Painlevé's argument was enough to persuade Poincaré to call a conference for 6 April of all the main figures in the drama, soldiers as well as politicians, British as well as French. The atmosphere at the meeting was apparently "very strained and gloomy."[6] Poincaré reproached Painlevé for asking the opinions of subordinate generals behind the back of the commander-in-chief. Painlevé countered by complaining that Nivelle had been talking to foreign governments without reference to him. Pétain "was quite impassive, presenting an exterior of ice as he always did on formal occasions."[7]

There was then, it appears, a good deal of shouting. The generals present were asked to give their opinion on the proposed offensive. When it came to Pétain's turn, he gave it emphatically but in his customary low voice. Nivelle interrupted him constantly, shouting at him so much that he was unable to finish his speech. Nivelle proclaimed loudly that since he was in agreement neither with the government nor with his subordinates the only course open to him was to resign. With that, he stood up and made to leave.

Poincaré, Ribot and Painlevé all said it was unthinkable that a commander-in-chief should resign on the eve of an offensive. Poincaré did his best to sum up.

What he said is even now not entirely clear, but it was ambiguous enough to allow Nivelle to interpret it as sanctioning his original plan.

As it turned out, the whole thing was a fiasco. To start with, the weather was appalling. On the eve of the assault there was rain and sleet. The troops of General Mangin's 6th Army, due to lead the assault, already numb with cold struggled to their positions through the mud. The noise of the barrage made sleep impossible, with the result that on the morning of 16 April the original enthusiasm for the battle had collapsed. It was then discovered that the creeping artillery barrage had moved forward too fast. The infantry were cruelly exposed to the German machine-gunners who had had time to come out of their dugouts.

Furthermore, the French guns had not succeeded in destroying all the German barbed wire. By then the artillery commanders had no idea where the infantry were. Some believed that the infantry had not yet left their trenches, and ordered their barrage to be brought back to the starting point. The soldiers in front were treated to the horrific spectacle of their own barrage gradually coming back to rain shells on them. French aircraft had also lost control of the air to the Germans.

Early in the afternoon, Nivelle sent his tanks forward. Instead of being the key to victory, they proved cumbersome and ineffective. They could only move at walking pace, were frequently bogged down in the mud or tipping into shell holes, and their armor was no protection against the armor-piercing bullets the Germans had invented nor German field artillery. Almost all the tanks were destroyed, and the infantry which followed them were killed almost to a man.

Then the German counterattack was launched. The forward French troops were halted—but the reserves kept on moving up behind them. The chaos from the subsequent telescoping of a large section of the French Army was unimaginable. Moreover, the French Army Medical Service, which had expected to receive no more than 15,000 wounded, found themselves quite unable to cope with the nearly 90,000 needing drastic attention by the time night fell.

For a few days, Nivelle tried to continue the offensive against the German positions on the Chemin des Dames. The battle meandered wearily on. Back at GQG Nivelle tried to blame Mangin for the failure—and then Micheler. But it was no good. They both knew, as did everybody else, that Nivelle's gamble had failed; and nobody knew that better than the *poilu* in the field.

On 16 April, the day of the attack, five soldiers and a corporal of the 151st Infantry Regiment had refused to go into battle. On 17 April men of the 108th Infantry Regiment deserted their post. The *"crise d'indiscipline"* had begun.[8] But there was much more to come. On 18 April the survivors of the 2nd Battalion of the 18th Regiment of infantry, which had been first into the attack on 16 April, staggered into miserable billets just outside Soissons. They were told that they were going to another area of the front, the border with Alsace. But by 16 April the battalion had been reconstituted, and was told that they were going back to their original position for a further assault on the German positions on the Chemin des Dames. This was the last straw.

The men of the 2nd Battalion went on the rampage. They roamed around their quarters in drunken rage, shouting that they were fed up with the war and wanted no longer to have anything to do with it. By the time they had sobered up the damage had been done. As they marched off yet again to the front, a few of their number were hauled out of the ranks—as suspected ringleaders—and arrested. After a trial with no more than what turned out to be uncertain evidence, five men were summarily shot.

Meanwhile, Nivelle himself was being called to account. Someone had to take responsibility for the fiasco, and he tried again to put the blame on Mangin and Micheler. On 27 April Nivelle arrived in Châlons to see Pétain. He started by reproaching Pétain for his caution, but ended up by offering him a job as his chief of staff. Pétain, not unnaturally, refused.

Two days later, on the day the men of the 2nd Battalion went on the rampage, Pétain was summoned to Paris to see Premier Ribot. Pétain was not one to neglect an opportunity; Nini was told, in a letter of 28 April, that it was possible that he would be in Paris the following day, but "was unlikely to be able to have dinner with you."[9] Nevertheless, she was summoned to an after-dinner rendezvous at the Buffet Hotel. The following day the message became more urgent. He would now be staying at the Continental Hotel (Room 222), and would she please turn up in his room some time after 10 P.M.

Pétain duly met Ribot on 29 April. Ribot told him that the government had decided to revive an old office—Chief of the Army General Staff, in other words immediate adviser to the minister of war—which had been dormant for many years. It was a way, Ribot pointed out, of dislodging Nivelle without admitting that the offensive had been a disastrous failure. Furthermore, it was widely believed that any Pétain appointment to the highest levels of military command would meet with resistance.

So it was. The British, particularly Lieutenant General Sir Henry Wilson, head of the British Mission to GQG, objected on the grounds that a Pétain appointment would mark a diminished French interest in any offensive. The politicians in Paris objected that Pétain was now so widely known for his dislike of politicians in general, and of President Poincaré in particular, that he would be a threat to the Constitution. Maginot, a former infantry sergeant who had lost his leg earlier in the war at Verdun, apparently threw his crutch on the table in disgust at the prospect.

But in the end Painlevé had his way. The British noted the reaction of the Parisian press, which came out on Pétain's side—although the British ambassador commented, perhaps rather oddly, that "the fact of his being a practicing Catholic causes him to be 'persona grata' in conservative circles."[10] But there is no evidence that Pétain had resumed his devotion to the Catholic faith. He was much more interested in Nini—although custom at the time had it that devotion to the one did not at all exclude devotion to the other. Nevertheless, the fact that Nivelle was a Protestant and that his fellow generals, Castelnau, Franchet d'Esperey, Micheler and others were devout Catholics may well have led Pétain to resume regular observance. It would have been the sensible thing to do.

Pétain moved into his new office, a magnificent affair decorated in the full pomp of the Second Empire, on 1 May 1917. Since the office of chief of the army general staff had been in abeyance for such a long time, nobody was quite sure what the holder of the office was meant to do. But on 3 May Painlevé received a document from Pétain setting out his views on his new duties: to be the delegate of the War Committee (of the Council of Ministers). He would take command of the allied armies on the Franco–British (Western) front and in the Balkans. He would "ensure the co-ordination of those operations with that of allied armies in other theatres."[11] In other words, Pétain was saying he would run the war. Painlevé lost no time in cutting Pétain down to size. The chief of the army general staff was to be subordinate to the minister of war and no more than a technical adviser to the government. He was not to be in direct command of anything.

Even so, there was much to be done. On 4 May Lloyd George, accompanied by Robertson, Haig and Admiral Jellicoe, arrived in Paris with their respective staffs for a conference about the future conduct of the war. On the French side were Ribot, Painlevé, Nivelle, Pétain and Vice Admiral Le Bon. The Italian and Russian governments were represented by their ambassadors. Pétain managed to persuade the others that it was no longer realistic to mount an offensive designed to secure a "breakthrough." The French Army simply no longer had the men to do it. Even Haig, forever wishing to go on the offensive, agreed that the French would only attack "vigorously to wear out and retain the enemy on their front."[12]

This conclusion was relayed to the political leaders the same afternoon. The only worry which was expressed was by Lloyd George, who wished to continue offensive action toward the Belgian ports to stop their use by the Germans as bases for their submarine war in the Atlantic. This was agreed, but it was pointed out that the United States, now an active belligerent, had come to the aid of the antisubmarine campaign by putting its Atlantic fleet at the disposal of the Allies. It was also noted that America was even then sending over a detachment— admittedly small but nevertheless symbolic of its commitment—of the United States Army. "Waiting for the Americans" was creeping onto the agenda of both Allies.

Meanwhile, Russia was in disarray. The Tsar had been compelled to abdicate and give way to a more populist government. In his first pronouncement to the Russian *Duma* the new leader, Alexander Kerenski, struck a reassuring note. He proclaimed to the Allies that Russia would continue to fight. Nevertheless, it was already clear that the tensions inside Russia made her future contribution to the war a matter of serious doubt. The arrival of two Russian brigades on the Western

Front brought with it first-hand accounts of the agitation in Russia. Equally, news of the impending arrival of the American saviors spread quickly to the French soldiers in the trenches. The conclusion, on the face of it, was simple. There was no cause for them to be hurled into battle to no purpose, when the Russians were giving up and the Americans would soon be coming to take over the burden.

On 15 May 1917 Pétain replaced Nivelle as commander-in-chief of the armies of the north and northeast. Pétain's appointment was supported both by Foch, who took over Pétain's position as chief of army general staff—thus completing his rehabilitation after his failures on the Somme in the offensive of July 1916—and by other generals, including—most important—Castelnau. The Parisian press were all on Pétain's side, at least for the moment.

So it was that the peasant boy rose to become commander-in-chief of a French army of more than a million men. In that sense, it was a personal triumph. But there was no time for gloating, or, for that matter, even telling Nini. Pétain was much too busy. On 17 May he moved in to GQG at Compiègne, where he occupied Nivelle's room in the Compiègne palace—the room which apparently had previously been occupied by Marie Antoinette. He felt able to write to Nini on 21 May that he found his accommodation "charming"[13] Surviving letters, however, demonstrate that Pétain was far from faithful to Nini in the distribution of his favors, and that his favors were enthusiastically accepted by those on whom they were conferred. Even at the age of 61, Pétain was still absorbingly attractive to women, particularly, of course, to those whose menfolk were away at the front. With the position of authority which he now had, Pétain looked—and sounded—the part of a successful and confident military commander. "None approached nearer than he," wrote one of his staff officers in GQG, "to what the Latins termed 'Great Men.' "[14]

Pétain, as the new commander-in-chief on the Western Front, had two immediate tasks. The first was to get to know the British; the second was to deal with the indiscipline in the army which by then was reaching alarming proportions. The British were certainly a problem. In Paris their ambassador, Lord Bertie of Thame (known, because of his aggressive manner, as "The Bull"), verged on eccentricity. He sported not just a white moustache but long and flowing white hair. Apart from his habit of riding around Paris in his state coach, he was remarkable in his capacity for telling a seemingly endless number of obscene jokes. He also disliked intensely his military attaché, Colonel Herman LeRoy-Lewis, who was not only bad-tempered but also regarded Bertie as an old fool; he much preferred to report to Lord Esher, who lived in Paris but had no position at all—except that he had the ear of the King. For Pétain, this whole situation was made easier by the return to France in May of the by-then Major Spears. Pétain had taken to him in 1914 and was certainly glad to see him back again. Spears was appointed in May as liaison officer reporting directly to the British War Office.

Pétain's first contact as commander-in-chief with his opposite number in the British Army, by then acclaimed as Field Marshal Sir Douglas Haig, was in a visit paid to Haig at Amiens on 18 May. Pétain made what he thought would be a friendly gesture by offering to put six French divisions at Haig's disposal for his proposed offensive in Flanders. Haig was, as always toward the French, patronizing. He found, as he recorded, Pétain "businesslike, knowledgeable and brief of speech . . . a rare quality in Frenchmen," but he received Pétain's offer well.[15] Yet Serrigny noted that the British were deeply suspicious. Pétain's reputation as a cautious military commander had gone before him. Haig put the question: "Will you take the offensive?"[16] The question was repeated. The minute of the meeting puts it more politely. On receipt of Pétain's proposals for four separate but limited attacks, Haig "saw no objection to the proposals, which were workable provided that there was determination and goodwill on the part of all concerned."[17] Pétain was indeed evasive, for two good reasons: first, he did not believe in hurling live bodies at barbed wire and machine guns; and, second, he knew perfectly well that the troops in his command would not obey orders to do so. What he was unwilling to do, of course, was to explain to his patronizing British allies that a substantial part of the French Army was in a state of disarray.

During the second week of May there had been further sporadic outbreaks of protest, amounting to mutiny, among the infantry divisions lined up along the front of the Chemin des Dames and the reserve divisions who were soon to go up—yet again—to the trenches. As Pétain fully understood, the real problem lay in the way the men were treated. Their trenches were little more than rivers of mud, urine and excrement. Their food was cold and maggot-ridden; their "rest areas" behind the front were squalid and rat-infested; the army medical service could not cope with the diseases, let alone the wounded; they were expected to go into battle at short notice with no clear idea what they were fighting about—only that they would be lucky if they survived. Above all, they were infuriated at being denied their proper entitlement to home leave.

In addition to dreadful conditions was the knowledge that there was growing disenchantment with the war throughout France. Even the severe censorship of press and post was unable to disguise the fact that the failure of the Nivelle offensive had demoralized not just the army but the civilian population as well. If the civilian population was supportive the army would do its job; if morale in the army collapsed, the collapse quickly spread to the civilian population. And this is what had happened. There were strikes in major industries and defeatist talk in Paris. The British were scathing in their comments about the "jelly fish who just now sit in the French Ministries."[18] The soldiers at the front wanted to know what was going on at home—but the arrangements for leave were at best uncertain and at worst random, and in any event cancelable at short notice. This was the grievance around which all other grievances coalesced. The men simply wanted to go home. Furthermore, those at home wanted to have them back.

By May it was clear that there was something near what can only be described as a general mutiny in the French armies along the line of the Chemin des Dames. General Maistre, the new commander of the 6th Army, postponed an attack because "we risk having the men refuse to leave the trenches." When he asked for fresh troops, Franchet d'Esperey promised five divisions but added "they are in a state of wretched morale."[19] On 26 May four battalions of the 158th Infantry Division refused to accept orders to go to the front. Troops stormed railway stations demanding trains to take them home. Even when they arrived in Paris, soldiers on leave proceeded to wreck the railway stations and insult those Parisians who had been unwise enough to greet them on their return from the front.

Nothing can be worse, as Serrigny remarked, than to take command of an army only to find that it is disappearing under your feet. Pétain was precisely in this situation. Although the common view of the rebels was that they would defend their trenches against an enemy attack but would not go on the attack themselves, and although the Germans seemed to have no perception of the state of French morale, it was immediately clear that Pétain had to assert the authority of command or disappear in inglorious defeat.

His first act was to issue a formal Directive. It was addressed to the generals commanding the three army groups and nine armies, and one army corps. The language was terse and to the point. The balance of forces on the front of the north and northeast did not allow, for the moment, for a breakthrough. Efforts should therefore be directed to wearing down the enemy with the minimum of losses. "To secure such attrition," the Directive went on, "it is wholly unnecessary to mount huge attacks with distant objectives."[20] In the future, attacks would have limited objectives, be conducted with maximum artillery support, make use of surprise, cover different sectors of the front and follow each other rapidly so as to deny to the enemy his freedom of action.

It was all quite revolutionary—and also extremely sensible. It recognized the extent of the losses that the French Army had suffered since the beginning of the war and the need to economize on future losses to allow time for the build-up of American troop numbers. It also recognized one of the grievances of the rebellious soldiers. But as the situation became more volatile, direct action was necessary. First, Pétain set out to reform GQG. The Nivelle supporters were sent packing. Alcohol in the mess was strictly limited. Officers only spoke when they were spoken to—meals often passing in silence unless Pétain himself thought he would tell an anecdote from his military past. He himself stayed up late in the evening, reading military history or the plays of Corneille—or writing to Nini. High living in GQG was no longer on the agenda.

Then there were the men. On 23 May Pétain wrote to Nini that he was "going away for several days. Don't worry if you hear nothing from me."[21] He was concentrating on the problem at hand. There was no time for frivolities, however attractive they might be. First of all, leave arrangements had to be improved. GQG issued an instruction that seven days leave must be granted every four months without exception. The number of trains for those going on leave was increased. Reception facilities at the Paris terminals were overhauled, and the French Red Cross was asked to set up canteens for arriving soldiers.

But all this took time to set up, and in the meantime the virus was spreading. Furthermore, the eruptions of indiscipline were taking on a much more sinister form. In short, what could hitherto possibly have been described as "military strikes," in the sense of simple refusal to obey orders, had become what can reasonably be termed "mutinies," in the sense of taking over direct leadership of military units. The protests of May, which were largely about the conditions under which soldiers were required to live, assumed in early June clear overtones of social revolution. "Down with the War!" "Throw down your arms!" were slogans heard more and more frequently. Whole companies were disappearing into the forests. By the time of the emergency cabinet meeting on Sunday 3 June, it was glumly noted in the ministry of war that between Paris and the front of Chemin des Dames there were only two divisions which could be "absolutely and wholly relied on."[22]

Pétain was still not prepared to come clean with the British. On 27 May he repeated his promise to Haig to provide six divisions for a British-led Flanders offensive, but by then the British were becoming aware that something was badly wrong. Spears, in particular, was reporting to London that the situation in the French Army was much more serious than they let on, and by the end of May Haig was convinced—vaingloriously, as it turned out—that the British would have to win the war on their own. Pétain himself went to see Haig on 7 June, admitted that some recalcitrants had been shot, but left the impression that the troubles were confined to two divisions only. He clearly was not prepared to tell Haig the whole truth. Indeed, he admitted as much to Haig after the end of the war.

Apart from what he did or did not tell the British, Pétain had a domestic political problem. In order to suppress the mutinies a proper and efficient system of justice was essential. After the Dreyfus affair the old system of courts-martial had been replaced by a system of *conseils de guerre*. This allowed any soldier convicted of a crime to appeal to a civil court and, in the case of the imposition of the death penalty, to appeal directly to the president of the republic. That system obviously would not work when it was necessary to deal quickly with major collective events such as mutinies. Pétain saw this clearly and, stretching his legal powers to the limit, on 1 June gave the armies in his command the authority to summon *conseils de guerre* without reference to a higher command. Painlevé—who throughout the whole affair was to be much more lenient than Pétain—noted the action, but urged caution.

On 9 June, he got what he really wanted: an order from Painlevé abolishing the right of review of sentences in cases of "collective disobedience." At that point, he felt able to send out a ferocious message to the commanders of army groups and armies that "all officers, from the commander of a platoon to the commander of an army corps, must have the same sense of duty. It is necessary that all realize that they must exercise their responsibilities or else they will themselves be brought before *conseils de guerre*."[23]

By the time calm was restored, approximately 40,000 troops had been involved in episodes ranging from indiscipline to outright mutiny. Some 50 divisions were affected in one way or another, almost half the French Army. In all, 554 men were condemned to death by *conseils de guerre*, of whom 49 were actually shot. Nearly 1,400 were sentenced to deportation and forced labor. Fierce as it was, it was part of the price Pétain was prepared to pay—not just to whip his army into shape but for the "public cause," the restoration of civil morale.

By then visible help was at hand. An American advance force had arrived at Liverpool on the morning of 8 June. It and its general, John J. Pershing, were greeted with what can only be called hysterical enthusiasm. The Americans were, to a war-weary crowd, to be the saviors of all that was decent in the world—particularly the lives of British men still engaged in the seemingly endless battle. On their arrival in London, Pershing and his men were greeted by the great dignitaries of the realm led by no less a figure than King George V. "It has always been my wish," the King intoned to the assembled company, "that the great English speaking peoples unite in the pursuit of a great cause." "The Anglo-Saxon race," he went on, "must save civilisation."[24] (Nobody apparently remarked that King George V was of largely German blood and was born with the surname of Saxe-Coburg-Gotha.)

On 16 June Pershing arrived at Compiègne to meet Pétain over lunch and to explain the American position. "He has a kindly expression," Pershing noted, "[and] is most agreeable, but not especially talkative. His keen sense of humor became apparent from the jokes he told at the expense of some of his staff."[25] Pershing did not record what Pétain had said to him about the condition of the French Army—or even if, as is more likely, he said nothing at all.

Almost every day Pétain set out from Compiègne in his car to drive to one or another divisional headquarters. His day was always the same: discussion with senior commanders, an address to the troops—standing on a mound or on a tree stump—in which he reiterated, time after time, his strategy of holding ground with limited and well-prepared offensives until the French industrial base had been fully converted to build the machinery of modern warfare—guns, tanks and planes—and until the Americans arrived to give the Allies superiority in manpower. As a speech it was perhaps not very eloquent. But there is no doubt that his speech, repeated over and over again, hit the mark with the *poilus*. At least, they thought, they had one general on their side.

The round of visits—perhaps to as many as 90 units—bore fruit. By mid-July outbreaks of indiscipline were on the wane. A violent German assault on the Chemin des Dames front was contained. The 77th Infantry Division had been mutinous throughout May and June, but the troublemakers had been weeded out, the division had been to one of the newly improved rest camps and was back in the trenches. On 19 July it not only survived a heavy German bombardment but was able to counterattack and repel a fierce infantry offensive.

It was now time to demonstrate that the French Army was still a fighting force—that, with proper direction, it was as good as, if not better than, the German or British armies. The six divisions which Pétain had promised Haig were collected under the command of one of Pétain's most trusted officers, General Anthoine, and dispatched to Flanders to fill the gap to the south of the Belgian Army and to the north of the British. Haig was curmudgeonly: "I am afraid that Anthoine and his Frenchmen will be a terrible drag until the enemy begin to fall back."[26] In fact, Anthoine's operation was a spectacular success. His troops built some 30 kilometers of roads, laid 80 kilometers of rail track, set up three field hospitals, assembled large quantities of ammunition to service the 900 guns which were moved up to the front. The French barrage started on 15 July with heavy artillery followed by howitzers and trench mortars. By the time the infantry attacked, on 31 July, the German lines were a tangled mess. By the end of the day, the French had captured the German third line. On hearing that the Germans were moving in reinforcements, Anthoine ordered his troops to dig in and hold what they had. In the assault, he had lost only 180 men. Haig was (reluctantly) impressed.

Three weeks later, on 20 August, the French went on the attack again, this time with eight divisions striking north of Verdun on both banks of the Meuse. The objectives were the forts which had been lost the year before and the heights of Mort Homme and Hill 304. Again the limited operation was a success. Once the objectives had been achieved and the infantry appeared to wish to advance beyond the range of the artillery, Pétain called a halt. French casualties were again low.

The third major action, the largest since the mutinies, was in October. General Maistre's 6th Army attacked on a 20 kilometer front north of Soissons at Malmaison—precisely the area where Nivelle had failed so disastrously in April. There was a preparatory barrage lasting a full ten days before the infantry assault on 26 October. Again, the attack had limited objectives (to drive the Germans out of the Chemin des Dames), and again was a success. General Pershing, who had been invited by Pétain to observe the event, was suitably impressed.

It was by then time to start planning for 1918. But two events intervened. The first was the battle of Caporetto, at which the Italian Army was broken, leaving a dangerous southern French flank. The second was the Bolshevik revolution in Russia. It was in the light of these two events that Pétain put forward a draft plan to Haig, based on what would now be called a working hypothesis. If Russia made a separate peace, the Germans might increase their forces on the Western Front by as much as 50 divisions. On the other hand, if Russia stayed in the war, there could, and should, be a general offensive in the spring of 1918 by all the Allied forces, including the Americans. It followed that, if Russia pulled out, there should be only limited offensives with local objectives, until the time came, probably in the late summer, when there would be a more general offensive on a broader front.

It was quickly noted by Haig that Pétain's anxiety related only to the defensive security of the French line. Haig took the view that even if Russia pulled out "the vigorous prosecution of our [British] offensive would still be not only possible but the wisest military policy."[27] At that point, it was clear that a difference between Pétain and Haig was starting to open up. Pétain, in short, had been much affected by the 1916 experience of Verdun. Haig, on the other hand, seemed hardly to have been affected at all by the 1917 experience of Passchendaele.

But although Haig continued to mutter into his diary that the French were a broken reed—and that General Pershing had perceived as much, which, of course, was untrue—he felt able to write, on 17 December 1917, that he was "much struck with the different bearing and attitude of the present Officers at GQG. The present ones seem much more simple, more natural than their predecessors, and are more frank in their dealings with the British. In fact, the relations between GQG and GHQ are better than I have ever known them."[28] 1918, of course, would tell a different story.

Total War

"L'armée française est ce qu'elle doit être, ce que je voulais qu'elle fût."

The war at the end of 1917 was very different from the war of 1914. Russia had collapsed, to be replaced by the United States as an open belligerent. Austria-Hungary was suing for peace. Italy was only just holding a line on the river Piave and could no longer be considered a serious force. In short, Germany had won in the east and could now turn her attention to the west. All now turned on America. America, in the Allied view, was to provide the resources which would win the war for them. As it happened, the German High Command had arrived at the same view. One way or another, 1918 would be the decisive year. Either the Germans would destroy the British and French armies in 1918 before the American forces could be fully deployed or the weight of American manpower would turn the tide against Germany and force her into surrender in 1919.

But nobody on either side had yet found the solution to the main military problem. The truth was that the stabilization of the front in late 1914 had led to a new and unexpected form of warfare. It was discovered that the combination of the machine gun and barbed wire ruled the field. Offensives and counteroffensives came and went, but turned out to be little more than bursts of murderous fighting over narrow strips of territory. The lines on the Western Front, give or take a few kilometers, were more or less where they had been at the beginning of 1915.

Pétain had also changed his view of war. In 1914 he was a commander on the offensive. But the battles around Arras in 1915 had been enough to show him the futility of uncontrolled and ill-timed infantry attacks. He, unlike others, had then applied his accumulated military skill and experience to the problem. True, the solutions he developed were cautious, and were considered by most of his fellow generals to be "pessimistic"—an epithet that was more and more used against him—but there were few who would stand up to deny their logic.

The war had also changed for the French civilian population; 1916—and Verdun—had brought much greater civilian involvement. Almost every family in France by then had lost a son, a husband or a brother. Many had seen their menfolk return from battle either with grotesque physical wounds or, perhaps even worse, mentally deranged. War could no longer be quietly ignored.

The war was also coming ever closer to home. By the second half of 1917, German Zeppelins and Gotha bombers could reach Paris or London to unload their own form of destruction. British and French planes could in turn reach the Ruhr. Whistles announcing an air raid became a common event in London and Paris. Shelters were manufactured on the spur of the moment to cope with the resulting panic. In London, bugles announced the end of an air raid. In Paris it was another blast of whistles. Such was the danger that Pétain was constantly advising Nini that she should not return from the south to Paris, whatever they both might wish. It was too dangerous. She should stay away.

Civilians were also subjected to intensive propaganda in a way unimaginable in 1914. By the beginning of 1918 all sides had learned the techniques of psychological warfare, of the use of grotesque images of enemy sins to stiffen the resolve of their people and to undermine the enemy's morale. The relatively courteous war of 1914 had become a ferocious and uncompromising struggle to the death. The press itself had become a weapon of war. Also, as might be expected in what was perceived to be a great cause, God was invoked by all sides—German soldiers had *Gott mit uns* carved into the buckle of their belts while English bishops pronounced, from pulpit after pulpit, that theirs was a just war. In short, the whole of Europe was beginning to learn the meaning of "Total War."

Pétain fully understood the necessity for all this, and, indeed, played his part. But as far as God was concerned, Pétain was at a distinct disadvantage compared with his heavily Catholic fellow generals, or even his devout British Protestant counterpart, Field Marshal Haig. They all seemed to believe that men killed in battle would go immediately to a heavenly Valhalla as martyrs in a just cause. Pétain's agnosticism did not allow him to see them as such. To him they were just festering corpses hanging on the barbed wire.

Such was the dispiriting nature of the conflict that it comes as little surprise to learn that by then all the participants, in one way or another, were becoming tired of it. Soviet Russia signed a humiliating armistice in December 1917. Heads of government, however, continued to talk war. Clemenceau, at the age of 76, became premier and minister of war in November 1917 with a promise of "war—nothing but war."[1] But in spite of all the bravado, many senior figures in all countries continued to whisper peace in private. The problem was that nobody seemed to have a clear idea how to achieve it.

At a conference in Rapallo on 5 November 1917, the Allies decided to create a coordinating unit for the Western Front, to be known as the Supreme War Council, to which the military were little more than advisers. (The ubiquitous Spears was to be its master of ceremonies.) This, it need hardly be said, was not to Pétain's taste. The creation of the council brought increased political interference in what Pétain regarded as purely military matters. It was already enough that he had had to defend himself against attacks from politicians who thought that he was being too cautious. But Pétain saw a further menace in the council. Foch, rather than he, was invited to become its French military representative. Foch declined, since he wanted to stay as chief of the general staff, but he managed to put in his deputy, General Maxime Weygand, in his place. Pétain suspected, rightly as it happened, that Foch was using the post as a stepping stone toward a higher appointment as Allied commander-in-chief. Although Pétain did not object in principle to there being an Allied commander-in-chief (in fact, he had himself earlier suggested it), he clearly thought that he rather than Foch should get the job.

Pétain took this view not just out of distrust of Foch or dislike of Weygand. It was because he had complete confidence in his military policy, in spite of the buffetings it had received. It was, indeed, clear, simple and straightforward. There was to be no major spring offensive in 1918. Soviet Russia's acceptance of peace would allow the transfer of troops from the east to the west. A German spring offensive was therefore confidently expected. This was to be resisted by a strategy of defense combined with limited tactical offensives where appropriate. The overall objective was to contain the Germans until the American Expeditionary Force was strong enough to participate fully in a final strategic offensive. To contain the Germans, of course, the French Army had to be up to the task, in a high state of morale and with enough tanks, aircraft and artillery to be able to face the German onslaught with confidence. This was the task Pétain set himself in the winter of 1917–1918. It was a task that he accomplished with diligence, method and success.

Pétain's success in reestablishing the fighting spirit of the French Army and in re-equipping was an achievement which ranks with his settling of the 1917 mutinies as a high point of his war. It has been little understood by British historians, who have tended to accept Haig's dismissive view that "it is doubtful whether the French Army can now withstand for long, a resolute and continued offensive on the part of the enemy."[2] (In fact, it was the British Army which broke in March 1918.) The restored state of morale was demonstrated by the regular studies which Pétain commissioned.

There was then the matter of equipment. First of all, Pétain gave attention to the artillery. By the end of 1917 French factories were turning out guns and munitions at a high rate, although, of course, slower than he hoped. Heavy artillery was organized half into a formidable general reserve which could be moved wherever most needed and half into divisional batteries. Then there were the tanks. The battle of Malmaison in October 1917 had shown that the lighter Schneider tanks were the most effective. Pétain asked for 3,500 of them (a quite unrealistic figure). After that came the aircraft. By January 1918 Bréguet and Hispano were producing more than 400 fighters and nearly 300 bombers a month. Pétain organized them, for the first time, into squadrons and gave them specific instructions on their tasks. Once more, speedy transfer to the part of the front where they were most needed was to be the guiding principle.

Pétain's next concern was to make sure that all these forces were correctly deployed. On 22 December 1917, he issued Directive No. 4, setting out the principle of successful defense. The first line of defense, the directive stated, should not be manned in force. There should only be enough troops to slow the enemy's advance. The second line, however, should be fully manned. It would be out of range of the enemy field artillery and therefore able to halt decisively the enemy advance. Reserves should then be used to attack the enemy in his flank as he went forward. The directive caused something near to uproar. The idea that a retreat from the front line—even if only for tactical reasons—was officially sanctioned by the commander-in-chief was, to generals trained in the doctrine of the offensive, wholly unacceptable. General Micheler even appealed to Poincaré on the matter. The upshot was that Pétain was obliged to visit all his army headquarters to explain and clarify what he was up to. But it was not by any means an easy ride. In fact, it was only eight days later that Foch made his views known to the military representatives at the Supreme War Council in Versailles. In the end Pétain got his way, thanks to Clemenceau's—perhaps unexpected—support. Strong defense was now official policy. The line of trenches on the French section of the front, particularly the stretch from Soissons to the Somme, was reinforced. Instead of relatively shallow trenches from which attacks could be launched, the "second line" was constructed with deep trenches on the model of the trenches in the Hindenburg Line. To do this Pétain asked for, and obtained, no fewer than 60,000 workers from Italy whose sole purpose was to dig. (Haig was very envious of this success. He asked Pétain if he could let him have up to 26,000 of them—which Pétain agreed to—and requested another 60,000 from Italy, a request which was politely refused by the Italian government.)

Pétain's efforts, however, were under constant attack throughout the winter—as, indeed, was Pétain himself. Mangin, who been sacked after the failure of the Nivelle offensive but who was reinstated as an army commander by Clemenceau, nursed a deep dislike of Pétain. Joffre, now in semiretirement in his small house at Auteuil, lost no opportunity of explaining that Pétain's tactics were far too cautious. Micheler was not afraid to talk to ministers behind Pétain's back. Pétain gave as good as he got, denigrating the efforts of his subordinate generals when they were slow to follow his instructions.

Apart from his travails with fellow generals, and the odd spat with politicians, Pétain's winter was relatively calm. He visited London in late December—where he flirted with the Duchess of Sutherland—and Belgium in early

January—where he flirted with the Queen. But most important of all was his relationship with Nini. By then, it had taken on the air of permanence. His letters are still full of passion, but instead of requiring her to meet him in various seedy hotels, he had rented an apartment in Paris in the Square de Latour-Maubourg.

On 31 January, the Supreme War Council met at Versailles. It was not an easy meeting. Haig complained to Lloyd George that the shortage of men was hampering his operations. Foch, too, reproached the British for not providing more troops, claiming, rightly, that France had called up many more classes than Britain and had trained more men in each class. Lloyd George attempted to demonstrate that resources were adequate and suggested a diversionary attack on Turkey, whereupon Clemenceau gave him "a real good dressing-down"—most of which Lloyd George, who did not understand French, was able to ignore.[3]

The meeting at Versailles came to one conclusion that suited Pétain. Foch argued, just as he had at a meeting of the military commands at Compiègne a week earlier, that the way to halt a German offensive was to launch a powerful counteroffensive. He claimed that the pressure on Verdun in 1916 had been to a large extent relieved by the offensive on the Somme. Both Haig and Pétain disagreed, Haig on the grounds that his troops were exhausted and that he had no reserves, Pétain on the grounds that the situation in 1918 was quite different from 1916. In the end, they persuaded both Foch and the council. It was decided to "adopt a defensive attitude for the present"—much to Pétain's satisfaction.[4]

The carefully constructed alliance between Pétain and Haig did not end there. They had even made a pact to come to each other's assistance. Haig made the deal clear in his note to the Supreme War Council rejecting the whole notion of an Interallied General Reserve. "In the event," runs the text, "of the enemy making a sustained attack in great force on any of the Allied Armies on the Western front it might be necessary to dispatch a considerable force to the assistance of the Army attacked. . . . For such a purpose . . . I have arranged . . . with the Commander-in-Chief of the French Armies for all preparations to be made for the rapid dispatch of a force from six to eight British divisions with a proportional amount of artillery and subsidiary services to his assistance. General Pétain has made similar arrangements for relief or intervention of French troops on the British front."[5]

The conclusion of the alliance with Haig was the last piece in Pétain's jigsaw to restore the French Army to fighting fitness. By the middle of March 1918 everything had been put in place. Army morale was high; there was a clear statement of purpose; both the political and military leadership were resolute; the French had no fewer than 4,000 aircraft; the Schneider light tanks were performing well in exercises; and the Franco-British alliance was cemented. The general state of French military preparedness was of a standard that could not possibly have been predicted at the height of the mutinies nine months earlier. Moreover, Pétain could reasonably claim the credit for himself. The French Army, in short, was by then Pétain's army. Furthermore, it was as ready as it could be to resist the impending German offensive—far readier, as it turned out, than the British.

On 19 March, in fact, Haig himself was prepared to throw in the towel. He told his visitors of the day, Winston Churchill, the Duke of Westminster and General Birch, that he was ready for peace. Churchill asked his views. "I stated," he replied, "that from the point of view of British interests alone, if the enemy will give the terms Lloyd George recently laid down, we ought to accept them at once; even some modification of our demands for Alsace Lorraine might be given way on."[6] Haig certainly had a point. In fact, whatever the subsequent bluster, Haig had now joined the peace party. He knew that a German offensive was coming. He knew that his whole army was tired. He knew that they could not hold out against the imminent German offensive without massive American reinforcements—which were not yet there.

At first light on 21 March 1918, General Erich Ludendorff, the commander of the German armies in the field, launched the long-awaited offensive. Just at the point where the British and French Armies met, along a front of some 70 kilometers, 76 German divisions followed a barrage, lasting no more than five hours, of high explosive, chlorine, phosgene and tear gas shells. The surprise was complete—the Allies were used to a much longer artillery barrage to start an attack—and there was dense fog on that morning. Storm troopers, assembled the night before in the greatest secrecy, burst through the first line of Sir Hubert Gough's 5th Army. By the end of the day, the German infantry in their wake had occupied Gough's second line. His Army had lost over 7,000 killed and, much worse in terms of morale, 21,000 taken prisoner. As a fighting force, the British 5th Army no longer existed.

Haig's reaction to the day is, even to this day, astonishing. In spite of authorizing Gough to withdraw, he sent a message of congratulation to the 5th Army, just as it was disintegrating, on a "highly creditable" result.[7] As it happened, however, Pétain knew better. Before Haig had even asked for help, he put three infantry divisions, a battalion of chasseurs and a regiment of heavy artillery on alert to move into the gap which was left by the virtual disintegration of the British front. On the following day Haig made his request, and the French troops went immediately into battle. But it was too little, too late. A breach was opening up between the two armies.

On 23 March, Pétain went to see Haig at his headquarters. Haig told him that, much to his surprise, he had learnt that Gough and the remnants of the 5th Army had withdrawn behind the Somme. He asked Pétain to concentrate a French force of 20 divisions to protect Amiens. Pétain replied that he would do what he could to help, and in particular to keep the two armies in touch, but he expected the Germans to attack to the south along the line of the Chemin des Dames. He could not leave that front too weak, since a German breakthrough there would open the route to Paris. Haig spoke openly of a crisis.

Haig's problem was that he had never fought a defensive battle. The BEF of 1914 which had fought at Mons and the Marne no longer existed. Haig had been used to ordering his troops to attack. Neither he nor they were accustomed to defend. The absence of a clear plan to manage retreat led to the breakdown of communications. Whole units wandered about in confusion and men, not knowing what to do, simply dropped their rifles or left their guns and ran away or surrendered. That was what had happened to Gough's 5th Army.

Pétain, on the other hand, was the master of defense. But it is precisely because of this that he understood the true gravity of the situation in a way which Haig did not. If his carefully constructed defensive strategy was overturned and the Germans had succeeded in rediscovering the war of movement, Pétain had no solution. There was nothing—no plan at all—to stop the Germans chasing the French and British armies, the one to Paris and the other all the way to the sea. Once a breakthrough had occurred, after all those years of static defense, nobody knew how to deal with it. In fact, it was precisely the danger of such a situation that had confronted Joffre and Sir John French in 1914. Then Joffre had accepted that in the event of a German breakthrough the British were bound to protect the Channel ports and the French were bound to protect Paris. Pétain saw this happening in front of him precisely as Joffre had imagined. He had no answer. Nor, for that matter, did Haig.

On the 24th Haig and Pétain met again. Haig noted that Pétain looked badly shaken, and so he was. The Germans had crossed the Somme south of Péronne. Pétain told Haig that all available French reserves were in battle, that further reserves were coming by rail, lorry or on foot from around Rheims and Belfort— distances of 150 to 250 kilometers, to be assembled under the overall command of General Fayolle. He said that he was doing all he could. He had issued an order to Fayolle that his reserve force should not be detached from the rest of the army, and that, if possible, the liaison with the British should be maintained. But he was still worried about weakening his front along the Chemin des Dames, where he expected a German attack at any time.

That simply fanned the flames. Pétain was acknowledging that the two armies might be separated. At that point, and in something of a panic, Haig signaled London for help. The two armies must not be separated. French morale, he thought, needed stiffening. Furthermore, he had finally come around to the view that there should be a supreme allied commander. He asked Wilson and Lord Milner, the British war minister, to come immediately to France "to arrange that General Foch, or some other determined General who would fight, should be given supreme control of the operations in France."[8] The "some other general" was obviously not to be Pétain. Apart from the by now clear breakdown in the relationship between the two men, to have allowed Pétain to become supreme commander over his head would have been an admission by Haig that he had been defeated in battle and was in consequence being demoted.

That evening Clemenceau and his chief adviser General Henri Mordacq
arrived for dinner at Compiègne. Pétain was at his most gloomy—he was suffering from a recurrence of the influenza which had made him so ill in February
and about which he had moaned to Nini. Moreover, it was far from a quiet
evening. The German attack had made it necessary to move GQG to the little,
and hitherto sleepy, town of Provins, and lorries full of files were churning up
the mud around the palace. German bombs were falling at regular intervals on
the railway station and the nearby crossroads. In the middle of this noise Pétain
told Clemenceau that, although he now had command of the vital part of the
front, including the remnants of the British 5th Army, the British 3rd Army were
retreating northward. Since he could not give orders to Haig, the situation was
not one which he could control. Moreover, his greatest concern was that the
Germans were planning a second attack in Champagne.

As soon as Clemenceau and Mordacq had left, however, Pétain's mood
improved. He immediately ordered an air strike by all available aircraft on the
German divisions preparing to move into the gap left by the disintegration of the
British 5th Army. On the following morning, 25 March, Fayolle found Pétain
calm. But by the time Clemenceau returned to Compiègne at about midday, this
time with Poincaré, Foch and Lord Milner, Pétain had descended again into
gloom. He claimed that he had no more reserves, that the British 5th Army no
longer existed and that Haig was fighting a losing battle. Indeed, by the end of
the day the German advance had reached a point 33 kilometers from the initial
line of attack. Clemenceau and Milner, after a long private talk, agreed on another
conference, this time to include Haig and Wilson, to be held at Doullens.

The conference immediately agreed that the key railway center of Amiens
must be held at all costs. If the Germans took Amiens the British would have to
run for the Channel ports and the French would have to fall back toward Paris.
The war would then in practice have been lost. Clemenceau asked Haig what he
intended to do. Haig replied that he would hold the territory north of the river
Somme, but that the area south of the Somme should be a matter for the French—
he had already put his 5th Army under Pétain's command. Pétain intervened to
reiterate that the 5th Army no longer existed, and went on to compare the whole
British Army with the Italian army at Caporetto. Foch could hardly contain his
anger; Wilson kept on interrupting with snide remarks. Pétain said that he had
already sent 24 divisions into the Amiens area, and turned the question back to
Haig: what would he do. Haig replied that he had no more men fit to go into the
line. The meeting fell into ominous silence.

There were then several whispered conversations in the corner of the room.
When the meeting reconvened, Clemenceau played his hand with the greatest
skill. He announced that it was agreed to make a stand in front of Amiens with
a joint Franco-British force. He went on to allow Milner to propose that Foch
should be appointed to coordinate the operation. As Clemenceau hoped, Haig
immediately saw the flaw in this proposal. Foch would be responsible to Pétain

and himself. Haig considered it vital that Foch should control Pétain. He therefore recommended at once that "Foch should coordinate the action of all the Allied Armies on the Western front."[9] The meeting agreed to this with a sense of relief, and promptly broke up for lunch. Haig had sandwiches out of his lunchbox. Clemenceau and his French colleagues crossed the street to lunch at the Hôtel des Quatre Fils Aymon. As they sat down, Clemenceau told Foch, "Well, you've got the job you so much wanted."[10] Foch was not amused.

By nightfall on 26 March the German advance had reached 43 kilometers from its starting point. The French 1st Army, which was being assembled hurriedly as Fayolle's main strike force, was not yet in place. General Byng's 3rd Army was retreating. The gap between the two Armies was opening wider. Yet even at that point Fayolle started to believe that the Germans could, after all, be held. The critical days would be the 28th and the 29th. Foch bullied his generals into moving their exhausted troops to new positions around Beauvais. It was very high-risk, since it left Amiens exposed to the north. Nonetheless, the tactic was successful. On Good Friday 29 March, the first French counterattacks went in. The German advance was halted.

The next day Pétain received a visit from the British minister for munitions, Winston Churchill. Churchill had been sent by Lloyd George (although Lloyd George—too late—thought better of his instruction and tried to reverse it) to report on the situation at the front. Churchill and Clemenceau went first to Amiens and then drove back to Beauvais, where Pétain was waiting for them in the French headquarters train, and conducted them, as Churchill recorded, into the "sumptuous saloons of this traveling military palace, and a simple but excellent dinner was served in faultless style."[11] Pétain had quite clearly recovered his composure. "All was calm and orderly . . . said Pétain at one moment, 'A battle like this runs through regular phases. The first phase through which we are now passing is forming a front of any kind. It is the phase of men. The second phase is that of guns. We are entering upon that. In forty-eight hours we shall have strong artillery organizations. The next is ammunition supplies. This will be fully provided in four days. The next phase is roads. All the roads will be breaking up under the traffic in a week's time. But we are opening our quarries this evening. We ought just to be in time with the roads, if the front holds where it is. If it recedes, we shall have to begin over again.' "[12]

Churchill was mightily impressed. Pétain was showing the determination which seemed to be missing in the British generals. Nor was his confidence misplaced. The German advance on that front was held. But it was not to be long before the German Army delivered its next hammer blow—precisely where Pétain had expected it, along the Chemin des Dames.

Pétain, Architect of Victory

"Est-il possible qu'on me refuse cela?"

On 27 May Ludendorff launched the last—and most dangerous—German offensive of the war. After a short artillery barrage, 18 divisions swarmed onto the Allied lines on the Chemin des Dames. Of the six Allied divisions left to face the German attack, three were British—the remnants of Gough's 5th Army, which had been retired to what was considered to be a "quiet" part of the front—and three French. They were the only defenders of a line of 55 kilometers. It is little wonder that by the evening of the 27th the German infantry had crossed the river Aisne and had almost reached the town of Fismes, some 18 kilometers from their starting point.

Oddly enough, Ludendorff's attack on the Chemin des Dames had at first been no more than a diversion. His main thrust was to have been against the British between Arras and the Somme. He thought he had the British on the run, and that with one more push he could roll them back to the Channel and into the sea. Foch's analysis was the same. He had decided that the main sector which needed reinforcing was the British sector in front of Amiens. Hence the continued movement of French troops to the north—and the virtual denuding of the Chemin des Dames sector to the south.

In fact, Ludendorff had already tried an assault on the British and Belgian positions in Flanders on 9 April. Haig had then appealed to Foch to send even more French divisions to shore up his position. Foch responded that he would maintain a reserve of 15 French divisions to support the British, but to do so he would have to put "tired British Divisions" on the Chemin des Dames front in place of the French divisions required to support Haig.[1] Haig, supported by Lord Milner, replied that he accepted Foch's offer, but there could be no question of mixing French and British units on other than a temporary basis. Pétain, Fayolle and Franchet d'Esperey, the generals on the other Allied fronts, were furious and amazed at the same time.

This whole episode, in fact, had shown the limitations of Foch's position. Although he had been nominated as supreme commander, the Beauvais meeting had specified that if any individual commander-in-chief objected to his instructions he had a right of appeal to his own government. In practice, this did not apply to Pétain since Foch was a French general and as such Pétain's superior. He could therefore give orders to Pétain but only make requests to Haig and Pershing. Whether they accepted his requests was then a matter of negotiation.

But there had been then a further shift in positions at a conference of the Supreme War Council held at Abbeville on 2 May. Lloyd George and Clemenceau complained that the Americans were being too slow in building up their force. But on the major question of the day, whether the British and French armies should be treated as one strategic unit or as two separate fighting forces, the meeting was unanimous in insisting that the main strategic priority was not to allow a breach between the two armies.

There was, however, a sting to the conclusion. If necessary to keep the two armies together, the meeting went on in its conclusion, the Channel ports would have to be abandoned and a retreat would be made southwards toward the Somme. In other words, Haig and the British government were accepting something which had been unacceptable to them only a few weeks before— Pétain and the French government's view that the defense of Paris was the strategic priority of last resort. But the question then raised, which Foch was unable to answer, was why French divisions were protecting the British when they might have been guarding the route to Paris—which lay precisely through the line of the Chemin des Dames.

On 5 May Foch had issued a general instruction virtually countermanding Pétain's Directive No. 4. All ground, he insisted, should be held. The front line should be fully manned and the second line only lightly manned. "Defense of territory, foot by foot, must be the priority."[2] General Duchêne, commanding the 6th Army along the Chemin des Dames, was quick to follow Foch's instructions. Pétain accepted the instruction of the supreme commander, much against his better judgement. Franchet d'Esperey, Duchêne's immediate superior as general commanding the Army Group, did the same.

The result was that Ludendorff's diversionary attack on the Chemin des Dames on 27 May achieved a surprising but immediately decisive breakthrough. Seeing this, Ludendorff cancelled plans for an attack in the British sector and moved further divisions south to support what had become his main thrust. Since there were virtually no Allied divisions in reserve, it was impossible to contain the German advance. It was not until 31 May that the advance came to a halt along the line of the river Marne. To the east, Reims itself was only held thanks to the heroic defensive action of Gouraud's 4th Army and the American 2nd and 3rd Divisions. As Fayolle wrote in his diary, "If we manage to surmount this crisis as well, it is only because God wishes to save us."[3] Pétain expressed himself doubtful about defending Paris. Even Foch said that he thought that the war might be lost.

The reaction in Paris to these events was one of panic. The government made plans to move to the Loire. Matters were made worse by the presence of three Krupp long-range cannon (known as "Fat Bertha" after Krupp's daughter) on the edge of the Forêt de Villers-Cotterets, able to lob shells into the center of Paris itself. There were angry scenes in the Assembly, many voices calling for the heads of both Foch and Pétain. In short, they wanted the government impeached. Clemenceau, when he finally managed to speak, was only able to resist the attacks by a virtuoso show of angry rhetoric (although he privately admitted to Poincaré that he thought both Foch and Pétain had made mistakes).

The panic in Paris spread to Versailles, where the Supreme War Council met on 1 June. The meeting was both bad-tempered and fruitless. Everybody agreed that the Americans should be asked to make more of an effort—President Wilson was to be asked to aim for 100 divisions. There was, however, a wrangle about where the American units should go. Haig wanted them to reinforce the British front, maintaining that it was a waste of time to relieve French divisions with Americans. Haig showed his by then customary contempt for his French allies, not even bothering to recognize that they had come to the rescue of his army after the defeat of 21 March. Foch just managed not to lose his temper, but countered with the justifiable complaint that reinforcements from Britain had been too slow in arriving.

It was just at that point that Ludendorff's attack had been halted on the Marne. In fact, although the Allies could not know it, he had already decided that he would call a halt to the attack on 3 June, since he calculated that by that time his infantry would be at the limit of its supply chain. Nevertheless, it took a resolute combination of French and American troops to prevent a further breakthrough. The Americans, for the first time, played a full part. Pétain, in particular, admired the new verve and spirit they brought with them. Pétain was so impressed that he predicted that "if we can hold on till the end of June, our situation will be excellent. In July we can resume the offensive: after that, victory will be ours."[4]

The line of the Marne may have been held, but Ludendorff's offensive was far from ended. On 9 June, his supply columns having caught up with his infantry, he switched the direction of attack, driving westward along the line of the small river Matz and then the larger Oise toward Compiègne. This time, however, the maneuver was less successful. To be sure, it started well. The French 3rd Army, under General Humbert, followed Foch's defensive formula—to hold the first line at whatever cost. Again it was easily broken. Pétain lost his temper, and—unusually, given his normally quiet manner—gave Humbert a loud dressing down in front of his subordinate commanders. Humbert could only reply that he had been following Foch's directive. Needless to say, an undignified row ensued, Pétain claiming that he and he alone was commander-in-chief and that his generals should obey him in all operational matters. Fortunately for everybody, at that point Foch ordered a counterattack. It was organized—with his customary ferocity—by Mangin, by then commander of the 9th Army Corps and Humbert's superior commander. By 13 June, Mangin had successfully used his tank squadrons to reclaim ground and throw the Germans onto the defensive.

By that time, all French reserve divisions had been brought into front-line battle. At Fayolle's insistence, Pétain asked Foch for British divisions to be placed as reserve to support the French front line. On receiving Foch's request Haig replied that he wished to consult his government. In his now customary fashion, he insisted that he was receiving "a dismal picture of the French troops. But this I knew in August 1914. The Somme battle confirmed my view that much of the French good name as efficient fighters was the result of newspaper puffs."[5] In short, he used every tactic to resist having to move British troops to support the ally who was being attacked. Pétain could only note—with some bitterness—that Haig's response to him on 13 June was in marked contrast to his own response to Haig on 21 March.

In part, of course, Haig's reluctance to help may have been because he was aware that Pétain's own position was now threatened. Rumors were rife. It was freely said that Fayolle was to succeed him. He himself wrote to Nini on 28 June that "it might happen that my services will no longer be required, since I am not supple enough to endure humiliation. . . . But I view such an eventuality," he went on, "with imperturbable calm."[6] But, instead of Pétain, it was Anthoine, Pétain's chief of staff, who was sent on "rest leave" for advancing "defeatist notions."[7]

It was in this mist of uncertainty about his own position that Pétain was left to face the fifth—and, as it happened, the last—German attack. In spite of his heavy losses and a near epidemic of Spanish influenza on 15 July Ludendorff launched his remaining 54 divisions against the French 5th and 4th armies around Rheims. It was to be the final assault leading to victory—the *Friedensturm*, the Germans named it. But yet again he was to be disappointed. To the east of the city of Rheims Gouraud held firm. His army had adopted the formula of Pétain's 4th directive—a weak first line and a strong second line. The result was that the German opening barrage fell, as predicted, largely on open territory. The infantry attack was then slowed by the first line, and by the time that was overrun the infantry had lost touch with the creeping barrage—which had moved on ahead but had not the range to reach Gouraud's second line. The infantry advance was then halted and thrown back by a well-judged counterattack. It was, as the official history points out, "proof of the value of Pétain's defensive method."[8]

General Berthelot's 5th Army, to the west of Reims, fared much less well. Berthelot himself, a creature of Joffre and an even greater believer in the "offensive," was now required to fight an essentially defensive battle for which he was poorly equipped. True to form, he followed Foch's instruction to keep a strong first line and not on any account to surrender territory. Equally true to form, his army was quickly overrun. Nevertheless, Gouraud's resistance to the east of Rheims, and the fact that the city itself remained in French hands, meant that a headlong German advance to the south and west ran the risk of a French counterattack.

Ludendorff was slow, or perhaps even failed, to realize the danger he was now in. He had established a large salient, along the line of the Marne from Château-Thierry in the west to Epernay in the east, but with a large and exposed western flank from Château-Thierry in the south, across the rivers Ourcq and Aisne as far as the Oise to the north. It was against that flank that Foch ordered his counterattack. On the morning of 18 July, while Ludendorff was in Mons discussing a transfer of German troops to the north for a further attack on the Flanders front, the French 10th and 6th Armies, under Generals Mangin and Degoutte, respectively, supported by five American divisions—each 28,000 strong—attacked along the line of the Ourcq. At the same time, Pétain ordered the 9th, 5th and 4th Armies, ranged along the southern and eastern boundaries of the German salient, to prepare for a general offensive.

The Second Battle of the Marne lasted some three weeks. It was fierce— Mangin saw to that—and ultimately successful. But the going was slow. The territory which Ludendorff had gained since 27 May was won back again, but only after weeks of tenacious defense. Yet it was not only the disciplined German retreat which held up the French and American advance. The truth is that the Allied command and control was far from perfect. Foch's uncertain role—he was supreme commander but without the power to give direct orders other than to the French Army, and even then Pétain had a good deal of latitude in their interpretation—turned out to be a recipe for confusion. It was difficult for generals in the field to know the difference between an "instruction" from the supreme commander (to the French) and a "request" from the supreme commander (to the Americans). Furthermore, Foch had a limited staff at his disposal and was therefore obliged to pester his fighting generals for information on which to make his decisions.

Similarly, it was far from clear at what level—Foch or Pétain—general directives on policy should be made. On 12 July, for instance, only six days before the major counterattack, Pétain issued his Directive No. 5. Pétain, as he had said at the end of May, had expected the German offensive finally to break its back on the rocks of French and American resistance. That being so, it was reasonable to expect—as was confirmed by prisoners taken at the front—that Ludendorff had run out of options. For Pétain, it was necessary in logic to spell out at that point his view of the new nature of offensive tactics.

Directive No. 5 has some familiar material. Attacks should be "audacious" and "rapid," the follow-up "immediate and far-reaching." None of that was new. It could easily have been drafted in 1914. What was new, however, was the method of attack. There should be a bombardment of the enemy lines "either by artillery or from the air" as short and as violent as possible. This should then lead quickly to an assault by heavy tanks "opening the way to the infantry and artillery." Lighter tanks should accompany the infantry to help it break down residual resistance and "repel counterattacks."[9] The directive was followed to the letter in the counterattack of 18 July: some 1,000 aircraft were deployed and some 750 tanks. (In fact, it is hard to think of a clearer description of what became known as the German *Blitzkrieg* of May 1940.)

Although Pétain's armies were prepared for offensive action along the whole of his front, Foch was surprisingly slow to allow them free rein. It was not until 24 July that he summoned Pétain, Haig and Pershing to his headquarters at Château Bombon to explain the conclusions he had drawn from the Second Battle of the Marne and the subsequent counterattack of 18 July. Somewhat surprisingly, they were modest. It was time, Foch thought, generally to adopt a more offensive attitude. He hoped to achieve some "useful" results, with the possibility of launching a more general offensive in late summer or autumn. In the meantime, he requested Haig to prepare for an attack in front of Amiens and into the old battlefields of the Somme.

As it happened, Foch was made a marshal on the day of the British attack. (Pétain was awarded France's highest military honor, the Médaille Militaire. This was added to recognition by the British in the form of the Grand Cross of the Order of the Bath.) On the morning of 8 August, 530 British and 70 French tanks, 10 divisions of the Canadian and Anzac Corps and 8 French divisions from Fayolle's Army Group attacked on a front of 30 kilometers. It was a stunning, almost a decisive, blow. Within four days most of the old Somme battlefield had been retaken and the Germans were in full retreat toward the Hindenburg Line. On the evening of 12 August, Foch, Pétain and Fayolle were invited to meet King George V to receive his congratulations. Haig, apparently, was "very friendly."[10] Since he had been in command of the eight French divisions it is perhaps not hard to see why.

That might have been a moment of bonhomie, but it did not last long. The now deep mutual distrust between Pétain and Haig continued to bedevil Allied operations right up until the November armistice. Nor, for that matter, were Pétain's relations with Foch particularly good at the time—although this was due to differences of opinion over tactics rather than personal animosity. The first point of disagreement was about what Pétain perceived to be Foch's tendency to favor the British over the French. The second point of disagreement concerned the Americans and the use to which American forces might be put. Pétain took the view that they were not sufficiently trained to embark on a sustained offensive operation. He believed that they should be kept in defensive positions or in reserve until properly trained for attack. Foch took the opposite view—that the enthusiasm of the American soldier made up for his lack of experience, and that he should be put on the offensive straightaway. General Pershing, it need hardly be said, agreed with Foch.

At their meeting of 24 July in Bombon, Foch had instructed Pershing to assemble his troops for the reduction of the small salient of Saint-Mihiel on the Verdun front. This Pershing had done. In fact, he had been quietly planning the Saint-Mihiel operation with Pétain—who had to suppress his doubts—and his staff for some weeks. True, he had no tanks, but that problem was solved by Pétain allocating six divisions from Castelnau's Army Group of the East to reinforce the American left. But on 30 August Foch changed his instruction. The major thrust of the attack was to be northwards. Saint-Mihiel was to be a secondary operation. As it turned out, Foch was right; the success of the Canadian and Anzac offensive of 8 August had opened up new possibilities—the chance of a major encircling movement, with a Franco-American push northwards from Verdun and a British push eastwards toward the Ardennes. If the two pincer movements could unite, the German Army would be trapped and surrounded on the Hindenburg Line.

A limited Saint-Mihiel offensive started only two days behind the original schedule on 12 September, and Saint-Mihiel was taken within two days. Congratulations poured in. Pétain was accordingly almost forced to reverse his previously held view. The Saint-Mihiel action had persuaded everybody else that the Americans were fully able to take offensive action. He could only bow to that judgement. Accordingly, he requested Pershing to transfer his army from the right to the left bank of the Meuse, ready to participate in the major push northwards which Foch now planned for 26 September.

When the day came, however, the American First Army was badly held up. They had been instructed to attack northwards, and that they did. What Foch had perhaps not appreciated was that the route north toward Mézières and Sedan leading up the west bank of the Meuse and into the Argonne forest was by far the most difficult territory to attack and by far the easiest to defend outside the Vosges. The failure of the American troops to meet their targets on the Meuse-Argonne front had follow-on effects. Gouraud's 4th Army was also held up, and this in turn threatened disequilibrium along the whole front—the attack of 26 September had, after all, been mounted simultaneously by British, French, Belgian and American armies, with a total of 180 divisions. It was not the time for one sector to flag while another moved on, and the British were making excellent progress in Flanders and on the Somme to the north. They had even succeeded in piercing the Hindenburg Line.

What none of them knew at the time was that German morale was starting to crack badly. On 28 September Ludendorff had had something of a breakdown. Later he went to Hindenburg and told him that there was no alternative but to seek an armistice. The following day, when it became known that Bulgaria was opening negotiations for peace, the Kaiser was told firmly by a delegation from the Reichstag that Germany should prepare for her own negotiation by moving to greater democracy. On 3 October he accordingly appointed Prince Max von Baden, a known moderate and an advocate of peace, as chancellor.

On 6 October, somewhat to his surprise, Foch read in the Paris newspapers the text of a note from Austria-Hungary, Germany and Turkey. It requested an immediate armistice and discussions of peace conditions on the basis of President Wilson's Fourteen Points. The note, it appeared, had been sent to the U.S. government by the intermediation of the Swiss. The German tactic was clear: they thought that could get a better deal from Wilson than the French and the British, who had borne the brunt of the struggle. But it is little wonder that not only Foch but both Clemenceau and Lloyd George were badly put out.

On 9 October there was a meeting of the Supreme War Council to respond to the German request for an armistice. Clemenceau and Lloyd George insisted on harsh conditions, tantamount to unconditional surrender. Pershing was in favor of precisely that. Nonetheless, no decisions were taken, but it was agreed that there would be further consultation with other belligerents, and in particular that Foch would sound out the views of the Allied commanders-in-chief. But it was not until 25 October that Foch was able to call a conference of Haig, Pétain and Pershing. Haig proposed that the terms of the armistice should be minimal: (a) immediate evacuation of Belgium and occupied French territory; (b) Metz and Strasbourg to be at once occupied by the Allied Armies and Alsace-Lorraine to be "vacated by the enemy"; and (c) Belgian and French rolling stock "to be returned and inhabitants restored."[11] It could hardly have been more insulting to the French or, for that matter, to the Americans. France had, after all, been the main victim of the war. The battle had been fought largely on her territory, much of which was no more than a mangled desert. The French Army had fought battles, particularly at Verdun, in defense of its own land, which the British Army had never had to fight. Finally, although itself mourning the loss of more than a million of its sons, the French Army had come to the rescue of the defeated British Army in March 1918. The idea that France would agree lamely to lay down her arms on Haig's terms was one which every French officer, including Foch, found deeply offensive.

At the meeting, Pétain spread out on a table a map of the Western Front, on which he had marked out in red lines a progressive withdrawal of German troops from their present positions to the Rhine. He recommended immediate and prompt German withdrawal on the timetable he had prepared. If this happened, he argued, the Germans would be unable to remove their heavy guns and ammunition. Further, he recommended that the Germans should surrender to the Allies 5,000 locomotives and 100,000 freight cars. When all that was completed, their armies should withdraw to the east of the Rhine and the Allies should establish bridgeheads at Mainz, Koblenz and Cologne. For good measure, he threw in the suggestion that Germany should pay a large indemnity to the Allies whose territory had been laid waste.

Pershing, when he came to speak, showed his irritation at Haig's performance. He endorsed all that Pétain had said, and added for good measure that U-boats and U-boat bases should be put under the control of a neutral power "until their disposition is otherwise determined." At that point Haig bridled. "That is none of our affair," he said, "It is a matter for the Admiralty to decide."[12] But Haig was outvoted. Foch, Pétain and Pershing were firm. They were there to have their pound of German flesh.

Pétain had already hatched another plan. By the third week in October he and his staff were preparing a major offensive in Lorraine, which, passing to the east of the heavy fortifications on the Metz-Thionville axis, would strike—for the first time in the war—into German territory beyond the Saar, thus destroying communications between the homeland and the remaining German Army on the Western Front. German capitulation would then have been inevitable—and unconditional.

In Pétain's eyes, this was to be the last offensive of the war—the coup de grâce. Not only that, but it would be the French Army which would be seen to have delivered the mortal blow. Instead of having to share the glory of victory with the British and Americans, France could claim to have resisted the German onslaught in the first place, to have fought through the miserable middle years of the war and, finally, to have landed the knockout punch.

By 20 October Foch was coming round to the idea, so he asked Pétain to explain the plan in detail the following day. This he did, with supporting memoranda from his staff. On 27 October Pétain was able to give Castelnau instructions for the French 7th, 8th and 10th Armies and to invite Pershing to do the same for the 2nd American Army. But time was running out. On 3 November, the German sailors in Kiel mutinied. Germany itself was descending into chaos, crowds of armed soldiers roaming the streets of the major cities and near revolution in Berlin. Prince Max von Baden gave way to Friedrich Ebert as Chancellor, who immediately said that the Kaiser, by then in the army headquarters at Spa, must abdicate. On 9 November the Kaiser accepted what had by then become inevitable. At that point, the German armistice delegation, which had already crossed into France, arrived at Rethondes in the Forest of Compiègne.

The terms of the Armistice were all that Foch, Pétain and Pershing had wished. Pétain should have been pleased. Yet the evidence suggests otherwise. He may have exaggerated when he claimed later in life to have pleaded in tears with Foch to postpone the Armistice, but it is impossible to dismiss the evidence of an extreme reluctance to give up his Lorraine offensive—due to start on

14 November. As Charles de Gaulle later pointed out, "the hasty end to the combats . . . on 11 November 1918 came just at the moment when we were about to harvest the fruits of victory."[13] Above all, in Pétain's eyes, it allowed Haig and the British to claim to be the true victors of the Great War.

Thus ended Pétain's war. From an obscure beginning he had risen to be one of France's greatest military heroes. He was also, without a doubt, the most accomplished defensive tactician of any army, French, British, Russian, Austrian, Italian or Turkish. (The only possible rival would be Ataturk for his defense of the Gallipoli peninsula in 1915.) Pétain's defensive system held firm from the time it was devised in 1917 to the end of the war. For that, and for organizing the defense of Verdun at a critical moment, he was undoubtedly worthy of his Marshal's baton, formally presented to him by President Poincaré on 8 December 1918.

Nonetheless, it would be wrong to suggest that Pétain was a perfect all-around military commander. There were moments, particularly in March 1918, when his courage deserted him, and his natural caution took on an air of gloom and despondency. Moreover, he found it difficult to summon up the enthusiasm for battle which leads men to put their lives at risk for a cause. Fayolle summed it up well. "If Pétain had been alone [in command]," he wrote in his diary, "we would not have attacked. We owe everything to Foch. It is not that he organised this series of victories, but he gave the order to fight. It is always the same thing: Foch said 'Attack!'; Pétain provided the means."[14] Perhaps he did not quite have the ruthlessness to pursue his own ambition to the end at the expense of others and perhaps because his built-in caution did not allow for the dash needed to inspire men to attack. Furthermore, he was forever the outsider—a peasant in the company of swordsmen, a bachelor in the company of husbands, a lapsed believer in the company of devout Catholics. Yet, as a general, he was certainly superior in intelligent analysis, in tactical awareness and, above all, in humanity to both his colleagues and his opponents. He was not a Napoleon or a Wellington, but he comes very high in the ranks just below them.

T W E L V E

Nini, the Wife Next Door

"je constate que je t'aime profondément . . . ."

There is no denying that Eugénie Hardon was, in her prime, a particularly beautiful woman. True, in her mid-forties, when her relationship with Pétain blossomed, she was what kindly observers would describe as "statuesque" and the less kindly as "large and plump" (she was all of 5′10″ tall—the same height as Pétain—and was possessed of an imposing bosom), but her face was still her undoubted glory. A photograph taken at the time tells the story. Her face is shaped as an almost perfect oval. In the style of the day, her hair—a deep brunette—is done in ringlets kept in place by a discreet silver band. One of the ringlets drops down her forehead, to a point just above where her dark eyebrows—the right arched quizzically, the left slightly lower but slanting upwards as though in challenge—frame a narrow indentation at the top of her nose. Above all, however, her face frames, and guides the onlooker toward, her brown, passionate and inviting eyes.

Men found her irresistible. So, by all accounts, did she find men. Her main lover during the latter part of the war was General Pétain. There were certainly others, in the same way, indeed, as Pétain had other women. But in the first flush of their renewed relationship, at the time of Verdun, Pétain's craving for her company—or rather, not to put too fine a point on it, for her body—was passionate. His letters to her are quite explicit in their assertion of his desire. By the end of the war, however, his letters seem to have become rather more mechanical in their expressions of devotion. The relationship was certainly settling down; Nini's outbursts of affronted dignity at her lover's peccadilloes were less convincing; and above all, hanging over the whole affair, there was talk of marriage.

The idea was not altogether welcome to Pétain. It was one thing to have a successful relationship with an attractive, but divorced, mistress. It was perhaps something to boast about, as Pétain did from time to time. It was quite another thing to marry her. For a start, there was the matter of his almost certain excommunication for living in sin with an adulteress, since they could not, of course, be married in the Catholic Church. Although Pétain acknowledged the loss of his childhood faith, there were residual emotional hang-ups—and then there was the social problem. Nini could not possibly be introduced into society as his wife. She, and consequently he, would be shunned. Lastly, there was the problem of what to do with Nini's son Pierre. Pétain certainly did not want a stepson. It would be an intolerable encumbrance. Besides, Pierre was not an easy child, and his mother seemed overprotective of him.

Pétain himself had come out of the war as one of the two marshals of France who were generally regarded as the architects of victory. In the public eye, in fact, Pétain even outshone Foch. The "Victor of Verdun" was fêted wherever he went. It helped, of course, that he was extremely good-looking. He kept himself fit—a daily hour on horseback, walking long distances, fencing skillfully with foil, épée and sabre—so much so that his doctors could not believe that he had recently come through four years of war. But it was not only his good looks. His reading was by then widely drawn, by preference Corneille but extending to more modern authors as well. He made friends of Paris intellectuals, of Paul Valéry, Maurice Donnay, Pol Neveux, of the diplomat Maurice Paléologue and of the satirist Forain. Two literary clubs were happy to invite him to membership: the Déjeuner Paul Hervieu and the Dîner Bixio.

Nor was his company confined to intellectuals. At a time when *le Tout Paris* was trying to forget the war and determined to forget the lost years in a self-indulgent spasm of enjoyment, Pétain was quite prepared to join in. He frequented the *salons*, joined the Jockey Club, lunched almost every day with one or other of the society lionesses who decorated the *vie mondaine*. He was invited to stay at the castle of his friends the Marquis de Chasseloup-Loubat and his wife, and at the luxurious home of the Citroën family. He was regularly invited by the de Rothschilds. Of course, Mme. de Chasseloup-Loubat, the Citroëns and the de Rothschilds were all Jewish, but that did not seem to matter. In fact, at one point it was alleged that he was the natural father of a son to the Jewish wife of a prominent industrialist. Among his amours, Germaine Lubin, a striking operatic soprano celebrated for her performance of Isolde in Wagner's *Tristan*, was certainly a target—although she probably managed to escape Pétain's ultimate intentions by pleading an unfashionable fidelity to her husband. Jacqueline de Castex, the widow of one of Pétain's officers who had been killed at La Malmaison, was another. Marie-Louise Regad, by then grey-haired and stout, reappeared from Besançon and almost threw herself at him.

There was no particular reason that Pétain could identify why he should hurry to get married. Once the war had ended, of course, his excuse that he could not possibly get married while it was still on was no longer valid. Nini therefore redoubled her efforts. She started to follow him around the country when he was on official business. He could hardly prevent her, but he certainly did not want her showing up in public.

Nini kept up the pressure. By March 1919 Pétain was consulting his old friend Guide about "our projects"[1]—namely the purchase of a property in Provence. At first, Guide was pessimistic about finding anything suitable, but he started a search and soon produced one or two possibilities. Their preferred area was the hills above Antibes and Nice. Pétain had walked about those hills many years before when he was a young officer at Villefranche, and Nini's family had spent a good deal of time in Monaco. Since the Pas de Calais—which Pétain had chosen before the war for his retirement—had become a large coal-mining area and as a result had lost whatever agricultural charm it might have had, Provence was an obvious choice. Pétain himself, indeed, imagined himself retiring there to keep chickens.

But he was still a Marshal of France, and still on the active list. In fact, until peace was signed in June 1919 he was still commander-in-chief of the French armies in the west. There was much to be done to convert a wartime establishment into an arm of peace. The French Army at the end of 1918 was a formidable fighting force. More than a million men were under arms; the Hotchkiss machine gun was superior to all its rivals; there were some 6,000 75 mm field pieces and 7,000 heavy guns; 2,500 light Renault and 100 heavy Schneider tanks. Moreover, the French air arm was more numerous and better than any Allied rival.

Clemenceau considered that the Armistice had finished the war and that there should be substantial demobilization. At the same time, Foch was required to produce a military plan which could be put into action in the event of Germany refusing to accept the Allied peace terms. On top of all this was the need for some hard thought about the configuration of a future peacetime army. There was still a threat from Germany but, worse even than that, was the danger from the great new enemy—Bolshevism. In June 1919, only two weeks before the signature of the peace, French metal workers went on strike. They followed the miners of Lorraine, bank employees and shop workers in demanding Soviet-style political change. Clemenceau promptly ordered tanks onto the streets of Paris and a force of 17,000 men behind them. The strikers were dispersed, but not before the fear of Bolshevism had become a reality in the minds of senior officers.

Addressing the question of what sort of army should emerge, Pétain at the beginning of 1919, even while his present army was being demobilized, had made his views clear. He asked for the next mobilization to be of "6,785 tanks . . . under separate command . . . it is much to ask for, but the future belongs to those who have the greatest number of armored warriors."[2] Furthermore, along with Joffre, Pétain urged the importance of air power. The airplane, he had argued to Pershing as long ago as December 1917, could be the weapon of decision.

Demobilization was little short of chaotic. Units were stripped of men seemingly at random, without much thought of merging them to give a rational structure to the army which was to emerge. On Clemenceau's direct and explicit instruction, Pétain reluctantly dissolved 22 divisions between 10 January and 10 February, and a further 24 between 22 February and 31 March. By the end of September there were only 41 divisions left in France—little more than one-third of the army of a year earlier.

The peace treaty was signed in the Hall of Mirrors at Versailles on 28 June. Pétain was there, summoned, as he told Nini, back from Metz for the occasion, but Foch was conspicuously absent. It was no accident. Foch and Mangin had argued throughout the negotiations for a separate Rhineland state to be a buffer between Germany and France in the future. Foch had gone so far as to write about his plan in the press and to speak out at a meeting of the Peace Conference on 6 May. Lloyd George thought that he had gone off his head. Clemenceau was furious; Wilson was simply baffled. The period leading up to the signature of the treaty was marked by bad-tempered bickering among the Allies.

After the signature of the treaty France returned to its prewar form of political supervision of the armed forces. Pétain's job was to be wound up as soon as demobilization had been satisfactorily achieved. The Conseil Supérieur de la Guerre was revived, along with the Conseil Supérieur de la Defense Nationale. After Foch's antics at the Peace Conference there was no question of his getting the top military job, the vice-chairmanship of the Conseil Supérieur de la Guerre. That naturally fell to Pétain. On 23 January 1920 his appointment was announced.

For the whole of 1919 Pétain had managed to fend off Nini. True, he was away from Paris a great deal, leaving her with her son Pierre in a small house which she had bought in the rue Desaix—an unfashionable part of Paris. She had spent September with Pierre in England—in Bournemouth, to be precise, where she was thoroughly bored. In her absence Pétain seems to have renewed contacts with his sister Sara—they had met again at the funeral of their elder sister Adélaïde "whom I never used to see"[3]—who clearly warned him against unsuitable relationships.

But by early 1920 Pétain's resistance to marriage was breaking down. Nini sold her house in the rue Desaix, advised on the sale by her lover. The previous September, Guide had found what seemed to be the perfect retirement home. Named, somewhat banally, L'Ermitage, it consisted of a modest two-story house, a stable for the owner's horses, a barn, a small house for a caretaker and a pigsty. Just outside the hamlet of Villeneuve-Loubet, high up on the road to Vence above Antibes in the Alpes Maritimes, it commanded a panoramic view of the Mediterranean below. The vendors were asking a price of 140,000 francs (roughly some 60,000 of today's euros). His annual salary as a marshal was 150,000 francs—but that would rise over the years to 300,000—which meant that he would have to borrow to do the deal. The vendors finally accepted an offer of 130,000. At the same time, however, he was asking Nini if he could see her portfolio—apparently to give her proper investment advice, but perhaps also to see whether she might be able to make a contribution toward the price of L'Ermitage. Pétain, the peasant, was always frugal with his money.

Pétain was by then virtually committed to marrying Nini. He had given up his pursuit of Madame Lubin. Madame de Castex was still on his list—he had apparently asked her to marry him when Nini was not looking, but she replied that she was not yet ready for a second marriage. Finally, there was Marie-Louise Regad, who was still not prepared to take "no" for an answer.

What followed has taken on the status of legend. A letter from a friend of Marie-Louise, Henriette Laurent, tells the story. Thinking that she had won Pétain over, Marie-Louise was one day dismayed to receive a message from him saying that "Everything is broken. All is finished." The message went on to express the thought that she might be owed some sort of explanation. He had, he said, wished to convey—as gently as possible—to Nini that the situation had changed. When he had tried to do so, his message went on, Nini had taken a revolver out of a drawer and, waving it at him, had simply said "It's going to be me or it will be a bullet for you."[4]

Whether the story is true or not, Nini certainly won the day. On 14 September 1920 the pair were married at the *mairie* of the 7th *arrondissement* in Paris. It was all very discreet. Fayolle, by then a marshal himself, was Pétain's witness. After the brief ceremony the motley party went off to lunch at the Café de Paris.

The marriage was not well received. Pétain's sister Sara said she had no intention of knowing her new sister-in-law. A number of Pétain's acquaintances cut him from their address books. Nevertheless, the thing was done, and the new maréchale had to be recognized. A larger number therefore wrote to Pétain with congratulations, promising to recognize Nini as the Marshal's rightful spouse. But it was not to be as easy as that. Pétain considered it unwise to take Nini to official functions. Her position as a divorced woman might lead to difficulty with the heavily Catholic officers' wives. Even entertaining friends at dinner at Pétain's apartment in the Square Latour-Maubourg was fraught with problems.

Pétain's solution to the problem was nothing if not ingenious. He acquired the apartment next door in the Square de Latour-Maubourg, No. 6, on the same level as his No. 8. A connecting door was installed, to be opened only from Pétain's side. When dinners were held, the door was kept firmly shut, and Nini was left to entertain herself as best she could. Next door, however, the hostess for the evening was selected by Pétain from among the ladies in attendance on that particular evening. Thus it was that Madame de Gaulle, the young—and very Catholic—wife of Captain de Gaulle, who had returned from his adventures in Poland to a job as assistant professor of history at Saint-Cyr and had become one of Pétain's staunchest admirers, frequently found herself hosting the Marshal's dinners at his own table.

Pétain himself also paid the inevitable penalties of marrying a divorcée. Although he had lapsed in his religious observance, he was certainly upset at being deprived the holy sacrament for living in what the law thought perfectly proper but in the eyes of the Church were—at least formally—sinful circumstances. In fact, it seems that in 1920 or 1921 he took to mingling unnoticed with crowds going in and out of Mass on Sundays. Official functions were also a difficulty. Pétain was frequently invited—and attended—without his wife. Even his closest friends found the whole situation embarrassing. Pétain's grander friends, the Chasseloup-Loubats, the Citroëns and the de Rothschilds, certainly would not have Nini, given her rackety past, in their grand houses—so Pétain went alone. It was a strange existence. Pétain, one of the most powerful men in France, was required—and perhaps secretly wanted—to ignore his wife for a large part of his own life.

There is little mention of the great affairs of the day in Pétain's letters, yet much was happening in the wider world. By the time the two were married, Clemenceau had retired. After the elections of November 1919 had produced a right-wing government, he had tried and failed to get himself elected president. The National Assembly elected Paul Deschanel instead, leaving Clemenceau to walk out in disgust. Alexandre Millerand became prime minister. But without Clemenceau's personal authority government became more diffuse and uncertain. The war had drained French resources to the point where the public finances were only propped up by massive short-term borrowing. Speedy demobilization had thrown large numbers onto the labor market. Finally, by the autumn of 1920 the French economy had moved decisively into recession.

It was this deterioration in the public finances which put an end to Pétain's proposals for a large tank and air force. At a meeting of the Conseil Supérieur de la Défense Nationale of 12 March 1920, the finance minister, François Marsal, announced that although Pétain's proposals were undoubtedly excellent they could not be afforded. Deschanel announced the conclusion. Savings were to be made in the air force. Some 55 infantry divisions were necessary as the main weapon for national defense. There was hardly a mention of tanks. These conclusions were reaffirmed at meetings on 27 October and 13 December, except that, under pressure from Marsal, it was agreed to reduce the 55 divisions to 30. After that, it was left to the marshals—Pétain, Joffre and Foch—to pick up the pieces and to devise an alternative strategy.

The task was not easy. The occupation of the Rhineland, which served as a buffer against a future German attack, had a finite life. When the occupying forces withdrew, as they were bound to do under the Versailles Treaty, Germany would again be in a position to strike quickly at the industrial basin of Lorraine and from there progress to the northern French plain. If the French Army was to be drastically reduced in numbers and if French superiority in tanks and aviation was to be thrown away, a method had to devised which would make best use of the resources which would be left.

The general staff had begun to think seriously about a line of forts along the frontier with Germany. A report was first considered at a meeting of the Conseil Supérieur de la Guerre on 22 May 1922. It rejected the idea that in a future war ground might be ceded to the enemy and later recovered at the moment of victory in favor of the doctrine of "inviolability of the [national] territory."[5] The way to achieve this was to construct a line similar to the line of Séré de Rivières in the previous century. The idea was supported in the end by Joffre (surprisingly, in view of his hostility to forts when he was commander-in-chief) as long as they were sited in a manner which was consistent with an overall operational plan. The meeting was unanimous in resolving to adopt the principle of a line of forts along the frontier.

At first sight, it seems astonishing that all three marshals present, even Joffre and Foch, agreed on a strategy which was precisely that of a defeated France in 1871. All of them, in one way or another and with varying degrees of enthusiasm, had been proponents of the doctrine of the offensive in 1914, and all of them had seen the results of 1918. Indeed, both Joffre and Foch—Foch with greater conviction than Joffre—had argued at the meeting in favor of a more offensive strategy. Nevertheless, they were all forced in the end to grapple with the problem of resources. Reductions in defense spending dictated their conclusions. If there were to be a shortage of tanks and planes, the main strike weapons of the future, it was obviously no good devising an offensive strategy at the outset of a war. By the force of circumstance, France was in 1922 already locked into a defensive strategy. In fact, this logic would become even more obvious in the 1930s.

Pétain's ascendancy over his fellow marshals was confirmed by his appointment as inspector general of the army in February 1922. He was now not only the commander designate of the French Army in time of war, but also the supervisor of all military establishments, domestic or foreign. His position was further strengthened in 1923 by the appointment of General Marie-Eugène Debeney as chief of the general staff. Debeney had been a fellow cadet of Pétain at Saint-Cyr and a fellow junior officer at Besançon. Moreover, they were friends (both of them enjoying the same style of risqué joke).

The result of this new cooperation was the emergence of a new army manual, portentously entitled *Provisional Instruction on the Tactical Employment of Large Units*, which soon became known as the "Bible." It was certainly weighty enough—much larger than the 1913 manual which it replaced. The strategy for a new war which it set out was clear enough. Given the financial constraints imposed by the government, the emphasis was very much on defense. But this was not the only point which it stressed. The shortage of tanks meant that an autonomous tank force was out of the question and that therefore tanks would have to be dispersed and become a support arm for the infantry. Similarly, if there were to be a reduced air force, the planes that were available should be used for observation, reconnaissance and spotting for the artillery. Powerful fire-power in defense was "the preponderant factor of combat."[6] As a matter of record, the document was approved by both the Conseil Supérieur de la Guerre and the Conseil de la Défense Nationale (which included all the surviving marshals).

More problematic was the effect of demobilization and financial stringency on the infantry itself. This was first shown up in 1923, when French and Belgian troops were sent to occupy the Ruhr in an ill-judged protest about German fail-ure to meet its obligations to pay reparations for the damage inflicted in the war. But it was not until 1925 and the campaign on the Rif in Morocco that the weak-nesses became clear for all to see. It was this unsatisfactory army that Pétain was to command in what was to be his last venture on the field of battle. But, oddly enough, if 1925 was to mark the end of his active military career it was also coincidentally to mark his venture into serious politics. Needless to say, when this shift in Pétain's ambitions occurred, Nini was to be little more than a bystander.

THIRTEEN

Saving the Spanish in Morocco

"Le Maréchal est un grand homme qui . . . est mort en 1925."

It is difficult to convey to the modern reader the esteem in which the victorious French marshals were held in the years following the end of the First World War. Whatever the bickering among them during the conflict, they were perceived after the war as a united body of heroes of Homeric valor. To be sure, the three who had received their marshal's baton before the end of 1918, Joffre, Foch and Pétain, were held in particular respect. Of the three heroes, if there were to be carping, perhaps Joffre, the "Victor of the Marne," was thought to be a bit past it, and perhaps Foch had been too hysterical in his attacks on Clemenceau in the run up to the armistice and during the Versailles peace conference. But there was no denying Pétain—the "Victor of Verdun," as he was universally known, by himself.

In many ways, 1925 was the apogee of Pétain's whole life. (As de Gaulle was later to imply, it might have been better if it had ended there.) Wherever he went he was fêted. The weekly magazines were full of his exploits, of the speeches he made to veterans' associations, of the prize-givings, of the parades, and of the openings of official buildings and even of the dedications of the streets which carried his name—at least one in every town that considered itself of any importance.

Pétain certainly enjoyed these attentions. But in 1925 he was to encounter attentions which put even the Homeric worship of a Marshal of France into shade. Moreover, as a hitherto political naïf, he was to encounter a régime which appealed to all the instincts of a respectful peasant educated into the grand tradition of the French Army. In short, he was to meet Spain.

Don Miguel Primo de Rivera y Orbaneja, the second Marqués de Estella, was thick-set and heavily built. Born in 1870, he led a boisterous career in the Spanish Army in Morocco, Cuba and the Philippines. Eventually he found his way back, first to his native Andalucía as military governor of Cádiz and then to Catalonia as captain general of Barcelona. While there, he gained a reputation for unnecessary brutality in putting down any sign of civil disturbance—proclaiming, nevertheless, his affection for his fellow citizens. He also gained an equally deserved reputation for sexual prowess and his ability to drink his fellow officers under the table. To the Spaniards of the day, male and female, he was irresistible.

In September 1923 Primo de Rivera led a coup on a manifesto of "Country, Religion, Monarchy." King Alfonso XIII, who was conveniently on holiday in San Sebastián at the time, returned to Madrid and "invited" Primo de Rivera to establish what was tantamount to a dictatorship under no more than the nominal authority of the monarch. The directorate which he set up was composed entirely of military figures, but there was no doubt who ran it. Once in place, it quickly set about suspending all constitutional guarantees, outlawing the Communist Party and forcing trade unions to arbitration at the risk of being disbanded; it also added further to the existing privileges of the army officers who had supported the coup. Rivera was enthusiastically supported by those who held the reins of Spanish finance—and by the Catholic hierarchy. But it so happened that, in the course of this constitutional hijack, he also declared himself high commissioner for Morocco.

The history of the Spanish Protectorate of Morocco, set up by the Treaty of Fez in 1912, had been little short of disastrous. Many areas had remained out of Spanish control. In fact, over the years the Spanish army had only been able to advance by slow steps into the Moroccan hinterland. In 1921, however, the policy had changed. The Berber tribe of Beni Urriaguel had succeeded in forming a series of alliances with neighboring tribes along the extended ridge of mountainous country in northern Morocco known as the Rif. They were threatening to declare independence from the sultan, who was under the protection of Spain.

The Beni Urriaguel had acquired two charismatic leaders, the brothers Mohamed and Mhamed Abd el Krim. Contrary to the Spanish propaganda of the time, both Abd el Kim brothers were men of intelligence and education. The confrontation between the brothers Abd el Krim's Berbers and their Spanish protectors came to its first climax in 1921. The Spaniards launched an army of some 20,000 men under General Manuel Fernandez Silvestre. But on 17 July 1921, at first light, the Berbers attacked, ferociously and in waves, all along a Spanish line defending a small settlement by the name of Anual. In the ensuing rout, those Spaniards who failed to surrender—and some even if they did—were either hacked to pieces or, in extreme cases, disemboweled and strangled with their own intestines. Silvestre's body was never found.

Not only was it a human tragedy; 1,100 men had surrendered but, worse still, the Berbers captured some 19,000 rifles, about 400 machine guns and 129 cannon. The Spanish prisoners were ransomed for a large sum of money, which allowed the Abd el Krim brothers to buy even more weapons and ammunition. Finally, in the enthusiasm of victory, Mohamed proclaimed the independent Republic of the Rif, with himself as president.

Liberal opinion throughout Europe—and in particular the French Communist Party—pronounced the Berbers to be honorable natives who had thrown off the colonial yoke. Not unnaturally, Primo de Rivera took a different view. Anual had to be avenged and the Rif Republic suppressed. But the army had to be reorganized, and there were still some 40,000 men sitting in relative tranquility in the garrison of Chaouen, in the southern part of the protectorate. Primo de Rivera gave orders that they had to be brought back 65 kilometers northward to the capital Tetuan. But there was a problem. A protective line of 400 blockhouses standing a quarter of a mile apart—to be known as the "Primo Line"—still had to be built. And so it was not until September 1924 that the order could be given to evacuate Chaouen. The Riffians were waiting; the retreat from Chaouen turned into another Spanish disaster. The scale of losses has never been established, but by all accounts only half of the Chaouen garrison made it back to Tetuan. Furthermore, in all probability, casualties would have been much greater had it not been for the robust rearguard action of the Spanish Foreign Legion—known as the *Tercio*—under the command of the young Colonel Francisco Franco.

The Treaty of Fez had awarded France the protectorate of the southern—and by far the larger and richer—part of Morocco. The natural frontier to the north was the river Wergha, which rises in the mountains of the Rif and flows westwards. The legal frontier between the two protectorates, however, ran north of, and parallel to, the river. The French quickly realized that the Spanish withdrawal left the way open for the Riffians to make allies of the tribes within their protectorate between the legal frontier and the natural frontier of the Wergha, and to assert their authority over land that the French regarded as their own.

There was hurried consultation in Fez. Some French officers there wanted a quick preemptive strike against the Riffians, but the resident-general, Marshal Hubert Lyautey, disagreed. His policy was, and remained, one of peace. Lyautey's answer to the Riffian threat was to construct small forts in the territory between the Wergha and the frontier with the Spanish Protectorate. The strategy was a complete failure; on 13 April 1925 the Riffians, led by the younger Abd el Krim, overran the French forts in the west, hacked the defenders to pieces and put the villages of tribes which were friendly to France to the torch. The way to Fez itself was open.

The French establishment, both in Morocco and in Paris, was deeply shocked. After all, Pétain, in his capacity as inspector general, had the previous January reviewed the military arrangements and had apparently found them adequate. He had even been relaxed enough to invite Nini to visit Morocco in February—a move which the Lyauteys, surprisingly given their strict Catholicism, warmly welcomed. But by the middle of June the atmosphere had changed. In Paris, Lyautey was personally blamed for the April failure.

It was Painlevé, a figure from Pétain's past, and now once more minister for war (as well as prime minister), who started the campaign to undermine Lyautey. He and his colleagues decided that the only way forward in Morocco was in joint military operations with the Spanish. Lyautey had never thought that the Spaniards were anything other than boorish and brutal. Worse still from Lyautey's point of view was that Painlevé was preparing to negotiate with Abd el Krim. Indeed, peace terms were handed to Abd el Krim's agents in Tangier at the same time as Lyautey was replaced as commander of the French army in Morocco by a hitherto obscure general, Alphonse Naulin. Painlevé sent Pétain himself to make a detailed inspection of French forces and report back to him.

Pétain flew to Morocco, and at first he was welcomed by Lyautey. But it became clear, as his journey of inspection proceeded, that he was less than impressed with the conduct of affairs. "I am trying to arrive at a reasoned opinion," he wrote to Nini on 22 July, the day he sent off his report to Paris.[1]

Lyautey had been less than open in his reports to Paris on the extent of the Berber incursions, and Pétain's report came as a wake-up call. He described Abd el Krim as "the most powerful and best armed enemy that we have met in the course of our colonial operations,"[2] praised Lyautey's efforts—and then demanded massive reinforcements. During August and September troopships crisscrossed the Mediterranean loaded with men, animals and machinery.

Pétain's plan was to mount, together with the Spanish, a massive attack on Abd el Krim and remove him and his followers from the map. Once his report to Painlevé had been safely dispatched he therefore set off on 27 July from Casablanca to meet Primo de Rivera and to launch the process of planning a joint operation.

Primo de Rivera had sacked several generals and instituted a discipline which had brought the army to a peak of competence quite unknown to the ragged mob which was destroyed at Anual three years earlier. In Paris, of course, the Spanish Army was still seen as something of a bad joke. Pétain was anxious to correct that impression, confident that he could safely recommend to Painlevé a joint military operation with the Spaniards. On his return to Paris, he explained to Painlevé and other ministers that he wished to mount

not just the minor type of skirmishing favored by Lyautey, but a much more substantial attack designed to defeat Abd el Krim once for all. Painlevé agreed, but
insisted that Pétain himself should take charge of it. Pétain accepted the job, but
replied that he only wanted to run the military operation, not to replace Lyautey.
On 18 August Pétain left Paris again for Morocco. The terms of Painlevé's proposals had been published a few days earlier, together with Abd el Krim's rejec-
tion of them. The stage was set for a major military confrontation. The nature of
this was agreed between Pétain and Primo de Rivera; the Spaniards would
attack from the north and the French from the south.

On 3 September, the French government announced that Pétain had been
appointed sole commander of French forces in Morocco—without any responsibilities toward Lyautey as resident general. Lyautey's position was steadily being
undermined. Three weeks later, worried and depressed, he returned to Morocco.
He had finally recognized that the campaign to get rid of him was unstoppable.
Only a week after that he wrote a dignified letter of resignation. By that time, the
military operation was under way.

On 8 September, the Spaniards landed at the beaches of Cebadilla and
Ixdain in Alhucemas Bay, a point on the north coast half way between Ceuta
and Melilla. The landing turned out to be wholly successful; the Riffians had
expected a landing further to the west of Cebadilla beach and were taken by
surprise. The Spanish Legionnaires, under Colonel Franco, were able to establish
a bridgehead. By nightfall the Spaniards were off the beaches and encamped in
the hills behind. That was enough for Primo de Rivera to leave General José
Sanjurjo in charge and to head back to Tetuan. Progress from there, however,
was slow, and it was not until his return on 20 September, that the Spaniards
again took the initiative. On 2 October they were able to take Ajdir, Abd el Krim's
capital. On 8 October they met the French columns which had been advancing
in the territory north of the Wergha.

Five days earlier, Lyautey had left Morocco for the last time. He had had a
last meeting with Pétain on the 3rd. Privately, Lyautey thought that Pétain was
implicated in a plot to dislodge him. He certainly bore resentment toward Pétain
for some years afterwards. He also wrote a furious condemnation of Pétain's
plan of attack (which he had earlier approved).

On 14 October the rains came. Further military action was impossible, and
all sides dug in for the winter. The Rif was surrounded. Everybody, except perhaps the Riffians, knew that in the following spring the war would be concluded.
His mission apparently completed, on 2 November Pétain left for home. Two
weeks later he was again traveling—this time to inspect French troops in the
Rhineland.

When Pétain arrived back in Paris, he was appalled to learn that the French
government, under the pressure of public opinion, was ready to strike a deal with
Abd el Krim. He and Primo de Rivera had agreed that the Riffians had to be crushed
once and for all, not least to give the Spanish Army its full revenge for Anual.

Nevertheless, a peace conference was held at the end of April—at the town of Ujda, near the Moroccan–Algerian frontier. Both Pétain and Primo de Rivera urged their governments to be tough. Preconditions for a conference were therefore laid down: release of all prisoners and Riffian retreat from many of their most important strongholds. Although these preconditions were subsequently withdrawn, it proved impossible to establish any trust between the two sides, and the conference soon broke down.

It was then only a matter of time. On 7 May, a joint Franco-Spanish attack was launched. Although the Riffians fought bravely, by the end of May Abd el Krim had had enough. On 27 May he, his mother, his brother, his two wives and four children—with a mule train carrying all their possessions and, it was later alleged, a quarter of a million dollars—stole away from the main Riffian army and surrendered to the French. The Rif War was over.

There is no doubt that by then Pétain and Primo de Rivera had developed a strong personal friendship. Primo de Rivera obviously admired Pétain's war record. Pétain was impressed with what he perceived to be his friend's political skill. In fact, his dictatorship followed the same ideological line as the other military interventions in politics in both Spanish and Latin American history. The military in these events sees itself as the ultimate guarantor of national cohesion; parliamentary democracy is believed to lead to confusion and corruption; the nation state has to be defended as the most efficient and reliable political entity and source of pride; and the Catholic religion is to be revered since it ensured continuity of conservative purpose, with the additional advantage of promising to its adherents eternal life. All this was familiar ideological territory for Pétain. Like all French officers of the day he was familiar with the most effective voice of the Catholic, anti-Semitic, xenophobic and monarchist right, Action Française. Primo de Rivera did not follow the extremes of Action Française, but there was similarity between them. But although the ideology may have been familiar, Action Française had never been a political party, let alone taken power. In Primo de Rivera's Spain, Pétain saw in operation for the first time a political system which answered to his instinctive—if as yet incoherent—political views. Moreover, it seemed to be working.

Not only that, but Primo de Rivera had created for himself a public image that even a Marshal of France could only envy. He had an extraordinary appeal to the Spaniard in the street or in the field, and was known as "the savior of the fatherland," even a "Christ, who carries the cross on his shoulders," "the Messiah who carries the sun of justice in his right hand in order to illuminate the beloved Spanish soil."[3] No Marshal of France, however great his reputation as a Homeric hero, could have dreamed of such accolades.

It is little wonder that the 70-year-old Pétain was impressed, even to the point where, as de Gaulle later pointed out, he started to think that he might, in the future, follow Primo de Rivera's example. Indeed, he seems to have let slip as much himself, at a dinner given to him after their meeting in Algeciras on

21 August 1925. Under the headline "Alleged toast by Pétain," the Madrid agent of the New York Times reported carefully. "Details received here of the banquet given by General Primo de Rivera to Marshal Pétain," he wrote, "reveal a curious toast which the French Commander-in-Chief is alleged to have tendered to the head of the Spanish Directorate. He is quoted as saying: 'I toast Primo de Rivera who through his intelligence and patriotism was able to re-establish discipline and order in Spain. Perhaps circumstances may make it necessary to do in France as was done in Spain."[4] As a manifesto for the future, Pétain's toast could hardly be bettered.

The Politics of Peace

"Je n'avais jamais subi une telle avalanche de questions en trois jours."

The *Ossuaire* at Douaumont is a truly dreadful monument. For a start, the architecture can conveniently be described as proto-Stalinist. But if the outside isn't bad enough, the inside is even worse. Row upon row of unidentified skulls and random bones lie in mute but furious testimony to the battle in which they had fought and died. And yet it is strangely moving. Pétain, as was fitting for the "Victor of Verdun," was Président d'Honneur du Comité de l'Ossuaire. On 17 September 1927 it was his duty to preside over the transfer of the 52 coffins—each representing one of the 52 sectors of the battle—from the temporary building where they had lain to the new building. Pétain did not normally display emotions, least of all on public occasions, but his speech in this case is redolent of the memory of human suffering to which he himself had borne witness. He could not, nor would he ever, forget it; nor, indeed, would France.

France in the 1920s found the postwar adjustment particularly difficult. It is not hard to see why. The loss in terms of killed, wounded, blinded or mentally damaged in the four years of conflict had been fearful. In total, according to official statistics, the war had cost France 1,382,400 male dead or missing in action. A further 3,594,889 men were wounded. Moreover, all classes had suffered equally. The officer class had, in fact, been somewhat worse hit—20 percent of the 1894–1918 promotions of the École de Guerre, for instance, had lost their lives. But the peasantry was not far behind—nearly 700,000 were killed and some 500,000 wounded. Admittedly, the statistics are far from reliable, but it is certainly true that almost every family had scars to bear. The lines of cemeteries in almost every village and town, with flowers withering on the graves, still remain as silent witnesses to the tragedy which was played out during those years on the plains of eastern France.

By the mid-1920s there was a general feeling that the apparently glorious victory of 1918 was not producing the rewards which the survivors felt they deserved. True, there was an outbreak of somewhat forced gaiety in the early years after the war. It a was long time since anybody had had anything which resembled a good time, and a good time people—at least in Paris—seemed determined to have. But the memories were still haunting. Painting, for instance, had changed to darker, surrealist colors and shapes. Music, apart from the frenetic dance music of the day, became more fractured and dissonant. The arts reflected the atmosphere of frenetic unease.

So did politics. All sorts of groups were formed—most notably, of course, the Veterans Associations, but also communist and anticommunist factions, trade unions, and groups of apparently well-meaning men who wished to set the world to rights. *Redressement français* was one such group. Its founder was the industrialist Ernest Mercier. In its early days—it was founded in 1925—the task was to develop a coherent program for applying the concept of "scientific management" to the economy and the political system. The role of the state was to be reduced, education reformed, agriculture made more efficient, and the banking system overhauled. In terms of a political stance, Marxism was a particular enemy. To fight it off, strong government was needed, perhaps by successful senior military figures who had shown themselves to be capable of running large units during the war. If this meant a suspension of democracy and civil rights, it was a price worth paying. To lend suitable dignity, Foch was the group's honorary president.

It is not clear precisely when Pétain decided to form part of this group. He had known Mercier during the war, and his experience of Primo de Rivera's Spain confirmed Pétain in the views which were the basis of Mercier's political attitudes. It is not too much to say that this was Pétain's first introduction to what might be called political theory.

For the moment, however, this was a minor preoccupation. What was worrying him much more was the state of the French Army. Morocco and the Riffians had shown him how badly it had deteriorated since the end of the war. The length of national service had been reduced from the two years fixed in December 1921 to 18 months. It was impossible to retain an army of 32 divisions on that basis. A larger and larger part of the army was taken by native colonial regiments. Most drastically from the point of view of Pétain and his fellow generals, a majority of the National Assembly had been elected in 1924 on a platform of reducing the length of service even further, to one year.

The campaign for the reduction in army numbers was given impetus by the signature, in October 1925 at the Swiss town of Locarno, of a treaty. Under its terms, France, Belgium and Germany made a solemn commitment to the frontiers settled by the Treaty of Versailles, to the permanent demilitarization of the Rhineland and to Germany's admission to the League of Nations. It need hardly be said that the Locarno Treaty was hugely popular in all the capitals of Europe. This was, it was widely proclaimed, the final peace between the nations of Europe. The three main architects, Austen Chamberlain, the British foreign secretary, Aristide Briand, his French opposite number, and Gustav Stresemann, the German chancellor, were fêted as heroes. In fact, in spite of the euphoria in Paris and London, the real winner was Stresemann. He had given no guarantee about Germany's eastern frontier with Poland and Czechoslovakia. Moreover, he had managed to secure a further reduction in the Allied forces occupying the Rhineland. All the French had achieved was a rather reluctant reaffirmation by Britain of her guarantee, already promised at Versailles, of Rhineland demilitarization—which, in the event, was to prove worthless.

The Locarno Treaty was precisely what French campaigners for a reduction in the length of national service required. In January 1926 Chief-of-Staff General Debeney put forward a radical proposal. Only 20 infantry divisions could be maintained on a standing basis. On mobilization the three most recently discharged groups would have to be recalled. Officers from the standing army would then be posted to command and run the 20 further divisions thus formed. Thereafter, a further group of 20 divisions would be raised by recalling older reservists to the colors (known as "Series B" reservists). The standing army would be little more than an educational institution designed to train enough adult males to form on mobilization an army of 60 divisions. Debeney's proposals were agreed.

Pétain, of course, disapproved, pointing out rather plaintively that, after all, North Africa still had to be defended, and that in itself required a substantial standing army. But his cause was by then lost in the post-Locarno euphoria.

The Army Organization Law of 1927 was complemented by the One Year Law, finally passed in January 1928. At each stage in the debates, Pétain's name was cited and his reputation invoked—as it happened, by both proponents and opponents of each particular clause. Pétain himself kept his own counsel, at least in public, but recognized in private that the tide was flowing strongly against him and his fellow generals.

Meanwhile, Captain Charles de Gaulle had joined Pétain's staff in July 1925. He had, of course, been one of Pétain's subalterns in the 33rd in Arras in 1910. But he had had an indifferent war—wounded twice in the early phases and then wounded again at Verdun, he was captured and spent the remaining years of the war in a prison camp. Nevertheless, he had struck Pétain as an officer both of courage and of original views. It was de Gaulle's poor mark in his subsequent passage through the École de Guerre which prompted Pétain not only to take de Gaulle on to his staff but to invite him to give a series of three lectures at the École itself. It was unprecedented, but such was Pétain's prestige that nobody dared to say him nay.

De Gaulle's first lecture came on 7 April 1927. The great hall at the École de Guerre was packed. The crowd separated to let Pétain through, but Pétain pushed de Gaulle in front of him to give him pride of place—and to show that the lecturer was authorized by the Marshal himself to say whatever he wished. De Gaulle, in full dress uniform, strode up to the podium and, after Pétain's brief introduction, began his lecture—on military leadership.

"Powerful personalities," he proclaimed, looking directly at Pétain, "organized for conflict, crises, great events, do not always possess the easy manners and superficially attractive qualities which go down well in ordinary life. They are usually blunt and uncompromising, without social graces. Although deep down the masses may obscurely do them justice, recognizing their superiority, they are rarely loved and in consequence rarely find an easy way to the top. Selection boards are inclined to go more on personal charm than on merit."[1]

There was a good deal of muttering in the audience at the audacity of this young man who had never even commanded a company, and yet presumed to lecture them on leadership. In de Gaulle's second lecture, delivered a week later, he spoke at length about the real and lasting foundations of a true man of character. He went so far as to quote Admiral Fisher's judgement on Admiral Jellicoe after his failure to rout the German Grand Fleet at Jutland in 1916: "He has all Nelson's qualities except one: he does not know how to disobey."[2] By then, his audience had become used to the young and inflammatory lecturer. His third lecture, on the nature of prestige, was received in sullen silence. Senior officers in the audience simply referred to him as "Pétain's foal."

Later, in 1932, de Gaulle assembled the three lectures in the form of a book. It was dedicated to Pétain. "This work," de Gaulle wrote, "could only be dedicated to you, *Monsieur le Maréchal*, since nothing demonstrates better than your glory what virtue can be brought to action through the illumination of pure thought."[3] There can hardly ever have been a dedicatory note of greater adulation. Nor had the adulation been at a distance. During the years up to 1927 the social and family relationship had been very close. The de Gaulles were frequently to be seen at dinner at Square de Latour-Maubourg—Nini, of course, being excluded from the party so as not to offend Madame de Gaulle's religious sensitivities.

But by the end of 1927 the adulation was starting to wane. In December de Gaulle left Pétain's staff to command a battalion of Chasseurs Alpins stationed at Trier in Germany. By the time he had completed his two years at Trier, there were the beginnings of what turned out to be a serious dispute between the "foal" and his previously idolized mare.

Oddly enough, none of de Gaulle's lectures mentioned the burning military issue of the moment—the reduction of national service to one year. The reaction, of course, was to counter the proposed decline in manpower by stepping up preparatory work on a line of fortifications along the eastern frontier. In July 1927 Pétain himself went to reconnoiter the whole area. Having spent a good deal of time at Belfort and Metz, marching up and down hills waving his walking stick in the air, he returned to Paris with a revised plan. It was this which was finally adopted by the Conseil Supérieur de la Guerre (CSG) in October.

The Maginot Line, as it came to be called, occupied a good deal of Pétain's attention during 1928. Indeed, 1928 was a year in which he traveled extensively. In March there was a visit to Rome for the obsequies of his wartime colleague the Italian Marshal Diaz—followed by lunch with Benito Mussolini and a tour of St. Peter's, the Janiculum and the Villa Medici. In November he made a visit to Madrid to see his old friend Primo de Rivera, and in December he traveled to London to see his other old friend Louis Spears, by then a member of the House of Commons.

By December 1928, however, it seems that Pétain started to think that he had had enough, both of traveling and being asked too many questions about every aspect of army policy. He let it be known that he wished to retire from the posts of vice-president of the Conseil Supérieur de la Guerre and inspector-general of the army. He was tired; he was approaching 75; and he wanted to spend his remaining years in tranquility at L'Ermitage. In fact, de Gaulle even remarked that those who knew him well had started to notice "small periods of emptiness"[4] and "senile disinterest in everything." Tired and senile he might look to some—though others, particularly his female acquaintances, claimed that he was in full possession of all his faculties. But the burning question was who would succeed him.

General Weygand was the leading candidate for Pétain's job. There was no doubt about his credentials. He had, after all, been Foch's chief-of-staff. Not only that, but he had almost been in love with Foch. "When I knew him," Weygand is reported as saying, "I loved him, and it is natural to do all one can for someone one loves."[5] The difficulty was that he was small in stature, ugly, with the face of a fox—he reminded one Englishman of an "aged jockey"[6]—was bad-tempered and a bigoted Catholic ("up to his neck in priests").[7] Pétain, it need hardly be said, loathed him.

It therefore comes as something of a surprise that Pétain always had Weygand in mind as his successor. Yet, in truth, Pétain's endorsement of Weygand had always been conditional. Weygand was, to his mind, the best man for the job—such as it was at the time. It was Maginot, the one-legged war hero, by then minister of war, who took the matter in hand. Not only did he support Weygand; he wanted to give him complete authority over the Army. He proposed to return to the system enjoyed by Joffre between 1914 and 1916, in which the posts of chief of the general staff and vice president of the Conseil Supérieur de la Guerre (and therefore commander-in-chief of the army in wartime) were united in one person. Pétain objected to Maginot's proposals on the grounds that the two jobs were fundamentally different. The staff function was planning; the command function was directing troops on the battlefield. Pétain won the argument. The upshot was that Weygand was nominated as vice president of the

Conseil Supérieur de la Guerre and General Maurice Gamelin—one of Joffre's protégés—was nominated assistant chief of the general staff. Furthermore, Pétain, to general surprise, insisted on himself being nominated Inspector General of Air Defense. Retirement, apparently, even at the age of 75, was no longer on his agenda.

On the face of it, Pétain's choice of air defense seems an odd one. In spite of his retirement as vice president of the Conseil Supérieur de la Guerre he was still a member, and by virtue of his rank he could command access to ministers at any time, and was by far the most influential voice on the committee. The most likely explanation for his acceptance of what was, after all, an inferior post is the simplest: Like many old men, he just could not let go.

In September 1928 the first of the great French marshals of the First World War died. It was Pétain's old friend and witness at his wedding, Emile Fayolle. Not long afterward, on 20 March 1929, Foch himself died. (Joffre survived until January 1931.) In Foch's death there was a particular consequence for Pétain. Foch had been a member of that most distinguished of bodies, the Académie Française. His death created a vacancy among the membership—strictly limited to 40—and Pétain was duly elected in his place. This, needless to say, gave him great pleasure.

But another event caused Pétain great sadness. His old friend Primo de Rivera had been forced out of office on 26 January 1930. His dictatorship had come to an unhappy end. In the first week of March, suffering from heart trouble and advanced diabetes, Primo de Rivera arrived in Paris for treatment. Eight days later he died in the hotel where he was staying, his gaze apparently "fixed on the church of St. Thomas Aquinas" opposite his hotel.[8]

Official notice of Pétain's and Weygand's appointments came on 9 February 1931. Pétain surrendered his office at 4 *bis* Boulevard des Invalides and moved the short distance to Foch's old office at No. 8. It was very much less grand than his previous office, although almost as big. He also recruited a new member of staff, Lieutenant Colonel Paul Vauthier, whose recently published book *Le danger aérien et l'avenir du pays* had been well received. At least there would be someone on Pétain's staff who was aware of the potential of air warfare.

As 1931 drifted into 1932, Pétain found himself able to spend more time with Nini at L'Ermitage. The house was by then simply but comfortably equipped, both for winter indoors and for sitting out in summer on the terrace. There was plenty of book space, many photographs of the pair together—and even more of Pétain by himself. Yet times were hard. Economic gloom was settling on all Europe. Pétain was growing old. As Emile Laure confided to a colleague, "the memory is weakening. For events of the past, the Marshal's memory is perfect. As for new events, he does not take them in or, if he does, he takes them in badly."[9]

De Gaulle, too, thought Pétain "gnawed" by old age.[10] One of his staff officers, Commandant George Loustanau-Lacau, was even more forthright. "He has seen so many things and men," he wrote, "so many good and bad times, ups and downs, great matters and small, that the arrival of the car he is waiting for interests him as much or as little as the fall of a ministry or the death of a friend."[11] But Pétain, old and perhaps tired as he might be, was to show that he had certainly not lost what de Gaulle was to call his senile ambition. Interestingly enough, and in the context of future events, his first report on Air Defense, written, no doubt by Vauthier (and advocating, of course, increased expenditure), was submitted in July 1931 to the Premier of the day, one Pierre Laval.

It should be remembered that France in 1931 was a country at a summit of power and influence. As one distinguished historian has put it, "France was the dominant military power in Europe in the air as well as on land; she was executing a naval program . . . which was causing unease to the [British] Admiralty in Whitehall. Above all, she had extended her potency into the field of international finance. In 1931, the Bank of England was shocked to find itself dependent on the Banque de France, and the Federal Reserve Bank [of New York] to find itself not altogether independent of French good will."[12] It was only during the decade of the 1930s that France slipped toward weakness. But then it is not for nothing that these years were to become known as "the hollow years"; and Pétain was to be part of them.

The Hollow Years

"Je n'ai jamais fait de la politique et je ne veux pas en faire."

Pétain's domestic arrangements in the 1930s verge on the bizarre. Until May 1939 Nini was kept in seemingly permanent isolation from her husband in her own apartment at 6 Square de Latour-Maubourg. She was rarely allowed to accompany Pétain when he went out, and never to official functions. Nor, indeed, were Pétain's friends allowed to meet her. Henry Lémery, a friend and colleague of Pétain's when he became a minister, was only one of many when he recalled that "I never knew the Maréchale before Vichy."[1] Moreover, even when they might have been alone together, Pétain very rarely invited her to have her meals with him, preferring to go out by himself to a restaurant. In short, Pétain was clearly distancing himself from what had become an uncomfortable marriage.

By way of compensation, Nini spent a good deal of time away from Paris with her son Pierre—whom Pétain gave every appearance of disliking. But as if the separation of their two lives was not bad enough, Pétain would from time to time graphically demonstrate it by—quite suddenly and without notice—simply disappearing. Sometimes it was with a mistress, as, for instance, to Rouen in 1932, but more frequently it was to see his family—sisters, nephews and nieces and, in turn, their children—to whom, as he grew older, he became closer. Nini was never allowed to meet them nor they her—not that either they or she wished to do so.

By 1932 the economic skies had perceptibly darkened. Moreover, in that year a government of the center-left was elected. For the military, in fact, it could hardly have been worse. Pay was reduced, conditions worsened, and orders for new weapons systems all but dried up. Furthermore, in 1932 and 1933 the summer maneuvers were canceled for lack of funds. Recruitment to the armed forces consequently fell off, to the point where Weygand, supported by Gamelin, warned vociferously and publicly of impending disaster.

But it was not just the customary bleating. France was about to enter what became known as the "hollow years" for army recruitment. The birth rate between 1915 and 1919, for obvious wartime reasons, had been only half the normal rate of a peacetime adult population. The unavoidable result was that 18 to 21 years later there would a shortage of men of military age. By 1933, Weygand could reasonably claim, as he did, that the French Army was no longer a serious fighting force.

Weygand's claim was met by the government, by then led by Daladier, with something near to contempt. Almost by way of retaliation, they introduced measures to reduce the number of officers in the army and to cut military pensions and pay. The measures were justified, in the government's eyes, not just by financial stringency but by the new spirit of international cooperation shown in the Disarmament Conference, finally taking place, after long delays, in Geneva.

The row reached a pitch of ferocity when, to general consternation, Germany, under the chancellorship of Adolf Hitler, walked out on both the disarmament conference and the League of Nations. At that point, it was clear that both in Germany and in France the cast on the political stage was changing. Hitler had come to power; the old French warriors of the Great War had disappeared. Clemenceau, Poincaré, Briand, Painlevé and Maginot had all died by 1934. Paul Doumer, elected president in 1931 in succession to Gaston Doumergue, only served a year in office before being assassinated by a White Russian émigré.

All in all, the French political leaders of the first half of the decade of the thirties were pretty much of a job lot. Édouard Daladier, the son of a baker—known as the "Bull of Vaucluse"—had fought the entire war at the front, but by the end of it had only achieved the rank of lieutenant. Subsequently, he had become leader of the left wing of the Radical Party, but, as a staunch supporter of the union of the left, was continually irritated by—and irritating about—his failure to induce the Socialists to join a Radical government. Laval, the streetwise trade union lawyer from the Auvergne, who had spoken up for peace in 1917 but had gradually moved to the right as he accumulated a large fortune through his investments in radio and the press, was personally charming enough—and clever—but fickle in his political allegiances. Léon Blum had undoubted ability, but he presided over a fissiparous socialist movement which had not only refused to join the 1924 and 1932 center-left governments but was also uncertain—to say the least—about its political ideology.

Faced with the gravest of economic crises and international confusion, not least the problem of how to contain a resurgent Germany, none of these governments pursued policies of any detectable strength or determination. Politics descended to the level of personal bickering. If the Third Republic had been the longest surviving republic up to that point, it needs little imagination to see in the personalities who inhabited the political world at the time the start of its disintegration.

The first true political crisis came in 1934. On 8 January, a small-time crook by the name of Serge Stavisky was found dead in a villa near Chamonix. He had become rich through shady dealing in securities. It turned out that Stavisky had been under police surveillance for the previous six years, but his contacts in high places had ensured that on at least nine occasions he had avoided prosecution. These contacts were mainly drawn from the pool of senators and deputies of the Radical Party. The right-wing press immediately pronounced that the premier of the day, the Radical Camille Chautemps, had had Stavisky murdered to shut him up.

Chautemps thereupon threw in his hand, and Daladier was called back to form a government to sort out the mess. In order to win the support of the Socialists for his government, he decided to sack the—admittedly overenthusiastic—prefect of police, Jean Chiappe. This sparked the fury of the right wing, and a riot took place outside the Chamber of Deputies. The police fired without warning into the crowd, killing 14 and wounding a further 236.

Paris fell into almost catatonic shock. Still in the political subconscious was the folk memory of the anarchy of 1789, of the "glorious days" of 1830 and 1848 and of the Paris Commune of 1871. Politicians believed that the riot had been carefully organized by right-wing groups intent on establishing a dictatorship along the lines of Mussolini's Italy. It need hardly be said that there were no conceivable grounds for this belief. But Daladier, instead of standing up to fight, resigned the following day. The 71-year-old Gaston Doumergue was dragged out of retirement by President Albert Lebrun and invited to form a government of national unity. So it was that, on 8 February, Petain's aide, Colonel Emile Laure, was sent for and asked to put formally to Pétain the invitation to accept the Ministry of War.

Pétain was preparing to go to bed when Laure arrived. At first, he grumbled at being disturbed. Then, after no more than a moment's reflection, he refused the offer. The administration of a department would be too much for him. Besides, he foresaw uncomfortable rows with the Chamber of Deputies. The following morning, however, Doumergue sent another message: France had need of Pétain. Then Weygand turned up at Pétain's home and begged him to accept the job. The army, he said, had need of strong ministerial leadership. Pétain relented. After accepting the post, he said "The Prime Minister . . . said that the country had need of me. I did not hide, but I have never practiced politics and I do not wish to do so."[2] The remark sounds pompous, and it was. But it is no more than an indication of Pétain's growing sense of self-importance.

Petain intensely disliked the rough-and-tumble of parliamentary debate—in fact, he only appeared once in front of the Chamber of Deputies during his ten months in office. His main ally was Foreign Minister Louis Barthou. Extremely able and cultured, but with a roughness of tone which made many enemies,

Barthou at least attempted to create a circle of allies to surround Germany. His difficulty was that the most obvious player in that game was the Soviet Union, and he pursued negotiations with the Soviets with enthusiasm. His chosen vehicle was a proposed Franco-Soviet mutual defense pact. At that point he completely lost Pétain's sympathy. Communists always had pride of place in Pétain's demonology.

All in all, Pétain was not an effective minister. On the major issue, that the army's manpower needed reinforcement, he made no headway. On the other hand, he managed to reverse Daladier's decision of February 1933 reducing the number of officers; he improved the recruitment program for specialists; and he lengthened the training period by reducing holiday and leave entitlements.

The one matter on which Pétain could claim to have made progress was the Maginot Line. Although his initial argument, that the line should consist of a series of "lighter but unbroken prepared battlefields"[3] had been lost in favor of Foch's "discontinuous fortified zones," he was prepared to adopt the generally agreed formula. In fact, owing to the shortfall in predicted army recruitment, it was undoubtedly the best option. Not only was the construction of the line underway; Pétain even secured an increase in the budget.

Nevertheless, there were two—interlinked—problems. The first was the matter of how far the line should extend; the second was what, if anything, should be done to protect France's northern frontiers. Some suggested that the line should be extended to run along France's northern frontier with Belgium, on the grounds that Belgium was an unreliable ally and could easily fall into German hands as it had in 1914. Others argued that the terrain along the northern frontier was too soft, that the industrial complex around the Lille coal basin was too close to the frontier for comfort, that Belgium would consider itself abandoned and, finally, that a defensive line would negate the main strategy of moving a sizeable force into Belgium at the outbreak of war with Germany.

Pétain was convinced by the second set of arguments. On the other hand, he recognized that it might be unwise to rely on Belgium forever being willing to invite a French army to march into and across its territory. He therefore favored a scheme originally put forward by André Tardieu when he was premier from February to May 1932. The idea was to persuade the Belgians to erect a line of fortifications similar to those of the Maginot Line along their eastern frontier with Germany. The cost was to be met by a loan to Belgium of one billion French francs. Pétain revived the scheme; it was bold, and could easily have been effective. But the financial climate was even less promising in 1934 than in 1932 and it came to nothing.

The strategy which emerged was therefore neither one thing nor the other. The Maginot Line would not be extended but would be defended in strength; Belgium would be assumed ready to invite France to send in an army to man the Liège forts and line up along the Albert Canal and the Belgian section of the river Meuse—the underlying threat being that the French Army would go in whatever the Belgians said; and the "hinge" around which two operations would revolve would be the Ardennes. The possibility that the Ardennes might provide the platform for a massive tank attack was never seriously entertained by any high-ranking French officer, from Weygand downward (and certainly not by de Gaulle). Pétain himself ruled out the possibility. Nobody, then or later, disagreed with him.

In 1934, de Gaulle sent Pétain a letter announcing the publication of his book *Le Fil de l'Epée*, with the suggested dedication to him. Pétain was irritated first that de Gaulle was publishing the book at all, and, second, that de Gaulle, as a serving officer, was putting forward views which were contrary to official army policy. Not only did Pétain refuse to reply to de Gaulle's letter but he cancelled all their luncheon arrangements forthwith. De Gaulle retaliated by publishing his book regardless but with the dedication he had originally drafted.

The autumn maneuvers of 1934, reinstated by Pétain after the cancellations in 1932 and 1933, made it clear that officers were poorly instructed, had little basic knowledge and no confidence. Noncommissioned officers had no sense of leadership and the soldiers had "forgotten everything."[4] At that point Pétain did make an effort to secure further funds for the Army, but the Doumergue government was starting to look very shaky. On 6 October King Alexander I of Yugoslavia was assassinated in Marseilles by a Croatian nationalist. In the hail of bullets, Barthou was badly wounded and died soon after. There was a reshuffling of ministers, the most notable change being the appointment of Laval, who was eager to make alliance with Mussolini's Italy, as foreign minister. Negotiations with the Soviets continued but, without Barthou, with diminished enthusiasm. The press were certain that it was only a matter of time before the government fell. Pétain accompanied President Lebrun to Belgrade for the funeral of King Alexander. While there he made a new acquaintance: Hermann Göring. Göring had been a heroic aviator—perhaps the bravest after Baron von Richthofen—in the First World War. As old soldiers from opposite sides frequently do, the two got on famously, reminiscing about their experiences. Indeed, when he returned to Germany Göring spoke admiringly of Pétain, going out of his way to describe him as a "man of honor."[5]

The Doumergue ministry finally tottered to its end in early November. Doumergue had made a series of proposals for constitutional reform, one of which was to ban strikes by government employees. This was too much for Édouard Herriot and his fellow Radicals, who promptly walked out. Pétain was furious with Herriot for bringing down the government, but pleased to be no longer a minister. In fact when Pierre-Etienne Flandin formed a government and asked him to stay as minister of war, he refused. He left the offices in the rue Saint-Dominique and returned to his old office in the Boulevard des Invalides. As he entered the familiar surroundings he was reported to be smiling.

Pétain's influence on military policy was undiminished; no longer shackled by collective governmental responsibility, and made a member by name of the High Military Committee on its reorganization on 11 December 1934, he could be much more forthright in his views. Weygand retired on 21 January 1935, and at the first meeting of the High Military Committee on 23 January, with Gamelin now commander-in-chief designate, Pétain took up Weygand's reports on the state of the British army. Pétain claimed that Britain was militarily so weak that it would be fruitless to look for assistance there in the event of a German attack. Weygand—and others—had been particularly impressed by the professionalism and imagination of the British exercises on Salisbury plain between 1927 and 1931. But the maneuvers which Weygand had watched at Tidworth in June 1934 were altogether a different matter. Weygand was shocked at the extent of the deterioration. He "shook his head and walked away," went one British report, "hoping that we really had something better."[6]

The inevitable conclusion was that France would have to go it alone. True, Laval had on 7 January signed an agreement in Rome with Mussolini which purported to resolve all outstanding differences with Italy, but even then it was far from clear that Mussolini would prove a reliable ally. (In fact, Mussolini interpreted the Rome Agreements as freedom to invade Abyssinia in October.)

Pétain pursued his campaign with an article in the *Revue des deux Mondes* of 1 March 1935. He (or perhaps, more truthfully, the officer who ghosted it for him) reviewed the history of the army since it had effectively been reconstituted in 1927–1928. At that time, he argued, the arrangement was adequate given the restraints on German rearmament in the Treaty of Versailles. But those conditions no longer obtained. Germany was rearming. The militia system could not possibly cope with a sudden attack by an enemy using armor and air power. This type of warfare could only be met by a standing army of trained soldiers. The only solution was to reinstate a compulsory two-year national service.

Pétain's article appeared only five days before Hitler, in the first of what became known as his "Saturday Surprises," announced that Germany had a newly constructed air force. One week later, he announced that he would no longer abide by the military clauses of the Treaty of Versailles and was expanding the German Army from its treaty strength of 100,000 to a force of 36 divisions comprising some 550,000 men.

The news could only add irresistible force to Pétain's campaign. But it also, at least in the mind of the press, endowed the Marshal with the quality of uncanny and almost superhuman prescience. If he could read the future so clearly where others were blind, then surely he was the man who should be leading France at this dangerous time. The idea, of course, was not new. There had been a move immediately after the fall of the Doumergue government by *Le Petit Journal*, a popular newspaper of generally right-wing circulation, to promote Pétain as a candidate for dictatorship.

The theme was taken up by Gustav Hervé in *La Victoire*. On 14 February the paper produced an article with the headline "*C'EST PÉTAIN QU'IL NOUS FAUT!*"[7] The theme was taken up by *Le Jour* and, in April—after Hitler's two Saturday Surprises—by *L'Action Française* (particularly by the fiercely anti-Semitic Léon Daudet). Whatever Pétain did, wherever he went, provided material for eulogistic commentary.

Pétain's campaign to increase the length of military service to two years was a success—thanks to Hitler, the Parisian press and some deft parliamentary footwork by new Minister of War Louis Maurin. When the Flandin government fell at the end of May, therefore, Pétain felt able to respond to the call of Fernand Buisson to take ministerial office again. This decision was greeted with almost hysterical delight by his rightwing sycophants. But Buisson's government fell after only three days in office. Hervé took this as a sign that democracy had failed—and that the answer, without any further doubt, was a Pétain dictatorship.

Apart from *L'Action Française*, none of the press campaigns need be taken too seriously. Certainly, Pétain did not take them too seriously. Laval formed a government without Pétain—and without much clamor for Pétain to be included—and in August, Pétain went off to review works on the Maginot Line. Whatever else he was doing, he certainly was not angling for a political job. As a matter of fact, he stayed away from ministerial office until the crisis of May 1940.

But the press agitation in favor of a Pétain dictatorship did not die down. Indeed it even gained in momentum—fueled by the prospect of general elections in May 1936. The British naval pact with Germany, which allowed the Germans to construct a surface fleet a third the size of Britain's (but with parity in submarine strength), concluded in June by Britain without even bothering to consult the French, added fuel to the flames. Hitler's decision to build the *Westwall*, a line of heavy fortifications along the German western border to counter the Maginot Line, was equally disturbing. Moreover, it became clear that the general elections might well produce a French government which included communists. Finally, the growth in strength and influence of the paramilitary *Ligues* added to the fear of civil unrest.

By the second half of 1935 there were several of these paramilitary or near paramilitary organizations. Action Française was intellectually the most powerful, Catholic, anti-Semitic, authoritarian and monarchist, but the Croix de Feu, with its veteran base, could summon up more bodies if strenuous action was on the agenda. There was no doubt that if they combined forces they could pose a very grave threat to civil order. Pétain, in common with other veterans of the Great War, was sympathetic to the Croix de Feu. When a minister, he went to church services and other celebrations organized by the movement, but he was careful not to endorse either their political program or their roughhouse tactics. Although he read—intermittently—the newspaper *L'Action Française*, he was careful to keep his distance from the organization itself.

It was this distance from the activities of the *Ligues* which inspired the most surprising endorsement of Pétain as the prime candidate to take charge of France and bring it to its senses. It appeared in a special edition in November of the left-wing journal *Vu*, and was written by the former minister for air in Daladier's Radical government of 1933, Pierre Cot. As such, he had known Pétain well as Inspector General for Air Defense. Although he was a politician of the left (some claimed that he was a Soviet agent) and hence not to Pétain's political liking, Cot had impressed Pétain, and others, with his grasp of detail and his ability to assemble around him experts from any political affiliation or none.

In his article Cot claimed that the army would never seek to overturn the republic, but that if a crisis occurred, the president of the republic had the right to appoint to the highest office someone of proven record and loyalty to the republic who would take the reins firmly in hand for the duration of the crisis. "Does such a man exist?," Cot went on. "Such a man does exist. It is Marshal Pétain."[8] By the end of 1935, Radicals, Socialists and Communists had agreed on a platform on which to fight the general election of the spring of 1936 under Léon Blum. As the campaign got under way, hysteria took over. The Franco-Soviet pact, by then initialed but not yet signed, was waiting ratification by the Chamber of Deputies—the debates becoming even more acrimonious and violent. The British were pressing for the imposition of economic sanctions (except for oil) against Italy as punishment for the assault on Abyssinia. The French right-wing press lashed out all round. Blum himself was savagely beaten up on 13 February by an Action Française mob. To add to the political mayhem, Hitler seized his chance to spring another "Saturday Surprise." On 7 March, German troops marched into the Rhineland. As justification, the German government cited the Franco-Soviet pact—which made Locarno no more than a dead letter.

The first round of elections, on 26 April 1936, showed 5.5 million votes for the left against 4.5 million for the right on an 84 percent turn out. Pétain immediately decided to break cover. He gave an interview before the second round, due on 3 May, to the journalist Jean Martet of *Le Journal*. He made an unconvincing effort to pretend that he was not party political, but after a short and rather tedious introduction about military organization he launched into an attack on the Franco-Soviet pact, on communism in general, and on those who allowed communists intellectual respectability. He praised the Croix de Feu, not least because they "occupy themselves with the moral and spiritual improvement of youth." He claimed that both Germany and Italy were happier and had greater confidence than France. "We have lost faith in our destiny, that is all. We are like sailors without a steersman, without a rudder." When asked by Martet whether he could pass on his warning to the French people, Pétain replied—astonishingly—"No. That would be politics."[9]

Pétain knew perfectly well that his words would be reported and he knew what slant the public would put on them. But they had no effect. The result of the second count was equally crushing, and the Popular Front government was born. Pétain had entered his eightieth year; he had also entered an arena which he had hitherto shunned. In the Martet interview he had crossed the threshold into party politics. Far from being a soldier who would serve whatever government was legitimately elected, he had almost overnight openly associated himself with the political right. It was a move, however misjudged, of which his old friend Primo de Rivera would certainly have approved.

The Unpopular Front

"Si le baromètre annonce la pluie, est-ce le baromètre qui a tort?"

"We have a rotten government and I want to tell you that the French people won't fight."[1] Thus ran Pétain's early verdict on the Popular Front government. He was not alone. The arrival of the Blum administration was greeted with a cacophony of poisonous abuse not just from the right-wing press, but also from the aristocrats of industry and banking, many of whom were among Pétain's acquaintance.

Admittedly, Blum got off to a bad start. Forever legalistic, he waited for more than a month for the previous chamber to reach its constitutional term instead of seizing the initiative immediately after his election victory. However noble Blum's motives, the result was that the intervening month saw the worst demonstration of working-class discontent that France had ever witnessed. There was at the same time a prolonged capital flight. The mere idea that Communists would be supporting a French government, if only from the sidelines, was more than any of the bankers of the day could stomach. In the end, Blum was obliged to settle the strikes by approving pay rises of up to 15 percent, by recognizing the rights of trade unions, by instituting a system of compulsory collective bargaining and—the last straw for Pétain and his friends—introducing a 40-hour week and paid holidays. By September, in an attempt to satisfy the bankers and to stem the capital flight, Blum was forced to devalue the franc.

Pétain's objections to the new government led him into what was, for him, strange territory. For the first time, he felt it necessary to explain—if only to himself—what his political views really were. This required many hours of unusual introspection. After much thought, he chose to explain himself at the place with which he was most associated—Verdun. The occasion was to be the twentieth anniversary of the battle, to be celebrated on 21 June 1936. He could be sure that his words from there would be heard, but, to make quite certain, he made a request that his speech should be broadcast live on radio to the French nation.

Pétain prepared himself carefully, in dialogue with his godson (and, after the father's death in 1936, his doctor) Bernard Ménétrel. But the preparation for the event turned out to be far from easy. He felt it only right to submit a draft of his speech to Blum. His most dramatic pronouncement—in draft—that "having won the War [France] is on the point of losing the peace" was promptly struck out. Blum also vetoed the radio broadcast. Pétain's reaction was one of uncharacteristic fury. "Here is a government," he raged to one his aides, "which is stopping me from saying and broadcasting what needs to be said."[2]

As finally delivered, Pétain's speech no doubt lacked the determined force of his draft, but it was nonetheless powerful. He started conventionally enough, by stressing the importance of remaining strong. "Whatever policy is dictated by external circumstances, we have the duty to develop to the maximum our armed forces—land, sea and air. Force ensures independence, attracts alliances and maintains friendship." So far, of course, it was all fairly routine stuff. But he then went on to more dangerous ground—domestic politics. "The physical and mental health of the French people require important reforms. . . . The family is the essential cell which must be not only preserved but sustained and magnified. . . . If the laws had defended it with care, the social disequilibrium which rages at the moment would not have assumed worrying proportions. . . . There is a whole program to be revived: family, school and army . . . the three guiding steps which make the child into a man."[3]

It was certainly powerful, but not particularly original. Indeed, most of it had been said before in Spain by his friend Primo de Rivera. But, unlike Primo de Rivera, Petain was firmly opposed to a coup d'état. He was far too deeply grounded in the old military tradition of service to the legitimate government, however distasteful that government might be. If he was destined to serve his country in public life, he had to be called to do so.

There was one man who was fully prepared to do the calling. Pierre Laval had been Pétain's colleague in the Doumergue government. Pétain, almost in spite of himself, recognized Laval's ability, while Laval saw great use in Pétain's prestige as a marshal. After the Popular Front government's measure to outlaw the *Ligues* (although François de la Rocque, one of the leaders of the Croix de Feu, was astute enough to convert into a fully fledged political party), Laval became convinced that there had to be an alternative to the system which had thrown up an administration of such disgraceful revolutionary socialism. In an interview with two American journalists, Laval claimed that he "was convinced that the era of popular governments by parliaments was doomed."[4]

This conclusion struck a chord with Pétain, and in the middle of 1936 Laval renewed contact. There was also a personal connection. His daughter was married to Pétain's other godson, Count René de Chambrun. Moreover, de Chambrun's father was not only a friend of Pétain but also a colleague, having persuaded Pétain in 1935 to become president of the French Information Centre in the United States. Laval, whatever else was subsequently said, was quite open about his intentions, although in the end they came to nothing. But they allowed Laval to conclude that Pétain "had seemed disposed, if the occasion were to present itself to him, to accept the responsibility of power."[5]

Whatever the nature and extent of Laval's contacts with Pétain, there was never any question of planning a coup d'état. Nevertheless, what Pétain seems not to have realized at the time was that even within his own office there was similar political ferment. Loustaunau-Lacau had come to the (doubtful) conclusion that communists were infiltrating the army. Together with others, including Pétain's ever-faithful aide de camp Captain Léon Bonhomme, he organized a counter-effort. They set up a network of officers, both active and reserve, who would gather information about their colleagues and report any sinister left-wing sentiments. The network was known, somewhat obscurely, as Corvignolles. Corvignolles enjoyed almost immediate success. It was not long before there was at least one member in every army battalion, every air base and every armaments factory. And it was not very long before Pétain got to hear of it. When he did so, he insisted on seeing the reports. He did not help to finance the network—he was much too careful with his money for that—nor was he formally a member, but he did from time to time provide helpful information.

Much more sinister, however, was the Mouvement Social d'Action Révolutionnaire, commonly known as La Cagoule ("The Hood"). For a start, the committee which ran it, the CSAR, headed by a former naval engineer by the name of Eugène Deloncle, was quite prepared to use violence. Groups of carefully organized thugs were regularly sent to break up communist meetings. By the autumn of 1936 the movement had attracted the attention—and the cash—of Franchet d'Esperey, and by the end of the year Pétain himself was showing curiosity. He sent Loustaunau-Lacau to see General Duseigneur, who had recently retired but who was making a new career with Deloncle and La Cagoule. Duseigneur told Loustaunau-Lacau that indeed the group had arms, was well financed, and was in the process of organizing attacks on communists. There is no suggestion, nor has there ever been any serious suggestion (apart from the prosecutor at his trial), that Pétain was a member of either Corvignolles or La Cagoule. There were, of course, rumors, particularly when made a botched attempt at a coup d'état on 15 November 1937, that both Pétain and Franchet d'Esperey, the two surviving marshals, were up to their necks in both movements. But, at least in Pétain's case, these were no more than an attempt by his detractors to find guilt where there was none. On all the evidence, he was no more than an interested bystander (unlike Franchet d'Esperey).

Pétain's hostility to the Blum government was by then open. Apart from his general objections to the whole nature of the government, he also believed (unfairly) that Blum disliked him personally. His hostility was given further impetus by the government's reaction to the outbreak of civil war in Spain on 15 July 1936. Pétain's view was quite simple: his royal Spanish patron, Alfonso XIII, had been forced to abdicate in 1931 in favor of a parliamentary republic; the new republic had failed to deal with the problems with which it was confronted, and had allowed the elections of February 1936 to produce a Frente Popular which had won a parliamentary majority on a minority of votes cast; following the assassinations of José del Castillo and José Calvo Sotelo on 12 and 13 July, there had been a military uprising; the leading figure in this was the hard-faced young general whom Pétain had known in the Rif, Francisco Franco. It followed that France should either support Franco or keep out of the affair.

Personally, Blum was in favor of supporting the Frente Popular. But under pressure from the British government (which disapproved of the new Spanish government) and from his own ministers, he agreed that they should not be supported openly—with the proviso that they should be sent clandestine military aid. The decision, taken as it was in haste, managed to incur the odium of both sides. The right screamed that Blum was a traitor and the left shouted that he was a coward. The communists even refused to support the government when it came to a vote in the Chamber of Deputies in December. In the event, the policy itself fizzled out, after the export to Spain of 150 obsolete aircraft.

In the course of all this, Blum and his colleagues recognized that the frontier with Spain needed, if everything went wrong, to be defended. They were also sensitive to the continued bleat from Gamelin and his fellow generals—and Pétain—that France's field forces needed substantial reinforcing and reequipping. German rearmament and the remilitarization of the Rhineland had strengthened the generals' case. Daladier, the minister for war, finally accepted the argument, and managed to persuade his colleagues—and a surprisingly sympathetic Blum—to adopt a four-year plan at the total expense of 14 billion francs. It was indeed an ambitious project—perhaps too ambitious, as the future would show. By 1938 national defense claimed a third of the whole French budget and absorbed 50 percent of tax receipts, an almost unsupportable burden for a government committed to social reform. But to Pétain, at least, it was a welcome recognition that the defense of France had been put in peril by successive governments and needed to be addressed.

It was only a month after the rearmament program was announced that the whole French strategy for a future war with Germany was thrown into disarray. On 14 October King Leopold III of the Belgians declared that Belgium in the future would follow an independent foreign policy. Everybody knew what this meant in practice—Belgium would remain neutral in any future war. For the French strategists, it was a bad blow. In all their plans, they had relied on active and complete Belgian cooperation for a quick French move into the Low Countries in the event of war.

French reactions to the Belgian declaration were, to say the least, confused. Gamelin tried to make a secret deal with his Belgian opposite number (and enthusiastic francophile) General Édouard Van den Bergen. The two quickly agreed that the Belgian Army, in the event of war, would immediately appeal to the French for help. As far as it went, that was all very well. But the problem with the deal was that Belgian generals, unlike their French counterparts, had no political clout. For Daladier, the solution was to extend the Maginot Line along the Franco-Belgian border as far as the English Channel. France would then be protected along her whole frontier from Switzerland to the Atlantic. But as soon as serious study got under way, the familiar problems emerged, and Pétain again stressed them.

By then, Pétain's own thinking had moved on. Already, in a speech to the École de Guerre in April 1935, he had proclaimed that "the military art is the swiftest moving of all the arts. It would be ridiculous to be stuck in a study of the past without looking at the future. . . . While remaining attentive to progress in chemistry and electricity or any other science, it is necessary to take full account of the perspectives opened by the tank and the aeroplane."[6] This was followed by a preface written to General Sikorski's book *The Modern War*. "The possibilities of tanks," Pétain wrote, "are so vast that we can say that the tank will perhaps become tomorrow the principal arm [of warfare]."[7] He considered that the tank was best used in counterattack, but he went further in a speech at St. Quentin on 4 October 1936. "The concept of the defensive army has had its day . . . modern means of offense are the only ones capable of ensuring proper collaboration for an associate in danger." (By which, of course, he meant Belgium.)[8] Moreover, he was very much in favor of a strong attacking bomber force to carry the attack to the enemy in the opening phases of a war. He was very much in support of Pierre Cot's Plan II, launched in September 1936, which gave priority to the production of bombers over fighters by nearly two to one. Indeed, he was even prepared to argue, along with Cot, for an arrangement with the Soviet Union for the joint of manufacture airplanes.

In January 1937 an article appeared in the magazine *Revue militaire générale* under the name of General Debeney. It soon appeared that, even if the signature was Debeney's, the thoughts were those of Pétain. Entitled "The Mystique of our Officer Corps," the article set out to demonstrate the role of the Army in healing the social and political divisions of the nation. As a theme, of course, it was not particularly new. But it was given particular relevance by the disputes of the day, which threatened, in Debeney's view, to "become mortal."[9] In such a situation the army was to be seen as an active force, even "the true France," protecting the nation against the excesses of a political regime—by which was meant, of course, the Popular Front government.

Amid strikes and talk that the government was about to fall, Pétain took several days off at L'Ermitage in February. No sooner had Pétain escaped to the south of France than there was mayhem in Paris. In another attempt to pacify the bankers, Blum gave up his plans to introduce old age pensions for workers and to create a National Unemployment Fund. The communists, predictably, denounced the move as craven capitulation. On 16 March, when the government refused to ban a meeting of de la Rocque's new political party, the Parti Social Français, protesters tried to storm the cinema in Clichy where it was being held. In the ensuing clash with police, seven people were killed and several hundred injured. The largest trade union, the Confédération Générale du Travail, called a general strike. By then, it seemed clear that the Blum government was mortally wounded. Although it limped on for another three months, it was effectively powerless, and on 22 June 1937 Blum threw in his hand. The Popular Front experiment had, without any regret from Pétain, died its death.

It was not until mid-April that he returned to Paris. Even then, it was only because he had caught a cold at l'Ermitage and felt in need of treatment from Bernard Ménétrel that he came back. On his return, he duly underwent Ménétrel's treatment. Whether he knew with precision what he was letting himself in for is not at all clear. Ménétrel had inherited from his father some strange medical practices. One of his specialties was to treat gout and arthritis by attaching a copper cylinder to the patient's skin and heating the air inside to as much as 200 degrees Celsius. Another was to inject oxygen into the patient and a third, apparently favored in Pétain's case, was bleeding. On this particular occasion, Pétain's cold was treated by Ménétrel, as he reported to Nini, with "blue rays." What these were is something of a mystery, but certainly he thought they did him some good, since on the following day he was coughing "noticeably less."[10]

The new government of June 1937, under the Radical—but intellectually bereft—Camille Chautemps, seemed to have little for Pétain to do. He therefore left Paris again in May for an extended tour of the Maginot Line. But soon there were new developments in Germany. On 9 March 1937 the Reichstag passed a law "concerning the security of the frontiers and concerning reprisals."[11] This was the formal authority for the building of the *Westwall*. The "reprisals" referred to possible French retaliatory action after the remilitarization of the Rhineland—and, looking ahead, after future German territorial expansion to the east. The *Westwall* was designed to mirror the Maginot Line—but, it was said, with superior German construction—along the whole length of the Franco-German frontier.

It is not clear whether Pétain either heard, or, if he heard, took any serious note of, the news. Certainly neither he nor any of his French colleagues are on record as drawing any conclusions from the news, let alone the right ones. So concentrated were they on a French response to a future German attack that they failed to understand that the Germans were equally worried about their own response to a possible future French attack. The German High Command had assumed that France would intervene in the Rhineland. That not having happened, they assumed that at some point a superior French army would march into Germany on any suitable pretext. By the middle of 1937, it should have been clear to Pétain and the French General Staff that both they and their German counterparts were engaged in a very similar defensive strategy. Maginot and Siegfried (as the *Westwall* came to be known) were, in truth, two of a kind.

In fact, German intelligence had been quick to understand the consequences of the Belgian declaration of October 1936. Their conclusion was that a French drive into a neutral Belgium could only be the prelude to an attack across the plain of east Belgium and southern Holland to strike directly at the Ruhr. The German High Command therefore started to badger Hitler to extend the *Westwall* northward along the frontiers with Holland, Belgium and Luxembourg. Hitler gave the order 9 March 1938.

Three days after that order was given, German troops moved to seal the annexation of Austria into the Reich. The reaction in France was, to say the least, surprisingly muted. But by then the Chautemps administration was on its knees. The Socialists had abandoned it in January in protest against the erratic—and pro-German—behavior of Georges Bonnet, who had been brought back from the Washington embassy by Chautemps to be his foreign minister. In March 1938, the Socialists struck again, voting against the Chautemps government and bringing it down. In the confusion of the moment, a further Blum administration was formed—and lasted no more than a month.

The way was then open for a further attempt at something approaching a government of national unity which could face up to what was now perceived to be the threat from Germany. President Lebrun gave the task to an old parliamentary veteran, calling on Daladier to see what he could do. As it turned out, it was a good choice. Daladier had already served in no fewer than 15 governments and had been premier 3 times. He was also extremely popular, with a view of democracy which was widely shared (not least by Pétain), patriotic and, once a mandate had been given, authoritarian. Daladier shifted the political center of gravity sharply to the right. He brought in Paul Reynaud as his finance minister to torpedo the 40-hour week and Bonnet to pursue his policy of avoiding war until France was ready. The rearmament program, which had badly lost momentum, was given new vigor, with the result that in the 18 months after Daladier's arrival in office, average monthly airplane production rose from just over 40 to just under 300, and average monthly tank production from just over 30 to just under 100.

But although the Daladier government was supported by a large majority in the Chamber and in the Senate, the fissiparous nature of the French politics of the time ensured that there was no guarantee that it would last. As Pétain in March wrote to his recently acquired friend—and prolific correspondent—Marie-Antoine

Pardee, "a new political crisis is beginning, and it worries me because it might become serious."[12] As it happened, Pétain himself was one of the candidates offered to Lebrun as an alternative to Daladier, not least by Laval. But Pétain refused to play the game, and even went so far to tell Lémery, who was peddling the same line in his newspaper *L'Indépendant*, to stop writing such "stupidities." Whatever Daladier turned out to be, Pétain, at least for the time being, was going to support him.

As in 1937, in the summer of 1938 Pétain preferred to be out of Paris. But he was far from idle. On 19 July, King George VI and Queen Elizabeth embarked on a four-day state visit to France. They arrived at Boulogne. There was an obvious point to the state visit: Daladier and Bonnet needed allies in the west of Europe. After Mussolini had declared the "Axis" of Rome–Berlin and Franco had virtually won the Spanish Civil War, the only place to look was toward their old— and unreliable—ally, Great Britain.

It was in Boulogne that Pétain, as befitted an old marshal of France, gave the most fulsome speech in praise of the "*Entente*." But Pétain was only delivering what was appropriate for the moment. His views about Britain, ever since his dispute with Haig in 1918 and his conviction that the British had stopped him from occupying the Rhineland and destroying the German Army, had, in private, been quite clear. Pétain's view had been expressed most explicitly in an informal conversation with the Italian ambassador to Paris two years earlier. "England," he stated, "has always been France's most implacable enemy." She only waged war at France's side because this served her own interests and then she backed Germany. (This was a clear reference to his belief that Britain had rushed the Armistice to prevent France annexing the Rhineland.) "For all these reasons," he went on, "I believe that France has two hereditary enemies, the English and the Germans, but the former are older and more perfidious; that is why I would favor an alliance with the Germans which would guarantee absolute peace in Europe."[13]

Daladier's minister of finance, Reynaud, had come to a different view. He still believed that Nazi Germany was the main threat to the peace of Europe and had to be resisted by all means available. De Gaulle, Reynaud's political protégé, was of the same view. But de Gaulle was about to embark on the final stage of the simmering dispute which had stood between him and his erstwhile patron Pétain. On 2 August 1938, de Gaulle wrote to Pétain about the book he was due to publish. Pétain was in no mood to be generous—and curtly refused.

After a further exchange of letters, de Gaulle and Pétain finally met. De Gaulle set out to persuade Pétain to lend his name to the book, and in the end Pétain agreed to do so. On 5 September, therefore, Pétain produced a carefully written dedication. De Gaulle took this as a draft, rewrote it in a manner which subtly suggested that the publication was at Pétain's initiative—and sent it direct to his publishers. Pétain, as he often reminded others on future occasions, regarded this as a breach of trust; he wrote to de Gaulle's publishers to tell them so. De Gaulle brushed aside Pétain's objections as an irritating nuisance, and demanded that his publishers proceed as planned. By then it was clear that the breach between the two had become what can only described as a chasm. But this conflict was as nothing compared with the crisis which was about to occupy the politicians of all Europe.

Hitler, in Nuremberg on 12 September, delivered a violent and vituperative attack on the Czech government. "I have no intention," Hitler screamed, "of allowing a second Palestine to be formed here in the heart of Germany by the labors of other statesmen. . . . The Germans in Czechoslovakia are neither defenseless nor abandoned."[14] Apparently undeterred by Hitler's histrionics, on 14 September Pétain wrote to Nini that "I do not think that we can be caught up in the Czech row; our leaders would really have had to lose their compass bearing" (in other words, their mind).[15] In the early hours of 30 September, Daladier, Chamberlain, Mussolini and Hitler met at Munich and signed an agreement which would deprive Czechoslovakia of a large slice of its population, its most important industrial sites—and its means of frontier defense against a German attack.

The Munich agreement was immensely popular in France, as it was in Britain. Daladier, who had expected to be booed in the streets, suddenly found himself a popular hero. From every town he received telegrams of congratulation. Tens of thousands signed books recording their enthusiasm, and there were subscription lists which collected substantial sums in appreciation of the government's action. In the Chamber of Deputies, the agreement was approved by 535 votes to 75 (73 of which were Communist). Pétain echoed the public mood when, a few days later, he spoke to Bonnet. "You have rendered a great service to France," he said. "I know how you have struggled to avoid war; you were right; we would have been beaten."[16]

Nor was that the end of it. The anti-Semitic tide in France was flowing again, swept on by Action Française and the even more outspoken *L'Ère Nouvelle* newspaper. But it was not so much the wave of anti-Semitism that worried Pétain as what he perceived to be the general disintegration of French society. In November, he spoke at Metz for the twentieth anniversary of its liberation in 1918. He again returned to great themes he had annunciated at Verdun two years earlier. France was gripped by material pleasures and desires; the benefits of the peace had been lost; spiritual life had been abandoned in the education and behavior of the nation. As a result, France would no longer be able to defend herself. From then on those themes were constantly repeated. If anybody objected, he would say what he had said when Blum tried to water down his Verdun speech: "If the barometer announces rain, is it the barometer which is wrong?"[17]

1. The young officer

2. With Joffre at Verdun (*Keystone*)

3. With Primo de Rivera, Tetuan, 1925

4. Decorated by King Alfonso XIII (*Keystone*)

5. Pétain (center) and de Gaulle (behind Pétain) in 1926 (*Giraudon/Bridgeman Art Library*)

6. The handshake at Montoire (with Ribbentrop in the background) (*Hulton Archive*)

7. Pétain and Darlan in Marseille, January 1941 (*Bettman/Corbis*)

8. Pétain and Darlan with Franco at Montpellier, February 1941 (*Keystone*)

9. With Göring in December 1941 (*Keystone*)

10. Leahy taking leave of Pétain, April 1942 (*Keystone*)

11. Paris, April 1944 (*Keystone*)

12. The trial: Isorni pleads (*AFP*)

Ambassador to Spain

"I do not believe that Pétain had, at that time, any sympathy for Germany beyond the reluctant admiration which all of us have felt, at one time or another, for her method and powers of organisation."

"Yesterday evening I saw Monsieur Daladier and I agreed to go to Burgos for three or four months in order to redress French affairs in Spain or, at least, to help to do so. It was agreed that I should take two of my officers as well as civilian personnel. No women. Departure in 15 days."[1] Thus Pétain's crisp announcement to his wife Nini on 1 March 1939. Almost as an afterthought, he added that in the evening he was to dine with Senator Léon Bérard.

Bérard had been a central figure in the complicated political dance which led to Pétain's appointment as French ambassador to Spain. Sensing that the Spanish Civil War was gradually, if painfully, coming to an end, he went on his own initiative to Burgos, then the capital of the new nationalist government, to see an old friend and francophile, Lieutenant General Francisco Gomez Jordana. The Bérard-Jordana agreements, as they came to be known, marked an important first step in the French effort to claw back the political ground lost by the Blum government's unofficial support of what turned out to be the losing side in the civil war.

The agreements had seven main points. The most important, in Spanish eyes, were those requiring the release of gold deposited by the Republican government, contracted to the Banque de France as security for a loan; and the repatriation of all military matériel, in particular the naval vessels and the fishing fleet which were held in French ports, and all lorries and other vehicles which had found their way to France during the conflict. The French, for their part, wanted to be rid of the 500,000 or so refugees who had fled Spain and who were housed, if that is the right word, in refugee camps at the French taxpayers' expense. They also wanted landing rights for Air France.

Until he took the ambassadorial job, Pétain knew nothing of the Bérard-Jordana agreements, which were only announced on the day he saw Daladier. He was not privy, after all, to political secrets; nor had he shown any particular interest in Spain since the outbreak of the civil war. He had met Jordana, with Franco, in Morocco in 1925, and he knew that Jordana was now Foreign Minister in Franco's government, but that was about the sum of it. Moreover, Daladier's offer had been unexpected. Indeed, Pétain was not even the first choice for the job.

But from Daladier's point of view the move was sensible. Pétain had fought alongside Franco in the Rif, and his name was well known and honored in Spain. If anybody could build bridges the old marshal was the best candidate. Besides, with another war with Germany in prospect, the French frontier along the Pyrenees had to be secured. In simple terms, this meant that in the event of a conflict Spain should be persuaded to remain neutral. Furthermore, by sending Pétain to Spain, Daladier could push aside a figure who still had influence but was, in his view, given to moaning too much about France's lack of preparedness for battle.

For Pétain there were no such advantages. He was old, he claimed to be going deaf, he tired easily and openly admitted that he could not maintain a consistent work rate. But the truth is that he was also getting bored. Even at the age of 83 he was, in his sharper moments, perfectly capable of serious thought and, if necessary, action. Furthermore, by accepting a relatively lowly position he would be officially in touch with political affairs rather than watching from the sidelines. Finally, to judge from the tone of his letters, he was quite happy to have a bit of time off from Nini.

On 16 March, Pétain arrived in Spain. Pétain's staff was quite small given the importance of the embassy. His own officers were Vauthier and Bonhomme, and his financial adviser was a young official from the Ministry of Finance, Henri du Moulin de Labarthète. The professional diplomatic staff was led by Armand Gazel, holding the rank of counselor. Settling in was to prove difficult. Pétain had forgotten his Spanish medals and his marshal's baton and wrote urgently to Nini in Paris to have them sent on. That apart, the house he was allocated, the Villa Zinza, in what before the civil war had been an elegant suburb of San Sebastián, was in disrepair.

There was, however, one good reason to be away from Paris: the election for the presidency. Lémery was canvassing Pétain's name in the Senate; others were doing the same in the Chamber of Deputies. The object of this attention was adamant. He wrote to Lémery telling him not to pursue the matter, and to a deputy who was proposing to come to San Sebastián to sell him the idea, that he should not bother. By 2 April, he was able to write to Nini that he had read in the newspapers "some efforts at combinations in which I have refused to participate . . . besides, it is quite amusing to look from afar at the game of parties and individuals."[2] In the event, Lebrun was reelected unanimously.

Such was the Spanish displeasure, not at him personally but at France in general, that Pétain was not received in Burgos until 24 March. He was conveyed there by a special train. The ceremony was splendid in its choreography, but was spoiled by Franco's evident coldness. "Franco didn't say a word, or hardly," reported Gazel later.[3] When—after the ceremony—he did, he pointed out to Pétain the failings of France in not supporting him in the civil war. But he was at least grudgingly complimentary to Pétain himself, who, he said, "having accumulated treasures of military virtue, is in the best position to understand the lofty sentiments of the new Spain, and cannot be indifferent to the proof of heroism and sacrifice which our people has given in this grandiose epic for the defense of its ideals and of Western civilisation."[4]

Pétain made a friend of the new British ambassador, Maurice Peterson. The Marshal, Peterson recorded, "made a great impression on me. Of medium height, holding himself erect whether seated or on foot, the healthy color in his face and the firm regard of blue eyes, made him appear, even in mufti, the very type of the great French soldier." Peterson noted, however, that "vigorous and alert as I invariably found him in the morning, it was a different story if I had occasion to see him later in the day. For by then his age was almost painfully apparent and he looked more—though never wholly—like the figure which caricaturists have since made of him."[5] Peterson obviously liked Pétain; and Pétain obviously liked Peterson. Moreover, Peterson never found Pétain "defeatist."

Pétain set out on a series of trips around Spain. It was while he was on this journey that his preliminary report was delivered to Bonnet. It described the legacy of the civil war, speculated about the country's future and expressed doubts whether it would ever be possible to determine what Franco really thought. The Falange, a semi-fascist movement founded by Primo de Rivera's son in 1934, preached a message of nationalism and regeneration in close alliance with the Catholic Church. Franco was believed to be sympathetic, but was unwilling to commit himself too deeply. He was also showing some sympathy toward the monarchists. As for foreign policy, Pétain noted that Franco was very appreciative of those who had come to his aid in the civil war—and correspondingly hostile to those who had turned away from him. Nevertheless, the report's conclusion was clear. Franco, in spite of powerful pressure from Germany and Italy, would wish to keep Spain out of any future conflict.

The conclusion was thrown into doubt by the news that Franco had authorized the building of fortifications along the frontier of the Pyrenees. It was a bad blow to Pétain's efforts which, at least in the matter of the gold to be released back to Spain under the Bérard-Jordana agreements, were beginning to show results. Pétain had hoped that this would open the door—hitherto no more than ajar—to a fruitful relationship between the two neighboring countries which the Bérard-Jordana agreements had proclaimed as the ultimate objective. But the fortifications on the line of the Pyrenees were ominous.

On hearing the news, Pétain wrote directly to Franco. Writing as "soldier to soldier," he assured him that France had no intentions that could remotely be called aggressive. "Have confidence in a proven friend of Spain," he went on, "who would not have agreed to come to your country were it not to tell the truth."[6] Pétain's plea seems to have convinced Franco, since little more was heard of the Spanish fortifications. Moreover, in a spirit of unaccustomed generosity, Franco invited Pétain to another interview. "The operations relative to the deposit of gold in Mont de Marsan happily concluded," announced the Falangist newspaper *Arriba*, "in which Marshal Pétain, the French ambassador, has so nobly and energetically intervened, His Excellency the Head of State received him this morning."[7]

While Pétain was whiling away the time in Spain, there was much activity in the Square de Latour-Maubourg. The apartment in No. 8 which was to be Nini's had been secured. It was then a matter of making the necessary arrangements to their joint satisfaction. The delicate matter of communication between the two apartments resolved, Pétain decided in May 1939 that the necessary construction and decoration work should go ahead.

He also wrote that he wished to set a date for the end of his ambassadorship to Spain. He wanted to get back to L'Ermitage to supervise the vintage in September. He also felt that he had done as much as he could. The Spanish gold had been released. Negotiations for a commercial treaty between the two countries were underway. It would not be long before the government moved to Madrid, and the thought of the move—and setting up a whole new office—was daunting. In short, he felt that the time had come for him to end his mission and come home.

Nevertheless, he was still in San Sebastián when war broke out on September 3. The event itself, of course, was momentous, but in France there was none of the enthusiasm which had greeted the outbreak of war in 1914. It was more a resigned belief that a job, however unpleasant, had to be done. But Pétain was even less enthusiastic than his compatriots. He did "not approve the act of beginning the war and he had serious concerns about how it would be waged, given the still defective organization of relations between the High Command and the government."[8] In truth, he had a point. The previously strong relationship between Daladier and Gamelin had become very tense—and there were even doubts about Daladier himself. Interestingly enough, Pétain seems to have recognized that the rearmament program was starting to bear fruit. In a few months France might have at least most of the equipment for war, if not the leadership. But the extra few months were badly needed.

The onset of war had an immediate effect on the kaleidoscope of French domestic politics. Straightaway, Daladier made an effort to recreate the *union sacrée* of 1914. He decided to invite representation from all parties (except the communists) into a new administration. It almost went without saying that one of the first to be invited was the old and dignified hero of Verdun, Marshal Pétain. Pétain was duly summoned to Paris on 8 September and offered the post of minister of war.

Pétain turned the job down. The reasons he gave in his letter to Daladier were that the government of national unity which Daladier proposed was merely a political roundup. What was needed was something much broader. "This decision firmly arrived at," he went on, "allows me to be freer to tell you my thought about the cabinet you have in mind. The presence of certain politicians will be an obstacle to proper relations with Spain and Italy, and will have a deplorable effect on the morale of the country and the army."[9] He was, of course, referring primarily to Herriot, whom he considered had sabotaged the Doumergue government of 1934. But he was also having doubts about Daladier himself, let alone Gamelin. Moreover, as the Italian ambassador to Paris pointed out in his dispatch at the time, Pétain confessed himself a very reluctant warrior.

Having delivered his broadside to Daladier, Pétain took the train back to Spain. This was not, however, a signal that he was about to abandon his customary close observation of the Parisian political scene. Quite the contrary. Loustanau-Lacau was buzzing to and fro between Paris and San Sebastián, as was Bernard Ménétrel. Pétain retained a "liaison officer" in Paris, Colonel Henri Pellissier de Féligonde, whose task was to observe and report. Then, on 8 October, Lémery arrived in San Sebastián and spent two days with Pétain trying to convince him that a new government was an absolute necessity, and that only he, Pétain, could form an administration which would be able to continue the war. Moreover, he claimed that there was a substantial bloc, in the Chamber as well as the Senate, in favor of such a scheme. But Pétain was not persuaded. He would be quite happy, he replied, to take the war portfolio in an administration which was not party political, but he would not head it. A premier, he pointed out, had to be able to answer questions on a multitude of topics, from agriculture to the merchant marine. He would only look foolish trying to do so.

Lémery, however, did not give up. Pétain's reply had been firm enough in what he said, but he was not wholly convincing in the way he said it. Besides, he had entertained himself by composing a list of possible members of a future cabinet, which he had shown to Gazel (it was absurdly injudicious to show it to a civil servant if it was meant to be taken seriously—and most unlike the cautious and usually secretive Pétain). Daladier's finance minister, Paul Reynaud, later wrote that in his view Pétain was conspiring against the government during his ambassadorship in Spain. All that can be said is that if Pétain was conspiring he was a conspicuously bad conspirator. Much more probable is that he was doing what he had always done—waiting on uncertain outcomes while observing most closely the confused march of events. Indeed, it is no more than reasonable to take the view, along with André François-Poncet in his 1953 speech to the Académie Française after Pétain's death, that in the period of his ambassadorship he "psychologically became accustomed to the idea that in a great crisis he would some day save the nation."[10]

Be that as it may, Daladier was certainly full of suspicion about Pétain's intentions. When Pétain in mid-October asked whether he could be relieved of his post in order to take up his position in the Comité de Guerre, Daladier told him to stay put. This had for Pétain a number of unpleasant practical consequences. It was not just a matter of missing the vintage at L'Ermitage—for the first time since he had bought the property. Even worse than that, the Franco government had set up shop in Madrid. All embassies had to transfer there forthwith.

Once established in Madrid, Pétain had to undertake the task of visiting ministers, city authorities and ambassadorial colleagues, a task which he much disliked, particularly when there was another mountain of mail which needed answering. Pétain's letters become increasingly critical of his hosts as the winter wore on. The New Year came and went. There was a splendid dinner at the Palacio Real, but the high point of the season was the transfer of the remains of José Antonio Primo de Rivera, the founder of the Falange, to the Escorial. The eldest son of Pétain's old friend, he had been executed by the Republican authorities in November 1936 and had become something of a martyr for Franco and his followers. Pétain, of course, felt obliged to be there. But there were those who noted that as he entered the basilica of the Escorial the whole diplomatic corps, led by the German ambassador, rose to its feet. Furthermore, when he left, the German Youth of Spain saluted him by lowering their swastika flags in homage.

In fact, Pétain had become rather friendly with the German ambassador, Dr. Eberhard von Stohrer. He had advised von Stohrer on his French holiday plans before war broke out, and even when the two countries were at war the two ambassadors remained on reasonably cordial terms. At the ceremony at which Franco's ministers took their oath of allegiance, on 19 October 1939, Pétain seemed to go out of his way to shake hands with von Stohrer, a gesture which brought much critical comment in the French press, but which he regarded as no more than a simple act of courtesy to an ambassadorial colleague. (This courtesy, however, did not prevent von Stohrer from making some unfriendly comments about Pétain in his dispatches to Berlin.) Moreover, Peterson overheard Pétain's remark to an ambassadorial colleague: "I always shake hands with those whom I intend to strike."[11]

As the winter of 1939–1940 moved slowly toward spring, it became clear in Paris that the Daladier government was in trouble. At the beginning of February Daladier, without consulting his British allies, suddenly announced that he would send 100 planes and 50,000 troops by the end of the month to help the Finns in their resistance to a Soviet invasion. Nobody knew where these forces were to be found. It was widely said that Daladier was drinking too much. That this was so became clear in a debate on 13 March in the Chamber. During his speech he made remarks which were so crude and offensive that they were struck from the official record. In the Senate, in a parallel debate, Laval made a most effective speech opposing the war and demanding an immediate peace. On 20 March, Daladier called for a motion of confidence. By then, as it happened, the Finns had signed an armistice with the Soviets, and there was no longer an obvious and urgent danger. But still, in the event, no fewer than 300 out of 540 deputies abstained on the substantive motion. For Daladier, there was no alternative to resignation.

Daladier's obvious successor was his finance minister, Paul Reynaud. Reynaud, in fact, had been doing his best in the previous weeks to undermine his own government's position. He had been hostile to the Munich agreement and he loathed Daladier personally. The sentiment was reciprocated. Indeed, during the month of February the two men were unable even to speak to one another, communicating only by way of notes. Yet such was the parliamentary arithmetic that Reynaud was obliged to have Daladier in the cabinet which Lebrun asked him to form—as minister of defense. He was also obliged to accommodate others, such as Chautemps and the banker Paul Baudouin, who were known opponents of the war. Even so, when it came to parliamentary endorsement of his administration, Reynaud's overall majority was down to one.

In the first weeks of his administration Reynaud was all fireworks. He thought himself the Clemenceau of his day, with a mission to hector the generals and the country into a much more energetic pursuit of the war. There was much shouting—but to little effect. However intelligent he was, and however enthusiastic about the war, Reynaud had not the precious gift of being able to inspire men. But whatever the failings of Reynaud's own character there is no doubt that he was continually being wounded by Daladier's unceasing and sulky sniping at his flank.

Although the dispute between the two was primarily personal, there was an element of disagreement over war policy. French strategic planning in the 1930s was based on the experience of the First World War. An initial German attack was to be soaked up by vigorous defense (as at the Marne in 1914). This would be followed by stalemate. After a period the superior industrial might of France and Britain would wear down the enemy and lead to eventual victory. This was known as the strategy of the "long war." But there were those in Paris, particularly around Reynaud (but not around Daladier) who were worried that time, rather than working for the French, would in fact work against them. Such was the pace of German arms manufacture, they argued, that the longer the war lasted the worse it would be for France. The Germans, of course, were planning a very short war indeed.

By the end of March Reynaud was becoming convinced that Daladier was a serious liability. So too, he thought, was Gamelin. The fiasco of Norway—the south of the country was overrun by the Germans in April in a matter of days—allowed Reynaud to start dislodging Gamelin. When Daladier leapt to his defense Reynaud decided that he would have, one way or another, to be rid of him, too. Nevertheless, he knew that the only possible way he could secure a parliamentary majority for a new administration, in which Daladier would no longer be involved in the conduct of the war, would be if he could assemble a cabinet which the Chamber and the Senate could not possibly reject; and the key to this was the "Victor of Verdun," Marshal Philippe Pétain.

On 29 April Reynaud summoned Pétain back from Madrid. Reynaud immediately offered him the post of minister of state in his cabinet. Pétain asked for a little time, but after consulting a few of his friends he telephoned his acceptance to Reynaud—provided he could return to Spain to settle his affairs— which he did on 9 May. On 10 May, at first light, the Germans launched their attack into Holland and Belgium. On 13 May they followed up with an assault through the Luxembourg Ardennes. The real war had started.

The pace of events quickened. On 16 May Pétain was summoned back from Madrid with immediate effect. He arrived in Paris at eight o'clock on the morning of 18 May at the Gare d'Austerlitz, to be told by Colonel Pellissier de Féligonde that the German army had broken through the Meuse front and was heading for the sea. He went straight from the station to see Reynaud, who told him that he was personally taking over the direction of the war and offered him the post of vice-president of his cabinet—in other words, deputy premier. Pétain hesitated, but Reynaud wanted an immediate answer, as he was to announce the new members of the government that evening. He then went on to tell Pétain that Gamelin was to go, and to be replaced by Weygand. When Pétain said that he did not much care for Weygand, Reynaud brushed his objection aside. He said that Pétain would soon come round to the idea that "Reynaud and Weygand" would sound well with the army. Pétain was left perplexed at such frivolity.

Later, after the war, Reynaud claimed that previously he knew very little about Pétain. He was not telling the truth. He knew perfectly well, since it had never been a secret, that Pétain had been opposed to the war in the first place; that he believed the politicians, above all those of the Popular Front, to be responsible for the mess that France was in; that he thought that France had not been ready for war and that the present group of politicians were not up to fighting it. If there is any doubt about what Reynaud knew or did not know, on 26 May, when he went to see the new British prime minister, Winston Churchill, he told Churchill that if France were "entirely invaded" they "must reckon on the possibility of a move by Marshal Pétain in favor of an armistice."[12] The truth is that Reynaud made Pétain vice-premier simply to trump Daladier. He only had himself to blame if the consequences of his petty maneuver turned out not to his taste.

Defeat

"Je fais à la France le don de ma personne pour atténuer son malheur."

When Pétain arrived in Paris on 18 May 1940 in response to Reynaud's summons, there is little doubt he had persuaded himself that, if suitably called, he could lead France in her current travail. If he had any doubts, his supporters had been, and still were, enthusiastic on his behalf. His reception by the Parisian press, and the standing ovation given to him by the Senate three days later, confirmed the general impression that he was destined to be the latest member of that illustrious band who had saved France by their mere presence on the scene—Joan of Arc, Napoleon, various saints and so on. When on 16 June he was invited by President Lebrun to form a government, with well-prepared confidence he produced, like a magician producing a rabbit out of a hat, a list of ministers, proclaiming firmly "Here is my government."[1]

The previous four and a half weeks had been hectic. Pétain's moods had swung with the flow of the events. Moreover, at the age of 84, his attention span was far from reliable. The faithful Bonhomme, for instance, thought that he "was very, very old. His thought no longer puts action into gear."[2] Even Spears, his old friend, appearing yet again on the scene on 25 May as Churchill's special emissary, found at their first meeting that very day that "the long fair moustache, although whiter, was the same, but he seemed dead, in the sense that a figure that gives no impression of being alive can be said to be dead."[3] Spears, not for the first or the last time, read his man correctly. Pétain was not saying much to Spears about what he really thought. In fact, he was not saying much to anyone—other than to his doctor, Bernard Ménétrel. This was no accident. By then Ménétrel had become much more than his doctor. He had become what would, in modern jargon, be called Pétain's "minder." His job was now to make the old man's life—in all its respects—easier. There was even more to it than that. Ménétrel can best be described, in the hackneyed phrase, as the son that Pétain never had. Some went even further, asserting firmly that Pétain's relations with Ménétrel's mother had been such that Bernard was without a shadow of doubt the Marshal's natural son. Certainly, the dates and the history lend support to the assertion. Bernard was born in 1906, when Pétain was no more than 50 years old. His relationship with Ménétrel's mother was well known. Furthermore, ever since his childhood Bernard had been the object of the Marshal's particular affection, in marked contrast to his unfortunate stepson, Pierre.

In 1937, Ménétrel moved from the Left to the Right Bank to a larger apartment at 5 Avenue Montaigne—then, as now, one of the richest streets in the whole of Paris. It was this suite that Pétain occupied during late May and early June 1940. He had persuaded Ménétrel, who had joined up on mobilization and had been posted to a cardiological center at Chauvry-en-Oise, to transfer to his own staff as his personal doctor. That done, Ménétrel was able to devote all his attention to Pétain's health and well-being. Moreover, he became Pétain's favored companion. Of all the people he could talk to without restraint, Ménétrel was without a doubt at the top of the (admittedly very short) list.

If Ménétrel helped with Pétain's domestic arrangements, it was Raphaël Alibert—much disliked by Ménétrel—who took charge of Pétain's office. It was set up in Pétain's old premises at 8 Boulevard des Invalides. Staff were recruited, both military and civil, to assist him in fending off persistent visitors—and seemingly hourly messages from Laval, possibly encouraged by Alibert, claiming that the war was lost and that Pétain should get up and say as much. The main activity seemed to be little more than continual dialogue with his colleagues about the conduct of the war and daily meetings with Reynaud—held, as often as possible, with Weygand in attendance.

The German panzers had broken through at Sedan on 15 May and by the time he arrived in Paris they had made their way as far as the English Channel. Their "corridor," as it was called, stretched from Sedan in the east to Abbeville, at the mouth of the river Somme, in the west. The French 1st and 8th Armies, and almost the whole of the British Expeditionary Force under General Lord (known as "Boy") Gort, seemed to be in an inescapable trap.

But Weygand, as Pétain soon found out, had a plan: to attack the German corridor in a pincer movement from both north and south. Churchill, on a visit to Paris on 22 May, approved. Yet Weygand's plan was based on little more than optimism. It had been inherited from Gamelin, and relied on what can only be described as phantom armies. The British were not, any more than a newly constituted French army on the Somme, in a fit state to execute any plan, let alone

Weygand's. Furthermore, communications, and trust, between the two armies had long since vanished. As a result, the whole plan collapsed in general acrimony on 24 May. Reynaud, promptly and much to Pétain's annoyance, sacked 16 French generals and then fired off two telegrams to Churchill complaining that the British were retreating much too far and much too fast. Weygand, too, felt betrayed by the British. Gort said stoutly that the French were plainly not up to fighting a war. The ghosts of 1918 seemed to be stalking the stage.

Reynaud's War Committee met in the evening of 25 May to decide what to do next. Lebrun started by asking what their reaction should be if the Germans offered some sort of settlement which would lead to a way out of the war. Weygand and Reynaud, unusually, were in tandem. Both said that any offer should be discussed with Britain. Reynaud then agreed to go to London the following day. Weygand told him firmly to ask for more assistance. Pétain reinforced Weygand's demand by pointing out that the British had only put 10 divisions in the field against France's 80. Finally, they approved Weygand's next plan, to set a defensive line from the mouth of the Somme, along the rivers Ailette and Aisne to Montmédy in the east, to be held "without thought of retreat." It seemed firm enough as an idea, but Weygand certainly spoiled his presentation by remarking that if the army fought to the end it would in all probability lead to the total destruction of all French armed forces. On that note of gloom the meeting broke up.

It was on the night of 25 May that Pétain gave up hope. In the morning, he confessed to Baudouin that he had spent a sleepless night. It would be wrong, he said, for France to fight to the death. At least part of the army had to be saved to maintain order. The roads were clogged with refugees from the north. Weygand was worried about a possible communist uprising in Paris. The British were of no help: they refused to send aircraft to France, desperately needed to support Weygand's attempt to secure the Somme-Aisne line, and were busy getting their troops back home. It was all getting too much, and much too much for someone in his 84th year, and—here Pétain was near to tears—it was time to put a stop to it.

There was worse, much worse, to come. On the morning of 28 May, Weygand and Pétain met. Much as they disliked one another personally—Weygand was, after all, Foch's creature, and the old rivalry died hard—they were of one mind. By then, they had heard the news that the Belgians had asked for a ceasefire and that the British had started to embark troops at Dunkirk. For the first time, they raised between themselves the possibility of an armistice. Weygand was willing to write a fierce memorandum to Reynaud. He wanted to be sure that Pétain shared his views. They were simple: should the Somme-Aisne line be broken, the battle for France was lost—and the British should be told as much. Pétain heard Weygand out, and then gave his opinion. He agreed.

Weygand's memorandum was presented to Reynaud that evening. Reynaud raised no objection, on Pétain's insistence, to inviting the British without delay to another meeting. On 31 May, Churchill arrived in Paris. There was a great deal to talk about—apart from the Dunkirk evacuation, there was the matter of the repatriation of French troops who had been sent to Norway and who were trapped in an enclave around the port of Narvik; and there was, above all, the French request for British air reinforcements—necessary, Weygand said yet again, if the Somme-Aisne line was to be held. There was also the matter of Italy and what should happen if Mussolini declared war. The agenda was, at length, disposed of, and Churchill wound up the meeting with a fine rhetorical flourish. Reynaud replied in the same vein but, as the British ambassador reported, "one felt that it came rather from his head than from his heart."[4]

Whatever the formal business, there is no doubt about the undercurrents. Churchill wanted to stiffen Reynaud's spine—while limiting the number of aircraft sent to France in case they were needed for the defense of Britain itself following a French collapse. There was no need to remind the French government of the solemn undertaking given to the British on 28 March 1940 that neither country would make peace without the consent of the other. (That reminder would come in due course.) The French, on the other hand, wanted to be assured of British readiness to commit themselves fully to the battle for France.

Throughout the whole meeting Pétain was silent. But, after the meeting, he found himself standing in the bay window of Reynaud's office overlooking the rue St. Dominique with Churchill, Spears and the young French diplomat Roland de Margerie, who was talking volubly about fighting on in North Africa if France fell. Pétain's attitude was, as Churchill later wrote, "detached and somber, giving me the feeling that he would face a separate peace . . . his reputation, his serene acceptance of the march of adverse events, apart from any words he used, was almost overpowering to those under his spell."[5] Pétain's conclusion was evident to everybody present: a French defeat could not now be avoided. Nor was he the only one; Churchill and Spears had arrived at the same conclusion.

On 3 June Paris was bombed for the first time. On 5 June Dunkirk fell. Reynaud reshuffled his government—finally, much to Pétain's satisfaction, getting rid of Daladier and, much to Pétain's disgust, bringing de Gaulle into the Council of Ministers. But there was little time for Pétain's continued grievance about de Gaulle and his book, much as he was still complaining about it. That very day the Germans launched their attack on the Somme-Aisne line. Churchill refused to send further aircraft to help out the French. On hearing this, Pétain told Reynaud "well, there is nothing left but to make peace. If you do not want to do it you can hand over to me."[6]

On 6 June the Somme line was breached, and the Aisne line was to give way soon afterwards. On 9 June the German army was in Rouen. At that point, everything seemed to be in the Germans' favor, even the weather—in seemingly endless days of clear sunshine, perfect for tank attacks. Pétain's mood, in contrast to the weather, was far from sunny. On 6 June he told Ambassador Bullitt, but without any conviction, that the only hope for France was immediate and decisive intervention by the United States. When Spears came to see him later in the morning, Pétain led him to a map on the wall. "He adjusted his pince-nez, and his strong forefinger with its straight cut nail began to follow the line along which the battle was raging." Pétain told him that there were no reserves. "No doubt the men are fighting well, they have got over their surprise as they did in 1914, but they are fighting one against two."[7]

On the morning of 9 June, Pétain saw Reynaud at their customary daily meeting. Clearly doubtful about his ability to recall all his thoughts, he had prepared a written memorandum, which he proceeded to read out. It stressed the necessity of the government remaining in Paris. But it was already badly out of date. When the Council of Ministers met the same evening, they decided to decamp to a series of châteaux along the river Loire.

At 3 A.M. on the morning of 10 June, the cavalcade arrived at the river Loire and the little town of Gien. But there was not time for more than three hours sleep. In the early morning they set off again. It was only at midday on 11 June that they were able to unpack and to start to get settled at their new perch, the château de Saint-Amand-en Puisaye, near Briare on the middle reaches of the Loire. No sooner had they arrived at the new perch than Pétain was summoned to a meeting of the War Committee at the château de Vaugereau, some 20 kilometers away. On his arrival, he was told that they were all waiting for Churchill. Next, the meeting was moved in haste to the nearby, but more spacious, château de Muguet.

Churchill, with Anthony Eden, his minister for war, and a full complement of other ministers, officials and generals—and, of course, Spears—arrived late in the afternoon of the 11th at Briare airport. At 7 P.M., the meeting began. Churchill did his best to rally the French—he returned to an idea, which had been going the rounds, of a retreat to the Brittany peninsula. Churchill cited the example of the British defense of the lines of Torres Vedras in the Napoleonic Wars as an example of what he meant. Weygand, rightly, dismissed the idea as impractical. Churchill reminded Pétain of their meeting in Beauvais in March 1918 and Pétain's determination then to resist the German advance. It was to no avail. Seeing that both Weygand and Pétain were unreceptive to any and every scheme he could put forward, Churchill made one last, impassioned effort. If France were defeated, he said, Britain would fight on—in the air, with her unbeaten navy and with the blockade weapon. If Reynaud was encouraged by Churchill's speech, Weygand was unmoved and Pétain was "mockingly incredulous. Although he said nothing his attitude was obviously 'C'est de la blague' (It's a joke)."[8]

The next morning Churchill made yet another effort, but it was to no avail. Pétain did not even go to the meeting. He knew what would be said. As far as he was concerned it was all too late. When Spears saw Pétain later that day he found the Marshal in a mood of quiet resignation. Spears suddenly realized that "if the French could but be made to believe we could fight on successfully, then many of them would stand by us."[9] It was with that sudden and depressing—but vital—insight that Spears left for Tours. (It was also, as it happened, the last time that Spears spoke to Pétain in private.)

At the château de Cangé, where Lebrun was staying, on the evening of 12 June, Weygand came out openly with a request for an armistice. He told the assembled Council of Ministers that if fighting continued French forces would be cut to pieces. There would be confusion and disorder—not merely military disorder, but general disorder. The response was one of shock. For most ministers, it was the first time they had been confronted with the stark military reality. After all, they said among themselves, the government had abandoned Paris in 1914. That had been followed by the heroic battle of the Marne. Weygand told them that there was no longer any question of a second Marne. He also implied that Britain could not possibly hold out and that consequently any retreat to Brittany or North Africa—or anywhere else for that matter—would be pointless. Pétain supported Weygand, but there was little agreement among the rest, and little sympathy for an immediate request for an armistice. Nevertheless, since the matter had been formally raised by the commander-in-chief, it could not just be ignored. On Chautemps' proposal, it was agreed to invite Churchill to France again for yet another discussion. That done, Pétain left Cangé for his new perch, the château de Nitray, near Azay-sur-Cher, where Ménétrel had dutifully prepared a bed for him.

At midnight on 12 June Reynaud telephoned Churchill. He asked Churchill to come immediately to France. "This looks," noted Churchill's private secretary, John Colville, "as if the French mean to give in."[10] As it happened, this was not yet the case. At Tours, where the two men met, Reynaud reported the discussion of the night before, adding that there had been no majority in favor of an armistice—but that many ministers were now veering that way. Churchill replied that he fully understood the problem and that he was much affected by French suffering. Nevertheless, he went on, Britain was not ready to release France from her formal undertaking of 28 March. The upshot was that it was agreed between the two of them that Reynaud would send a telegram to President Franklin Roosevelt requesting United States intervention, and that no decision would be made before Roosevelt's reply.

Later that afternoon the Council of Ministers met again at Cangé. Everybody present expected to see Churchill, and there was much irritation, directed at Reynaud, when it was announced that he had gone back to London. They were hardly pacified when Reynaud told them that no decision had been taken at his meeting in Tours other than to appeal to President Franklin Roosevelt. Pétain then delivered a statement, which he had had in his pocket for two or three days and which he had polished—in his own hand—that afternoon. As it was getting dark, and in order better to read his own writing, he moved his chair nearer to the bay window so that he could see better, put on his pince-nez and delivered what amounted to a body blow to the Reynaud government.

If the government did not ask for an armistice, his statement made clear, the army would probably stop obeying orders and give way to panic. It went on to assert the absolute necessity of the government remaining in France. As far as he was concerned, he preferred to stay and "accept the suffering" which would ensue. The "renewal of France" would be "the fruit of that suffering." There were only two options open: to seek an armistice or to leave. "I declare," Pétain read solemnly, "that, as for myself, I will refuse to leave metropolitan France— [I will stay] if necessary out of the government. I will stay among the people of France to share their trials and misfortunes. The armistice is in my view the necessary condition for the continued existence of eternal France."[11]

In itself the assertion was dramatic, but it is far from clear whether Pétain really meant what he said or whether he was simply aiming for drama in asserting his own patriotism at the expense of others who would leave. But in making the assertion he maneuvered himself into a political corner. He could not subsequently leave France without an embarrassing—and politically damaging— change of tack. In fact, he did admit, in his very old age and in prison, that the assertion was no more than a rhetorical flourish. But the flourish itself gained a life of its own.

There was then, as might be imagined, a bad-tempered argument. The only thing on which they could all agree was to send a plaintive telegram to Roosevelt. Weygand lost his temper and marched out of the room, slamming the door behind him. But before leaving he had told them all that the German Army was about to enter Paris and would soon be on its way to the Loire. It was thus that, without any decision of substance, a divided and straggling government concluded that they had better retreat further. Their destination was to be the haven in the southwest—Bordeaux.

Unlike the departure from Paris for the Loire, the move to Bordeaux had been well planned in advance. Pétain was to stay in an apartment on the (aptly named) boulevard du Président Wilson and his office was to be alongside that of the military commander of the region. Nevertheless, whatever the arrangements, Pétain's mind was made up. There had to be a decision. It was no longer possible to delay.

While ministers had been scattered around in different châtaux on the rivers Loire and Cher, with uncertain communications and almost no contact between them other than the formal meetings of the council, it was impossible for them to swap views in anything resembling informality. In consequence, it was equally impossible to hatch a conspiracy. Once in Bordeaux, however, all that changed. There could be meetings in cafés, bars, parks or hotels or discussions on those telephones which worked. Bordeaux at the time became no less than a political hothouse.

Laval continued to bombard Pétain with messages. Pétain—in irritation— refused to read them. But although he agreed with Laval on the need for a quick decision about an armistice, there had been an unfortunate delay. Pétain had the support of at least a third of the council for an immediate armistice. Reynaud and Lebrun, on their side, had the support of another third in insisting that they should all wait for Roosevelt's reply. Reynaud then made another proposal: that they should follow the Dutch example and negotiate a cease-fire and carry on the war as a government in exile in London. Weygand rejected the idea out of hand. It would, Weygand had said, be no more than a capitulation. There was, once more, deadlock.

Chautemps then came up with what seemed like a clever scheme. He suggested that a neutral party, perhaps the Pope or the president of the United States, should sound out the Germans on what their terms might be for an armistice. If the terms were reasonable they should be discussed with the British; if, on the other hand, the terms were dishonorable, then France should fight on. Pétain immediately accepted the proposal, saying that in any event he had always envisaged an honorable armistice. Reynaud, of course, immediately saw the flaw in Chautemps' proposal. As soon as it became known that the approach from the "neutral" had come at the request of the French government the game would be up. But when Reynaud took a vote, 13 voted in favor of the proposal and only 6 against. Reynaud immediately offered his resignation. Lebrun, at this point shouting, refused to accept it. Reynaud, in his turn, then had second thoughts. If he threw in the towel now, he quickly realized that there would be a Pétain or a Chautemps government which would immediately request an armistice.

In this angry debate, there was one voice which was decisive—François Darlan. "There is plenty of evidence," one account goes, "to show that, right up until 15 June, Darlan was prepared to sail away with the fleet if any attempt was made to seek an armistice. Had he done so, he would in Churchill's own words have become the master of all French interests beyond German control . . . [and] the chief of the French Resistance with a mighty weapon in his hand. . . . The whole French empire would have rallied to him. Nothing could have prevented him from being the Liberator of France."[12]

Darlan had no particular love for the British and he too believed in the inevitability of a British defeat. He could rightly claim that he had been responsible for the French fleet's undoubted reputation as France's most efficient armed force, equal in stature with the German, British and United States navies. Besides, it was undefeated. In the event, Darlan decided to go with Pétain—provided that "his" fleet would not be surrendered to the Germans. Pétain agreed. So, up to a point, did Reynaud, who then informed the British government of the decision of "the majority of the council," asking their advice—but promising that under no circumstances would the French fleet be part of any deal.

During the evening of Saturday 15 June 1940 there was any amount of muttering in Bordeaux. Generally, the mood was gloomy, but there were two threads: the first was a distrust of England—always referred to as "England" rather than "Britain." Old rivalries had not died. The second was a crude anti-Semitism. Jews were somehow believed to be responsible both for the war and, at the same time, for the failure to resist the invader. There was no logic either in anglophobia or anti-Semitism; but logic, in those tense days, was, to say the least, in short supply.

During the evening Pétain drafted, or, more likely, asked Alibert or even Ménétrel to draft, a letter submitting his resignation from the Reynaud government. At the meeting of the Council of Ministers on the morning of 16 June, he proceeded to read it out. Lebrun took him aside and managed to talk him out of immediate resignation. But Pétain, in agreeing, replied that he would only wait until the British reply to the Chautemps proposal was received. Reynaud then read out Roosevelt's response to his telegram. It was full of sympathy, and Roosevelt promised to continue to send equipment as long as France remained in the fight; but there was no possibility of any military commitment. Nor could there be; only Congress could make such a commitment.

The meeting then adjourned to await the British reply on the Chautemps proposal. It arrived early on that Sunday afternoon. Carefully considered, it said that, on all the balance, Britain would agree to the French request provided that the French fleet was sent immediately to British ports. In fact, this condition was at best unrealistic and at worst absurd. As Darlan was quick to point out, the maneuver would leave French North Africa at the mercy of an Italian attack.

At half past four, however, Reynaud was summoned to the telephone to hear an even more ridiculous proposal. At the other end of the line was de Gaulle, who had been sent to London to ask the British for assistance in moving the French government to Algiers. He was in a state of high excitement. The British Cabinet, he explained, had decided to offer a full "and indissoluble" union of the two countries and peoples.[13] Moreover, Reynaud, if he wished, could become prime minister of the new union. It was all very exciting. In fact, such was the excitement that it was hardly noticed that King George VI of England had not been informed of the proposed disposal of his empire.

In yet another stormy meeting, Georges Mandel accused his ministerial colleagues of outright cowardice. Pétain, after his first intervention, kept his silence. He knew perfectly well that Reynaud had lost the battle. The only option left was the Chautemps proposal. Reynaud, by now exhausted, said that he would submit his resignation to Lebrun. On that note, the council adjourned. They were to meet again at 11 P.M.

The meeting never took place. Lebrun, as was his constitutional duty, sought the advice of Herriot and Jeanneney, the presidents of the two houses of parliament, on who should be the new head of government. Both answered "Reynaud." That said—and rejected—they replied that it was Lebrun's problem. There was, in truth, only one candidate. As ministers were waiting uneasily for the meeting, Reynaud walked passed them saying abruptly that Marshal Pétain was even then forming a government. It was true. Lebrun had had no choice.

Pétain had been preparing carefully for the moment. Like others before him and others since, the thought, which had been in his mind in Spain, had become a wish. At the age of 84, he believed he was the right person to rescue his country in her distress. He was not, perhaps, a new Joan of Arc, but he thought himself to be the next best thing. Oddly enough, his former protégé and now his antagonist, General de Gaulle, at the same time, but in a different place, felt precisely the same about himself.

The Road to Vichy

"Il arrive qu'un paysan de chez nous voie son champ dévasté par la grêle. Il ne
désespère de la moisson prochaine."

It was all to be so very simple. Pétain would form what was to be no more than
an interim administration. Once Britain had surrendered there would be a
peace treaty. France would be herself again, governed from her historic capital,
Paris. The spirit of 1871 would be revived, and France would, as she had before,
regain her status as a major power in Europe and the world. Once that was all
on course, Pétain himself would retire to L'Ermitage, secure of his place in history as another savior of his country in her need. It may, even at the time, have
sounded all too easy; but there were no more than a handful of those involved
who had doubts. Pétain himself was certainly not one of them.

There were, to be sure, some inconveniences. The Germans turned out to be
unexpectedly unpleasant; but, as Laval continued to assure those who listened to
him, Nazism would in the course of time wither away. France herself, too, had to
be cured of the mistakes of the 1930s; but this could be done by the program
Pétain had announced at Verdun in 1936 (with a nod to Primo de Rivera's Spain).
Of course, those who were to blame for France's defeat had to be brought to
book, a matter which, in the event, became muddled up with the fashionable
attack on Jews and Freemasons; but that could be done by some—admittedly
dimly perceived—procedure of justice. There would without a doubt be a peace
treaty before long, but there was no certainty when that would be. Nonetheless,
as one of the German negotiators of the armistice, General Karl-Heinrich von

Stülpnagel, pointed out, no more than confirming the general opinion, the British collapse could be expected "in mid-August" of 1940.[1] A peace treaty would follow soon thereafter as the day follows the night.

Such was Pétain's acknowledged prestige as a marshal of France that few in the political inner circle, least of all himself, believed that these minor inconveniences could not be overcome. Pétain, gratified as he was by the constant expression of devotion from both politicians and public, certainly believed that he was up to the job. But what he (and others) failed to take into account was the frailty of what de Gaulle was later to describe as the "shipwreck of old age." The age of 84 was hardly the time to assume the leadership of a country even in the most healthy state, let alone one which had just suffered the worst defeat in its history. It was also hardly an age to resist the flattery, amounting almost to adoration, to which he had become accustomed in his role as a great savior of France.

On the surface, of course, Pétain seemed reasonably fit. Yet old age takes its toll on the mind as well as the body. Mentally, he could be either extremely alert or almost vacant. Only Ménétrel seemed to be able to read the signs. He was also going deaf, as he himself admitted, and was tiring more easily. Nevertheless, in spite of all, Pétain still stubbornly believed that it was his destiny to lead a defeated France into future, and calmer, waters.

But the one attribute necessary to accomplish the task, political judgement, was missing. As a result, even in the process of forming what he thought would be an interim administration Pétain managed to make a series of blunders. Moreover, through a combination of old age, susceptibility to flattery and political naïveté, he managed to surround himself with a dubious group of failed politicians of the Third Republic; to encourage the petty jealousies; and to upset both his potential allies and his declared enemies.

Pétain's first blunder came when he produced his list of government ministers to Lebrun on the evening of 16 June. The major surprise was that Laval was not given the job of foreign affairs but was offered justice minister instead. When Laval got wind of this, he marched into Pétain's office—and after ten minutes came out announcing that he was after all to be given foreign affairs. Immediately thereafter, Weygand, with François Charles-Roux, the civil servant head of the department, in tow, marched into Pétain's office and, banging on the table, told Pétain that Laval's appointment would be disastrous for future relations with Britain and the United States. Pétain then changed tack again and gave Baudouin the job. Laval remonstrated again, but Pétain, old and obviously confused, told him that he could not change his mind yet again. Laval stormed out, slamming the door behind him.

Another blunder, of course, was not to put de Gaulle on his ministerial list. In fact, it was later claimed that in an earlier Pétain version de Gaulle's name had indeed been on the list—and that it was only out of pique at its subsequent removal that de Gaulle decided to stay in London. The claim, although made even now by Pétain's supporters, has yet to be substantiated by any documentary evidence.

Pétain had thus at the outset managed to upset almost everyone. But there was almost immediately another blunder. On the morning of 17 June somebody—it is still unclear who—told Pétain that Mandel was at the center of an armed plot against the government. Pétain, without any delay, ordered his immediate arrest. Mandel was picked up while having lunch at a restaurant. The news spread quickly. When they heard about it, Herriot and Jeanneney went to see Lebrun. As guardians of parliamentary immunity they told him, correctly, that Mandel's arrest was illegal. At the same time, two of Pétain's new ministers, Charles Pomaret and Ludovic-Oscar Frossard, formed up to Pétain and told him he was making a grave mistake. Pétain, faced with an attack from both sides, climbed down yet again, changed tack, summoned Mandel and wrote him a grovelingly apologetic letter.

By that time, Baudouin had requested the Spanish ambassador, José Felix Lequerica, to ask the Spanish government "to transmit to Germany with all speed the request to cease hostilities at once and at the same time to make known the peace terms proposed by Germany."[2] Without delay, the request was relayed to Berlin. Pétain then made another, even more serious, blunder. At about the time Mandel was being arrested, he made a radio broadcast. He announced that, at the request of the president of the Republic, he had that day taken on the leadership of the government of France. He went on to say that "it is with a heavy heart that I tell you today that it is necessary to cease fighting."[3]

The effect on those listening to him—throughout the whole of France—was of stunned silence, and then of almost unimaginable confusion. Although the text was amended the following day in the official press release to read "try to cease fighting,"[4] the damage had been done. There was complete confusion. Platoons, companies, and sometimes battalions, of brave men, who were even then mounting an effective—and locally successful—resistance against a German Army which was tiring and at the end of a long supply chain, surrendered on the spot. Others fought on—pending further news. Those who fought on found that a unit on their defensive flank had laid down its arms. Just when French commanders and the troops on the ground had started to inflict serious damage on the hitherto all-conquering German army, their efforts were undermined.

Even the Germans were perplexed. Their armies in the field sent urgent requests for further orders. In the event, the official German response to the French request for an armistice was not received until 6:30 A.M. on 19 June. A whole day and a half had gone by between Pétain's radio announcement of a cease-fire and the German agreement to negotiate an armistice. Pétain's blunder had thus cost, at best, a chance to negotiate an armistice on better terms than those finally achieved, and, at worst, many courageous French lives.

If Pétain had been less reckless in his announcement, he could have made out a perfectly good case for an armistice. Had he known the figures, he could have pointed out that no fewer than 112,000 French soldiers had died in six weeks—more than in any six-week period at Verdun in 1916—and a further 200,000 to 250,000 had been wounded. True, the army had been defeated, but it had been an honorable defeat and not a rout. Under the circumstances, an armistice was a perfectly honorable way—in fact, the only honorable way—of stopping unnecessary slaughter.

The armistice negotiations were led, on the French side, by General Charles Huntziger. In fact, there was little room for negotiation. The Germans had already made up their mind about the terms. These were certainly harsh, but not unduly so. Two-thirds of metropolitan France was to be occupied by the victors, including Paris and the whole of the western coast; the remaining third would be self-governing; France was to pay the costs of the German occupying force; all French forces, except for those required for the maintenance of law and order, were to be disarmed and demobilized; the French fleet was to remain in its home ports and be disarmed under German and Italian supervision; finally, there was to be a simultaneous armistice with Italy.

The terms were considered by the Council of Ministers in Bordeaux during the night of 21 June and into the following morning. Various amendments were proposed, but, apart from two of little consequence, General Wilhelm Keitel, the chief German negotiator, brushed them aside. While all that was going on, Weygand was asking the commander-in-chief in North Africa, General Auguste Noguès, about the possibilities of continuing the fight there (and getting a surprisingly positive answer), and Pétain had finally decided to bring both Laval and Adrien Marquet, the mayor of Bordeaux, into his government.

On the face of it, Pétain's decision was rather odd. After all, he did not like Laval. It was not just Laval's louche appearance—a badly groomed moustache, a crumpled suit and, usually, a smudged white necktie. It was worse than that. As Laval became more confident, he became more insolent to the old man, at times treating him almost with scorn. In particular, he had developed a habit of blowing cigarette smoke in Pétain's face when talking to him. Nevertheless, once the governmental circus had arrived in Bordeaux, Laval had started to play, as it were, on his home ground. He and Marquet often seemed better informed about events than government ministers. Certainly, they had the ear of senators and deputies stranded in the unhappy streets of Marquet's city; and Laval's tongue was silvery and persuasive.

Pétain, in spite of the personal dislike, was impressed by Laval's ability to persuade reluctant deputies. Moreover, he recognized that Laval's voice was one which he needed to be with him rather than against him. Apparently without consulting any of his ministerial colleagues, he therefore decided that Laval and Marquet were essential to his government and sent a message to Lebrun asking him to sign the necessary decree. The message did not go down well. Lebrun protested, on the reasonable grounds that the president of the council should make the case in person. On the morning of 23 June, therefore, Pétain duly presented himself to Lebrun and the decree was signed without further ado.

Later that morning, Laval and Marquet turned up to their first session of the Council of Ministers—much to the surprise of those who learned of their appointment a few minutes before. In fact, the matter under discussion was close to Laval's heart—an armistice with Italy—but Laval, wisely, did not intervene. In the event, the discussion, which spilled over into the next day, resulted in an accommodation which allowed the Italian armistice to be signed at 7:15 P.M. on the evening of 24 June and for the armistice with Germany to come into effect at 12:35 A.M. on the morning of 25 June.

There was then the question of what to do next. Under the terms of the Armistice agreement, Bordeaux was to be part of the Occupied Zone. It could not possibly be the seat of the government of France. On the morning of 27 June, therefore, a long procession assembled to leave Bordeaux for Clermont-Ferrand, much favored by Laval, who owned the local newspaper and a radio station. Once there, however, the procession found that the place was impossible. There was no proper accommodation for ministers—let alone parliamentarians—and no office facilities in which a government could be properly conducted. Lyon was suggested, but Pétain refused to go there on the grounds that its mayor was none other than Édouard Herriot. There was only one solution: an old, somewhat decrepit spa resort some 60 kilometers north of Clermont-Ferrand, by the name of Vichy.

In fact, Vichy turned out to be almost perfect for the purpose of an interim administration. The resident population was no more than 25,000, but in the summer the population grew to some 150,000. The result was that there were spacious hotels, a casino, an attractive park along the river Allier surrounded by cafés and tea salons, and, for those who felt the need, baths in the reviving waters.

During their stop at Clermont-Ferrand Laval had gone on the offensive. He had seized on Pétain's own ideas on the way the country should be run, by a small group of honest (that is, not political) men. On 30 June Laval suggested to Pétain, Baudouin and Alibert that the Senate and the Chamber of Deputies should be called together in joint session and, to put it shortly, invited to vote themselves out of office. Baudouin was against the proposal, on the grounds that "you do not change the constitution of a country whose capital is in enemy hands."[5] Pétain sided with Baudouin and raised the problem of Lebrun. Laval claimed that he was able to fix Lebrun, and went off to see him. An hour later he came back claiming that Lebrun agreed. Astonished at Laval's negotiating skills, Pétain gave him his personal authority to go ahead.

In fact, none of the ministers closest to Pétain were opposed to Laval's project. Baudouin, Yves Bouthillier (the finance minister), Weygand and Darlan all supported it, although with varying degrees of enthusiasm. But they all equally agreed that if the project failed Laval would be discredited—which was no bad thing. If the project succeeded, of course, Pétain would claim the credit. Pétain himself seemed almost uninterested. On the following day he went with Laval to see Lebrun about it all and hardly said a word. At a small meeting of ministers on 2 July he endorsed the project, but apparently without enthusiasm.

On 3 July Laval had a stroke of luck. Although the Armistice agreement explicitly stated that the German government had no intention of using "for its own purposes in the war the French fleet which is in ports under German supervision,"[6] Churchill had no faith either in German assurances or in French consistency of purpose, and ordered that as many units of the French fleet as possible should be secured or rendered harmless. The most dramatic result of this order was at Mers el-Kébir near Oran in Algeria, where a large French battle fleet was berthed. A British naval task force stood off Mers el-Kébir and issued an ultimatum to the French admiral requiring him to sail his whole fleet immediately to a British port or to ports in the Caribbean or, alternatively, to scuttle his ships. A signal was sent to the admiralty in Vichy asking for instructions, but it only mentioned the last alternative. The response was that the French should stand firm and that three cruisers were setting sail from Toulon to help. On direct orders from London, the British opened fire on the stationary French ships. In the ensuing orgy of destruction, 1,297 French officers and men were killed and 351 wounded.

The effect of Mers el-Kébir at Vichy was politically decisive. There was general and vociferous outrage at this act of blatant treachery. Darlan, for instance, switched overnight from being moderately anti-German to being ferociously anti-British. He, and others, wanted immediate reprisals. Gibraltar should be bombed. A French task force should sail from Toulon to engage the British in the Mediterranean. Diplomatic relations with Britain were broken off. Much more powerful was the popular response in unoccupied France. Mers el-Kébir was burned into people's hearts as a prime example of British perfidy. The thought of France working together with Germany in the future became that much more palatable.

Laval rode his luck. When the Council of Ministers met in Vichy on 4 July, they approved the proposed constitutional change. But he did not have it all his way. When they heard of it, a group of ex-service senators decided to go directly to Pétain to express their anxiety. To do so, however, they had to get past Alibert—who was on Laval's side of the argument and was worried that Pétain would give in to them. It was not until 6:15 P.M. on 6 July that they finally found a way in. An obviously tired Pétain listened to them and responded that "he did not intend to transform the nation without consulting [parliamentarians] in the process."[7] He then asked them to prepare a text of a resolution, and all of them went away suitably reassured.

The resistance to Laval's project did not stop there. On 7 July Flandin arrived in Vichy. He argued that there was no need for radical constitutional change; all that was needed was for Lebrun to resign and for Pétain to be elected president in his place. Pétain would thus combine in himself the jobs of president of the Republic and president of the Council of Ministers. The idea met with general approval, and Flandin went to see Laval about it. Laval rubbished the whole idea, stating firmly that Pétain would never approve. Flandin then went directly to

Pétain who, unsurprisingly, thought the idea excellent. All he wanted, he said, "was to be granted full powers until the conclusion of peace without being accountable to the Assembly in the meantime."[8] Armed with this expression of approval Flandin went off to see Lebrun. There, unfortunately for Flandin, the proposal ran into the ground. Lebrun refused to take any decision until he had seen Herriot and Jeanneney. They advised him to sit tight—which he did.

By then, Laval had made up his mind—rightly—that Pétain was not to be relied on. He was obviously agreeing, not for the first or the last time, with the last person who had spoken to him. On 8 July, therefore, Laval told Pétain that he could not manage the business unless he had clear and unequivocal authority. Yet again Pétain changed tack. He wrote a letter in his own hand, saying that as it was difficult for him to take part in the debates, Laval was to represent him. Furthermore, the passing of the measure which the government was putting before the National Assembly appeared to him to be essential to ensure the salvation of the country. Armed with this letter, Laval went off to explain to assembled senators and deputies what the government had in mind. He said that, now that France had been defeated, they must work together loyally with Germany and Italy and become integrated, sincerely and in good faith, in a reorganized continental Europe. The memorandum which accompanied the constitutional reform bill even mentioned a "national revolution" to reinvigorate the country as a viable partner in the new Europe.

The formal debates in the National Assembly took place in the Grand Casino at Vichy on Tuesday and Wednesday, 9 and 10 July 1940. Laval's opening speech was generally agreed to have been one of exceptional parliamentary skill. If the assembly was not immediately dissolved and a new constitution introduced, he told the Chamber of Deputies, the Germans would occupy the rest of France. If that did not happen, Weygand's soldiers at Clermont-Ferrand would simply take them all over. The result of Laval's performance was that on that Tuesday afternoon, the Chamber of Deputies carried, by 395 to 3, a motion to endorse the principle of constitutional reform. The same motion was later carried in the Senate by 229 to 1. That decided, on the next morning there was an informal debate on where to go from there. Various proposals were made—Laval's proposal, the ex-service senators' proposal (by then produced in text), and yet another proposal, put forward by the Radical deputy Vincent Badie, accepting the need to give Pétain full powers but rejecting the notion that the Third Republic should be wound up. But when the full National Assembly, the Chamber of Deputies and Senate met in joint session, thanks to Laval's tactical agility, it was faced with two procedural motions: the first, that the government's bill should be voted on before any amendments were called and that if the bill was accepted all amendments would automatically fall, and the second, that passage should only require a simple majority of those present. Almost without demur, the assembly accepted both these motions. The government bill was carried by 569 to 80, and so all amendments, including that of the ex-service senators, then fell. The "collective suicide," as it became known, had been accomplished with a minimum of fuss.

Throughout all these parliamentary antics, Pétain remained detached. He had been glad to see his former—and much valued—subordinate Serrigny, who had turned up in Vichy on 6 July. They discussed how the Vichy government could administer occupied France. "It was not acceptable," Serrigny claimed, "that the Führer should administer [occupied France], contrary to the armistice treaty." But Pétain had hardly given the point much thought. Pétain suggested that he would send a "high commissioner" to Paris. That was to be all. A clearly deflated Serrigny could only note: "I have the impression that he is too feeble for the task in hand; it is a question of character, not intelligence."[9]

Detached or not, on the evening of 10 July, after a long and tiring day, Pétain signed three "constitutional acts," drafted by Alibert. The first announced that he himself was taking over the functions of the "French State"—in other words, that he was becoming "Head of State." The second gave the head of state complete and overall power, both executive and legislative. The third adjourned the chamber and the Senate *sine die*; they could only be reconvened by order of the head of state. There it was. Pétain, as Laval was to remark, had been granted more powers than Louis XIV.

On 11 July Pétain made another radio broadcast, in which he explained his new powers and how he proposed to exercise them. He had appointed a group of 12 ministers as his Council of Ministers. Laval was to be vice-premier, Baudouin was to continue at foreign affairs, Marquet was to be at interior, Bouthillier at finance and Weygand at defense. France would thus be properly organized, with discipline and justice. Above all, the status of the family would be protected. Almost as an afterthought, he added that the Germans had been asked to move out of Versailles so that French ministers could be seen to run not just unoccupied France but the whole country.

What Pétain did not mention was that there was still one constitutional matter which remained to be settled—the succession. He was, yet again, wavering. On 12 July he told Baudouin that he thought that the successor should be chosen by the Council of Ministers. He even suggested that Baudouin himself was the candidate that he favored. Later that evening, however, Baudouin was astonished to learn that Pétain had changed his mind and had decided to make Laval his successor.

Constitutional Act No. 4, appointing Laval as Pétain's successor if he was ever "hindered" from doing the job properly, was duly signed on the evening of 12 July. Weygand was furious, not at the emasculation of the Third Republic—far from it—but at Pétain's choice of his successor. Weygand had a point. One of the many ironies of a supremely ironic period in modern French history was that the day on which Frenchmen woke up to the news that the emasculated corpse of the republic had been put, as it were, in deep freeze, turned out to be Bastille day—14 July.

The Royal "We"

"Cette politique est la mienne . . . C'est moi seul que l'histoire jugera."

The modern town of Vichy reveals little evidence of Marshal Pétain and his government. Indeed, one can find a Place Charles de Gaulle, Place Victor Hugo, a rue du maréchal Joffre, a rue du maréchal Lyautey, and an Avenue du Président Doumer. There is even a Place de la Victoire, presumably commemorating the victory of 1918 rather than the defeat of 1940. Pétain himself gets little more than a footnote in the tourist literature of the town. Even the hotel where he stayed for all those years, the Hôtel du Parc, has been turned into apartments (Pétain's own, on the third floor, is preserved in its wartime state by those who still honor his memory).

None of this should be a matter of surprise. History moves on; but there is a particular ability in France to rub out the names of those once prominent and even glorious who have ended up on the wrong side of history. Nevertheless, there was a period, between 1940 and 1942, when Vichy was at or near the center of the attention of Europe and, at times, even of the wider world. The little spa town, hitherto ignored, suddenly became exciting—full of senators, deputies, ambassadors, officials, ministers, the mistresses of all of them, hangers-on, and, it almost goes without saying, spies. A whole government apparatus, with all its accompanying baggage, settled in the town during the summer of 1940. Pétain, in the early days, was the hub around which all revolved. In the first Constitutional Act he had adopted the royal "we." On the face of it, it was an odd thing to do. He certainly believed that responsibility for the defeat of the spring of 1940 should be laid firmly at the door of republican politicians, but he never wished to assume the mantle of a Caesar. He himself claimed that he only wanted to serve until a peace treaty with Germany had been signed and he could retire to L'Ermitage.

The reason why he did so can be traced to the drafter of the acts, Raphaël Alibert. At the outset, Pétain had impressed on his ministers that they must give the new administration a guiding theme, and Alibert, one of the most intense followers of Charles Maurras and Action Française, took up the challenge. Action Française, among other things, required a monarch; failing a credible descendant of the Bourbon or Orléans lines, a marshal of France was the next best thing. In turn, Pétain was quite prepared to assume the role of surrogate monarch; he considered himself a worthy monarch to look after his own people—whom, as though by way of asserting his monarchical role, he had started to refer to as his "children."

This was not the only matter on which Action Française had a decisive influence in the early Vichy. In fact, it had been Weygand who had set out the fundamental message, almost aping Maurras, in a letter to Pétain of 28 June. Weygand's message was then taken up by Alibert. France must be reborn; the Catholic religion was to be restored to its proper place; the family was the fundamental unit of society; education was to have the highest priority; there should be a return to the land, to the values of the peasant; cooperation was to replace capitalism. The whole message was to be described as the National Revolution (a phrase which Pétain did not care for—he preferred "National Renovation") and could be summed up in the words *Travail, Famille, Patrie* (Work, Family, Fatherland).

Pétain set up his office and his living quarters—Nini joined him in late July—on the main floor of the best hotel in the town, the Hôtel du Parc. Ménétrel was given an office next door to Pétain, to protect his patient from unwanted visitors and to be ready with immediate medical attention if required. Bonhomme, Pétain's faithful orderly officer, was also nearby. In the early days of Vichy, Pétain's staff was headed by General Charles Brécard, under whom there were a military cabinet led by General Krantz and a civil cabinet led by du Moulin de Labarthète. His speeches were drafted by the former journalist Emmanuel Berl (who was, as it happened, of half-Jewish parentage). On the floor below Pétain was Laval with his own staff. The two would usually meet each morning after Pétain's walk along the banks of the Allier, with Weygand, Baudouin, Bouthillier, Darlan and Alibert in attendance, in Pétain's office. There was not enough room there for the full council meetings, which were held in the nearby Pavillon Sévigné.

Pétain's government showed surprising energy, after the grim days and demoralization of May and June. Pétain himself seemed a new man. His old friend Serrigny noticed the difference. "He is in excellent form. . . . A curious thing: this silent man has become talkative. Before, you had all the trouble in the world to drag three words out of him. He really was the silent marshal. Here he is transformed."[1] Others reported the same. Decisions came with unaccustomed speed.

There were, indeed, many decisions to make. Ministries had to be staffed and premises found. Senior officials who had served the Third Republic loyally were not welcome in what was to be the new order. (Some, in fact, particularly in the Foreign Office, were given two or even three months salary and told to stay away.) Judges, too, were not easy to find to staff the supreme court which was set up by Constitutional Act No. 5 of 30 July—to sit in Riom, a smaller town some 20 kilometers south of Vichy. Military officers, on the other hand, there were in plenty. There was no difficulty in staffing the military tribunal set up in Clermont-Ferrand to try deserters (including de Gaulle). Indeed, the military could enjoy the most sympathetic régime for 50 years.

Action Française seemed to have set the agenda for the National Revolution. It also played its part in the virulent anti-Semitism of the day. Pétain himself was not, nor had he ever been, a follower of Maurras, but, in truth, he had never been one for ideology in any form. He was certainly anti-Semitic in the sense that most army officers—and many others—in France then were anti-Semitic. But he was not anti-Semitic in the Nazi sense, regarding all Jews as a biologically inferior race. If he ever thought about it in recognizably intellectual terms, he would have told himself, as had many others, that there were two sorts of Jews—in short, those you knew and those you did not. The "good Jews," that is those who were his prewar friends or others, such as Berl, whom he knew personally, or still others who had fought bravely in the First World War, were to be protected. The general, unknown and unidentified mass of what the Catholics called "deicide" Jewry, particularly those of foreign origin, were not to be given any special protection. The distinction is, of course, wholly bogus; but it appealed to many contemporaries—not least to Ménétrel, who wrote some notably unpleasant notes in the margins of letter about "*juifs*" while going out of his way to help those Jews that he knew personally.

On the other hand, Pétain, in blaming the Third Republic for the degeneration of France, accepted the view of many in the gentile middle class that Jews had not only come to dominate the heights of industry and finance but were conspiring to reap the benefits for themselves rather than the community at large. Others even believed that there was a general conspiracy between Jews and Freemasons—although how that was organized was never made entirely clear. In fact, for Pétain, communists were a much more immediate—and permanent—target.

It was later said by du Moulin that Pétain signed the decrees which Alibert had drafted only with reluctance. That may be so; but he took a close interest in the drafting, and Baudouin reported that Pétain showed himself to be among the hawks. Legislation then came in, as it were, on the tide. On 12 and 17 July anybody other than those of proven non-Jewish parenthood was barred from employment in the civil service. On 22 July a law appointed a commission to review concessions made under the naturalization law of 1927. On 13 August all secret societies were outlawed, with a special reference to masonic lodges. On 27 August the law which had been passed in April 1939 banning religious and racial defamation in the press was repealed.

This first wave of legislative action reached its climax in October with the *Statut des juifs*, which barred Jews from employment in the public sector and a large swath of the private sector. They were not allowed to edit newspapers or even write in them (other than in scientific journals). They were prohibited from holding any post of responsibility in the military, the cinema, theatre or radio. Jews were defined as those who had three Jewish grandparents, or only two if they were also married to a Jew. At the same time, a special police section was set up to deal with foreign Jews. Algerian Jews were deprived of their citizenship and there was a further order authorizing the internment of Jews born abroad in the camps created to house refugees from the Spanish Civil War.

During the debates about the legislation Pétain threw in a wild card. He instructed Alibert to exempt Jewish veterans of the First World War. He also, to put it bluntly, told Alibert to exempt his own friends who happened to be Jews. And he instructed Alibert to introduce a blanket exemption for anyone who had rendered exceptional services to the French state—in other words, anyone whom Pétain himself liked. As the result of Pétain's interventions, the legislation, however grotesque in principle, became impossible to apply with any degree of rationality, as almost immediately became apparent.

At this point, Laval's efforts to move Vichy closer to Germany had stalled. But the British and Free French attack on Dakar, on the western coast of French Africa, in the last week of September 1940, gave him his chance. Pétain was persuaded to agree that there should be further and more detailed negotiations with the Germans, with the objective that France's fleet and the North and West African colonies would not be handed over to Italy (or Germany, for that matter) in any peace treaty. That decided, the negotiations were duly put in train through two separate channels: the military commission set up to monitor the armistice, headed respectively by Field Marshal Walther von Brauchitsch and General Huntziger, and the diplomatic contacts between Laval and the German ambassador to Paris, Otto Abetz.

The name of Otto Abetz runs through the whole history of Vichy almost like a Wagnerian *leitmotiv*. On the surface, the Abetz *leitmotiv* was Francophile. Born near Mannheim in 1903, he started a career as a secondary school art teacher. Actively engaged in youth work, he discovered a vocation for encouraging Franco-German friendship, and set about arranging meetings between French and German youth organizations in his native Baden. In 1934, after a brief spell in the Hitler Youth, he was recruited by the future German Foreign Minister, Joachim von Ribbentrop, to become the head of the French section of his personal research staff, although it was not until 1937 that he summoned enough enthusiasm to join the Nazi Party. During a stay in Paris in the summer of 1939, he was accused (wrongly) of being a German agent and was expelled, only to return a few months later as Ribbentrop's personal representative. In July 1940 he was rewarded by being raised to the rank of ambassador.

Although the *leitmotiv* was Francophile on the surface, Abetz nevertheless believed that, as he put it in a memorandum to Hitler before he became ambassador, France should be reduced to "a satellite state."[2] But this policy, he went on, should not be openly espoused because it would provoke a too hostile French resistance. The correct attitude, he concluded, was to encourage French aspirations for an *entente cordiale* with Germany—and then play on the divisions thereby caused. Hitler thought that Abetz's view was eminently sensible. The ground for Abetz's negotiation with Laval was clear—and was officially endorsed by the Führer himself.

The growing friendship between Laval and Abetz helped to keep Laval in Pétain's government when he reconstructed it in early September. The reshuffle, if it can be called such, was in fact no more than the consequence of the demise of the Third Republic. Pétain had always had in mind to dispense with the parliamentarians; the only one to survive in the government was Laval. Weygand, too, although in no sense a parliamentarian, was a casualty—on the grounds that he was distrusted by Abetz as being pro-British. He was packed off to North Africa as governor with what amounted to proconsular powers. But, even while confirming Laval's status in his government, Pétain was starting to have doubts about Laval himself. Pétain realized, however reluctantly, that the relationship with Abetz was an asset to his government, but Laval was far from popular with his colleagues and was consistently impertinent to Pétain himself. Pétain, an old man used to unquestioning obedience, did not like it. In fact, he had even started to doubt the wisdom of having made Laval heir to his throne. Pétain's personal dislike of Laval led him in strange directions. In what appears to be a calculated attempt to undermine Laval, Pétain tried to open up his own line of communication with the Germans. On 15 September he sent a coded message to an old friend—a dashing aviator of the First World War—colonel René Fonck, who was in Paris at the time. Pétain asked Fonck to get in touch with Göring, with whom he had swapped stories of derring-do in the years immediately after the war, to see whether a meeting between him and Hitler could be arranged. Fonck passed the message on to Abetz. Abetz thought Fonck's project ridiculous, but said, reluctantly, that since the request had come from Pétain he would nevertheless pass it request on to Berlin. In the end, Fonck's mission came to nothing—much to the relief of Serrigny, who thought that "the Führer will play with [Pétain] as a cat plays with a mouse."[3]

Such was the result of the Fonck mission, and the air of secrecy that had seemed to surround it, that Pétain felt it necessary to spell out his views in a radio broadcast on 11 October. "France," he said, "is prepared to work together with all her neighbors. She knows as well that whatever the political map of

Europe and the world, the problem of Franco-German relations, so criminally dealt with in the past, will continue to determine her future."[4] Germany had a choice between imposing a peace or constructing a peace based on cooperation. "The choice is first of all one for the victor; it depends too on the vanquished." All that may have been true as Pétain saw it at the time. But at the time, too, he was also going behind Laval's back in contacting the British. Whatever the secrecy of the botched Fonck mission to the Germans, there was more secrecy to come in a new approach to Britain.

It all started improbably. On 17 October 1940 there arrived in the office of Paul Baudouin a 50-year-old French Canadian professor of philosophy from the university of Besançon, by the name of Louis Rougier. Rougier claimed that he had a way of getting to London, and asked Baudouin to arrange a meeting for him with Pétain. Baudouin agreed, but the arrangements turned out not to be easy. Three days later Rougier was still waiting. He only got his chance when he was in the Pavillon Sévigné explaining his case to one of Pétain's aides, René Gillouin. Pétain himself suddenly came out of a council meeting to smoke a— somewhat unusual—cigarette. Gillouin immediately seized the occasion to present Rougier and tell Pétain what was happening. Without checking any of Rougier's credentials or discussing the matter with any of his colleagues, Pétain, equally suddenly, told Rougier to go and negotiate with the British on his behalf.

On 22 October Rougier arrived in London. He first saw William Strang, then in charge of French affairs in the British Foreign Office. The interview went well enough for a further meeting to be arranged the next day with Lord Halifax. Finally, on 25 October, Rougier saw Halifax and Churchill together. Rougier suggested that there should be agreement whereby Vichy would agree not to try to recapture any of its colonies which had declared for de Gaulle, and de Gaulle would agree not to invade colonies which had stayed loyal to Vichy. Furthermore, Pétain would undertake not to hand French ships and French naval bases over to the Germans or the Italians provided Britain relaxed the blockade—and provided that Churchill and his ministers would stop being rude about Pétain himself in the House of Commons and in BBC broadcasts. (In fact, the British had already come to the conclusion that personal attacks on Pétain were counterproductive.)

The day after Rougier's arrival in London, however, Franco–German relations took a new turn when, on one of his visits to Paris, Laval had been told by Abetz that he was to meet Ribbentrop, only to find out that he was in fact going to meet Hitler himself. The meeting duly took place at the railway halt of Montoire-sur-le-Loir, where Hitler's train had stopped as he was on his way to see Franco to try to persuade him to bring Spain into the war. Hitler raised a number of points with Laval about Vichy's attitude toward the war with Britain, and Laval spoke of Franco–German cooperation and an honorable peace. Nothing was settled—except that Hitler said he would like to meet Pétain at Montoire on his way back.

The Council of Ministers met in Vichy on the evening of 23 October to discuss the proposal. Baudouin warned that Hitler would probably ask Pétain to declare war on Britain and said that he should be resisted. Pétain agreed and asked Baudouin to go with him. At this Laval objected, claiming that Abetz had specified that only he should accompany Pétain. Pétain then gave in to Laval—whereupon Baudouin wrote his note of resignation. Laval, as he had always wished, was duly appointed in his place.

At about seven o'clock on the morning of 24 October two cars set off from Vichy. The first was for Pétain, Laval and Ménétrel—dressed unusually in the uniform of captain, Pétain wearing the by-then rather shabby marshal's regalia. The second car was for Fernand de Brinon, an old friend both of Laval and Abetz (and a conspicuous Nazi sympathizer), and du Moulin. (François Charles-Roux had refused to go; he objected to the policy of cooperation with the Germans and resigned on the spot.) By six o'clock they were at Montoire. Hitler's train had arrived. Only Pétain and Laval were allowed to go near Hitler's own carriage; the others were banished to the restaurant car, where Ménétrel spent the time chatting to Hitler's personal doctor. When all were settled down, Pétain and Laval were ushered in to see the Führer himself.

But by that time Pétain was tired. He immediately started to explain that he wished to cooperate with Germany, but he could not go into details on how that desirable objective might be achieved. Hitler replied with an extensive analysis of the military situation, and pronounced that Britain would soon surrender. The conversation then stalled. Laval intervened to try to give some flesh to the bones of Pétain's generalities about cooperation, but to little effect. Hitler then summed up the whole affair as follows: "Marshal Pétain says that he is prepared in principle to consider cooperation"—the German word is *Zusammenarbeit*, literally "working together"—"with Germany as outlined by the Führer. The conditions of this cooperation would be established and settled in detail from case to case. Marshal Pétain expects from this a more advantageous outcome of the war for France. The Führer declares that he is in agreement."[5]

Before leaving, Pétain made another political blunder. He had shaken Hitler's hand. The Germans were no fools. They understood perfectly well the propaganda value of what seemed to the old marshal to be no more than courtesy. As a result, the photograph of the handshake was sent around the world—and it arrived in London precisely on the evening before Churchill was due to have his second meeting with Rougier.

The effect was volcanic. Churchill started shouting at Rougier as soon as he arrived in the morning. Pétain, he claimed, had signed a peace treaty with Hitler at Montoire. He would send the Royal Air Force to bomb Vichy and he would broadcast to the people of France to tell them that their government of traitors would be pursued wherever they go. Rougier managed to calm him down, but it was some little time before their negotiations were able to proceed.

Rougier was able to assure Churchill that nothing very much had happened at Montoire. This was no more than the truth. Pétain had achieved the release from prison camp of the ever-faithful General Laure, but that was hardly a major victory. But Pétain was seen—displayed by the world's press in one of the most famous photographs of the whole war—to have shaken the hand of the Nazi dictator and conqueror of France.

In the end, the Rougier mission did not amount to very much. Rougier, with the help of Strang, drafted notes on his meeting with Churchill. They were amended, with Churchill's approval. The notes still exist; but what is clear is that they were originally intended as a message to Weygand, whom Rougier was shortly to see. Somehow—it is not entirely clear how—the notes lost the name of Weygand in their heading. It was heavily crossed out. But Churchill did write, in his own hand, across the top of Rougier's notes, "If General Weygand will raise the standard in North Africa, he can count on the renewal of the whole-hearted collaboration of the governments and peoples of the British Empire, and on a share of the assistance afforded by the US."[6] Armed with this, Rougier went off to see Weygand, who would have none of it. Whatever his sympathies, Weygand was not prepared to allow himself to become a traitor to France. Rougier then reported back to Pétain, having at some point gratuitously added a second page to his note—and fraudulently attributed it to Churchill—which was much more explicit about an agreement between the two sides.

In the end, the Rougier mission did not amount to very much. But after the war the whole "Rougier affair" became a matter of controversy, not least because Pétain claimed that he had in truth made a deal with Churchill. Flandin, who was appointed by Pétain to the government in December, also claimed that he would not have joined the Vichy government had he not thought that there was a "secret agreement" between Churchill and Pétain.[7] Churchill was forced to make a statement to the House of Commons in 1945, and there was a British White Paper on the whole matter, categorically denying any agreement of any sort. Nevertheless, when the circumstances were reviewed in 1964 by the British Foreign Office, a considered memorandum was cautious enough to state that "[the White Paper's] complete repudiation of any sort of agreement was couched in unduly strong terms."[8] However, it is safe to say that the British were in fact prepared to do a deal with their former ally—and that Pétain was more than prepared, behind Laval's back, to do some sort of deal with them—and had Weygand come over, or had Pétain been more experienced in diplomacy, a deal might have been done.

None of this should be called, as some historians have called it, a "double game." All that Pétain was trying to do was to keep open lines of communication with the British. They were, after all, however much he distrusted them, his former ally and generally preferable to the Nazis. All that the British were trying to do was to keep the French fleet out of German hands and, if at all possible, to detach Weygand in North Africa. But the Rougier affair was only on the periphery of the main events. What lasted from all the to-ing and fro-ing between the various sides was the aftershock of Pétain's handshake with Hitler.

There followed an almost desperate program of damage control. On 30 October a chastened Pétain made yet another broadcast. He sounded nervous, not least because he had an irritating cough which Ménétrel had been unable to cure. "Last Thursday," he started, "I met the Chancellor of the Reich. This meeting has raised hopes and has caused anxieties; I owe you, on this matter, some explanation."[9] This he went on to give. He claimed that sincere working together with Germany was the only possible policy for France. The armistice was not peace. France remained sovereign. "This policy is mine. Ministers are responsible only to me. It is me alone that history will judge."[10]

The Rougier and Montoire episodes, although both were eccentric—to put it mildly—in their diplomatic method, showed that Pétain had gone to some trouble to think through his government's uncomfortable position, caught, as it was, between the former ally Britain and the victorious Germany. The course was difficult to steer. Nevertheless, Göring himself was later to say that the armistice was Hitler's greatest mistake. Like Abetz and many others, he believed that France should have been reduced to no more than a satellite. Similarly, Cecil von Renthe-Fink, who was to play his own role in Vichy's later stages, said after the war that for him Montoire constituted the greatest defeat of the entire German policy toward France; that Germany obtained nothing and almost lost what she had; that France was not won over to the German cause nor was the whole of French territory occupied; and that if there had been no Montoire, there would probably have been no Allied landing in North Africa and no German defeat thereafter.

On the other side, the British at the time were taking a relatively benign view of Vichy. "The French," Colville wrote in his diary, "have two great levers against Germany: their fleet and their Colonies."[11] Churchill himself put his finger on it in January 1941. He conceived "Marshal Pétain's main object," as he commented to the War Cabinet, "to be to keep the Germans out of Unoccupied France by threatening that if they came in the fleet and North Africa would join this country." But he then added, presciently, that it remained to be seen "how long he could keep the Germans in play."[12]

Rougier, the self-appointed ambassador, had opened up a dialogue. Certainly, the method was more eccentric even than Montoire. But when Rougier left the scene, the baton was taken up by others. King George VI had already sent a carefully drafted message to Pétain on 25 October, during Rougier's visit to London. It soon became the turn of Pierre Dupuy, the Canadian chargé d'affaires in Vichy, to act as Britain's—and Vichy's—unofficial ambassador.

By the end of November, the premise on which Petain's whole international policy was based was starting to change. Britain had—unexpectedly—survived. The Luftwaffe had been defeated in the air and the German invasion of England had not taken place. At the same time, although German armies were victorious on all fronts, the Italians were not performing well. In short, it was even—just—possible to imagine a British victory and a German defeat. "I have no love for the British," Pétain told the American chargé d'affaires on 16 November, "and I shall defend French territory against them. But their victory is much better for France than that of Germany."[13]

In light of all that, it made perfect sense for Pétain to pursue contacts with Britain (behind Laval's back) and to play down Laval's efforts at single-minded collaboration with Germany. It so happened that Laval was pursuing these efforts even more energetically than before. In late October, he had instructed the French directors of the Bor copper mines in Yugoslavia to sell out to the Germans. In late November, gold which had been deposited with the Banque de France for safekeeping and had been subsequently ferried to French West Africa was brought back and handed over to the Germans on Laval's sole signature. Laval was at the same time, together with Huntziger and Darlan, having conversations in Paris with the German general Walter Warlimont about a possible military attempt to recover Chad for Vichy.

On 12 December Laval telephoned Vichy from Paris. Hitler was sending an invitation to Pétain to come to Paris on 15 December, the anniversary of the return of Napoleon's remains from St. Helena. This time it was the turn of the ashes of Napoleon's son, the Duke of Reichstadt, to be repatriated. Pétain was invited to attend the ceremony, to be held at night with the full panoply of searchlights sweeping the sky and swastika flags waving in the breeze. In Vichy, however, the invitation was seen as a trap—to get Pétain to Versailles by himself and force him there to sign over the entire government to Laval. There would then be a new government, which would include Marcel Déat, editor of the openly fascist newspaper *L'Oeuvre* and the author of a number of hostile articles. Pétain therefore refused to go. The next day Laval arrived in Vichy, determined to fetch him. At first Pétain resisted, but he then buckled under Laval's pressure and agreed to go, provided he was able to carry out some sort of ceremonial tour of towns in the Occupied Zone.

When they heard this news, Bouthillier, Darlan and Huntziger—quickly joined by Marcel Peyrouton, the interior minister, and Alibert—met in du Moulin's office at 4 P.M. to decide their tactics. Their aim was simple. Pétain had to be protected. It followed that Laval had to be sacked—immediately. They then marched into Pétain's office and told him so. Peyrouton was armed with information that the Germans wanted a "more docile" French government.[14] The meeting was brief. Pétain was persuaded to immediate action. He summoned a council meeting for 8 P.M. and asked all his ministers for their resignations (as was the custom in government reshuffles of the Third Republic). Pétain then left the room for a short while, came back and announced that the resignations of Laval and Georges Ripert, the minister for education, were the only ones to be accepted. In short, it was a clear political coup.

Laval was—understandably—furious. He demanded to know the reason. Pétain replied that it was because he did not make proper reports, because he was opposed to the transfer of the government to Versailles and because he was behind the Déat articles. None of that was particularly convincing. Finally, Pétain said simply that he had lost confidence in him. But that was not the end of it. As he was preparing to go back to Paris with his wife and daughter, Laval was told by an American journalist that his chauffeur had been arrested and his car removed. He tried again to get in touch with Pétain. In order to avoid having to talk to him Pétain instructed Ménétrel to tell Laval that he was asleep. By that time the building had been surrounded by police—and by some members of Pétain's personal bodyguards, many of whom were ex-*Cagoulards*. Laval feared the worst when he saw them with "revolvers; they were showing them; they were threatening," and was relieved when the chief of the official police came into his office to tell him that he had orders from Pétain to escort him to his home at Chateldon some ten kilometers from Vichy.[15]

Pétain announced Laval's sacking in a radio broadcast on the evening of 14 December. The following day Abetz, at the ceremony to mark the transfer of the Duke of Reichstadt's ashes to Paris, told Darlan and Laure, whom Pétain had sent to represent him, that the action of the French government was unacceptable. He reinforced this by traveling to Vichy on the next day, with ten heavily armed SS guards as his escort. He told Pétain that Laval's dismissal had been taken by Hitler as a personal affront. He demanded a wholesale reconstruction of the French government—to include Laval—and said that if that was refused Germany would not continue the policy of cooperation.

Pétain replied that since he had already announced Laval's sacking he could not go back on it; but he was quite prepared to discuss the possibility of other changes in his government. Abetz then demanded to see Laval and said he was shocked to hear that he was under arrest. Pétain professed to know nothing of Laval's arrest and ordered his immediate release. There was a further meeting when Laval arrived. Pétain offered to reinstate him either as minister of agriculture or minister of labor. Laval yet again lost his temper, accused Pétain of "insincerity and double-dealing with England,"[16] became more and more insulting and finally had to be restrained by Abetz himself. At that point it was clear to everybody that Laval had put Pétain in an impossible position. Abetz left for Paris, and Darlan was sent to explain the matter to Hitler, which he did on Christmas Day in a meeting in Hitler's train—emphasizing, however, that it was "the formal wish of the Marshal and his government to pursue the policy of co-operation."[17]

Laval's sacking went down well in London. On 21 December, Churchill gave a dinner at Chequers for Dupuy. Dupuy told him that "Pétain, Darlan and . . . Huntziger had spoken to him about the possibility of co-operation in North Africa and Continental France," provided that "the present atmosphere of tension" between Britain and Vichy could be maintained "as a smoke screen, behind which contacts could be made and information exchanged." Churchill replied that "he was ready to enter into a procedure along the lines suggested above" and that he wished Dupuy "to inform the French Government of his readiness to send divisions to North Africa in case the French Government should decide to abandon the metropolitan territory or considered it opportune to receive British support in North Africa."[18]

In spite of leaks to the press, Dupuy went about his mission. Back in Vichy, he sent a report to the Canadian prime minister, Mackenzie King, saying that Pétain was fully aware and "was still hoping for a British victory."[19] (The awareness was perhaps overstated. Dupuy added later that Pétain had nodded off three times during their conversation and he had had to wake him up by pronouncing the name of General de Gaulle in a loud voice—a procedure which enjoyed immediate success.) Moreover, Dupuy went on to write, on 27 December, to Eden that Pétain, Darlan and Huntziger were at one in suggesting negotiations on commercial matters but "with the hope that such negotiations might lead to closer collaboration between the two countries." Dupuy further reported three weeks later. Churchill drafted a note for Dupuy, stressing the need for urgency, on the grounds that "the Germans may, by force or favor, come down through Spain, render unusable the anchorage at Gibraltar . . . most important that the Government of Marshal Pétain should realize that we are able and willing to give powerful and growing aid. But this may presently pass beyond our power."[20]

Dupuy finally reported in mid-January 1941. Neither Weygand nor Pétain had responded to Churchill's note, but he had found Pétain "much more alert than we had supposed, and anxious for a British victory."[21] Huntziger, too, was doing "excellent work behind the scenes, in preparation for the day of liberation," and even Darlan "was determined not to let his personal animosity against the British Admiralty make him work against a British victory."[22] There, for the moment, it rested.

As 1940 ended, Pétain, in spite of the blunders, the eccentric diplomacy, the plotting and the sheer bitchiness of Vichy politics, could claim that he had a number of points to his credit. The policy of cooperation with Germany, however wobbly in practice, was still on course. The infrastructure of government was in place. Dialogue with the British had been re-established—in fact, even while Dupuy was playing the go-between another official, in the ministry of education, Jacques Chevalier, had been in touch with his old friend Lord Halifax. The legitimacy of the Vichy government was not (apart from the interventions of de Gaulle in London) seriously challenged. Above all, he himself had retained the respect, admiration and devotion of his "children."

On the debit side, of course, Pétain had had to concede that the sovereignty of France was, to a large measure, dependent on German goodwill. Moreover, the main plank of his early foreign policy—the imminent collapse of Britain—was starting to look dangerously unstable. Finally, the dream of moving to Versailles or Paris to become the leader of all France had faded as the morning mist. Abetz no longer wanted to see Pétain in or near Paris. Vichy, however small and provincial, whatever the boredom of the place and however bitter the waters—in every sense—was to be his home for the foreseeable future.

TWENTY-ONE

The Germans, Darlan, and the Jewish Question

"Le chef, c'est celui qui sait à la fois se faire obéir et se faire aimer."

The winter of 1940–1941 in Vichy was cold to the marrow. Those who had long family memories said that there had been nothing like it for 90 years. The politicians and diplomats, of course, were able to survive without much trouble, but others without the privilege of rank or position were suffering—not just from the cold but from a shortage of food and clothing. Moreover, those whose menfolk had surrendered and were in prison camps were starting to complain that there seemed to be no prospect of them coming home. In short, at the beginning of 1941, Pétain's "children" were cold, undernourished and fractious.

The political climate was as cold as the weather. After Laval's sacking, the German government, at all levels, was instructed that the policy of cooperation outlined at Montoire was now null and void. Hitler had decided that Pétain was not worth bothering about and that it was better to keep Laval in Paris, with a view to setting up a rival government to Vichy if it seemed worthwhile. Besides, as he told Darlan at their meeting on Christmas Day 1940, it was a matter of indifference to him who was and who was not in the French government. The German attitude was clear. It was called *die kalte Schulter*—the cold shoulder.

The one shoulder which remained relatively warm toward Vichy was that of Abetz. Acting on his own initiative, he tried throughout January 1941 to get

Laval reinstated. By way of justifying himself to his superiors in Berlin, he maintained that "the question of Laval has assumed the character of a test of strength."[1] Furthermore, he told Baron Jacques Benoist-Méchin, a Germanophile intellectual who found himself in the improbable position of representing French prisoners of war in Berlin, that he was—equally improbably—only trying to negotiate Laval's reinstatement out of a deep love of France. In Vichy, Abetz's insistence could not be ignored. But Pétain was in difficulty. His action in sacking Laval had restored the popularity which the Marshal had enjoyed before the unhappy photograph at Montoire. Letters of congratulation poured in, praising him for what appeared to be a decisive break in the pro-German policy. His difficulty was that he, along with the other members of his new directorate (Darlan, Huntziger and Flandin) was determined to continue precisely the same policy.

The upshot was that early in January 1941 Pétain agreed to see Benoist-Méchin to hear Abetz's case. When he heard that Laval's reinstatement was a necessary condition for Franco–German cooperation, he started, yet again, to waver. It looked as though there would have to be an embarrassing volte-face. Since both Darlan and Huntziger thought that Laval had been shabbily treated, they pressed Pétain to change direction; but they all wanted to know whether Laval really had the support of Berlin. Subject to that precondition, they proposed to Benoist-Méchin, for onward delivery, a package for Laval. In return for a letter of apology for his insulting behavior to Pétain, greater freedom of movement for Pétain in occupied France (in particular freedom to go to Versailles whenever he liked) and Vichy censorship of the Paris collaborationist press which was constantly attacking Pétain, Laval could return as a minister of state and a fourth member of the directorate.

When told by Benoist-Méchin that he was required to write a letter of apology, Laval exploded. It was he who had been wronged and it was therefore he who should receive a letter of apology from Pétain. It took some hours of patient argument to calm him down. In the end he agreed to write a letter, although it can hardly be said to read like a letter of apology. Nevertheless, it served its purpose, and Pétain agreed to meet Laval on 18 January—at yet another railway station.

Pétain's meeting with Laval came to nothing. Pétain restated his grievances: Laval's unpopularity, his methods, his failure to report properly, his mistrust of colleagues. Laval tried to justify himself, but Pétain still had in the forefront of his mind the intemperate language Laval had used to him the previous December. It was not the sort of thing that Pétain either easily forgot or easily forgave. The two men spent some time circling around Laval's future position, but then Laval spoilt everything by asserting that the Vichy government was not up to the job. Although that may well have been true, it was hardly the remark to endear him to the head of the Vichy government himself. The meeting ended with Pétain grumpily agreeing—for fear of more pressure from Abetz—to be reconciled, while pointing out acidly that Laval's return to a ministerial post might take more than a little time.

By that time, a new character had appeared on the Vichy stage. The United States—in truth, President Franklin Roosevelt—had decided that there was work to be done. In late November 1940, while enjoying a leisurely Sunday morning breakfast in the governor's residence in Puerto Rico, Fleet Admiral William D. Leahy had received a message from Roosevelt summoning him to Washington to become ambassador to France. The message, to say the least, had come as a surprise. Leahy was, at the age of 64, suitably parked in his retirement from public service with "Mrs. Leahy," as he always referred to her. But Leahy was an old friend of Roosevelt. He had known him when Roosevelt was a young assistant Secretary of the Navy in 1913. Above all, he was one of the few still surviving who had known Roosevelt before he was stricken with polio. Leahy was an old salt—and far from stupid. Roosevelt needed somebody to go to Vichy, somebody who was an old friend and who could also talk, as one old salt to another, as it were, with Pétain and Darlan.

The Leahys arrived finally at Vichy on 5 January 1941, to do their best to reconcile themselves to the bitter cold and to settle down. On the morning of 8 January Leahy presented his credentials to Pétain. He found Pétain in fine fettle, "a splendid, soldierly bearing for one of any age, and a pair of remarkably clear blue eyes."[2] Although Pétain understood some English, he preferred to speak to Leahy in his usual precise and articulate French. They talked about the food situation in unoccupied France and about what help the United States could give. Leahy tried his best to be encouraging. To that extent, their conversation went well.

The following day, however, Leahy spent another hour—in the late afternoon—with Pétain, this time with Flandin in attendance. "I was startled," Leahy reported, "by the contrast in Marshal's appearance. He showed none of the vitality of the day before. He seemed a tired old man." Leahy went on to report that "there were many times when I saw the Marshal in the late part of the day when he appeared thus,"[3] and made a mental note to himself to try to see Pétain in the morning rather than in the afternoon.

These conversations were followed with the closest attention in London. Churchill was still trying to persuade Weygand to raise his standard in North Africa. On 7 January he wrote to the British Chiefs-of-Staff that "We can but wait and see what Vichy will do. In the meantime, we enforce the blockade of France fitfully and as naval convenience offers, partly to assert the principle, partly to provide a 'smoke-screen' of Anglo-French friction, and especially not to let the Vichy Government feel that life will be tolerable for them so far as we are concerned if they do nothing."[4] This message had, in fact, been delivered to Pétain by Leahy on the afternoon of 8 January.

Leahy's experience was shared by many others. Pétain was alert in the mornings, less so in the afternoons and usually very tired by the evening. Laval had used this pattern to advantage, presenting laws for Pétain's signature first in the morning, then in the afternoon and finally, for the third time, in the evening when the old man would sign almost anything for a bit of peace. In fact, on a number of occasions Pétain is reported to have signed laws without even reading them through—and then to have been surprised at the result.

It was not just a problem of old age. Ménétrel was up to his old tricks. There was the usual treatment of warm air, oxygen and massages in the morning. But to all that Ménétrel, if other doctors at Vichy are to be believed, apparently added injections of benzedrine, ephedrine or even amphetamine. Weygand, who had no love for Ménétrel, used to say when he met him—with his customary sarcasm: "I don't need I don't know how many injections a day, eh? Nobody has given me an injection at all this morning."[5] The effect of Ménétrel's attentions, of course, was to brighten the morning—at the expense of a soporific afternoon and evening. Since Ménétrel controlled access to Pétain's suite, he could manage Pétain's visitors as he wished.

In giving his first impressions of Pétain to Roosevelt in a report dated 25 January, Leahy made only a glancing reference to Pétain's health. He did, however, write at some length about the burden of work which Pétain had assumed and which, in Leahy's view, was "beyond his physical capacity."[6] He went on to write that he thought that Pétain favored "something like the Fascist government of Italy without its expansionist policy."[7] This was not altogether true. There was none of Mussolini's bombast. A more accurate comparison would be the Spanish régime of Primo de Rivera, but without a monarch (the monarch, of course, being Pétain himself). For instance, the main vehicle for ensuring support for the government was the Légion Française des Combattants, an amalgam of the various ex-servicemen's organizations which had existed before the war. Pétain was much given to touring the main centers of unoccupied France and communing with crowds of his "children." In fact, it was the part of his job he liked best. These tours were organized by the Légion, whose job it was to distribute favorable literature and ensure that enough people—and the right sort of people—turned out to welcome the Marshal with the utmost enthusiasm. Such was Pétain's drawing power that by mid-1941 the Légion had no fewer than 1.7 million members.

There was also the matter of encouraging doubters to support the government. In this, too, Pétain's techniques owed more to Primo de Rivera than Goebbels. But it was clear where it was all leading. For instance, there was the role of what were called the "patriots," who were, in fact, both spreaders of the gospel and informers. The role was described, in a memorandum from the Organe du Comité de Propagande sociale du Maréchal—intercepted by Canadian intelligence in September 1941— as being in essence "propaganda by word of mouth." There were secret cells. Each cell had a head, who was responsible only to his superior in the central office in Vichy. Members of the cell were to be known only by their numbers and only the head would know their identity. The main duty of the members was to make reports of anything he or she had heard which could be construed as damaging to the government. In short, they were a form of amateur and secular secret police.[8]

There was also the carefully maneuvered support of the Catholic hierarchy. Heartened by the revival of religious education and Pétain's obvious belief—whatever his private views—that the Catholic Church was one of the bedrocks on which a properly ordered state rested, the assembly of cardinals and archbishops urged their flock to "venerate" the head of state in person and to support his government. There may have been some grumbling among the minor clergy but there was no doubting the enthusiasm of the hierarchy. As Cardinal Gerlier, the archbishop of Lyon, said, "Pétain is France and France, today, is Pétain."[9]

Then there were the youth organizations. In spite of pressure from the extreme fascists such as Déat, there was no equivalent to the Hitler Youth, any more than there was a single political party. Pétain himself had refused the idea of a single party; he also refused the idea of a single youth movement, and felt they should not be too militaristic. True, young men of the Chantiers de la Jeunesse, the compulsory youth movement, wore uniforms, were heavily indoctrinated in the themes of the National Revolution and were marched up and down, but their commander was a former Boy Scout whose ideas were little more than an adaptation of the British movement. But, in competition, there were the Compagnons de France, as well as another six scout groups, all officially authorized by Paul Marion, the minister in charge of propaganda—including, oddly enough, one specifically for Jewish boys. All Marion's efforts to politicize such groups came to nothing, but at least they were supportive of the regime and dedicated personally to Pétain.

Nevertheless, in spite of the Légion, the informers, the cardinals, the bishops and the young Boy Scouts, all was not well in Vichy. True, Pétain himself commanded wide popular support, and there was general approval—at least until the autumn of 1941—for the National Revolution and the purge of Freemasons and Jews. But it was cold, and basic foodstuffs were running short. If people are starving they want bread. What they did not want were lectures on how the new France was to arise from the ashes of the old, and to be told that the way to this was for them to buckle down and improve themselves as Christians, soldiers and fertile wives. For the first time since the armistice there was some audible muttering.

January 1941 confronted Pétain with some awkward truths. He had convinced himself that the armistice would lead to a peace treaty which would allow France to be reborn from the political rubble of the Third Republic. He had thought that it was his mission, until a peace treaty was duly signed, to lead France to the middle way—staving off the Germans while maintaining relations with the British. But there was more to it than that. He had also thought that his mission would be successful, that he was the man who could come to the rescue of his poor country just as others had done in its history. With the new order, France would regain her true position as the leader of the civilized world.

Perhaps for the first time, he was now starting to understand that the enemy with whom he was dealing was much more devious and aggressive than he had ever thought. "If I go against them," he told Leahy, "they will come down here, and that would be terrible for my people. They are my people. I am responsible for their welfare."[10] He was conscious that he had done little in the face of that threat for the 1.5 million French prisoners of war—for whom he felt a genuine and constant sense of responsibility. True, he still enjoyed the large crowds at the towns he visited on his travels, but there was no disguising the muttering in the background.

In fact, small shoots of organized resistance were developing. Gradually the groups, initially informal, coalesced into more structured organizations with identifiable leadership. Henri Frenay (known as "Charvet"), Pierre-Henri Teitgen (known as "Tristan") and Georges Bidault were early leaders. At first, their methods were harmless—small demonstrations, newsletters produced on primitive monotype, meetings in safe houses. Yet such was the atmosphere created by the network of informers set up by the ministry for propaganda that news of these activities soon reached the authorities—and Pétain himself.

Pétain's first reaction was one of disbelief. He had deluded himself—the expression is not too strong—that, as father of the nation, as a marshal of France and, above all, as the "Victor of Verdun," his popularity would remain forever undimmed. His second reaction, once his disbelief had been dispelled, was intense irritation. On 27 January 1941 Constitutional Act No. 7 was announced. It required all secretaries of state, high dignitaries and senior civil servants to swear an oath of personal loyalty to Pétain. The act gave specific powers to Pétain to order any breach of the oath to be punished either by incarceration or house arrest. Given the network of informers, from then on no senior official could consider himself safe. Moreover, the same officials were obliged, under their oath, to report any sign of anything which could conceivably be regarded as treachery.

Abetz, for one, thought this measure highly satisfactory. But he still was not satisfied with the directorate. He continued to press for Laval's return—as it happened, against specific instructions from Hitler. Abetz claimed to Ribbentrop (untruthfully) that it was Darlan who suggested he come to Paris to discuss purely administrative matters. On that basis Ribbentrop agreed to the Darlan visit—provided it was understood that Laval was not to return to Vichy. In the belief that Abetz had Ribbentrop's unqualified support, on 3 February Darlan arrived in Paris with a clear proposal for Laval—endorsed, of course, by Pétain. Laval could return to a ministerial post and membership of the directorate—but no more. Laval immediately rejected the proposal, replying that he would only return as premier with full powers. Darlan tried to negotiate, but there was no possible common ground. Darlan went back to Vichy convinced, probably rightly, that Laval had never wanted to return in the first place.

There was one further complication. While Darlan was in Paris, Abetz had, in passing, attacked Flandin with some unusually poisonous venom, on the grounds that he was wholly and irreconcilably opposed to Franco–German cooperation. It was, of course, quite untrue, but Abetz's disapproval was enough. Flandin had to go. Pétain meekly agreed; and on 9 February Flandin, equally meekly, resigned. This entailed yet another governmental reshuffle. Pétain then appointed Darlan deputy premier and minister of foreign affairs. (Darlan retained his existing posts of Navy Minister and commander-in-chief of the Navy.) The following day Pétain went further: he named Darlan his successor. "The Marshal has stripped himself of his powers," wailed Serrigny, "in favor of Darlan. . . . Pétain has become Lebrun."[11] Churchill, too, was horrified. He believed, with justification, that Darlan "nourishes abnormal and professional resentment against this country" and that "the matter is very serious in the light of the stories that Pétain at 84 is going to have an operation for prostate gland, which might well carry him off."[12]

The new ministers who assumed office on 9 February 1941 were of an altogether different brand to their predecessors. Out went Alibert, the ideologue of the National Revolution, and Peyrouton, one of the chief conspirators against Laval. In came Pierre Pucheu (from the Banque Worms) at the post of industrial production, Jacques Barnaud at Franco–German economic relations, and François Lehideux at the Ministry of Equipment. These were not ideologues—any more than Darlan himself. They were technocrats. They believed that the business of running the state was a matter of efficient planning. Moreover, planning required a disciplined approach to corporate governance, in which employers and workers would join together for the greater good. The "National Revolution" was still a useful tool since it struck a popular chord—but as a pious aspiration, not a program for action. For them, what mattered was efficiency, and efficiency could not be produced by Boy Scouts but by a carefully organized corporatist state. Only in that way would France be able to hold her head up in the new Europe.

Darlan seemed happy with his new team. His political ambition was to see France as an imperial—and naval—power within a German-dominated continental system. France, in the words of a memorandum drafted by Pucheu, Lehideux and Marion and submitted to Abetz, would be Europe's "Atlantic bridgehead."[13] For that to happen, France had to become a model of industrial efficiency and inter-class harmony. The new technocrats would make it happen. But there was no sign that the Germans were in the least interested in what Darlan was prepared to offer. No senior German figure could be bothered with what was or was not happening at Vichy. Until further notice, the cold shoulder was official policy.

Amid all the politicking, on 7 March 1941 Pétain and Nini were married— again. It was, to be sure, a strange affair. Thanks to the efforts of the Papal Nuncio and Brécard, by then Vichy ambassador to the Holy See, Nini's first marriage had been annulled by an ecclesiastical court in Rome. (The fact that she had borne a child to her lawfully wedded husband had been conveniently ignored.) This left Nini free to demand that her civil marriage be regularized by the proper and eternal rites of the Catholic Church. Pétain could hardly refuse. For a head of state of a supposedly Catholic country—and one which had promulgated the National Revolution so enthusiastically—to be living, as it were, in sin, was hardly acceptable if the alternative was available. On the other hand, a religious ceremony in Vichy, however private, would require Pétain to confess his sins in the usual manner. This, so the wags maintained, was altogether too daunting a prospect. Besides, the publicity would no doubt be unpleasant—the bridegroom not being precisely in the first flower of youth. The solution devised was very neat. He and Nini would be married by proxy. So it was that Nini set off for Paris on the appointed day clutching a sworn affidavit from her husband and, indeed, husband to be. Armed with this she appeared in the chapel of the archbishop in the cathedral of Notre-Dame, knelt solemnly by herself to be joined in holy matrimony to Henri Philippe Pétain, Marshal of France.

Pétain spent much of the rest of March and early April visiting the provincial towns—and then made another blunder. Against his—admittedly feeble—opposition, Darlan had succumbed to German demands to set up a Commission Général aux Questions Juives. By early April Xavier Vallat, a former deputy of pronounced anti-Semitic views, had become its first head. Its function was to enforce the existing law against Jews, to coordinate them with the ordinances issued by the German military governor in France—and to devise further laws. Vallat was to prove rigorous in his task, and there was little Pétain could or wanted to do to restrain him. Vallat's unpopularity was in time to rub off on Pétain himself. The announcement, and Vallat's appointment, were greeted in most of unoccupied France with outright hostility.

It was this hostility which encouraged the fledgling resistance groups to become bolder. In response, on 7 April Pétain delivered his first attack on the "dissidents," as he called them. In a radio broadcast he stressed the need for national unity, and went on to criticize "propaganda, subtle, insidious, inspired by Frenchmen. . . . Halted for a moment, the calls to dissidence take up again each day a tone which is ever more arrogant."[14] To shore up further the government's position, Darlan extended the application of the oath of personal allegiance to Pétain to magistrates and, above all, the army.

This was for Pétain a personal Rubicon. For the whole of his life, Pétain had been educated to believe that it was the duty of the army to obey the instructions of a duly constituted civil authority. If that authority changed complexion the army would obey the instructions of the new authority. That had been the rule which had proved a binding force in the turbulent French politics ever since the Revolution. That was now to change. From the most senior general to the humblest *poilu* all were solemnly bound to obey without hesitation or question Pétain's orders, however eccentric they might be and whether or not Pétain was the duly constituted civil authority. Of all the measures which Pétain signed at Vichy it is this measure which brought him—against everything he had learnt in his military career—into the ranks of Hitler, Mussolini and Franco.

On 10 May Pétain heard that Darlan was summoned to see Hitler the following day. As Pétain soon found out, the German cold shoulder was thawing quickly. The Germans found that they had need of French cooperation. This was no longer a matter of mutual agreement for economic or even political cooperation. It was now about the military conduct of the war. The Germans wanted military collaboration—not just civil cooperation—in the French protectorates of the Levant.

Since the outbreak of war the tranquil life of the French forces in the Levantine protectorates, Syria and Lebanon, had hardly been disturbed. They had, of course, welcomed the armistice, and followed instructions from Vichy. Their commander-in-chief was General Henri-Fernand Dentz, an Alsatian whose father had emigrated to France in 1871 to prevent his sons becoming German citizens. Dentz was a faithful supporter of Pétain's government, although he disliked the Germans, on the grounds that they had "germanized" Alsace in July 1940 and expelled many Alsatian refugees into unoccupied France.

Dentz had been rather put out in early February 1941 to receive a signal from Darlan instructing him to give all necessary facilities to two German intelligence agents, by the names of von Hintig and Rosen, who duly arrived disguised as commercial travelers. They were there to make contact with German sympathizers—and to survey the possibilities for German use of Syrian airfields.

For the next six months, Dentz's life became a misery. On 2 May the prime minister of Iraq, Rashid Ali, after prolonged German wooing, staged an anti-British coup d'état in Baghdad and laid siege to the British base at Habbaniya airport. The overland route to India, as well as the Iraqi oilfields, were in danger of being lost to the British. But Rashid Ali needed German help if he was to fight off the task force of British, Australian and Free French troops which was even then being mobilized in northern Palestine.

Abetz had sent for Darlan and had proposed a deal. Procedures at the demarcation line would be made less onerous, the costs of occupation payable by France would be reduced, prisoners of war who had fought in the First World War would be repatriated and there would be limited permission for rearmament of French naval vessels. In return, the French would provide arms for Rashid Ali and allow German planes to land, refuel and, if necessary be repaired, at French-controlled airfields in Syria.

On 6 May, without consulting the holidaying Pétain, Darlan agreed, and was invited to meet Hitler at Berchtesgaden. At the meeting, on 11 May, Darlan expected Hitler to express his gratitude for Darlan's efforts. Hitler, however, was not in that sort of mood. He snapped at Darlan that the sort of cooperation envisaged at Montoire was no longer on the agenda. Since Germany was certainly going to win the war, France had a decision to make: either she collaborated fully or she would suffer the consequences. In other words, she would be treated like Poland, as an appendage to the greater Reich. That, in his view, was the end of the matter.

Darlan returned to Vichy. His report was written out in full, and, as though by way of insurance, also sent to the governors of the French colonies. "If we favor Britain," he wrote, "France will be smashed, dismembered and will not survive as a nation. If we try to follow a balanced policy between the two adversaries . . . the eventual peace terms will be disastrous. If we collaborate with Germany, without agreeing to make war against England alongside her, we can save the French nation . . . and play an honorable, even important role in the Europe of the future."[15]

Pétain was yet again in a quandary, which was becoming familiar. He had agreed with the principle of a direct meeting between Darlan and Hitler. He had also been prepared for German aircraft to use French airfields in Syria. But he had not expected Darlan to go much further. This Darlan did, and Pétain, having given his initial approval, was unable to stop him. By 28 May he had signed three separate agreements. The first was to allow the Germans to use Syrian airfields; the second was to allow Bizerta and Sousse in Tunisia to be used as transshipment points for General Erwin Rommel's Afrika Corps in North Africa; and the third was to allow German submarines to use Dakar as a U-boat base from which to attack Allied merchant shipping in the Atlantic.

These agreements, known as the "Paris Protocols," were brought back by Darlan to Vichy for approval. It was immediately clear that they were a great deal more than the original agreement for the use of Syrian airfields. The second and third protocols were tantamount to wholesale military collaboration with the Germans, only just stopping short of a declaration of war against Britain. Darlan had wildly exceeded his brief. It was no doubt a bold initiative, but he still had to carry Pétain with him—and Pétain was not to be carried. There was no question of his approving the second and third protocols. On the other hand, he could not openly disavow Darlan's signature.

Pétain saw only one way out of the confusion. On 2 June he summoned Weygand from North Africa. As it happened, Weygand had heard about the protocols and had already decided to fight the battle in Vichy. Weygand marched into Pétain's offices and refused, as governor general, to put any base in North Africa at the disposal of the Germans or the Italians. French Africa, he went on, would defend itself against whoever attacks it, but France must not, he emphasized finally, deliberately go to war against her former ally.

On the morning of 3 June Pétain called together a small group of ministers, including Weygand. "I recall the scene," Berthelot said later. "Darlan made a cold exposé in an icy silence. He hadn't read the papers. He simply gave an analysis. Weygand was on the Marshal's left; I felt him boiling like a racehorse wanting to jump and Darlan had hardly finished before General Weygand took the offensive—and the word represents precisely what passed. The [Darlan] Protocols were killed on 3 June."[16]

Weygand went on to say that he would resign. That afternoon Pétain, Huntziger, Laure and others pleaded with him to withdraw. Weygand replied that he would only withdraw if the Germans were asked for concessions which they could not possibly grant: French sovereignty over the whole of France; liberation of all prisoners; guarantee of nonintervention in all French colonies; Alsace and Lorraine to be "ungermanized"; and so on. On 14 June Darlan sent a note to that effect to Abetz. Negotiations on the protocols were immediately broken off.

There has been much debate on whether Weygand was the decisive voice in forcing Darlan to abandon the military collaboration enshrined in the Paris Protocols, or whether Darlan himself was already having second thoughts; the matter even now remains in doubt. What is clear, however, is that Darlan drew back from the position he had taken and that, in doing so, he had the support of Pétain. Unless Berthelot's evidence at Pétain's trial is no more than fabrication—unlikely, since it was given under oath—Pétain's view at the time was plain and, unlike his views on previous (and future) occasions, unusually clear. He was not prepared to concede any more than the limited military collaboration already conceded—the use of the Syrian airfields.

As it happened, the Syrian airfields soon passed out of history, and Dentz's misery came to an end. On 8 June the motley Allied army in Palestine crossed into the Lebanon. Dentz's troops formed up to stop them. Although the Free French were led by a band playing the "Marseillaise" as loudly as possible, the Vichy soldiers were not impressed. One battalion of the Foreign Légion, on the Free French side, refused to fire on their Vichy opponents and had to be withdrawn. It was only when Rashid Ali's rebellion collapsed that the British General Archibald Wavell was able to send reinforcements into Syria. At that point Dentz had had enough, and sued for peace.

There was, however, a strange and revealing twist to the whole episode. On 20 June, while negotiations for an armistice in Syria and Lebanon were about to begin, Pétain decided to renew contact with the British. An emissary was smuggled from Vichy to London by the British secret services. He informed Churchill that Dentz's government had been instructed to "carry on with their duties in collaboration with the Free French Forces" after the British occupied Syria.[17] Both Pétain and Churchill were trying to keep lines of communication open, however unorthodox the means. But, as it turned out, there were greater—much greater—events about to take place in Eastern Europe. On 22 June 1941, at four o'clock in the morning, Hitler's armies invaded the Soviet Union. It was to mark, with all the necessary hindsight, a turning point in a war which had been until then a list of German military successes. Few suspected it at the time, but there was one man who understood very clearly what it meant. When Weygand heard the news, he immediately called Robert Murphy, Roosevelt's personal envoy to North Africa. "I found him minus his usual composure and in a state of exhilaration," Murphy later wrote. "He said without further ado: 'When we discussed the war and you expressed your belief that Britain would win in the end, I asked you where the divisions would come from. Now I know where they will come from—Russia. Germany has lost the war!'"[18]

The Specter of Communism

"J'ai des choses graves à vous dire."

Early in the evening of 12 August 1941 *le tout Vichy*, or at least those who could afford the tickets and the required elegance of dress, arrived at the Opera House for a performance of Mussorgsky's *Boris Godunov*. Ambassador Leahy and Mrs. Leahy were, of course, present. In the interval between the third and fourth acts there was an unexpected interruption. Marshal Pétain, it was announced, was to make a radio broadcast which was to be relayed direct to the Opera House.

By way of introduction to what became an extended address, Pétain began by announcing solemnly that he had "serious things to say." These included that cooperation with Germany was no short-term matter; patience was of the essence, since Germany was now embarked on the defense of Western civilization against the "Bolshevism" of the East. Pétain went on to speak about the sins of capitalism. "I intend that our country should be removed from the most untrustworthy guardianship: that of money." How this should be done was far from clear. Pétain rambled on. France, he said, could only be governed from Paris, but he himself could not take up his position there "until certain possibilities are offered to me."[1] Until that was done, France had to stand on her own feet and govern herself properly.

Thereupon, to the dismay of the opera audience, he proceeded to announce measures which were tantamount to the introduction of a police state. As Leahy listened, he "had a feeling that Hitler must have written the speech."[2] "Authority," Pétain asserted in his by then quavering voice, "no longer comes from below. It is only and entirely that which I grant and that which I delegate."[3] All political parties were abolished; no political meetings, either in public or in private, were to be held; political literature was no longer to be distributed; parliamentary immunity from prosecution was removed as of 30 September; no Freemason could hold any public office; the police budget would be doubled; the powers of regional *Préfets* were to be increased; all ministers and senior officials were to swear an oath of personal loyalty to himself. "This first series of measures will reassure Frenchmen who only think of the health of their country."[4] On that note, he ended—piously—"Vive la France!"

Most of those present, and certainly all the diplomats, understood that the Vichy government was entering a new phase. There was then a good deal of whispering before the final act of *Godunov*, in which, by the curious irony of which history is sometimes capable, they watched the destruction of a previously distinguished and popular military figure who had subsequently claimed for himself authoritarian power. To complete the irony, the language in which they were hearing it was Russian—the language which Pétain believed to be the true language of Bolshevism.

The German invasion of Russia had provided the backdrop for Pétain's hard, authoritarian, almost Tsarist, line. Not only had Darlan severed diplomatic relations with Moscow abruptly on 30 June (Leahy had had to intervene on behalf of his friend the Soviet ambassador Alexander Bogomolov to delay his departure on the grounds that he had a baby too small to travel), but, more important, the Soviets had released French communists from their previous obligation not to attack Germans and indeed encouraged them to use whatever means they chose to do precisely that. The specter of communism which Pétain—and others—had always feared seemed to be haunting not just Europe but France herself.

It was not only the communists. July 1941 had been an altogether uneasy month in Vichy. Vallat had produced further measures against Jews. They were to be excluded altogether from employment by banks and other financial institutions, and there was to be a ceiling on their numbers in law and in medicine. Darlan had reported to Pétain on 21 July that these measures were unpopular. So they were, but that was, to Pétain, neither here nor there. What was closer to home was Darlan's complaint about Ménétrel, that he was in league with a Colonel Georges Groussard, who, Darlan claimed, was in turn in league with the British and whom he had had arrested. In normal times, all that could be brushed aside as little more than domestic political froth. But these were not normal times, and a quarrel between his immediate deputy and his doctor (and confidant) was a nuisance, and perhaps more than a nuisance, to Pétain himself.

Internationally, Darlan had irritated the United States by conceding to Japan the use of French bases in Indo-China, and he had irritated the Germans by continuing to press for a permanent and comprehensive arrangement to replace the armistice, claiming that the French military collaboration in Syria merited sympathetic treatment from Berlin. He had thus failed to understand either the strength of American feeling about Japan or the German view that with the collapse of Vichy forces in Syria they no longer had any need of, or wish for, French cooperation.

In short, July had produced for Pétain no successes and a number of failures. The communists had been let out of their cage. It followed to Pétain's military mind that this was not a time to allow internal dissent. Order in "France" had to be maintained and strengthened. Treason was in the air—Freemasons, as always, apparently at the fore. It was no longer a matter of settling gently the mutinies of 1917, however much he referred to them in his speeches. A hard fist was now needed.

Pétain appointed Darlan to Weygand's old job of minister of defense, giving him overall control of the armed forces, including those in North Africa—much to Weygand's irritation. In short, Darlan was the one to apply the hard fist. Moreover, in order to win back favor with Berlin, both he and Darlan would both give tacit, and at times open, support to those members of the Legion who volunteered to join with the German army in the attack on the Soviet Union—even to the point of their swearing an oath of personal allegiance to Hitler.

Pétain's personal image had received something of a battering since the beginning of 1941. It now needed to be restored and, indeed, enhanced. Pétain wanted this under his own close control; and, to ensure this was so, he put Ménétrel in charge of it. Ménétrel, wholly unqualified though he was, turned out to be a surprisingly good choice. Photographs of Pétain, statuettes, portraits, porcelain carrying his portrait—all, of course, carefully vetted—were widely distributed. References to Pétain in news bulletins or newspapers were encouraged and required to emphasize his wise, patriotic and caring nature. (Nobody, for instance, was allowed to refer to Pétain in connection with the volunteers from the Legion who were fighting for the Germans in Russia. Even references to him as the "Victor of Verdun" were ruled out on the grounds that he would appear too militaristic.) There were pamphlets, calendars, children's stories and diaries—all with flattering portraits or potted biographies, or pictures to color in. To cap it all, a special medal was designed by a jeweler, to be known as *la francisque*, a miniature marshal's baton topped by a double-headed axe, to be awarded to those who showed particular and personal devotion to the Marshal. There is no doubt that for the 85-year-old Pétain all this was a matter of quiet satisfaction. But there was one ceremony he enjoyed above all. On two Thursdays in each month there was an opportunity for his "children" to come to the Hôtel du Parc to greet him. Groups of Boy Scouts, members of the Légion, school parties, workers' delegations and any other suitable body crowded in for the occasion. Pétain patted them on the head or shook their hand as appropriate and proceeded to give them all presents—usually portraits of himself in one form or another.

Pétain took a week off at L'Ermitage in early October. He wanted to reflect on what had happened since June 1940. Disappointingly, there had been no peace treaty. The whole premise on which the armistice was based—a quick German victory over Britain followed by a general European settlement, in which Germany would be the senior European ally to a France which, thanks to the National Revolution, would have sloughed off the political weaknesses of the past—seemed further away than ever from realization. But he still believed that cooperation with Germany was the only possible policy. As he had told Serrigny the previous May, "negotiations [with Germany] will certainly take a long time. But, in spite of everything, they must come to a conclusion. If the war is prolonged, we must be able to live and, above all, to eat. We can only do that with German permission."[5]

While at L'Ermitage, Pétain also decided that it was time to bring fully to book, as he put it, those responsible for France's defeat in the previous year. He had already authorized the creation of a Council of Political Justice—the members, of course, to be nominated by himself. On 15 October, by then back in Vichy, he announced that the council, made up mainly of veterans of the First World War, had concluded that Daladier, Blum and Gamelin were guilty and should be detained indefinitely, the most severe punishment allowed to the council. But this was not good enough. Pétain therefore decided to ignore the decision of the council and to refer the case to the judicial court at Riom. In doing so, he publicly expressed his clear understanding that the court would find them guilty and mete out severer punishment.

Even in Vichy, virtual police state as it had by then become, this procedure was, to say the least, unusual. It was one thing to ask for a trial. It was quite another thing for the head of state to announce the verdict of the trial in advance. So unusual was it that the presiding judge at Riom, even though he had sworn the oath of personal allegiance to Pétain, announced in open court, on the first day of the hearing, that he would act as though the proceedings in the Council of Political Justice (and, by implication, Pétain's intervention) had never occurred. This allowed the defendants to put up such a spirited defense—Blum's speech was particularly impressive—that the hearing only lasted a few weeks and was abandoned in April 1942, by which time the whole thing had descended into humiliating farce.

On the 22nd, the anniversary of Montoire, Pétain wrote what can only be described as a groveling letter to Hitler saying that the victory of the Germans over "Bolshevism" offered new hope for a Europe in which the peoples of Germany and France could unite their efforts. Hitler's response was contemptuous. None of that mattered, he replied. What mattered was the assassination of German troops on French territory.

The communist resistance had become active—and violent. On 21 August, their first effort, in Paris, had cost the life of a German soldier. It was only by setting up a special section within the courts with the power to condemn to death anybody found guilty of "subversion"—another product of the Vichy police state, proposed by Pucheu and approved by Pétain himself—that reprisal executions had been avoided. But just as Pétain's groveling letter to Hitler was being sent, a German officer was assassinated in Nantes. This time the German authorities were not to be deterred. Fifty hostages, randomly selected in Paris, Nantes and Châteaubriant, were to be shot immediately, and a further 50 in due course unless the culprits were surrendered immediately.

Pétain was having a quiet lunch with friends near Vichy when Ménétrel arrived to tell him the news. By all accounts, Pétain was obviously—upset. Innocent Frenchmen were to be murdered by the invader. That was bad enough. But, almost as bad as that, what he believed to be his and Darlan's carefully constructed efforts to join forces with Germany in the new Europe were being undermined by communist criminals. On 23 October he therefore made another broadcast. France, he said, had laid down her arms. She had no right to pick them up again to shoot Germans in the back. "One guilty man found," he said, "would save the lives of one hundred Frenchmen."[6]

The following morning, at seven o'clock, Ménétrel, du Moulin and Laure pushed their way into Pétain's bedroom to announce that the first 50 hostages had indeed been shot, that his broadcast had gone down badly and that public opinion was unanimous in condemning German brutality. Pétain was clearly distraught—almost in tears. He had, he said, spent a sleepless night. This was not at all meant to be the result of cooperation with Germany. Laure and du Moulin then explained their plan. Pétain would announce that he would surrender himself to the German authorities as a hostage in place of the next 50.

The plan was, quite simply, absurd. Nevertheless, all was prepared. Laure and Ménétrel were to accompany Pétain and stand with him on the Demarcation Line, which defined the border between the occupied and unoccupied Zones. But there was a snag. The government had to be informed. When they heard about the plan, Darlan and Pucheu said bluntly that it was quite ridiculous. Others agreed. Faced with this barrage, Pétain conceded and the project was called off. Pétain was reduced to sending a telegram to Hitler deploring the attacks on members of the army of occupation.

As if that was not enough, Pétain was worried about his own position, which was becoming more difficult. German pressure and petty jealousies among ministers created unpleasant diversions. On 8 November, for instance, Darlan delivered an ultimatum to Pétain: he would resign if Weygand was not sacked. At the funeral of General Huntziger, who had been killed on 11 November when his plane had tried to land at Vichy airport in bad visibility (and with obsolete radio equipment), Abetz handed Pétain a letter from Hitler stating bluntly that cooperation between the two countries was out of the question while Weygand was still there. Furthermore, Abetz said firmly that no German negotiator would even bother to sit down with a Frenchman unless

Weygand was removed. As though to emphasize his point, he went on to say that he was leaving in Vichy as consul general one of his closest associates, Roland Krug von Nidda.

Pétain, yet again, caved in. On 16 November Weygand was summoned once more to Vichy. He brought with him a memorandum pointing out the importance of keeping the Germans out of French North Africa. Pétain ignored this, again offered Weygand another job and, when that was refused, on 18 November told him that he was dismissed.

The following day Leahy requested, and was granted, an interview with Pétain—alone. Leahy pointed out "very clearly that the heretofore friendly and sympathetic attitude of the American Government was based on the assumption that he would not in his relations with the Axis powers go beyond the requirements of the Armistice Agreement and that a removal of General Weygand under German pressure cannot be considered by anybody to be necessitated by the Armistice Agreement." Pétain replied that the Germans had exerted increasing pressure, that they had sent him a "brutal diktat threatening in the event of refusal [to sack Weygand] to occupy all of France, to feed the army of occupation with French foodstuffs and to permit the native population to die of hunger." Faced with such a threat he claimed that he had could do no other than to yield to their demand.[7]

In his comments to Roosevelt on the interview, Leahy described Pétain as "a feeble, frightened old man . . . surrounded by conspirators . . . devoted to the Axis philosophy . . . Darlan . . . Pucheu . . . Benoist-Méchin . . . De Brinon . . . Marion . . . Bouthillier . . . Lehideux." Pucheu, in particular, not only wanted Pétain's job but "is busily engaged in building up via the Légion des Anciens Combattants what is intended to become an effective Ku-Klux Klan and which is already operating as such to some extent." Finally, his verdict on Pétain was equally harsh. "While one may be fully justified in looking at the difficulties of the Marshal's ending years with understanding sympathy, it seems necessary to reluctantly relinquish what was perhaps always a faint hope that it might be possible for me through friendly personal relations and pertinent advice to give some semblance of backbone to a jellyfish."[8]

Feeble and frightened he might have been, but Pétain thought that he had managed to secure one concession from the Germans. "The rumor of an interview between [Pétain] and Hitler is true," the Turkish ambassador to Vichy signaled Ankara (his message was intercepted by the British). "It will take place in Occupied France after the capture of Moscow."[9] It was not to be quite like that—in two respects: first, the Germans failed to capture Moscow and, second, it was not Hitler that Pétain was to meet but Göring.

The meeting took place on 1 December 1941 at Saint-Florentin in the department of the Yonne. Göring's train was a formidable sight. It was fully armored, with platforms for anti-aircraft canons and heavy machine guns. Around the station where it was parked a battalion of fully armed infantry patrolled, and a squadron of Messerschmitt 109 fighter aircraft flew up and down overhead. Göring wanted from Pétain both military collaboration and the use of North African bases. Pétain in turn wanted German concessions. He recited from a prepared paper, admitting that a head of state cannot govern without the consent of the governed and that he no longer had that support—because the policy of cooperation with Germany had not brought tangible results to his people. There followed a list of French requirements: the liberation of prisoners of war, the removal of the Demarcation Line, the rearming of the French Army and an end to German interference in French administrative matters. He claimed that Germany had broken the promises made at Montoire. Göring listened with impatience— finally saying: "But, Marshal, I thought that it was you who had been defeated."[10]

The meeting with Göring had, to say the least, not been a success. Pétain had somehow deluded himself that there could be a conversation between former military officers and between the two countries as equals. He had told Göring that Germany could not make peace without France. Göring found this impertinent. Pétain failed, yet again, to realize that Germany had no need of, and no particular affection for, France as such. The only reason the Germans were prepared to talk to the French was because of the French fleet and the North African colonies, which, if they were delivered to the Allies, would make the German military position in Libya untenable.

Matters were made very much more complicated by the German and Italian declaration of war on the United States on 11 December 1941, after the Japanese attack on Pearl Harbor. That, together with the failure of the German armies to break the Soviets in their first onslaught, gave both Pétain and Darlan pause. It was possible—just—that Germany would not, after all, win the war. Given that, they would have to decide where they stood—and they would have to decide quickly, since the Americans would want to know. Sure enough, Leahy was sent to sound them out. It was Darlan who answered, but Pétain clearly agreed. Vichy wished to remain neutral and outside what was now a world war but "they were powerless to resist German ultimatums."[11] Pétain intervened to say that the Germans could starve the French civilian population should they so choose. But they reiterated that they wished to remain neutral, and, by way of reassurance, they agreed to set out their position in writing. This was done, and Roosevelt, when he received it, expressed his "profound satisfaction."[12]

On 1 January 1942 Pétain broadcast a New Year message. "For the first time," wrote Serrigny, "he dared to tell the truth, that is to say that he is not free and traitors are to be found not only in London but also in Paris."[13] He also repeated the message he had given to Roosevelt on neutrality. He went on to say that France's position would be noticed by Germany—and he hoped that it would lead to a softening of the terms of the armistice. Finally, he warned his compatriots against giving any sympathy to those in the press or on the radio who both preached disunity and attacked the National Revolution (which, he was forced to admit, was not moving ahead with the speed he had hoped).

Du Moulin described the broadcast as signaling a policy of "wait and see." For their part, the Germans did not like it at all. Krug von Nidda and Abetz remarked that Pétain seemed not to have paid attention to Göring's message— that France had lost the war. But Pétain was unrepentant. In fact, he was rather pleased with himself, particularly since his broadcast had been well received in Unoccupied France.

But by the end of January Pétain's policy of remaining neutral in the world conflict was looking very frayed. American intelligence had noted that French ships were transporting heavy-duty lorries and even guns and oil to Rommel in North Africa. Leahy complained to Darlan, who replied that he was under an obligation to honor the agreement he had made with the Italians in December 1941 to make shipments of supplies on a regular basis in order to prevent the seizure of Bizerta. Leahy was then officially instructed to see Weygand and get him to agree to come out of retirement and return to North Africa under American protection. At the same time, Pétain was under relentless pressure from Abetz and, inside his own government, from Pucheu.[14] Abetz had hatched a plan, which may even have had Hitler's blessing, for a peace treaty if Vichy would declare public support for the German war effort. In practice, this meant either a declaration of war or a clear and unambiguous statement of support of Germany. The matter was discussed in Vichy in January, and there were those who were attracted by the idea. Even Darlan wavered. After all, a complete post-war settlement was exactly what he had been working for. Pétain only managed to fend off the plan's supporters by reciting the assurances of French neutrality he had personally given to Roosevelt.

On 24 February 1942, Krug von Nidda relayed a message from Abetz to Pétain. The message was blunt. Things were going wrong. Darlan had lost the confidence of the Germans. There was only one way to repair the damaged relations between France and Germany: Pierre Laval should be put back in charge. For Pétain the message was the worst possible news. Not only was Laval just as—if not more—scornful as Darlan about the National Revolution; he was rightly perceived as altogether too wedded to the policy of full cooperation with Germany. Pétain realized that his careful assurances to the Americans about French neutrality would go for nothing if Laval were to be put in charge.

Throughout the month of March rumors flew around Vichy. There was, it was said, to be a drastic ministerial reshuffle, the important ministerial posts to be given to German nominees. It was even hinted that the Germans were about to appoint a *Gauleiter*, who would take over from Pétain and run unoccupied France under instruction from Berlin. This particular rumor was confirmed when Laval's son-in-law—and emissary—René de Chambrun arrived in Vichy on 24 March. He saw Pétain briefly, but the main part of his message was delivered to Bonhomme. It was simple. The Germans were disenchanted with Darlan. Either Laval was brought back or the Germans would resort to "extreme measures (nomination of a *Gauleiter* etc . . .)."[15]

But Laval was no more likeable in the spring of 1942 than he had been in the winter of 1940. For the moment, Pétain refused to make any promises. It was not only Pétain who didn't want Laval back. Leahy was directed by Washington to tell Pétain that the appointment of Laval to any important post in the government would make it impossible for the United States to continue its generally sympathetic attitude toward France. (Privately, the Americans referred to Laval as "Black Peter.") The message was delivered on 30 March. The American threat had its effect. Pétain told Laval that he had given up the idea of recalling him. The Americans would not have it.

But Abetz was turning up the psychological heat. On 5 April an article appeared in *Le Nouveau Temps*, under the name of Jean Luchaire, stating that not a single day should be lost in putting a stop to American blackmail. It was a question, Luchaire went on, of choosing between Washington and Berlin. The article was broadcast on the Paris radio.

On 13 April Fernand de Brinon flew to Vichy to see Pétain. A quick decision, he said, was essential to avoid a German takeover. Darlan agreed. He would step down as vice-premier if Laval became premier, as long as he remained commander-in-chief of the armed forces. Pétain finally caved in. Darlan and de Brinon went off to see Laval, who, conveniently, was staying in his house at Chateldon. The deal was done, and was duly sealed in a meeting between Laval and Pétain the following morning. "The disquiet in the Marshal's entourage," Serrigny noted, "is very great, because of the feebleness shown by the Head of State in this affair as in many others."[16]

On 18 April 1942 the new government was announced. Laval became Head of Government, foreign minister, minister of the interior and minister of information. Constitutional Act No. 11 was produced to make it all official. It was clear enough. The effective direction of France's internal and external policy was to be assumed by the Head of Government, appointed by the Head of State and answerable only to him. In theory, Pétain was still able to dismiss the Head of Government. In practice, those around him knew that Pétain, if he had ever done such a thing, would be inviting a German occupation.

On 26 April Pétain entered his eighty-sixth year. In his old age, he was pleased, perhaps too pleased, that he was still the object of veneration. But he had been confronted with the truth: he was no longer in charge of events. Then, on the morning of Tuesday, 21 April 1942, just as Leahy was preparing to leave on his recall to Washington, Mrs. Leahy died from a post-operative embolism in La Pergola Clinic in Vichy. Pétain, to his credit, was courteous to the end. He sent flowers, and provided a special private car to take her body on the first stage of its journey back home to her final resting place in Arlington Cemetery. Leahy's departure was not just a matter of regret for Pétain. He had lost, in Leahy and Mrs. Leahy, two good and honest friends. In truth, he had few good and honest friends left.

The Trap

"Je vais lui mettre tellement de responsabilité sur le dos qu'il succombera."

In mid-April 1942 political Vichy was in a state of the highest excitement. On 19 April there was a flurry of announcements. The new government saw most of Pétain's ministers cleaned out, particularly those whom Laval suspected of involvement in the plot against him of December 1940. Pucheu, too, was out— too ambitious and not to be trusted, it was said. Finance went to Pierre Cathala, a known Laval loyalist. Also promoted were Benoist-Méchin and Marion. The ultra-collaborationist de Brinon was brought back from Paris to Vichy as a secretary of state and Abel Bonnard, who had developed a fascination for National Socialism in the 1930s, was given—to much wringing of hands in Pétain's entourage—the education portfolio.

Pétain put up no opposition to Laval's appointments. When asked by Serrigny why he had not protested he replied that "I had to concede; they had forced me." But in the same conversation he went on "The next months will reveal the game on the military chess board. We will know in October whether the Germans can be victorious. At that moment it will be up to us to decide."[1] Others, given their doubts about the old man's resolve, decided they had had enough. When they heard of Laval's appointments, du Moulin de Labarthète and Laure resigned. At that point, it was not only Pétain's remaining friends who were disappearing; his favorite trusties were disappearing as well. The fall-out from Laval's new government was that Pétain not only found his position much diminished but found himself even more dependent for companionship—if only for someone he could talk to—on his personal doctor, Bernard Ménétrel.

It had become a strange relationship. It was as though Ménétrel had assumed the role of a surrogate wife. He had, by mid-April 1942, become Pétain's only daily confidant. Their walks were a daily ritual. Even in the coldest weather Pétain and Ménétrel would set out, Pétain with his walking stick, black overcoat with an astrakhan collar, and a black Homburg hat sitting flat on his head, Ménétrel with a simpler, but equally black, overcoat and a trilby at a more rakish angle. Pétain's true wife, the neglected Nini, might, in terms of the politics of the day, just as well not have existed. Nor was she much welcome even as company. In fact, Pétain, true to form, preferred the company of younger women, of whom there were many in the Vichy of the day to sit at his feet.

In a broadcast on 21 April, Laval announced bluntly that France was faced with a choice. It was "either to be integrated in a new, pacified Europe . . . or resign ourselves to seeing the disappearance of our civilization. . . . No threat will prevent me from pursuing agreement and reconciliation with Germany."[2] "Pierre Laval," as Leahy remarked after their meeting on 27 April, "is definitely not on our side."[3]

On 4 May 1942 Laval made another move. He took over the personal direction of the Legion. That done, the Service d'Ordre Légionnaire, originally set up to keep order at the Légion's rallies, was given a wider role as a shadow police force. Its young recruits would appear in khaki shirts, black berets and ties, wielding thick batons whenever there was likely to be trouble on the streets of Vichy—or Lyon or Marseille or Toulouse. Joseph Darnand, its commander, was far from shy in the brutal use of force. In fact, Pétain himself approved of Darnand's hard hand, not least because the Légion's members were not only required to take the oath of personal loyalty to him (after an all-night vigil reminiscent of the rituals of medieval knighthood) but were dedicated to the fight against communism and for the National Revolution.

As might be imagined, the new authoritarian state was far from popular. Those who opposed the régime were becoming both more numerous and better organized. From the other side, however, came continued political attack—continual sniping from the Paris collaborationists, particularly Déat and Doriot, and also from Abetz and Krug von Nidda. There were thus attacks from all sides. But that was not the end of it. In this already heated atmosphere an event occurred which raised the political temperature to even higher levels. On 25 April 1942 there arrived in Vichy a most distinguished escaped prisoner, none other than General Henri Honoré Giraud.

Giraud was, without a doubt, a figure in the greatest of French traditions. He had been a hero in both wars. In the first he had been left for dead on the battlefield, had been captured, had escaped and then operated clandestinely behind enemy lines (his description of those adventures had enthralled Churchill when he visited Giraud's positions on the Maginot Line in 1937). In the second war, he had been in the northern sector, commanding first the 7th and then the 9th French armies, with as much distinction as was possible under the circumstances, until he was captured on 19 May 1940. A carefully guarded prisoner of war, on 17 April 1942 he slid down a 150-foot rope to escape from his prison in the fortress of Königstein on the river Elbe, in spite of lameness from an earlier wound which had healed badly. He had then made his way through Switzerland to unoccupied France—determined to carry on the fight against Germany.

Giraud's arrival in Vichy could hardly pass unnoticed. In that small community, as he walked around the streets, he commanded universal attention. He was very tall—some 6' 5" inches and he sported a truly magnificent moustache, curled in the form of a saber. True, there were those who whispered maliciously that his brain had not grown in the same proportion as his body, but he was a five-star general, and above all, a courageous Frenchman who had defied the enemy.

Pétain, of course, welcomed his fellow soldier with the hospitality he deserved "with a most generous lunch."[4] He was perhaps less pleased when Giraud told him roundly that Germany would certainly be defeated and that it was time to strike a deal with the Americans. Laval, for his part, was very much less pleased. Hitler had been furious at Giraud's escape, and Laval complained that it was a serious blow to his policy of Franco-German cooperation. He was also worried that the French prisoners of war still in Germany would suffer as a result.

Laval then came up with a plan: Giraud should return voluntarily to his German prison. The idea was that he would then be released again formally and without delay. The problem was that the idea needed Giraud's agreement, and Giraud was certainly not in a mood to agree. He would only return to Germany, he said, if all married prisoners of war were released. The proposition was put to Abetz, who pointed out that that meant some five or six hundred thousand prisoners and that Hitler would never agree to it. Giraud then replied that he would only return to prison if specifically ordered to by Pétain. He knew perfectly well that Pétain would never sign such an order; and when it was suggested to Pétain he did indeed refuse to do so. Giraud then broke off all negotiation on the matter and left for his house in Lyon. Only later did it emerge that when there he immediately started meeting an intermediary sent for the purpose by Roosevelt's envoy in North Africa, Robert Murphy.

Giraud was not the only one in touch with the Americans. As far back as March Darlan had come to the conclusion that Germany would not win the war. Even then, he had started to plan his escape route. He had asked one of his closest colleagues, Admiral Raymond Fénard, to get in touch with Murphy on his behalf. The conversations had been intermittent, but with Laval's return, Darlan had even greater reason to jump ship. Not only was he furious at his dismissal but he believed that Pétain had no control over Laval.

None of this helped Laval in his efforts to secure a solid basis for Franco-German cooperation. In fact, the whole Giraud episode led to what he had feared—the removal of a number of concessions to French prisoners of war. On 21 March Hitler had appointed Fritz Sauckel as commissar-general for labor, with a brief to oversee a program of milking occupied territories of workers to replace Germans who had left to join the armed forces. Sauckel was, not to put too fine a point on it, a deeply unpleasant Nazi bully. For him, there was no question of negotiation with the French, whether occupied or not. He proposed to transfer to Germany no fewer than 350,000 workers from both zones, half of whom would be skilled workers, mostly from metal-working firms. Laval argued that the way to get the idea accepted was for one prisoner of war to be released for every worker sent to Germany. Sauckel eventually agreed to reduce the total number to 250,000 and to accept a ratio of one prisoner for every three workers. As it turned out, the results were disappointing. By mid-August fewer than 40,000 workers had volunteered. As a result, no more than 11,000 prisoners of war returned. The Germans were in no mood to make any further concessions, and the scheme, rather than remaining purely voluntary, would be imposed later on in the year.

While all this was going on an even more sinister policy had been put in place. In January 1942, at a conference on the Wannsee in Berlin, the decision had been taken by a group of senior Nazis assembled under Heinrich Himmler to "cleanse" Europe of all Jews. Furthermore, Unoccupied France was not to be exempt. In mid-June the Germans demanded the deportation of 10,000 Jews from Vichy France. On 2 July Karl Oberg, the SS officer in charge of policing the occupied Zone, met the Vichy chief of police, René Bousquet, to organize the round-up. Bousquet pleaded that it would be something of an embarrassment if the French police were obliged to carry it out; Oberg then agreed that it would only be foreign Jews who would be arrested. The next day the government ratified the agreement, but only after Laval had insisted that children under 16, hitherto excluded, should be put on the list. The sight of screaming children separated from their parents would be politically intolerable; they all had to go together. Moreover, Laval told ministers that the Jews were to be transported to a Jewish state in Eastern Europe. He later claimed that he really did believe what he was saying.

The operation went ahead. By the end of August over 6,500 foreign Jews had been taken, many from the concentration camps where they had been interned at the armistice, to special transit camps, before being transferred to the death camps to the east. Although the destination of the deportees was not known, the result in Unoccupied France of the sight of trains rolling out with their desperate cargo was to activate the first serious resistance to Vichy. Solidarité, for instance, set up a Mouvement national contre le racisme to publish illegal pamphlets urging the French people to help the Jews and calling on Christian clergymen to open their churches to protect Jews who might be threatened. The Comité de Nîmes, made up of Catholic and Protestant Christian relief organizations, actively worked on behalf of the Jews. The Central Consistory, which represented the Jewish leadership, kept closely in touch with Catholic bishops. Clandestine communist groups sheltered those who were threatened— frequently alerted by broadcasts from London.

On 18 August the Protestant priest Marc Boegner noted in his diary that Cardinal Gerlier had protested vigorously to the Préfet at Lyon about "the foreign Jews being delivered to Germany and delivered in conditions of inhumanity which were truly scandalous." Cardinal Suhard, too, had written to Pétain on the matter. Gerlier was to follow suit in a further letter to Pétain. "He believes that given the facts as established the Churches can no longer keep silent." But he did not see any point in writing to Laval. "His information gave him to believe that the initiative for the Jewish deportations came from him."[5]

The clerical protests, the public outrage when news of the deportations leaked out, and the consequent sympathy for the Resistance groups had their effect. Pétain told Laval that the policy was damaging to the government and to the reputation of the head of state. On 2 September Laval saw Oberg again and asked not to be required to arrest more Jews. Yet the deportations continued throughout the month. On 9 September Pastor Boegner saw Laval himself and made a detailed complaint about what was happening. Laval claimed that he did not know about the conditions and that Bousquet was responsible. In any event, he was not going to be deflected from cooperating with Germany. Nonetheless, by the end of September the deportations ceased (apart from four in November) until the end of 1942.

Yet Pétain's protests about the Jewish deportations were neither particularly strong nor particularly principled. His carefully cultivated image with his "children" was being damaged by Laval. In this, at least, he was right. But Pétain himself had already by then gone a long way toward damaging his own image. It was no longer a question of foreign Jews but of the future of Franco-German cooperation. By the end of May 1942 he had come to the conclusion that sooner or later there would be Anglo-American attacks on French coasts and on French North and West Africa. He told Abetz that such attacks were "inevitable."[6] He therefore suggested joint Franco-German staff discussions to plan the defense, particularly of North Africa. The Germans were reluctant, preferring instead to concentrate on getting their hands on French ships stranded in neutral ports.

Pétain's prediction was well founded. On 19 August, British and Canadian commandos staged a raid on Dieppe. The whole operation was bungled, and the raid was repulsed with heavy Allied losses. But Pétain was able to use the Dieppe opportunity to reiterate his request that to Hitler that France be allowed to participate in the defense of her own territory. No original text of his letter has survived (which led to doubts about its existence at Pétain's trial) but there seems little doubt that it was sent. "After a meeting I have just had with President Laval," it read, "and because of the latest British aggression which occurred this month on our territory I propose that you envisage the participation by France in her own defense. . . . I ask you, Chancellor, to consider this proposal as the sincere expression of my willingness to make a French contribution to safeguarding Europe."[7]

The intention was perfectly reasonable. If Germany was going to win the war, as Pétain still expected, it was only right that France should join in the defense of her own territory. Yet it handed the Germans another propaganda weapon. On 24 August the German-controlled Radio Paris announced that "the Marshal had warmly congratulated the commander in chief of the German forces in the occupied territory on his success in the region of Dieppe."[8] In fact, it is far from clear whether Pétain ever authorized such a message. Nevertheless, Pétain, by even writing at all in terms which moved from cooperation to military collaboration, had allowed himself to be caught in a dangerous public relations trap.

Pétain was not alone in falling into the trap. Laval had also given voice, and not just to his belief that Germany would win the war. In his broadcast of 22 June about the scheme to exchange French workers for French prisoners of war he had, in the middle, said that he "wished for a German victory since, without it, bolshevism would tomorrow establish itself everywhere."[9] The phrase itself was picked up and used against both Laval and Pétain in 1945. In his pretrial hearing, Pétain claimed that he had protested violently when the speech was discussed at a later meeting of ministers. Laval countered by claiming that he had discussed the speech with Pétain beforehand and that Pétain had only asked him to omit the words "believe in" but did not object to the words "wish for," on the grounds that "believe in" was an expression of a military opinion which Laval was not in a position to give. When the whole row erupted at Pétain's trial, evidence from Charles Rochat, the head of the ministry of foreign affairs at the time, confirmed Laval's version. Pétain had quite clearly seen Laval's draft. At this point, it is important to avoid the benefits of hindsight. Pétain had told Serrigny that October 1942 would be the month of decision. To most observers, in the summer and early autumn of 1942, it was quite clear which side was winning the war. The German offensive in Russia had reached as far as the river Volga, and General Erwin Rommel was not very far from the gates of Cairo. The British effort at Dieppe had been swept aside, and the Americans appeared to be more interested in the Pacific war with Japan than in adventures in the European theater. Stalingrad, Alamein and the invasion of North Africa—code-named Torch— were all in the future. Only Darlan had the foresight to suspect that the tide might be turning, but even he, trimmer as he was, sent a message to Laval congratulating him on his "moving and courageous speech."[10]

Where Pétain's judgment failed was in forgetting the lessons of Saint-Cyr and the lessons of 1918. At Saint-Cyr, he had learnt that Napoleon's armies had been defeated by the Russian winter and by the strength of Mother Russia, when roused, to defend the homeland. In 1917 and 1918 he had learnt that the Great War would be won by the full mobilization of American strength. Both those lessons had in 1942 been forgotten.

In the early hours of Sunday 8 November, Allied troops landed at Algiers, Oran and Casablanca. On the same morning the U.S. chargé d'affaires in Vichy, Pinkney Tuck, called on Pétain. Pétain greeted him with the words: "Monsieur Tuck, I am deeply grieved by what is happening." Tuck made no reply, but handed Pétain the official message from Roosevelt announcing the landings. Pétain in turn handed Tuck the official French response. It was, he said, simple: "We are attacked. We defend ourselves." "Monsieur Tuck," he went on, "a long time ago we took the decision to defend our empire; we must now do what we have said we would do. It is French honor which is at stake."[11] He then shook Tuck's hand and Tuck left—in tears.

Pétain was not alone in showing defiance. At six o'clock on the same morning in London, de Gaulle was woken by his Chief of Staff, Pierre Billotte, to be told the news. It was not a task that Billotte enjoyed. "Well," shouted the general, as he put on his dressing gown, "I hope the Vichy people are going to throw them into the sea. You can't get into France by breaking and entering."[12] He then proceeded to give Billotte a foretaste of what he would say to Churchill when he saw him. It lasted two hours.

Thus, the reaction of two Frenchmen, on opposite sides in the war, was the same. The major question, at that point, was what each of them would do next.

The Collapse of the House of Cards

"Le Maréchal reste . . . inerte dans son fauteuil"

When Pétain was woken on the morning of 8 November 1942 to be told about the Allied landings and to be presented by Ménétrel with the formal protest— drafted mostly by Laval while he was still asleep—the news came to him as no particular surprise; and, unlike de Gaulle, he had had time to prepare himself. In his meeting that morning with Pinkney Tuck, Pétain dutifully made his formal gesture of defiance and handed over the formal protest. The French official minute of the meeting, equally dutifully, formally recorded the event. Nevertheless, the French minute differs from Tuck's own report to U.S. Secretary of State Cordell Hull. In Tuck's version, far from being in tears as the French minute describes, he rose to take what he considered to be a dignified leave. When he got up, Pétain grasped him by both hands and looked at him "steadfastly and smiling." He then paid Tuck the courtesy of escorting him to the ante-room and "turned briskly back to his office humming a little tune."[1]

Tuck took this to mean that Pétain was secretly rather pleased at the turn of events. In this he was at least partially right. Memories of the First World War were always in Pétain's mind. Indeed, all his stories about Verdun and the mutinies of 1917 were a constant source of conversation wherever he went. Above all, the memories came back of the flood of American young men arriving in 1917 and 1918. Once again the Yanks, in the words of their marching song in 1917, were coming.

Pétain's dilemma was only too evident. Until November 1942, he had looked to Germany, however unpleasant the Nazi régime, as the only protector of Europe against what he regarded as the ultimate peril of communism; but on 8 November 1942 a new anticommunist champion had appeared in the lists. Pétain's memories of 1918 told him that America, if she committed her resources and energy to the priority of winning a European war, would, as in 1918, undoubtedly win it—whatever the British or the Soviets might or might not do; and there is little doubt that, of the two champions in the lists, Germany and America, Pétain's preferred knight in armor was America. But much as he might have preferred the Americans, he could not simply disavow all that he had hitherto said and done. He had embarked on a policy of cooperation with a dominant Germany, and he had personally endorsed legislation which, on any reading, would not be to the American taste, let alone that of his now perceived rival General de Gaulle, who had been condemned by a Vichy court to death for treason.

On the morning of 8 November there was a meeting of the Council of Ministers. They were given a full report—full in so far as anybody knew what was going on. Giraud had apparently broken cover and had broadcast an appeal (from Gibraltar, where he was still negotiating his future position with the Americans) to all French forces in North Africa to join with the Allies. There had, it was said, been a Gaullist attempt at a *coup* in Morocco. The bewildering information duly received, the Council then heard Laval, who reported that he had early that morning asked Krug von Nidda for a German guarantee of French territorial integrity. That request, and the formal protest which Pétain had handed to Tuck, were approved. The German offer of air support, in response to a request from Darlan, was accepted. The business done, Pétain then went for his customary morning walk—this time, however, not with Ménétrel or even Nini, but with Jean Jardel, the secretary to his military group of advisers. On that walk there was, indeed, much to think about.

Laval's request for a German guarantee arrived on Hitler's desk just after noon on the same day. Hitler discussed it briefly on the telephone with Mussolini, who said that he would only join in if France declared war on the United States and Britain. A telegram to that effect was drafted by Abetz, who was unwise enough to add on his own initiative that if France declared war Germany would stand by her "through thick and thin." Laval at first saw it as tantamount to the guarantee which he had sought. With the telegram clutched in his hand he went immediately to see Pétain—who replied firmly that under no circumstances would he agree to declare war on anybody, let alone the United States.

The proposal for a declaration of war was finally buried when Weygand arrived in Vichy later in the afternoon. He was in time to attend the second council meeting of the day, which started just after six o'clock. He and Laval had an angry exchange. Laval was forced to admit that the Abetz telegram did not in reality amount to a guarantee. There was little more he could do. At the council meeting he did not even mention the German proposal for a declaration of war. He merely said that the Germans requested France to break off diplomatic relations with the United States. He did, however, manage to get the council to agree to authorize German aircraft to overfly unoccupied France.

Even as the council was meeting the military situation in North Africa was deteriorating. In the late evening Darlan sent a telegram announcing that he had authorized the French commander in North Africa, General Alphonse Juin, to sign a cease-fire for the city of Algiers and that "I am to meet the American General [Charles Ryder] who wishes to negotiate, at 10 am local time, a cease-fire for Algeria and Tunisia."[2] The Americans had suggested that the civil administration remain in place and that it should act under the control of the French government. Darlan had asked whether that meant the Vichy government. Ryder had not replied. The reply would come on the following day, from none other than General Mark Clark, chief-of-staff to General Dwight Eisenhower, the overall commander of Operation Torch.

On the morning of 9 November Darlan's telegram arrived and was decoded. It was read by ministers just at the moment when Laval was leaving for a meeting with Hitler in Munich, to which he had been summoned late the previous evening. The telegram, as it stood, threatened to sabotage the whole purpose of Laval's journey, which was to settle once for all with Hitler the future structure, and defense of, a Europe in which France would hold its position as a great country in its own right. Hitler's purpose, on the other hand, was quite different. It was to instruct France to declare war on the Allies or face the occupation of its unoccupied zone. When he heard about Darlan's telegram, Laval immediately set about persuading Pétain to reply to Darlan that in his absence in Munich, no negotiations with the Americans should take place. Pétain, faced by an angry Laval, agreed.

Thus instructed by a telegram from Pétain, Darlan duly postponed his meeting with Ryder, and contented himself with sending another telegram to Pétain requesting the immediate dismissal of General Mast (who had been acting for Giraud pending his arrival in Algiers) and four other officers for "having broken their oath of allegiance to the Marshal, having acted dishonorably and having voluntarily facilitated the invasion of [French] territory by a foreign army."[3] At that point, on 9 November, it seemed clear that Darlan had not yet jumped off the fence on which he had perched himself. His uncomfortable posture was, in fact, made even more painful by the news that Giraud had arrived in Algiers that same day and was claiming that he, and he alone, spoke for the Marshal.

Laval did not arrive at Munich until early in the morning of the 10th. But while he was slowly navigating his way, events in Algiers had been moving on. Just before seven o'clock on the evening of the 9th, Ryder and Murphy had presented Darlan with the terms of a cease-fire in Algeria, Tunisia and Morocco.

Darlan summarized the terms in a telegram to Pétain. Urgent as it was, by the time it arrived in Vichy Pétain had gone to bed—and, it went without saying, could not be disturbed.

On the morning of 10 November, at 11 A.M., without any response from Vichy to his earlier telegram, Darlan was summoned by the Americans. At the meeting, Darlan was confronted not by the gently spoken Ryder but by the irascible General Mark Clark, who had flown in to Algiers the previous evening. Clark kept shouting at Darlan and banging the table, saying, in the crudest language, that he was certainly not going to wait for instructions from Vichy and that if Darlan did not sign straightaway he, Clark, would personally put Darlan under immediate arrest and get Giraud to sign the cease-fire without further ado.

Faced with this unconventional—but effective—diplomacy, Darlan immediately signed the document which Clark had slammed on the table in front of him. He then, as the cease-fire document specified, sent instructions to all military commanders in Morocco, Algeria and Tunisia to lay down their arms. He also pronounced that he was acting on the full authority of "the Marshal." But his instructions were received with some suspicion by their recipients. The resident general in Morocco, for instance, General Auguste Noguès, received his instruction through his office at 2 P.M. but waited until 4:30 P.M. for a telephone call from Darlan, who, as he wrote two days later to Pétain, "in your name, ordered the suspension of hostilities for the whole of North Africa."[4]

Whatever the confusion among the generals in North Africa, it was nothing compared with the confusion among the politicians in Vichy. When the news of Darlan's signature of a cease-fire agreement reached Vichy, at about lunch time, the Council of Ministers was deliberating over the reply which they should send to Darlan's earlier message asking for instructions. Weygand was all in favor of a message endorsing Darlan's signature. Others were more doubtful. Rochat, for instance, thought that nothing should be done until Laval returned from Munich. In the middle of the meeting, Laval telephoned from Munich, shouting that he would resign immediately if the Darlan decision was endorsed. That was enough, yet again, to persuade Pétain to concede. A further telegram was sent to Darlan. The order to resist the aggressor, the telegram insisted, still stood.

But that was not the end of the story of 10 November. Radio intercepts were reporting that Darlan was a prisoner of the Americans in Algiers. Nonetheless, the official telegram was sent to him—at 3:14 P.M. Yet at 3:15 P.M., according to Ménétrel, another telegram was sent—in code. Ménétrel's notes record, "the Marshal sent a personal and secret message to Admiral Darlan whose exact terms I don't remember but whose sense was: 'Pay no attention to my official messages and orders to you, sent under duress. Am fully in agreement with you. . . .' "[5]

Ménétrel's notes have, since then, been the subject of dispute. He was, after all, writing after the end of the war, and may have made the whole thing up. Nevertheless, there now seems no doubt that a private telegram from Pétain to Darlan was in fact sent. Whatever its true text, there is equally no doubt that the telegram, such as it was, fits with Pétain's belief that 8 November, marking America's determined entry into the European war, had changed the whole military balance.

The official telegram ordering Darlan to rescind the cease-fire agreement was, as Weygand had pointed out, absurd. Officers on the ground, he went on, were told to fight from ten o'clock to midday, not to fight from midday until two o'clock and then to continue fighting. Darlan himself simply gave up. He issued the order, as instructed, to rescind the cease-fire he had signed and declared himself to be a prisoner of the Americans.

It was just at this time, on the evening of 10 November, that Laval was beginning his meeting with Hitler. As might have been predicted, it was not a success. Hitler went straight to the heart of the matter. France had to choose between complete collaboration with the Axis powers or the loss of her whole empire. Laval tried to explain his plans for a greater Europe. Hitler was not in the least interested. In order to try to sweeten the atmosphere Laval suggested that an ultimatum be sent to Vichy demanding a safe passage for German troops landing in Tunisia, and this was done. But it was not enough for Hitler. At 8:30 P.M. he gave the order to his generals to start the occupation of the rest of France on the following morning—Armistice Day.

By the time German troops crossed the Demarcation Line at 7 A.M. on 11 November 1942, resistance in Morocco had ceased. Noguès sent a telegram that same day to Pétain saying that he had already ordered a complete cease-fire, following Darlan's instruction of 10 November, and that he was to meet Clark on the 12th to discuss the conditions. Casablanca surrendered at the same time. Thus, almost by coincidence, while French North Africa was crumbling to the Americans, Unoccupied France and Corsica were falling to the Germans.

At an early meeting of the Council of Ministers that morning Weygand and Vice-Admiral Paul Auphan argued in favor of supporting the North African cease-fire and sending the fleet from Toulon to the African ports. Others argued that nothing should be done until Laval returned from Munich. Pétain was only half awake and when everybody turned to him for a decision he took refuge in the suggested compromise. They should, he pronounced, wait for Laval. In the end, the only point of general agreement was to approve the appointment of Noguès as the Marshal's sole representative in North Africa. Almost without being aware of what he had done, Pétain had burned what remained of his boats. He had refused to offer any resistance to the German invasion. Never mind the terms of the armistice; never mind the humiliations which France had suffered. In November 1942 Pétain was perceived by the outside world to have capitulated—in the true sense of the word—to Germany.

There was then the matter of what sort of protest to make to the German invaders. Negotiated with Laval on the telephone, it was the feeblest possible effort. It did no more than state the obvious—that Germany had violated the terms of the armistice. To be fair, Pétain's protest did have some effect.

It convinced the Germans that Pétain was a crucial element in maintaining order in France. It also gave some heart to those who profoundly resented the German occupation. Field Marshal Gerd Von Rundstedt conceded that Toulon would not be occupied and that no attempt would be made to seize the French fleet. Finally, it gave Darlan another opportunity to try to reach an agreement with Clark without risking being branded as disloyal to the Marshal. But Darlan was to get yet another shock. Almost at the same time as Pétain's protest was broadcast, a telegram arrived from Vichy announcing Noguès' appointment. To add to the confusion, this was followed immediately by a personal telegram from Pétain to Darlan explaining that the reason why Noguès had been appointed to the post of the "sole representative of the Marshal in North Africa" was because Darlan was believed to be a prisoner.

Laval arrived back in Vichy at two o'clock in the afternoon. The Council of Ministers was summoned yet again. Auphan argued in favor of a general cease-fire in North Africa. Laval argued against him, on the grounds that a cease-fire would inevitably lead to oppression in France and further maltreatment of the French prisoners of war in Germany. Pétain was, again, persuaded by Laval's argument—and another message was sent instructing Noguès, yet again, to resist the Allies. The result was little short of comic. In one day, French troops had been told to maintain neutrality, to attack the Germans and Italians, then to maintain neutrality—and finally to fight the Allies. All in all, by the end of 11 November, the situation both in Algiers and in Vichy could hardly have been more chaotic.

The urgent question there was what should be done about Weygand. Since Vichy had been occupied—the hotels had been given over to billeting German soldiers—it was clear that Weygand was in the greatest danger. Pétain asked Ménétrel to make sure that Weygand could evade arrest by providing an official car to take him out of Vichy to what was thought to be a safe place. Weygand's car, however, together with its escort, was followed by the Gestapo. He was stopped, arrested, and taken back to Vichy. Pétain protested, but his protest was brushed aside. Within a few hours, Weygand was whisked off to prison in Germany.

Weygand's arrest had its knock-on effect in Algiers. He was not personally popular as a Commanding Officer but he was respected by the officers and men of the army in North Africa, above all because he was seen to be resolute in his resistance to Nazi Germany. When Noguès arrived back in Algiers, there was a meeting with Darlan and five senior officers, including Juin. All present gave their opinion. It was unanimous: further resistance to the Allies was fruitless. But they were also unanimous on another point. Under no circumstances would they accept Giraud as their commanding officer. Weygand had cast his formidable shadow on the meeting.

It was at 9:30 P.M. on the evening of the 12th that Darlan and Noguès met Clark and Murphy. Clark started off by saying that the Americans wanted nothing to do with Noguès or—for that matter—Pétain himself. When Giraud came in, Noguès refused to shake hands. After some 20 minutes of wrangling, Clark delivered an ultimatum. Unless the three had arrived at an agreement by the next morning he would impose a military government.

On 13 November, after Clark had threatened to arrest Darlan and Noguès, a deal was done. Giraud would command the army, Darlan would be the political leader in North Africa and Noguès would go back to Morocco. Eisenhower arrived to give the deal his blessing. All that was now needed was the nod from Pétain. Noguès sent a long telegram to Pétain explaining the arrangement in detail, and asking him to reappoint Darlan to his former position. There was, in practice, nothing that Vichy could do but agree. The alternative would have been American military government. For the Germans, a North Africa under conditional French government was better than a North Africa under total American control. Pétain and Laval duly cabled their approval.

The "Darlan Deal," as it became known, was greeted with uproar both in Britain and the United States. In Britain, trade unions, Jewish organizations, the press and members of both houses of Parliament protested angrily and vociferously. The flood of mail to the White House in Washington was almost universally hostile. The very public reaction, of course, only served to convince the Germans that they had been right to agree to it.

Ever since 8 November Pétain had been under pressure from many of his ministerial colleagues to fly to Algiers and declare himself on the side of the Allies. This he refused to do. He gave different reasons at different times to different people. If he went, he said to one, he would be replaced by Déat, who would declare war on the English and Americans, and that he certainly did not want to happen. To another, he claimed that if he went, the whole of North Africa would erupt into war and be burnt to ashes. Finally, to a number of others he said he thought he would be shot.

That seems to have been the conclusive reason. Pétain thought he might fall into a trap—as he had thought when Hitler had brought the remains of the Duke of Reichstadt to Paris in 1940. Moreover, he knew that the British support for de Gaulle would bring their protégé finally, and in some sort of triumph, to Algiers—as indeed happened only a few months later. The confrontation between the two would be, to say the least, awkward. But, above all, Pétain feared for his life, either in a plane or from a bullet.

He can hardly be blamed for this. After all, it was only six weeks later that Darlan himself was assassinated by a young Gaullist with the assistance of the British Special Operations Executive. Although Darlan's assassination was in the future, Pétain knew enough about the mesh of Algiers intrigue to know that he would be without any doubt the target of a variety of groups—whether of hot-headed Gaullists or hot-headed Axis spies. In terms of preserving his own life, a journey to North Africa was not an option. Serrigny tried to persuade him that if he died in an airplane on the way to North Africa "you would join Joan of Arc in history. You would reconcile all Frenchmen behind your presumptive heir and de Gaulle, between whom an understanding would inevitably be made. It is sad to say it but France would lose nothing by this accident."[6] The same might have been true if Pétain had been assassinated in the same way as Darlan. But it was not, to say the least, a very attractive argument—even for an 86-year-old.

Other alternatives were suggested. He could surrender himself, like the King of the Belgians, as a prisoner; or he could send his ministers to Algiers and stay in France by himself; or he could dissolve his government and let civil servants run the country. None of these appealed to Pétain. He would stay where he was.

But Darlan could obviously no longer be Pétain's presumptive successor. Under the circumstances, the succession could only be passed to Laval. Furthermore, Laval claimed, with some justification, that he could not, as head of government, possibly continue to negotiate with Hitler and Ribbentrop if every move he made was subject to Pétain's approval.

By that time, Pétain was very tired. At a meeting of the Council of Ministers on the morning of 16 November, he is recorded as saying, apparently in a low and gloomy voice, that he "asked President Laval, renewing all his confidence in him, to take all decisions which the present circumstances require."[7] Then, immediately after the meeting, came a surprise: Nini had decided to intervene. Pétain had reached the point at which he was resigned to anything which might happen. Nini was worried that he would lose office—and perhaps, like Weygand, be arrested and packed off to Germany—if he detached himself from the Germans and tried to make it up with the Americans. She saw Laval, agreed that he was right to lift at least part of the burden from Pétain's shoulders. (Ménétrel went further, believing that Pétain should retire altogether.)

The rest of 16 November was devoted to the negotiation and drafting of a Constitutional Act appointing Laval as Pétain's successor as head of state for a period of one month if for any reason he was unable to exercise his functions. At the end of a month it would be for the Council of Ministers to decide on the definitive successor. But by then Pétain's health was giving Ménétrel serious cause for concern. In order to avoid triggering the procedure which would automatically make Laval head of state, he produced a medical certificate which advised Pétain to take a few days rest (but only a few—and certainly less than a month). Jardel, too, advised a week's rest.

They should have known better. Laval seized on the opportunity to press the case for a transfer of executive powers to him. Ménétrel and Jardel had thus become the unwitting allies of Laval in securing what amounted to Pétain's virtual abdication. Auphan and two other members of Pétain's staff, seeing the way the wind was blowing, immediately resigned.

There was, however, one more twist to it. Pétain made sure—he required Laval to sign a secret letter—that although he could make laws on his own signature Laval could not sign constitutional acts; he could not declare war; he could not appoint ministers without Pétain's approval; he would respect human rights and the French spiritual and philosophical traditions; and, a point Pétain made with special emphasis, he would guarantee the absolute personal and material security of the Alsatians and Lorrainers, the political detainees and all who had found refuge in France.

Pétain from then on did not attend council meetings. He was not even given sight of the agenda, nor did he know the dates. The only texts which he was asked to sign were those which compromised him even further. (For instance, he was required to copy out the verdict on Giraud, convicted of treason, in his own hand so that copies could be distributed by air over Algeria.) He was more and more seen as a prisoner in a country which was wholly occupied.

Events moved on as the month came to its end. On 23 November, French West Africa declared for Darlan and the Allies. Darlan tried, and failed, to bring the French fleet over to North Africa. On 27 November the Germans invaded the naval base at Toulon. Admiral de Laborde gave the order to scuttle the fleet. Within a few hours, 250,000 tons of shipping, including three battleships, seven cruisers and one aircraft carrier, were at the bottom of Toulon harbor.

It was the end of any pretense of Vichy independence. In 1940, Unoccupied France had been created as an artificial construct—a short-term arrangement to bridge the gap between the armistice and a peace treaty. The cards which were the foundation on which the whole ramshackle house had been built were North Africa and the fleet. North Africa was lost and the fleet largely at the bottom of the sea. There was no negotiating hand with which to resist the Germans. The house of cards had finally collapsed.

Be that as it may, Pétain's abdication of executive powers is more difficult to understand. True, he was tired and resigned. But he refused point blank to make a radio broadcast announcing the event. In other words, and on Nini's insistence, he wanted everybody to know that he was neither incapacitated nor dead.

Yet the last word on 1942 belongs to Serrigny. In his diary for 19 December he wrote that he had lunched with Pétain at the Hôtel du Parc the previous day. "The poor man," his diary reads, "does not appreciate the state of public opinion toward him. The demonstrations the *Préfets* organize for him with children, nuns and a few idiots give him still the illusion of popularity. . . . He believes that Germany will be defeated; he has repeated this to me for the last six months and he throws himself into Hitler's arms!"[8] In other words, the 86-year-old had started to wander into some sort of mental no-man's-land, with no clear sense of reality.

Occupied France

"Il est inutile maintenant d'essayer de galvaniser ce pauvre vieillard"

It was no more than, and no less than, an invasion all over again. German soldiers were out on patrol in the streets of Vichy. The Gestapo set up head-quarters in one of the most pleasant hotels in the town, overlooking the park leading down to the river Allier, and their officers went about their business of arresting, more or less randomly, anybody suspected of harboring enemy agents or foreign Jews. Deportations of Jews, with the help of the French police, were resumed. The Germans demanded more money from the French to pay for the occupation of their own territory, and Sauckel demanded a further 250,000 French workers to work in the German war machine.

For those living throughout what used to be unoccupied France, the effects of the occupation were, in the truest sense of the word, dreadful. Laval suggested, and the Germans agreed, that a special police force be set up to complement the already overstretched German SS. On 5 January 1943, therefore, the Service d'Ordre Légionaire adopted the new title of the Milice. Darnand's command was confirmed. That done, he set about recruiting young thugs from the Légion who were to form the core of the Milice, made them swear total loyalty to Pétain, and instructed them in the necessary techniques which were to be used in hunting down Jews, Freemasons and communists. At that point, a miasma of fear seemed to settle on what until then had at least given the appearance of being an independent France—a miasma which, in truth, was not to be blown away until the arrival of the fresh wind of the Liberation.

If only by default, Pétain, old as he was and with frequent episodes of attention failure in the afternoons, must bear his share of responsibility. He had, after all, decorated Darnand in the First World War and did not object to—and even encouraged—the Milice oath of personal loyalty. Moreover, he had written to Hitler with the idea of "a national police force to maintain order in the event of [Allied] occupation."[1] Seizing on this, Laval had gone much further. The Milice grew in strength—and in brutality. Pétain, for his part, simply took far too long to try to put a stop to it.

By then, Pétain himself was under German suspicion. In January 1943 he decided to spend a quiet few days at l'Ermitage. But for this he now needed official permission. The Germans, and the Italians who occupied Villeneuve-Loubet, thought that this was a deep plot by Ménétrel to spirit Pétain away to North Africa. Permission was therefore refused. Pétain then tried to get authorization from General Alexander von Neubronn, the military commander at Vichy. The response was, again, uncompromising. Not only would Pétain be required to stay in Vichy, but two Gestapo officers would be assigned to his bodyguard. Pétain was understandably furious, but there was nothing he could do about it.

By then, Pétain had reached what seemed to be a conclusion. The news of the surrender of the German 6th Army at Stalingrad and the German defeat at El Alamein did little more than confirm the general belief that Germany would lose the war. On 19 December 1942 Serrigny, puzzled about Pétain's frame of mind and his behavior, found only one explanation: "the hope of a compromise peace."[2] This, in fact, was Pétain's conclusion.

His reasoning was simple. The greatest threat to France—the great and historical France about which he had learnt from his earliest peasant childhood—was communism. It followed that the Christian West should unite to defeat that threat. In turn, that meant that France should be in itself united, and that Germany should be supported by a united France, Britain and, of course, the United States, in the same enterprise. Even at the time Serrigny was puzzled, Pétain was warning his old friend and colleague, Alfred Conquet, who had worked with him before the war in his old office in the Boulevard des Invalides, to be prepared to make overtures to de Gaulle "when the Allies have clearly won the match."[3]

The "compromise peace" thus became Pétain's new project. The problem, of course, was that he was unable to understand that he was in no position to bring his project to any sort of fruition. He still had not realized that he was now no more than a figurehead in a discredited and occupied state. Old age had brought with it not just a sense of self-importance but a diminishing grasp of reality. To cap it all, he either was unaware—or had not taken in—that the Allies in their conference at Casablanca in January 1943 had declared that they would accept nothing less than unconditional surrender.

There were, of course, several matters which had to be dealt with. On 16 February 1943 Laval promulgated a new law, the Service du Travail Obligatoire. Voluntary service in Germany had failed to meet Sauckel's targets.

Service therefore had to be made compulsory. As a matter of fact, Sauckel's targets were duly met, but there was a corresponding defection by young men who wished to avoid what was then a legal obligation. The result was the formation of bands in the hills—known as the *maquis* after the heather on the hills which they adopted as their home. In Pétain's view this was a mutiny against the proper legal authority like the mutinies of 1917, and had, as in 1917, to be suppressed. The result was an upsurge both in violent resistance and equally violent suppression by the Gestapo and the Milice.

The next matter was Laval himself. Apart from personal dislike, Pétain knew that Laval was unacceptable, in any form, either to the Allies or to Giraud—let alone de Gaulle. In fact, Laval shared Pétain's view that the sensible course for France was to work for a compromise peace. He even, like Pétain, believed that he had a role to play in such a negotiation. Nonetheless, Pétain was perfectly aware that, for any possibility of success in negotiations with either the Committee for National Liberation (CFLN) in Algiers or with the Allies, Laval had to go.

The third matter was how even to start approaching those whom Pétain would have as his allies in his project. Of course, there was no difficulty about the Germans—they were, after all, on his doorstep. But there were difficulties both about the Americans and the British, as well as with his compatriots in London and Algiers. The problem was how to persuade all possible participants that the Vichy government had legitimacy as a proper evolutionary survivor of the Third Republic. Without that, there could be no hope of French reunification in the postwar resistance to communism.

Whatever the frailty of old age, Pétain's analytical ability, when fully alert and concentrated on a specific problem, was undiminished. In the early months of 1943, Pétain was slowly digesting the conclusion that Germany would lose the war, and that the right course to follow was his new project of a compromise peace. The end was clear, but the means were, far from simple. At the very least, he had to devise a strategy.

At first, his strategy was simply to get rid of Laval while assuring the Germans that he was on their side. But word leaked out to Laval that Pétain wanted to be rid of him. Hitler wrote a stern letter to Pétain—telling him, in the clearest possible terms, to back off—and then, by way of support, summoned Laval to Berchtesgaden.

His first effort having failed, Pétain devised another. On 23 May 1943 he and Jardel met to discuss it. Jardel told him that the only weapon Pétain had left to defeat Laval was the power vested in him by the National Assembly in July 1940 to promulgate a new constitution. Pétain and Jardel therefore started to outline a new constitution designed both to neutralize Laval and to be acceptable to the Americans. This, indeed, was plan B. The National Assembly, like Lazarus emerging from his tomb, was to be brought back to life.

Three events prompted Pétain to make haste. On 30 May de Gaulle arrived in Algiers to set up, with Giraud, the Committee for National Liberation (CFLN).

On 10 July the Allies landed in Sicily; and on 25 July Mussolini was deposed. There was no time to lose. A small committee, chaired by one of Pétain's most faithful confidants, Lucien Romier, was put to work. Their remit was to write, in the shortest time possible, the new constitution.

But Pétain did not stop there. His project of a compromise peace also involved making contact both with the CFLN, jointly chaired at the time by Giraud and de Gaulle, and with the British in Algiers. For these tasks, without mentioning the matter to Ménétrel, Jardel or Romier, he selected a variety of intermediaries. One was Paul Dungler, an Alsatian member of the Resistance, who was summoned by Pétain in July and, by his own account, told to see Giraud and de Gaulle and tell them that Pétain "proposed that at the Liberation we meet at the Arc de Triomphe when I will transfer to them my powers without reservation."[4] But when he arrived in Algiers, Dungler seemed to spend more time in discussing the finances of the Resistance in Alsace than in fulfilling Pétain's commission.

Pétain sent another intermediary to make contact with the British. The proposal that his intermediary was to put was, as it happened, very much more ambitious. Whatever the attempts to satisfy the Germans, whatever the inconvenience of leaving his wife and his home in Vichy, whatever the "gift of his person" to his compatriots, and whatever the personal consequences, Pétain seems—and "seems" is the only possible word—to have decided that the best way forward for his project of a compromise peace was to leave France and place himself in the hands of the Allies. If that were done, he could make peace with de Gaulle, show the Germans that there was a united France—and manufacture the compromise peace in opposition to the Soviets.

This proposal was communicated to André Poniatowski, Giraud's ADC, by a certain Monsieur Schneider, a French industrialist and head of a resistance organization in Alsace. Poniatowski in turn relayed it Lord (Eric) Duncannon, the British staff officer acting as liaison with the CFLN in Algiers, who made it known to Roger Makins, assistant to the British resident minister at Allied Forces Headquarters, Mediterranean, Harold Macmillan. Poniatowski told Duncannon that Schneider had seen Pétain on 25 August just before leaving France via Spain for Algiers. "Pétain told him that he himself was now prepared to leave France and go anywhere except to North Africa."[5]

Macmillan's response was that "There are no advantages in Pétain's escape. The only reason for taking him out of France would be to execute him as an arch traitor. This is very dangerous stuff indeed."[6] A discussion between Macmillan and Makins took place. In spite of Schneider's claim that "the arrangement of Pétain's escape would not necessarily be a difficult operation" and his conviction that "if the Marshal escaped and ordered the nation to resist the Germans openly, his action would have a beneficial effect on the 25 to 50% of Frenchmen who still recognized him as their legitimate leader."[7] The result of the discussion was that Duncannon was instructed to inform Poniatowski that he, Duncannon, had mentioned the matter to his immediate superior, who saw no object in putting it up to the minister, whose view would most certainly be that he would have nothing whatever to do with it.

In the cold light of history, leaving aside all the emotions of war, the attitudes of Makins and Macmillan defy rational explanation. An intermediary, apparently authorized by Pétain himself, had indicated that Pétain was prepared to escape from France and release the French armed forces from their oath of loyalty to him. His only stipulation was that under no circumstances would he go to North Africa. Pétain would openly encourage his compatriots to resist the occupier, with all the prestige he still commanded. The remaining French armed forces would have been able to join openly with Fighting France. It is even possible that the ensuing battle for France would have been much more easily won. At all events, Pétain's suggestion, if genuine, deserved consideration at the highest Allied level. Such was the importance of the possible event—however unlikely it may have turned out to be—that Churchill would certainly have wished to have been immediately informed.

The most plausible explanation is that by August 1943 de Gaulle was in the process of outmaneuvering Giraud in the CFLN. In fact, on 25 September de Gaulle was elected sole president. Giraud was given the consolation prize of leading the force which was to liberate Corsica. In all this, Macmillan was a fervent supporter of de Gaulle. At the Casablanca conference in January 1943 he had done his best to persuade both Churchill and Roosevelt that de Gaulle was the only possible leader of a revived France. The emergence of Pétain as an alternative leader of France, in whatever form and however it was done, would have spoilt what Macmillan regarded as his own personal triumph. De Gaulle was Macmillan's favorite horse. Nothing, even an obligation to report to Churchill, was to stand in the way. Pétain had to recognize that any plan to escape from France, or even to make peace with Macmillan and de Gaulle, was doomed. That part of his project—the reconciliation of the different French factions in unity with the British—had failed.

Nevertheless, Pétain was not yet ready to give up. Auphan had, on Pétain's instruction, been working on a series of policy initiatives to complement the new constitution which Romier's committee was writing. On 13 September Auphan presented his results. Among other things he suggested that Laval should be replaced, STO scrapped or at least suspended, collaborationist parties outlawed, the anti-Jewish laws relaxed, and contacts made with non-communist Resistance groups. Auphan fully realized that the Germans would oppose practically everything he suggested, and that all those involved would probably be arrested. He considered, however, that this would not matter, and might in fact be a benefit, if Pétain set up a regency council with full authority to exercise his powers if he himself was for any reason prevented from do so.

Pétain, after a few days' reflection, agreed. On 27 September a new draft of Constitutional Act No. 4 was prepared. A regency council was to be set up along the lines Auphan had suggested. It was to be composed of seven men (surprisingly including Weygand—still in prison in Germany—and the Gaullist former ambassador Noël, and, unsurprisingly, Auphan himself). In the event of Pétain being permanently unable to or prevented from carrying out his tasks, his powers were to pass to the National Assembly, to be exercised by a regency council reporting directly to it.

That done (and kept secret), on 26 October Pétain summoned up the courage to tell Laval that he must resign. Reasonably enough, Laval asked for an explanation. Pétain, rather feebly, told him that he was too unpopular, was too close to the collaborationists Déat and de Brinon, and that the country was on the brink of revolution. What he might have added was that Corsica had been liberated by 5 October and was now in the hands of the Allies, that Allied forces had established a bridgehead at Anzio, that Italy had declared war on Germany, that the Resistance was now active everywhere and that passive opposition in the police and the administration was making the country ungovernable.

Laval immediately told Krug von Nidda of this conversation, claiming that the right way to solve the problem, if indeed there was a problem, was to purge Pétain's supporters—and in particular Auphan. When this got back to him, Pétain responded by preparing yet another draft of Constitutional Act No. 4. This was ready by 12 November. Pétain immediately sent for Laval and told him that he was going to publish the new act and explain it in a speech the following day. Pétain's new proposal was simple: "Today," the draft of his speech went, "I embody French legitimacy. I intend to preserve it as a sacred trust and to return it, upon my death, to the National Assembly from which I received it, if the new constitution is not by then ratified. . . . This is the purpose of the Constitutional Act which will be published in the *Journal Officiel*."[8]

Initially, Laval was quite satisfied with Pétain's proposal. He assumed that he could manipulate the National Assembly just as he had in the past. But he thought that, out of courtesy, Pétain should tell Krug von Nidda about it. This was done. But when the message was passed on to Berlin, Ribbentrop was horrified. At 6:30 P.M. on 13 November, one and a half hours before the by then pre-recorded speech was to be broadcast, de Brinon telephoned Pétain to say that the Germans were not allowing the speech under any circumstances. Moreover, to make doubly sure, German troops occupied the Vichy radio station and the offices of the *Journal Officiel*.

No more than an hour later Pétain made a protest to Krug von Nidda in the most formal terms. He was, he said, no longer able to exercise his constitutional functions. Until the broadcast was allowed, he would simply sit on his hands and do nothing. In other words, he was going on strike. There followed, as might be imagined, a series of rows. Laval had changed his mind and was determined to make Pétain withdraw his proposal in its entirety. Ménétrel and Jardel, and even Romier, were inclined to agree with Laval. But Pétain stood firm. He was determined not to concede to de Gaulle on where the legitimacy of France lay. It lay with him, and not with the rebel general.

Krug von Nidda had originally told Pétain that the embargo on his broadcast was only to last 48 hours. In fact, it was three weeks before the Germans finally responded—they needed the time to make their military dispositions in case of serious trouble. But during those weeks (in fact on 23 November), Serrigny arrived unexpectedly in Vichy. Pétain told Serrigny that he considered himself a prisoner, and that he would act as one. Serrigny pointed out in reply that he certainly was not acting as one at the moment, but that he should. "You go publicly to Mass every Sunday; you receive delegations; Laval reports to you on the meetings of his Council of Ministers. This is not the way the King of the Belgians behaves—with the result that he has the whole country behind him. Shut your door—to me as well as to the others. The greatest good fortune which could happen to you would be for a German sentry to mount guard in front of the Hôtel du Parc."[9]

Pétain replied that perhaps Serrigny was right but he could not do all that at the moment as people would think he was ill, and that he could not sack Laval since Berlin had told him that if he did they would send in a *Gauleiter*. "Marshal, you think too much about Frenchmen and not enough about France!," Serrigny expostulated.[10]

It was Abetz, resuming his role after a year of disgrace, who delivered the final German response to Pétain on 5 December. It was in the form of a long letter from Ribbentrop. The Reich, he wrote, rejected all idea of reviving the National Assembly. The letter then delivered what amounted to three ultimatums: first, all proposed alterations to laws must be submitted to the Reich authorities in good time; second, Laval must reorganize the French Council of Ministers in a way acceptable to the Reich authorities; and, third, the head of state must remove from the administration all elements hindering reconstruction and ensure their replacement by trustworthy people.

Initially, Pétain was minded to protest. He tried to play for time. But Ribbentrop was not deceived. He insisted on Pétain agreeing to these ultimatums in writing. On 15 December Abetz was told to see Laval and to give him the names of those who should be dismissed. Romier and Jardel were among them—Ménétrel was only allowed to stay if he confined himself to medicine. By 19 December, Laval had extracted a written pledge from Pétain that all proposed legislative changes would be submitted to the Reich authorities for approval. On 29 December Abetz received Pétain's written agreement not to oppose any of Laval's appointments or any German request for dismissals. Pétain's capitulation was complete. It was sealed by the appointment by the Germans of "Hitler's special diplomatic representative" to the French head of state, as minister plenipotentiary, Herr Cecil von Renthe-Fink. To be plain, Renthe-Fink was to be—again in the modern vernacular—Pétain's "minder." Serrigny's prediction had been fulfilled, but in the most humiliating way. The Germans had taken control of Vichy France not by sending in a *Gauleiter* but by ensuring that the existing machine worked entirely to their advantage. Pétain's project of a "compromise peace" had failed at every turn. He was left, as Auphan found when he saw him in January 1944, sad and alone—and depressed. Serrigny summed it up: "it is useless now to try to galvanize this poor old man."[11]

Vichy: The Final Act

". . . il n'y a de salut pour la France que dans la reconciliation Pétain-de Gaulle."

By the beginning of 1944, Pétain found himself as little more than a tired old warhorse performing ceremonial duties. Excluded from the process of government, he even had to endure the appointment of Darnand, at the insistence of the SS, as head of the French police, and the presence of two arch-collaborationists, Paul Marion and Philippe Henriot, in Laval's government. True, Laval had managed to deflect Déat by offering him a minor post (which was refused), and Doriot was fighting on the eastern front, but the balance of the government had shifted decisively, as the Germans had insisted, toward overt collaboration. "I knew," he wrote in January to his old friend Mrs. Pardee, "that a defeat had disastrous consequences, but I never thought the misfortune which was the result would be so prolonged."[1]

As "minders" go, Renthe-Fink was not wholly unpleasant, and, on occasion, he could be reasonably affable. Tall and clean-featured, he took pride in his East Prussian aristocratic ancestry, and considered himself a Prussian of what he would have called the old school. Nor did he have any position of distinction in the Nazi Party, which he had joined only in 1939. Renthe-Fink was therefore probably as surprised as anybody to find himself posted from the Berlin office for propaganda on the eastern front to become the *"Kindermädchen"* (nanny), as he himself put it, to the 87-year-old Marshal Pétain.[2] Nevertheless, although he was apt to shout at Pétain from time to time, Renthe-Fink seems to have got on well with his charge. They were both old-fashioned in their manners, and Pétain certainly recognized an aristocrat when he saw one. Renthe-Fink, for his part, called Pétain "an upright and good man"[3] and regretted being unable to be of help to him after the war.

But there it was. Pétain made up his mind—there was nothing else to do—to live with his nanny. He also had to get used to a new head of his personal staff. Jardel, on German instruction, was replaced by Jean Tracou, a former Préfet of Tours, who had been persuaded by Romier to join him in Vichy—only to find when he arrived on 6 January that Romier had died suddenly of a heart attack. Moreover, on January 19 Bonhomme, Pétain's faithful orderly officer for some 20 years, was killed in a car crash. Pétain had lost two of his most devoted supporters.

Tracou turned out to be a loyal servant. He in turn brought with him another loyal (and perhaps over-devoted) servant in Louis-Dominique Girard, previously the head of the staff of the Préfecture of Angers. Pétain put them to work on the only role of any consequence which was left to him: the work, left by Romier, on the proposed constitution. The result was not altogether happy. In fact, it was little more than a shambles. A draft was produced at the end of January which Pétain signed without reading it thoroughly (if at all). It was only when it was explained to him that there was to be a return to parliamentary government that he declared himself not at all content with it. As for Laval, when he was shown the document, he said it was ridiculous, rejected it out of hand—and said that he would produce his own proposals.

If the constitutional question was one of confusion, there was also confusion in the maintenance of order in Vichy France. There were constant battles between the resistance in the surrounding hills—the Maquis—and the Milice, particularly in the Haute Savoie, both sides showing such ferocity that it was difficult to tell at times which was the more frightening to ordinary people. The Milice used torture and summary executions, as well as turning over to the Gestapo many of their compatriot prisoners. The Maquis responded by shooting without ceremony anyone from the Milice who fell into their hands. One report to the CFLN in early 1944 described the country as in a state of "pre-civil war."[4] The Gestapo joined in with random arrests. Laure, Bouthillier, Bousquet and even Jean Borotra, the minister for sport, were all gathered in and packed off to Germany.

But the German pressure on Laval to be more collaborationist was unrelenting. Abetz insisted that Déat be brought into the government. Laval was no longer in a position to resist. On 17 March it was announced that Déat had been made Minister for Labor, with extensive powers to attend to Sauckel's requests for French workers for German factories. Pétain thought about resigning, changed his mind—yet again—and confined himself to a refusal to sign the official appointment. He just hoped that Déat would stay in Paris and not come anywhere near Vichy. Walter Stucki, the Swiss ambassador, reported to his government in Bern that the Déat appointment was the hardest pill for Pétain to swallow; he had openly told Stucki that his life was intolerable and that he hoped he would soon be allowed to die.

It was at that point, very late in the day, that the Americans made their approach. A message came from Roosevelt himself—although the method of delivery was tortuous. The context was simple. Roosevelt disliked and distrusted de Gaulle. De Gaulle was, in Roosevelt's own words, "a nut."[5] On no account, in Roosevelt's mind, should de Gaulle be allowed to walk into power in France on the back of an Allied landing in which he was not allowed to have any part. Furthermore, Roosevelt had his own plans for the postwar arrangements in France. Roosevelt had been impressed by his old friend Leahy, who had told him a month earlier that "when Allied troops enter France, the most reliable person to whom we could look for help in rallying the French was Pétain."[6] Roosevelt's proposal to Pétain was that he should resign and play no further part in Vichy. He should follow the example of the King of Denmark—remain in the country but be wholly inactive. When the Americans arrived, they would pick him up out of retirement and he would help them in the postwar reconstruction of his country.

It is not too much to say that Roosevelt's proposal was Pétain's last chance to come out on the right side of history. If he had accepted the proposal, the course of postwar France would certainly have been different. Quite how and in what particular it is fruitless to speculate, but there is no reason to doubt that at least a sizeable part of the population of France thought of Pétain even then both as a symbol of the country's successful military past and as the legitimate head of state.

Yet Pétain, once again, took the wrong turning. He replied that if he did as Roosevelt asked he would be leaving France in the hands of a dangerous group of men without the check which the legitimate head of state symbolized. Moreover, the Germans would certainly not allow him to get away with it. He would be arrested and deported to Germany. Both arguments were, of course, ill-founded. He had no effective control over Laval's government; and, if he had been deported to Germany, it would have been a positive advantage to him. But he went even further, claiming, as always self-importantly, that for him to leave his post would an act of betrayal. As might be imagined, Roosevelt's proposal was not renewed—indeed, it was not long afterwards that Roosevelt himself announced that the United States was prepared to recognize de Gaulle and the CFLN as the *de facto* authority in France.

As it happened, and purely coincidentally, Pétain's popularity within France made a surprising recovery. The prospect of civil war—the Maquis versus the Milice, as it were—led those in the middle to look again to Pétain as the figurehead which stood above the conflict and which would shield the innocent from brutality and death. It was, of course, no more than a flight from reality, but when Paris was bombed by the British on 20 April, leaving 651 dead and 461 wounded, General Brécard, by then grand chancellor of the Légion d'Honneur,

suggested that Pétain should go to Paris to honor the dead. There was, apparently, to be a service of remembrance at the Cathedral of Notre-Dame. Pétain
went and there addressed the crowd from the balcony of the Hôtel de Ville. What
he said was recorded. He apparently described himself as a "prisoner," but by the
time his words were broadcast the censorship had carefully edited them. In the
newsreels of the day all that was heard was "I come to pay you a visit . . . . I think
often of you . . . . But be sure that, as soon as I can do it, it will be an official
visit . . . . So, I will see you soon, I hope."[7] There were shouts of "Vive Pétain" and
the Marseillaise was sung. "The impression was strong and will be long-lasting,"
wrote an onlooker, "the Marshal finally came out of his shell to take sides."[8] The
mythology of the Marshal had not yet lost its potency. The welcome given to
Pétain in Orléans and Nancy on his way back was equally enthusiastic.

No sooner back in Vichy, however, Pétain spoiled most of the favorable image
he had created—and dented his popularity—by making a speech condemning the
Resistance. In fact, Renthe-Fink had been pressing Pétain to make such a speech
ever since February, but Pétain kept putting him off by claiming that it would lose
him all support among his compatriots. Several drafts were prepared by Tracou
and Henriot, with Renthe-Fink insisting that somewhere in the speech a sentence
should make it clear that Pétain believed that Germany was the only defender of
European civilization against the menace of communism.

Pétain finally agreed, and on 29 April 1944 the speech was made. The
Germans, however, were still not satisfied. Many in Berlin thought that Pétain
was in some way in league with the Allies and was preparing to go over to them
when they landed in France. Renthe-Fink had already told Tracou, and on 5 May
he told Pétain, that, for his own safety, he was to move—temporarily—out of
Vichy to a château near Paris. On the afternoon of 7 May Pétain, after a feeble
protest, left the Hôtel du Parc, accompanied by Nini and Ménétrel. The crowd
which turned out to see them leave assumed that they were being taken as
prisoners. Many were in tears.

The château in question was at Voisins, not very far from Rambouillet in
the Ile de France. It had been built in the middle of a dense wood, and the only
outlook was on one side to a small pond fed by a stream which managed to work
its way through the surrounding trees. As Serrigny remarked, "it seems more
suitable to shelter romantic lovers than an old man of eighty-eight years, who
hates solitude and prefers [proper] gardens to nature."[9] Into these gloomy
surroundings the Pétain party arrived on the morning of 8 May, having spent the
night at Rambouillet.

The following day, Abetz and de Brinon were the first visitors. Next came
Henriot. He was invited, for lack of any other entertainment, to stay for lunch. It
was not a wise move. That very evening Henriot broadcast—with German
encouragement—that "I earlier lunched with the Marshal" who was in occupied
territory "to be close to the people for whom he had the greatest care."[10] The
next day the headlines in the press, in both Paris and Vichy, repeated Henriot's

words. The Germans had not missed a trick. Pétain, the message conveyed, was not a prisoner but had elected to go to Voisins of his own free will. When Pétain wanted to talk to Ménétrel about it, he discovered that Ménétrel had disappeared—nobody knew where.

The charade continued. On 17 May, Déat was invited, at German request. The next day Laval turned up with his wife, and on the morning of the 19th Darnand arrived. They were all received with courtesy. Even von Rundstedt arrived to invite Pétain to inspect the Atlantic defenses. But Pétain was clearly uncertain how to react to his new position—as a reminder of a glorious past and thus a possible card to play in the German defense of France. He received visits from delegations—mayors, local councilors and so on—all carefully orchestrated.

On 19 May, however, there was a much more welcome event. Hearing that Pétain was cut off from communication with the outside world, on the 18th Serrigny, Pétain's old friend and companion in arms, had telephoned and spoken to Pétain's orderly officer at Voisins. When Pétain heard of this, he immediately invited Serrigny to lunch, together with another old friend from the First World War, General Anthoine. Upon arrival, they were astonished when Pétain almost ran toward them to "embrace them with emotion." "It is not a familiar gesture for him," Serrigny went on to comment drily.[11] Pétain told them that they were the first real friends he had seen since his arrival at Voisins. After the visit, Serrigny's verdict was that he had "the clear impression that the Head of State no longer at all enjoyed all his clarity of mind."[12] In other words, Serrigny, his old friend and admirer, thought that Pétain was finally descending into geriatric vacuity.

The stay at Voisins did not last long. On 26 May the party started to move back to Vichy. But the Germans did not trust Pétain to stay in the Hôtel du Parc. By 7 June, he and Nini had been brusquely moved to yet another château—Lonzat, some 17 kilometers away from Vichy. He was to be allowed to spend his days at his office in Vichy—but return to Lonzat every evening.

By the time Pétain and Nini had been parked at Lonzat, the long-awaited Allied landings had taken place. Pétain was persuaded, under some German duress, that he could not remain silent. He therefore broadcast on 6 June. The message was simple. The German and Allied armies were engaged in battle on French soil. France should remain neutral. Pétain was in Lyon when the news of the Allied landings came through. According to Tracou, he was delighted—he even starting singing "It's a long, long way to Tipperary." His reception in Lyon had been ecstatic. It was the same in Saint-Étienne on the morning of 7 June, in spite of, or even because of, his broadcast of the previous evening. But when he arrived back in Vichy, it was a different matter. It was reported that 5,000 Maquisards were marching toward the Hôtel du Parc, and 1,500 German infantry and a squadron of panzers were waiting for them. Renthe-Fink whisked Pétain off to Lonzat.

As it happened, his public appearance before a crowd at Saint-Étienne was to be the last of its kind. On 11 June, he was told by the Germans not to go to

Vichy at all, but to stay where he was until further notice. Those who wanted
to see him had to go to Lonzat. In short, he was by then truly a prisoner. On
14 June Darnand was promoted in ministerial rank without Pétain's consent. On
28 June, Henriot was assassinated by the Resistance. Renthe-Fink wanted
Pétain to express condemnation. He refused. On 10 July he wrote a letter
protesting at the behavior of German troops, who were killing innocent French
civilians as they retreated. It was torn up. On 20 July he refused to write to Hitler
congratulating him on escaping assassination by a group of his own officers.

By the beginning of July 1944, Pétain had been allowed back to Vichy. But
the visits were no more than day-trips. In the evening he was driven back to
Lonzat. On 5 July for instance, there was a memorial service for Henriot at the
church of Saint-Louis. Pétain was obliged to attend. On 9 July Petain arrived at
the Hotel du Parc to be confronted by Admiral Charles Platon who delivered a
manifesto signed by the ultra-collaborationists Déat, de Brinon, Doriot, Luchaire,
Benoist-Méchin and others in sympathy with them. It demanded the replacement
of Laval by a head of government irrevocably committed to supporting the
German war effort. Pétain simply told Platon to go away.

The political air in Vichy became ever more oppressive by the day. Since the
Normandy landings the Milice had become even more brutal. Jean Zay, who had
an education minister in the Popular Front government, was shot while being
transferred from one prison to another. On 7 July Georges Mandel was also murdered by the Milice in the same circumstances. By way of revenge for Henriot's
death Paul Touvier, the head of the Milice in Haute Savoie, rounded up and shot
seven Jews. At Saint-Amand-Montrond, some 40 kilometers south of Bourges,
the Maquis took hostages. The Germans and the Milice arrived two days later,
arrested anybody suspected of links with the Resistance and either shot them on
the spot or took them to Vichy to be tortured. The Maquis then hanged 13 of the
hostages, whereupon the leader of the Milice, Joseph Lécussan, a brute who carried in his wallet a Star of David from a Jew's skin, rounded up 80 Jews, had the
men pushed into a well and buried alive under bags of cement. It was far from
being an isolated incident. At Oradour-sur-Glane a whole village was massacred
in the most horrific way.

There is no doubt that Pétain was outraged by such incidents. He told
Renthe-Fink as much: "You burn villages, you massacre children, you desecrate
churches, you cover your country in shame. You are a nation of savages."[13] On
6 August Pétain wrote a long letter to Laval about the *Milice*. "I have talked to
you," it started, "on many occasions and I always hoped that I would hear of
improvements in the diverse activities of this political police. The contrary is
true . . . . Unacceptable and hateful facts are reported to me daily." Pétain then
listed some of them. "By these procedures, the Milice has succeeded in imposing
an atmosphere of police terror unknown in this country until now."[14] It was
certainly strong stuff, but it might at least have had some effect if it had come a
few months earlier.

It was by then clear, if it had not been for some time, that Pétain was trying to make his peace with the Allies. Odd as it may seem, Laval was trying to do the same. Laval's plan was to make France, as it were, presentable to the Americans. On 9 August he left for Paris, where he somehow managed to persuade Abetz that it would be a good idea to reconvene the National Assembly. The person to do that, he thought, was Herriot, who was detained in a lunatic asylum near Nancy (although he was perfectly sane). Abetz agreed that Laval himself should go and fetch Herriot, which he did. Herriot was dumbfounded by Laval's unexpected arrival on 12 August. He nevertheless accompanied him back to Paris. But, when there, Herriot said that he was not the president of the National Assembly. Laval should send for Jeanneney, the president of the Senate, who was living somewhere near Grenoble.

Laval did his best to convince Pétain to come to Paris and endorse the scheme. But Pétain had other ideas. General Brécard, who was in Paris as head of a group known as the "Friends of the Marshal," was convinced, as he was to tell Pastor Boegner later in the month, that "there is no salvation for France other than in the reconciliation of Pétain and de Gaulle."[15] The message was readily accepted by Pétain, who, on 11 August, signed a document giving authority to Auphan to negotiate on his behalf with the Americans and, if possible, to make contact with de Gaulle, with the aim of avoiding a civil war in France and for a transfer of his legitimate authority to de Gaulle. But it was all too late—and too naïve. Laval's plan failed on 16 August, when Herriot was rearrested on direct orders from Berlin, and Pétain's plan failed because, after the Allied break out in Normandy at the end of July and the swift advance thereafter, none of the Allies were interested in what Pétain had to say.

On 15 August an Allied force, including seven divisions of the 1st French Army under de Lattre de Tassigny, landed on the southern coast of France. In a matter of only a few days Toulon had fallen and Allied troops had started to move up the Rhone valley. The German 19th Army was in full retreat to avoid encirclement. Vichy itself was threatened. On 17 August Pétain, by then back in the Hôtel du Parc, was summoned by Renthe-Fink and told to pack his bags. He was to be moved northeastward to the frontier town of Belfort in the Jura, along with Laval and the whole of the Vichy government. Pétain protested; Ménétrel said that he should escape and join the Maquis, or even hide in a safe house in Vichy until the Germans moved out. But it was all to no avail. On the afternoon of 19 August von Neubronn received his orders. If necessary, he was to arrest Pétain that evening to move him out of Vichy by force. If there was any resistance, Vichy would be bombed. Once again, Pétain conceded.

At first light on the 20th Ménétrel was up and about, packing up. At 6 A.M. a detachment of German soldiers arrived in front of the Hôtel du Parc. Soon a solitary tank turned and parked opposite the entrance. At about seven o'clock the soldiers had lost patience. They brushed aside Pétain's bodyguard—Pétain had ordered them not to shoot—kicked down the door and found Pétain still getting ready. The German officer in charge was preparing to arrest him when Ménétrel intervened. Given the long journey which awaited him, and his age, he thought that at least the Marshal should have some breakfast. The officer gave his assent. Coffee and bread were brought in and eaten in silence—while Ménétrel was on the telephone to tell the Papal Nuncio and the Swiss ambassador about the turn of events.

At eight o'clock Pétain's personal car drew up in front of the entrance. "A small group of people," a bodyguard reported to his wife, "were present, in silence, to see the scene which was to be played out. The Marshal crossed the doorway, the revolving door having been demolished, went down the front steps; but his face remained calm; he raised his hat in greeting, as though to say 'adieu', and climbed into his car."[16] The curtain had finally fallen on the drama which was Vichy. Suitably, it was raining.

Reluctant Flight

"Des principes que j'enseignais, de toutes les choses que j'ai librement dit, je ne retire rien."

The Pétain of the autumn of 1944 and the early spring of 1945 cuts a sorry figure. It was not just a question of age, although he was feeling all of his 88 years. It was worse than that. On the pretext that his personal safety was in danger he had become, as he said himself, a German prisoner. He was no longer able to decide for himself or for his wife where he was to find any sort of a home, or where—or when—he might be directed to go to next. The only constant in this disrupted life was that he would under no circumstances be going back to Vichy.

In fact, he had already said his goodbyes to Vichy. His main goodbye, apart from yet another letter to Hitler protesting his treatment, had been in the form of a text, written by the old follower of Maurras, Henri Massis, and corrected in Pétain's own hand. The document was not published, but it was reproduced as a poster and put up in various places—although its life was short, since it was soon torn down either by German soldiers or by the Resistance. In it, Pétain recounted his version of events since the defeat of May 1940 and the signature of the armistice. He claimed that his whole objective had been to "preserve the body and soul of France." Not only that, but he asserted roundly that "if it is true that de Gaulle has boldly raised the sword of France, I have patiently been the shield [protecting] the French people."[1] Needless to say, he failed to point out that the shield had not been particularly effective, not just in the current state of near-anarchy in the country but—a permanent blot on his record—in the deportation, and in many cases subsequent extermination, of some 100,000 Jews.

Nonetheless, there was in the document a note of defiance. "Of the principles which I taught, of all the things which I have freely" (the word is worth noting) "said, I withdraw nothing. It remains true that our country has committed errors against herself which were nearly fatal and which leave its future, for a certain time, compromised. It remains true that, if it persists in the same errors, it will not recover either its rank or its strength. It remains true that France and Germany, condemned by geography to be neighbors to eternity, will have to look, in an effort of mutual understanding, for the conditions of a peace which will last. Germany has known that she is powerless against a coalition; France has known that she could not struggle alone against her neighbor to the east; it is time for the nations of Europe to make up their mind that they do not want to die."[2]

It was a bold statement. (In truth, it could have easily been written by de Gaulle himself. The historical irony, of course, is that it charted a course which de Gaulle followed in the postwar era.) But, even apart from this final show of defiance, Pétain had started to regain some of the stubbornness of character which had been lost in the feeble compromises of Vichy. On 25 August, he made it clear that he no longer considered himself a head of state, and in consequence would only draw the salary due to him as a Marshal of France. Moreover, he became much more hostile in his resentment toward those whom, at last, he was prepared to recognize as his jailers.

Pétain, much as he might have wished, and occasionally confused as he was, could not escape the circumstance of the time. The Germans wanted to keep him in their pocket. Indeed, on 26 August 1944, the very day of de Gaulle's triumphal march down the Champs-Elysées to a victory ceremony in Notre-Dame, Hitler had sent for Laval. Laval refused the invitation, such as it was. In his stead, Marion, Darnand, Déat, Doriot and de Brinon went off to see, first Ribbentrop, and then, on 1 September, Hitler himself. The message they were given was clear. With his new weapons, Hitler was confident that he would turn the tide of the war. There must therefore be a new government in France. De Brinon—no less—was given the job of seeing Pétain to demand, in the name of the Führer, his endorsement of the new government.

By that point, the formation of any sort of French government verged on the ridiculous. Not only was France itself largely in Allied hands, but by then de Gaulle had received the endorsement of the United States. It was General Dwight Eisenhower, acting on clear instruction from President Roosevelt, who awarded the accolade. Eisenhower's visit to de Gaulle—on Sunday 27 August 1944—was clear in its intent. "I went to call on General de Gaulle promptly," Eisenhower later wrote, "and I did this very deliberately as a kind of recognition of him as the provisional President of France."[3] The political die was thus cast. The United States, whatever Roosevelt's dislike of the man, had finally and unequivocally given its support to the unruly general, and de Gaulle, in turn, was quick to take his cue. By 5 September he had started to put together a government of "National Unity," and, on 9 September—after the customary haggling about ministerial posts—had announced his list of ministers.

But there was even more to it than that. When asked by Georges Bidault on 25 August, on the balcony of the Hôtel de Ville in Paris, to "proclaim the Republic" de Gaulle cut Bidault down. "The Republic," he said, "has never ceased to exist. . . . Why should I proclaim it?"[4] De Gaulle's view was clear. The vote of the National Assembly on 10 July 1940 was unconstitutional. It followed that the Vichy régime itself was constitutionally outside the law and was only a "parenthesis," as he put it, in the long history of the Third Republic. Whether de Gaulle's view was right or wrong—and it has, of course, been disputed down the years—there is no doubt that, in political reality, power in France had passed to de Gaulle and his new government.

In spite of all that was taking place in Paris—and in the real political world—the charade of the remains of what had been the Vichy government continued to play on what was by then a pantomime stage. But by early September 1944, General George Patton's tanks were perilously near to Belfort. The result was predictable. Yet again, Pétain and his motley party were told to pack their bags—they were to be transferred to Germany. Pétain wrote a furious letter of protest to Hitler, yet again to no avail, and Ménétrel wrote a farewell letter to his wife. On 7 September Pétain, Nini, Ménétrel and the accompanying party left Morvillars and were conveyed under heavy German escort across the frontier into Germany. They were followed by the group of so-called ministers in the new "French Governmental Delegation," headed by de Brinon. The journey was, once more, miserable. The next day, they arrived at a small town on the upper Danube.

Sigmaringen was, and still is, with all its beauty, a small and, in political terms, insignificant town. At the time, the population was no more than some 5,000. The war, as almost everything else over the centuries, seemed to have passed it by. The town itself was overlooked by a grand castle containing innumerable staircases and vast drawing rooms. They seemed to be no more than extended museums of medieval armor, hunting trophies, antique German furniture and large portraits of forgotten Prussian royalty. There was only one elevator (into which, it was said, a large motor car could be fitted). This was to be Pétain's new home. The last Marshal of France had thus become the unlikely resident of a Prussian castle.

Everybody in Sigmaringen knew what would happen to them if they fell into the hands of their liberated compatriots. As the Allies advanced there was much settling of scores in France. What was called the *épuration sauvage* of the summer and autumn of 1944 and the early months of 1945—a series of uncontrolled, random and mostly brutal attacks on those suspected of fraternizing with the German occupiers—claimed some 9,000 lives before order was properly restored. There were summary judgments and improvised courts-martial. By late 1944, show trials were under way. On 10 November 1944, de Gaulle's provisional government set up a high court of justice to try all members of the "governments or pseudo governments which had their seat on metropol-itan territory . . . for crimes or offenses committed in the exercise of or con-nected with their functions."[5] It all sounded very sinister. For Pétain himself, however, there was some comfort in an opinion poll of October 1944. Whatever may be the doubts about the sampling techniques of the time, the message it conveyed was clear: when asked whether Pétain should be punished, 32 percent of respondents relied "yes," but 58 percent replied "no" (10 percent did not know).

In the light of all this Pétain set to work to compile a series of memoranda in justification of all that he had done since the end of the First World War. His preliminary notes, in his own hand, cover his interventions in the Conseil Supérieur de la Guerre in the 1920, his period as a minister, his stay in Spain as ambassador and, finally, the events of May 1940. Work was interrupted, how-ever, when on 22 November Ménétrel was arrested by the SS while returning with Pétain from his daily walk. The arrest, in fact, hardly came as a surprise. Ménétrel had been a constant irritation to de Brinon and his colleagues, and Abetz suspected him of links with the Resistance. Pétain protested yet again—and yet again to no avail. Ménétrel was taken first to the little town of Scheer—and another castle—some 10 kilometers south of Sigmaringen, before being transferred in March 1945 to the SS camp at Eisenberg in Bohemia. Pétain was never to see him again.

Pétain had lost—forever—his doctor and his closest friend. Ménétrel's replacement as Pétain's doctor, the writer and collaborationist Louis-Ferdinand Céline, was not welcomed with any detectable warmth. Not only that, but the war, by the end of 1944 and the spring of 1945, had taken what was to be a decisive turn. On 16 December 1944 the German army launched its offensive in the Ardennes. Bold as it was, it was no more than a last throw. By Christmas it had stalled. On 30 January 1945 the Americans launched their own attack on the *Westwall*—the "Siegfried Line"—and breached it on 4 February. On 22 March they crossed the Rhine at Mainz. On 30 March de Lattre de Tassigny's 1st French Army followed suit and, on 7 April, took Karlsruhe, no more than 120 kilometers to the north of Sigmaringen. They were under orders from de Gaulle to head for Stuttgart and the south. In a week or two, if there was no resistance, they would arrive at the river Danube. In short, they would arrive at Sigmaringen.

Pétain had made up his mind. On 5 April he had learnt that all Vichy minis-ters, including himself, were to be tried by the High Court *in absentia*. This was wholly unsatisfactory. He was determined to return to France and be tried in person. He therefore would wait for whoever arrived first, French or Americans—it mattered little—at Sigmaringen. He would request whoever came to repatriate him to France. There were moments, too, when he still thought that he could make peace with the Allies and de Gaulle. But the Germans had also made up their minds. They would not let him out of their sight. On the evening of 20 April Otto Reinebeck and Kurt von Tannstein, the first a diplomat and the second an officer at Sigmaringen, who by then had replaced, respectively, Abetz and Renthe-Fink, told Pétain that he was going to be moved. The whole party left Sigmaringen the next morning. In the darkness, two Gestapo cars led the gloomy cavalcade. Just in case any of the French party should have any ideas about escaping, all four Gestapo cars bristled with machine guns. Pétain kept muttering that he wanted to go back to France. Nobody seemed to notice, or, indeed, to know, where they were going.

At nine o'clock, after taking four and a half hours to cover 120 kilometers, the party arrived at the small town of Wangen. They had arrived, as it happened, in a place of beauty. In peacetime, this small town, in the upper valley of the river Argen, would have been a pleasant enough place to alight. Pétain and his party, however, were in no mood to admire Wangen's attractions—they only wanted to know where they were to be going next. Their German escort was mute.

It was to be to Zeil. There was a fine castle there where they were to stay for the rest of the day and one night. Immediately, maps were brought out, and a consultation followed. The conclusion was clear. Far from going southwest to Bregenz and the Swiss frontier, as they had expected, they were going northeast toward Ulm. By now confused as well as distraught, they decided that they were to be taken to the Bavarian redoubt, where Pétain thought Hitler would make his last stand.

On the evening of 21 April, they were all escorted, with the now customary Gestapo cars and machine guns, to the Prince von Waldburg's castle at Zeil. In other times, they might have enjoyed the beautiful views from the terraces of the castle. But the next day they learnt that the Americans had taken Ulm and were advancing southward. It looked as though Pétain's group would be cut off from the Bavarian redoubt and soon overrun by the American forward detachments.

Pétain was quite happy to stay put, take a much needed rest, and wait for them. But at ten o'clock that evening, von Tannstein sent for Debeney and told him to get his party ready to move again. When he heard this, Pétain sent Debeney back to von Tannstein with a message. The message was simple. Pétain refused to move.

At midnight, von Tannstein demanded to see Pétain himself. The others could only listen at the door of Debeney's room where the meeting was to be held. It started off crisply enough. Von Tannstein explained that the military situation required an immediate departure. Pétain replied that he would not leave. He was firm. He would wait there for the arrival of French or American troops. Von Tannstein tried another tactic. He said that he had to obey orders and he pleaded with Pétain to allow him to do so.

At that point, Pétain lost his temper. It was one o'clock in the morning and he was tired. "It's useless," he almost shouted. "You have done nothing but lie to me since Vichy. Where do you want to take me?"[6] When von Tannstein replied that it was to the Swiss frontier, Pétain said he did not believe him, and would not believe him unless he could show that the Swiss authorities had given them permission to enter Switzerland. That could be arranged when they get there, was the reply. Pétain said again that he did not believe it, that he had no confidence in von Tannstein at all, that he had always been deceived, that Renthe-Fink had always lied to him. In short, he was staying put.

Von Tannstein became angry in his turn. There followed a heated discussion about German good faith, which lasted the best part of an hour. An aide, Admiral Bléhaut, as well as Nini, were now brought into the debate. Nini said that Pétain was tired and needed rest. Bléhaut said that he was sure that they were to be taken to the Bavarian redoubt. Finally, von Tannstein admitted that those were his orders, but that on their own initiative they had decided to deliver Pétain to the Swiss frontier. Nini asked what the German government would think of that. "There is no government any more," von Tannstein replied.[7]

At that point, in the middle of the night, their host the Prince von Waldburg suddenly—and unexpectedly—appeared. He came with the news, which he had heard on the telephone, that French tanks were only 20 kilometers from Zeil. The Prince's sudden appearance had an immediate effect. Pétain said again that he would wait for the French tanks, and that, moreover, he was now going to bed, and that was the end of the matter.

But he did not have much sleep. At a quarter to six, Reinebeck and von Tannstein burst into Pétain's bedroom. He must leave immediately. Pétain refused. Not only did he refuse; he refused even to get out of bed, saying that he was old and tired, and that he would stay where he was. Only if they could assure him that the Swiss authorities had given their consent would he budge. Reinebeck calmed him down by saying that consent had been requested and would arrive that afternoon. The reply was simple: until and unless the Swiss consent was given in proper form he, Pétain, would stay in bed for a much-needed rest.

Reinebeck was right. The consent from the Swiss Federal Council arrived at around seven in the evening, with the proviso that Pétain sign an assurance that he would stay in the premises allocated to him in Switzerland until the French authorities indicated that they were ready to receive him on French territory. At 10:30 P.M. the whole party gathered itself together, left Zeil, made its way through dense traffic—lorries pulled by tractors, horses, bicycles—and a mass of refugees, and arrived at Bregenz at 3 A.M. the following morning. Rooms were provided, with bad grace by the owner, in a small hotel. At 8 A.M. they were up, woken by bombs falling on Bregenz. By 9:30 A.M. the air raid had passed and it was safe to leave. They drove the last 10 kilometers to the Swiss frontier, fearful lest they be spotted by Allied aircraft. At 10 A.M. on 24 April 1945, almost on the hour, they crossed into Switzerland. That day, Pétain also entered into his eighty-ninth year.

Pétain's birthday arrival in Switzerland was duly reported to Paris. De Gaulle was immediately informed. For him, given their relationship in the old days, the matter was not easy. In truth, de Gaulle wanted Pétain just to go away and not reappear. But his own government thought itself obliged, such was the ferment of the time, to demand Pétain's extradition to France. De Gaulle then made it known—through the normal unidentifiable channels—that it would be welcome if the Swiss courts could refuse extradition. In that case, Pétain and his wife would pass the remainder of their days in the safety of Switzerland. It was even mooted that if there was a financial problem in maintaining a reasonable Pétain establishment in Switzerland the problem could be resolved without difficulty.

But the problem for the Swiss was that Pétain, far from opposing extradition, was only too anxious for it. The court in Bern took due note of this, and without delay approved an extradition order. Moreover, the order was to be executed immediately. Pétain was to be out of Switzerland as soon as possible.

The route was supposed to be a secret, but their journey was lined by crowds cheering him on, throwing flowers as he passed, and even giving him, just outside Brienne, a cask of wine, as a belated birthday present, for his picnic. They finally arrived, at 4:45 P.M. on the evening of 26 April at the Swiss frontier station of Vallorbe. Nini was asked by a French official whether she wished to accompany her husband as there was no warrant out for her arrest. She replied that under no circumstances would she be separated from him. So it was that at 7:26 P.M. precisely, Philippe Pétain and his wife Eugénie, leaving their Swiss escort behind, crossed into France. The Marshal of France, as he had said he would, had returned to defend his honor.

The Marshal of France Defends His Honor

"Le vieux Maréchal ne pouvait douter qu'il allait être condamné."

Pétain's decision to return to France in April 1945 to face his accusers in person was certainly courageous, as de Gaulle was later to write. Some would describe it as foolhardy. He knew perfectly well that as long ago as 3 September 1943 the CFLN in Algiers had, by decree under the signatures of Giraud and de Gaulle, proclaimed him guilty of treason for having sought, and agreed to, the armistice of 1940. Furthermore, on 9 August 1944 the CFLN had declared null and void "all constitutional acts . . . promulgated on continental territory after 16 June 1940"—the day de Gaulle had left for London.[1] Moreover, even if he had thought that he might surmount the judicial and political obstacles and do some sort of deal with de Gaulle, he had only to look at the fate of one of his ministers, Pierre Pucheu, who had arrived in Algiers under safe conduct signed by Giraud—but had been arrested, tried by a military court, convicted (on dubious evidence) and executed on 20 March 1944.

And yet, at the end of his trial, the three judges proposed Pétain's acquittal on all the charges laid against him. Furthermore, their joint advice and their own votes went against the death penalty, which, in the event, was passed by a majority of only one. Botched prosecution, rambling evidence and some clever and emotional defense almost achieved what at the outset appeared to be beyond the limits of any reasonable possibility. The result in itself was the stuff of drama, but, as it happened, the whole trial turned out to be one of the most extraordinary judicial, political—and theatrical—events in modern French history.

Early in the morning of 27 April the special train carrying Pétain and his wife arrived at the little station of Igny. They were then driven to the old fort of Montrouge, south of Paris. Pétain was locked in a small cell in which the only furniture was a bed, a cupboard and a bedside table. He was told by the governor, Joseph Simon, that he was to be given no special privileges and was not to be allowed to receive messages or presents. He was permitted to leave his cell for an hour each day for exercise. His food was standard prison fare, but, as a concession, a doctor was on hand if required. To his wife—and she certainly had a case—it seemed to be a deliberate attempt to humiliate a great figure, not least a Marshal of France.

The procedure leading to the trial was by today's standards, to put it mildly, far from satisfactory. The High Court of Justice, itself only appointed by a provisional government without any democratic mandate, had in turn nominated a commission to interrogate the accused. There was no public say on who should be members of the commission and how they should act. Nevertheless, on the afternoon of 30 April its chairman, Pierre Bouchardon, a convinced opponent of Pétain hauled out of retirement for the purpose, arrived at Montrouge to claim authority for the procedure of interrogation which was to follow. Pétain in reply asked Bouchardon for a list of lawyers from which he might select his defense counsel. This was promised. Yet on 8 May (coincidentally the day on which Germany surrendered), Bouchardon returned to Montrouge with a series of questions to which he required immediate replies. He omitted to tell Pétain that he was entitled to refuse to answer questions without the presence of a lawyer. Unaware of his rights, and as yet without legal advice, Pétain signed his consent.

Bouchardon's questioning was overtly hostile. He challenged Pétain immediately. There was, first of all, the vote of 10 July 1940. Bouchardon did not doubt the legitimacy of the vote but attacked the aftermath. Pétain's replies were long and confused. They were a combination of self-justification, in many respects inadvertently—or possibly deliberately—erroneous, and memory lapse—the two, as is frequent in old men, going together.

Bad as it then was, the situation had not gone beyond hope of retrieval. Bouchardon had transmitted Pétain's request for legal representation to Jacques Charpentier, the president of the Paris Bar. Charpentier visited Montrouge to discuss the matter with Pétain. Their final choice was Fernand Payen, a most distinguished former president of the Bar but who, at the age of 73, was perhaps past his best (apart from all else, he had developed a disconcerting facial tic). In turn, on the recommendation of Pétain's old friend Henry Lémery, Payen chose as his junior the 34-year-old Jacques Isorni, who had caught attention in leading a spirited—but unsuccessful—defense of the collaborationist writer René Brasillach.

On 16 May, Payen and Isorni attended Pétain's second interrogation at Montrouge. Bouchardon was even more aggressive and Pétain even more confused. The more intense the questioning, the less coherent were the prisoner's replies. He even looked appealingly at his lawyers in the hope that they would answer on his behalf. But Payen had decided that both lawyers should stay silent. This was no accident. His strategy for Pétain's defense was to plead senility, and to lay the whole blame for what had happened on Laval—at the time, conveniently, a refugee in Spain. As they left Montrouge, Payen, in the best of humors, was supremely confident in his strategy, pointing out to Isorni that the whole interview had been in itself no more and no less a complete justification of what he had been saying all along. Senility was the only proper defense.

Isorni did not agree. Without even bothering to request authorization from Payen, he bicycled to Montrouge early the next morning and demanded to see the prisoner. Simon allowed him in—and agreed to keep this sudden visit secret. Pétain was nervous, but when he joined Isorni in the room assigned for the interrogation he was relieved to find Isorni ready and willing to speak up frankly and freely. There was no question of silence. Isorni urged the old man to stand up for himself—to cease to look like "a gardener accused of stealing vegetables."[2] When Pétain asked what would be done with him, Isorni simply replied: "You will be condemned to death."[3]

Isorni's outspokenness brought Pétain back to life. In short, the old warrior at that point decided to fight. Immediately, the two sat down to plan the defense. Far from being confused, Pétain was now clear in his mind. True, there were lapses of memory, but otherwise he was completely lucid. Together, they went through the whole history of events. Isorni made notes, constantly jogging Pétain's failing memory. In turn, once Isorni had left, Pétain dutifully copied them out in his own hand—so that Payen, when he was presented with them, would think they were all his own work.

Over the next three days, usually in the mornings when Pétain was at his most alert, Isorni came back to Montrouge to spend many hours with the prisoner. Sometimes he made two trips a day. On 21 May, however, while he was closeted with his client patiently going through the history of events—and urging Pétain to try harder to remember precisely what had happened and when—Payen arrived unexpectedly. Furiously, he demanded to know what Isorni was doing there. Isorni had no reply, and was almost prepared to plead guilty. But it was Pétain himself who saved the day. Smiling at Payen, he said that he had not wished to disturb his senior counsel for matters of minor detail and had requested Simon to invite his junior. Whether Payen believed him or not will never be known. Nevertheless, there is no doubt that from that day onward there was no love lost between the two counsels. In fact, the choice of a third lawyer to complete the required three-man team for the defense was to show the extent of the differences between the senior and the junior.

By early June Pétain was very tired. The constant interrogations exhausted him, to the point where the prison doctor intervened to request Bouchardon not to insist on two sessions in one day. But there was more to come. On 1 June the whole commission turned up—20 judges, magistrates and members of the Resistance. The meeting was, understandably, chaotic. Everybody seemed to be talking at once. Nothing of consequence was achieved. There was a repeat performance on 8 June. Each commissioner, on both occasions, wanted to have his say, frequently at inordinate length. Most of the speeches consisted of assertions rather than questions. Payen tried his best, but to no effect, to deflect the attack by demanding in turn that other witnesses be heard, in particular Leahy and Stucki.

By then, the whole procedure was in confusion. Pétain was on the point of collapse, his lawyers were bickering, the commissioners were making speeches rather than putting questions, much of the proceedings liberally reported in the press and the communist newspapers filled their columns with repeated insistence that the only possible penalty for Pétain—already and quite obviously, of course, guilty of the most horrendous treason—was death by firing squad.

By early June Pétain had the third lawyer in his defense team. Isorni had wanted to recruit Pierre Véron, a well-known and well-liked former member of the Resistance. When sounded out, Véron agreed to join Pétain's team only on the understanding that he could not defend the race laws or the deportation of Jews. Both Isorni and Pétain accepted his conditions, and on 2 June Pétain wrote to him formally inviting him to act for him—with a copy to Payen. But Payen immediately interposed a veto. It was unacceptable, he said, for a supporter of de Gaulle to be part of Pétain's defense team. The next day he nominated, as replacement, his old friend Jean Lemaire.

Lemaire was, in character, the opposite to both Payen and Isorni. Where Payen was ponderous and heavy handed, Lemaire could easily dissolve into irreverent giggles. Where Isorni was intense and highly strung, Lemaire could be calm and dispassionate. Calmness and giggles were just what Isorni needed, and he and Lemaire immediately struck up a friendship—much to Payen's irritation. In fact, the two got on so well that Isorni told Lemaire of his confidential meetings with Pétain. Thereafter, the two went together to Montrouge, huddled together in Lemaire's small Simca car, laughing, apparently, most of the way.

But the serious business was about to get under way. On 17 June, the anniversary of de Gaulle's flight to London in 1940, the High Court assumed its full legal competence—to try those who had previously been deemed to be traitors. Nevertheless, whatever was or was not its constitutional competence, the court itself was a very odd affair. It consisted of a president, who was at the same time president of the highest court of appeal, two fellow judges sitting beside him, respectively the president of the criminal division of the court of appeal and the president of the court of appeal of Paris, and 24 lay members.

The lay members—*jurés* in French (translated conveniently but incorrectly into English as "jurors," since they were allowed to intervene in debates as full members of the court)—were selected by lot from two groups: the first was a group of 50, chosen by the Constituent Assembly from a list of the 80 parliamentarians who had voted against Pétain and Laval on 10 July 1940; the second was a group of 50, supposedly freely chosen by the Constituent Assembly but in practice with heavy reliance on a list of members of the Resistance put forward by the commission appointed to oversee the "cleansing of the state." Since the (unelected) assembly consisted of those who, one way or another, had escaped the Vichy régime, it is hardly surprising that the final lists, ratified on 24 February 1945, consisted entirely of Pétain's opponents. As Charpentier himself put it, "the jurors were mostly people of good faith, but what impartiality could the accused expect from somebody who had been deported and who had returned from Buchenwald or from a mother whose son had been shot by the Milice?"[4]

Matters were made more complicated by an unexpected difficulty in finding a president for the High Court. The sitting president of the court of appeal was himself in prison, and nobody else wanted to take on the job. It took seven refusals before somebody was found. The final choice was Paul Mongibeaux; and he was to be flanked by Judge Donat-Gigue and Judge Picard. The difficulty, of course, was that all three of them had taken an oath of allegiance to Pétain personally. Furthermore, Donat-Gigue was a personal friend of Pétain and his wife. Finally, it became evident that the public prosecutor who was to launch the case against Pétain, André Mornet, had not only prosecuted the alleged spy, the glamorous Mata Hari, in 1917—which much amused the Paris wags—but had applied to be a prosecutor in the Riom trials of the Vichy court. (Fortunately for him his request was turned down.)

On 21 July, two days before the trial started, the three defense lawyers attended the procedure of choosing by lot 24 jurors, 12 from each group. Lemaire objected to three of those chosen on the grounds that they were communist. One of those rejected shouted "that will not prevent the traitor Pétain from getting twelve bullets in the skin!"[5] There was then a near riot, and Mongibeaux had to intervene to calm things down. What none of the defense lawyers spotted, however, was that one of the parliamentarians was a communist. His party, supported by their own press, screamed daily for the death penalty. As it happened, the oversight was to prove a costly error.

Much to the indignation of the Parisian public, de Gaulle had decided that the trial should be in a relatively small hall—the First Chamber of the Court of Appeal. The public was expecting a grand event, similar, for instance, to the trials of the Revolution, but de Gaulle refused to allow Pétain to be subject to such indignity. In fact, he regarded the whole thing as a "painful business."[6] The daily reports to him during the trial from the minister of justice, Pierre-Henri Teitgen, were received in the deepest gloom.

On 22 July, Pétain and his wife were moved from Montrouge to rooms in the Palais de Justice. The previous day Pétain had summoned his notary to make a new will. He had heard nothing from his relatives in the Pas de Calais—as far as they were concerned he seemed to have ceased to exist. His new will was therefore quite simple. His family was to be cut out altogether and his whole estate was to go to Nini and, in the course of time, to his much disliked stepson, Pierre de Hérain.

The morning of 23 July 1945 dawned dry and hot. By mid-morning the courtroom in the Palais de Justice was an oven. But none of this deterred those who were determined to witness in person what the press called, rightly, an historic trial. At 1 P.M. precisely, Pétain entered the courtroom, followed by his three lawyers. On their advice, he appeared in a simple blue uniform, wearing only France's highest military honor, the Médaille Militaire. In his left hand he held his Marshal's képi and in his right a roll of paper. It was a dignified entrance. Old as he looked, he held himself upright as he walked to an armchair placed facing the bench on which the judges would sit. The chattering crowd suddenly fell silent, and then, one by one until it became a wave, stood up. Once arrived at his chair, Pétain sat down carefully, and placed his képi, gloves and the roll of paper on the table in front of him.

At ten past one the judges entered, robed in the manner required by the court—but sweating heavily in the heat. They were followed by a bustling Mornet, who climbed up to his seat and sat down "like a vulture settling in his nest."[7] Immediately, Mongibeaux opened the proceedings. He made what he called a "declaration."[8] He wished the trial to take place in serenity and dignity. With this—most optimistic—observation he told Pétain to stand up. This Pétain did and, when asked his name, replied simply: "Pétain, Philippe, Marshal of France."[9]

Payen intervened immediately. He made a long speech claiming that the court was not competent to judge the case. He argued that the 1875 Constitution, which was still in place, required that the Senate, sitting as a court, was the only body which could legitimately try the president, the head of state, for treason. The order of 13 November, setting up the present court, could not possibly alter that. Besides, the judges had taken a personal oath of allegiance to the defendant. On both those grounds, the court should declare itself not competent. Mornet, in reply, pointed out that the oath meant nothing. The judges then retired. At a quarter to three they returned with the decision that they were indeed competent to try the case, since they had been specifically instructed to do so. Right or wrong, Mongibeaux then ordered the indictment to be read.

The final indictment was a curious document, a mixture of fact, opinion and, on occasions, accusations of guilt by association. It was in two parts, the first drawn up in Algiers and the second reflecting Petain's subsequent interrogation. It started with a recital of events surrounding the armistice, went on to the vote of 10 July 1940 and then, suddenly, laid the charge that Pétain had been previously plotting against the republic for many years. As an illustration of the style of the indictment, it quoted an M. Winkler, director of a press agency, who "related the following conversation reported to him by one of the Marshal's guests—a conversation which he had during a luncheon with the son of Primo de Rivera: 'You judge us Frenchmen from the angle of the Popular Front. Wait till next spring; we, too, shall have our national revolution, in the same manner as yours.'"[10]

Oddly enough, there was in the indictments no mention at all of the three crimes of which Pétain's régime at Vichy could with justice be accused: the racial laws and subsequent deportation of Jews, the forced labor of Frenchmen sent to Germany to work in appalling conditions and the terror organized by the Milice. None of those appeared in the main indictment and its supplementary. Since there was no reference to them, Pétain's role in each of them was, at first sight, apparently not to be explored.

It need hardly be said that there were reasons for the omissions. There was, of course, a problem about the Jews. There was no reason to believe that "liberated France" would be less harsh in its general attitude toward Jews than Vichy. What was objectionable was the inhuman treatment to which they had been subjected. Yet none of the prosecutors in Pétain's trial felt able to bring the matter up. Mongibeaux himself had dispensed justice in Vichy, it was said, "with a serene conscience."[11] In other words, the whole subject was a matter of embarrassment, and was to be passed over.

The Service de Travail Obligatoire, the system which had obliged Frenchmen to go to work in Germany, was equally delicate. True, there is in the indictments a short paragraph reproaching "the Marshal's Government with having contributed to the working of the German war machine, by voluntarily supplying it with products and manpower," but there was no mention of the conditions under which the "manpower" was forced to work.[12] (In fact, it was the return of the forced laborers, in their bedraggled state, which turned public opinion, if the polls are to be believed, against Pétain.) The trial judges had—when they were at Vichy—made no recorded objection either to the legality of forced labor or to its consequences.

As for the Milice, the indictments are silent. Again, this was a matter of profound embarrassment to the three judges and the public prosecutor. They had been, after all, there on the spot. They knew what was going on as well as anybody and had failed to take a stand, even to the point of registering their objections. To bring the whole thing up at this stage would have offered to the defense an open line of attack on the very sustainable grounds of hypocrisy.

De Gaulle was not pleased with the indictments and with the conduct of the early stages of the trial. He believed, as he later wrote, that "the capital fault of Pétain and his government was to have concluded with the enemy, in the name of France, the so-called 'armistice' . . . [all the rest] flowed infallibly from this poisoned source."[13] Yet the trial went on regardless. At the end of the reading of the indictments, the clerk read out the list of those who were to be witnesses and, when they had been told to leave the court, Mongibeaux announced that he was proceeding, as was the custom, to the interrogation of the accused. He asked whether, in view of his great age, Pétain wanted a break. Payen replied that, far from wanting a break, the defendant wished to make a statement. Leave was granted.

Pétain's statement had been prepared—by Isorni—with the utmost care. It went through several drafts, had been revised in discussion, copied out by Pétain in large letters which he would be able to see without his spectacles—and then had been learnt by heart. It was long on his old assertion of his sacrifice to his country and short on explanations of why he had allowed what had been done in his name. He claimed, for instance, that "the Armistice had saved France and contributed to the victory of the Allies in ensuring a free Mediterranean and the integrity of the [French] Empire," that "For [the French people] I went as far as to sacrifice my prestige," and that "While General de Gaulle, outside our frontiers, continued the struggle, I prepared the ways to liberation, in conserving a France sad but alive."[14] There was no mention of the anti-Jewish laws and deportations, of forced labor or of the Milice (which was perhaps excusable given that they had not been mentioned in the indictment, but perhaps not sensible, in that they were on the minds of much of his audience).

Pétain's speech lasted seven minutes. He had opened by saying that he would make this one speech and then remain silent. He closed by saying that if he was condemned it would be the condemnation of an innocent who will bear the whole burden "since a Marshal of France asks pardon from nobody."[15]

He sat down to silence in the courtroom. Immediately thereafter, first Isorni and then Lemaire attacked, Isorni on the insufficient time given to prepare the trial and the fact that there were still trunkloads of relevant documents which had not even been unpacked, let alone shown to the defense, adding for good measure that Mornet had announced prior to the trial that he would be seeking the death penalty. Lemaire followed up by a personal attack on Mornet, quoting an interview given by Mornet on 28 April to the newspaper *L'Aurore*. Mornet tried to rebut Lemaire but when there was some shouting in the gallery he made the mistake of saying that "there are really too many Germans in this room,"[16] a remark which was greeted by uproar, some in the crowd applauding and others booing and hissing. There was a crescendo of noise, to the point where Mongibeaux ordered the suspension of the sitting and the public galleries to be cleared. In the general confusion a young captain with only one arm leapt over the barrier and ran to shake Pétain's hand. The lawyers withdrew in indignation to listen to the soothing mediation of Charpentier, who had been called in, as the sitting president of the Paris Bar, to settle the matter amicably.

When the court met again, Lemaire picked another row, this time with Mongibeaux himself. He cited an article which had appeared in the *Franc-Tireur* of 21 July, in which Mongibeaux said to a reporter that "it is necessary [M Mongibeaux told us] to dispel the equivocation which wishes to make Pétain the man who had tried to save what he could of our unfortunate country but, on the contrary, he who, to satisfy his personal ambition and his political views, advanced himself to the point of treason."[17] Lemaire wanted a formal denial from Mongibeaux that he had ever said what was reported. Mongibeaux tried to defend himself by saying that he was not in the habit of issuing denials about newspaper articles. But Lemaire, in spite of Payen's tugs at his gown to try to get him to shut up, persisted. Mornet then launched into another defense of the court. After that, the session was again suspended while Mongibeaux and his two colleagues considered the matter.

The upshot of their consideration was that the trial should proceed but that Mongibeaux should not proceed along the normal pattern of such trials, in setting out in detail the charges against the accused. Consequently, the first witness for the prosecution should be called. By that time, Pétain, who had tried to hear what was going on by cupping his hand over his only viable—left—ear, appeared to have fallen asleep.

The first witness for the prosecution was Paul Reynaud. But it soon became clear that he was only speaking in self-justification. After the first wearisome hours of his evidence, Mongibeaux decided to call it a day, and the court adjourned. Reynaud continued on the following day. In all, his evidence, admittedly with many interventions from the defense lawyers, lasted over five hours. Reynaud came out badly damaged—particularly when it was revealed that he had agreed to be Pétain's ambassador to the United States, until Laval's hostility to the idea made him change his mind. It was no surprise that the defense lawyers questioned him closely, and that the lay members of the court—let alone these in the public gallery—had barracked him throughout.

There were to be many such noisy scenes over the three weeks of the trial. There were also revelations of attempts by Pétain's supporters to coerce the jurors into a favorable decision. They were bombarded with hate mail (and worse). Their food had to be checked each day for possible poisoning. At one point the word spread that an unofficial commando group was going to kidnap the jurors, and they were all issued with revolvers and live ammunition. Mongibeaux's call for serenity had quite plainly fallen on deaf ears.

In spite of these diversions, the proceedings continued. Next in line was Daladier who, rightly, asserted that in May 1940 the French Army had not been short of the tools of warfare—tanks, artillery and so on. Their generals had just not known how to use them. Then it was the turn of Lebrun, followed by Jeanneney, Louis Marin, Armand Gazel (the counselor in Pétain's Madrid embassy), Blum (the most thoughtful and elegant of the prosecution witnesses), Charles-Roux, Michel Clemenceau, General Paul-André Doyen (the first head of the Armistice Commission in Wiesbaden) and a number of figures of lesser importance. Their evidence occupied the remainder of the first week of the trial, but, apart from rambling about, switching from prewar history to the armistice, to Vichy and back again to prewar history, did not add much to what was already known. Each was defending his—or on one occasion her—own role.

By the end of the first week boredom had set in. But the thing was none the less vicious. Anonymous letters poured in. The Veterans of Verdun demanded an immediate acquittal. All three defense lawyers received death threats—from both sides. In all this, it was noted that Pétain had not only said nothing ("a Maginot Line of silence," one newspaper commented but seemed not to hear very much of what was going on and at times was quite clearly asleep.[18]

When the court resumed on the following Monday 30 July, the last witness for the prosecution appeared. It was Édouard Herriot, yet another veteran of the Third Republic. In spite of a painful attack of gout—he was obliged to keep one of his feet in a slipper—he chose to give his evidence standing up. This was a mistake. In considerable pain, and breathing hard, he was "alternately vague, bombastic, short-winded, shrill and tearful."[19] He was no match for Isorni, who reminded him at length that it was he who had woken Pétain in the middle of the night of 17–18 June 1940 to demand that his home city of Lyon be declared an open city. Moreover, after the armistice, Herriot had made a speech in the Council of Ministers on 9 July to any recalcitrant colleagues that they should gather "around Marshal Pétain, united in the veneration which his name inspires in everybody. . . . Take care to avoid disturbing the accord which has been established under his authority."[20] It was very embarrassing for Herriot.

Then it was time for the defense to put their own witnesses forward—nearly 50 in all. But quantity did not make for quality, and their position was weakened by the irrelevance of much of the evidence they put forward. There was, however, a good start. The first witness, Loustanau-Lacau, said immediately that he owed Pétain nothing. Indeed, he had been sacked in early 1940 from Pétain's office, had been arrested by Weygand in May 1941, had escaped and taken to the hills, had been rearrested and handed over to the SS, had spent six months working in the caves of the notorious Commandant Geissler, had undergone 58 interrogations, had been condemned to death and transferred to the camp at Mauthausen. He was freed just in time, but not before his body had been broken and his face laced with scars. He was unable to walk without the aid of sticks. It was all the more impressive, then, when he asserted roundly that Pétain had never been involved with the Cagoule, that he had known nothing of the 1937 plot to overthrow the government of the day. He finished by saying that "as for Marshal Pétain, I wish to say that, although he dropped me in a disgusting manner, I ask here that everybody reflect that, for France's misfortune, the blood of Marie-Antoinette and Marshal Ney is enough."[21]

It was then time for Weygand, who took the stand in the afternoon of 31 July, saluting Pétain as he walked past him leaning on his stick. (Pétain returned the salute.) Weygand was, as usual—and in spite of his age and the fact that he had just come from the prison hospital—robust and direct. But he was also very long-winded, explaining in full the history of events leading up to the armistice and defending his actions and those of Pétain. His first statement lasted three hours. He did, however, manage to make perfectly clear the difference between "armistice" and "capitulation." Since the surrender of Marshal Bazaine at Metz in the Franco-Prussian War "capitulation" was the gravest offense a commander in the field could commit, punishable by death. In fact, he went on, if France had "capitulated" the whole country would have been occupied and the fleet seized. Not only that, but the way would have been open for the German Army to march through Spain—occupying Gibraltar and handing it to Spain as the reward—and to land in Morocco. The whole of North Africa would have been lost. The same would happened if the French Army had fought on and, as would have certainly have happened, been mopped up with heavy casualties. At the end of his evidence, for the first time, Pétain spoke up, to say that he had not heard much of what was going on, but that he considered Weygand somebody on whom the greatest reliance could be placed.

At that point Reynaud intervened. He had been listening to Weygand with mounting anger. His anger spilled over when Isorni asked Weygand whether it followed from his evidence that the first people to mention the armistice in the War Committee was not himself and Pétain but Lebrun and Reynaud. Weygand agreed that that was so. This was the start of bad-tempered row between Reynaud and Weygand, which nobody seemed able to stop. Each was trying to lay the blame for the defeat on the other. So heated did it become that Mongibeaux declared an end to it—until the following day.

The session of 1 August started with the second act of the row between Reynaud and Weygand. By that time the court—and the press—was getting bored with it, and was only brought to life by the arrival of a letter from Leahy, which was hastily produced by Payen. In spite of Payen's enthusiasm, it did not add much to the debate. Leahy reiterated the views he himself had expressed when in Vichy as American ambassador. He was certain, he wrote, that Pétain had resisted many of the demands of the Axis. "I was then, and I am now, convinced that your main aim was the well-being and protection of the French people who had been abandoned. On the other hand, I must in all honesty repeat my opinion expressed to you at the time, that a complete refusal to make the slightest concession to Axis demands, which might have led to greater punishment for your people, would not in the long term have been disadvantageous."[22] In truth, Leahy's letter did little more than give ammunition to both sides.

After several other witnesses, a rumor spread quickly around the court: Pierre Laval was back in Paris, and was to be called the next day. The rumor turned out to be true. Laval was indeed back in Paris. He had been sent back by Franco, after the three-month asylum which he had been granted. He was immediately arrested by American military police and delivered to the French authorities. When they heard the news, the defense lawyers were horrified. Laval, if he was allowed to give evidence, might lead the court they knew not where. It was essential, and Payen argued the case to Mongibeaux, that there should be a preliminary interrogation. Mongibeaux refused the argument and the request. Laval, he announced, would appear the following day.

Laval duly appeared, escorted by his guards. Gone was the confident street politician of the prewar years. Instead, there entered a shabby, almost dirty figure, in a crumpled grey suit, grubby white tie, his hair plastered flat, his moustache yellow from nicotine. Mongibeaux started proceedings by saying that he wished to ask no questions which would prejudice the subsequent interrogation of an accused person. He then went on to do precisely that. As Laval answered—the first question was directed at the origins of his political relationship with Pétain—he constantly looked around him at the audience in court, reading, as best he could, the temperature and the mood. As he spoke about the days of the 1930s and of French relations with Italy, his voice grew in confidence. He made more of his Auvergnat accent—the r's fully rolled (oddly enough, Hitler, the Austrian, had the same trick) until they became almost mesmeric. He spoke on, about his period as minister of foreign affairs in 1934, about the Duke of Windsor, the defense of the franc, his hatred of war.

All that took up 25 minutes. By then, Laval was into his stride. He swatted aside an intervention from a juror, and even sneered at Mongibeaux, who had started to muddle his dates and had to be corrected not just by defense lawyers but by the witness himself. The more Laval went on the more confident he became. Even the hostile journalists started to put down their pencils to admire what was a most impressive performance. When he saw this, Laval turned to a nearby journalist and asked if he could have some water. An usher was called. He went out and came back—with a bottle of Vichy water. Even the most hardened and hostile journalist could not resist a wry chuckle.

By the time the session was adjourned after two hours, much to the relief of the defense lawyers, it was clear Laval was not going to attack Pétain. In fact, he went out of his way to align himself with the positions Pétain had taken. True, he was concerned to protect his back—he pointed out, much to the general surprise, that the constitutional acts Pétain had signed were null and void since they lacked the essential words "After consultation with the Council of Ministers"[23]—but he went on to claim that that was no more than an example of Pétain's lack of political experience. He was also firm in his view that the National Assembly had constitutionally and in due form approved the armistice.

At the start of the next session, Laval had a nasty moment. The former secretary to the Senate, a Mr. de la Pommeraye, claimed that Laval had said, on signing the constitutional acts himself, "and that's how you throw over the Republic."[24] Laval said he could not possibly remember, and replied that he and de la Pommeraye disliked one another from the start. He drew more fire when he talked of Montoire, claiming—amidst general clamor—"Do you think that in 1940 any man of good sense could imagine anything other than a German victory?"[25] He also had to fend off accusations about his "wishing" for a German victory. In fact, his defense was ingenious. Having been required by Pétain to cut out the words "I believe" he still felt that a gesture was necessary to placate the Germans. Indeed, if Pétain had asked him to cut out the words "I wish," he would have argued strenuously for their retention. With that, and with a sentimental flourish about his love of France, his village of Chateldon and the Auvergne, he was ushered out.

Pétain immediately made one of his rare interventions. "I reacted very strongly," he said angrily, "when I heard, in the speech, this phrase of M. Laval . . . he said earlier that he had come to find me with M. Rochat of the Ministry of Foreign Affairs, to show me that phrase. Well, M. Rochat would never have accepted keeping that phrase in, and I agreed with him. And then when I heard it on the radio . . . I thought it was done, that he had arranged the matter . . . and when I heard that the phrase had been repeated on the radio, I jumped up. I hadn't realized. I believed that it had been left out. I am very sad that it was left in."[26] In fact, in truth it was yet another example of Pétain's selective memory. Laval's version was correct.

The second day of Laval's evidence, on Saturday 4 August, was much less theatrical. The press was still hostile but the journalists nonetheless were admiring his performance. By the time he had finished Laval had shown himself to have sided with Pétain but, more important, he had shown Pétain to have sided with him. "Like a patient, cunning spider," wrote one onlooker, "he had trussed up the Marshal in his statements and insinuations which could never be untied."[27]

Once Laval was off the stage, the press again lost interest. During the afternoon of 6 August the news suddenly spread that the Americans had dropped an atom bomb on Hiroshima. This, for the press, was a much more interesting story than the succession of generals and Vichy ministers who were wheeled out by the defense. In fact, by producing so many witnesses who had so little to say, the defense seemed to lose momentum. The following day, *Le Monde* devoted the whole of its front page to the Hiroshima bomb and one column on an inside page to the Pétain trial.

In truth, among the many defense witnesses who were heard, only three points of interest were raised. The first was in the evidence, on 7 August, of the former Vichy minister for national education, Jacques Chevalier. He reported Pétain telling him on 1 February 1941 that "I am caught between two policies: one, that of cooperation with the English, which I greatly prefer; the second the law of the victor which I am bound to submit to because the victor is there and he is imposing it on the people that I must defend from him. . . . I do not follow a policy of 'double game.' "[28]

A less charitable view, however, was put on 8 August by General Jacques Campet, the head of Pétain's military cabinet during 1941, 1942 and 1943. In the middle of an incoherent ramble he suddenly produced a sentence which startled the court. His job had been to brief Pétain on the military situation from day to day. "Questions of sentiment," he announced, "did not arise for the Marshal; only questions of practicality were important. It was not a question of knowing whether the Marshal desired the victory of the Allies or the Germans but of knowing who would win the war, in order to be able to stick close to the victor and to profit from his victory."[29]

The second point of interest was in the evidence of Captain Édouard Archambaud on the following day. He confirmed that he had been instrumental in putting into code the three telegrams sent to Darlan: on 10 November 1942, that he should understand that the order to defend North Africa "was necessary for current negotiations"; on 11 November, that he was not appointed the Marshal's representative in North Africa "only because you were thought to be a prisoner"; and on 13 November, in response to the proposals for a binding agreement with the Americans sent earlier by Darlan to Vichy, a telegram drafted by Auphan himself saying "Close agreement between Marshal and Laval but before answering you the occupying forces are to be consulted."[30] Archambaud went on to say that at that point Laval was on the telephone to Abetz. In other words, his message was that Pétain approved the American plan but Laval scuppered it.

The third point of interest was the written evidence of General Juin who, in November 1942, was one of the generals commanding in North Africa. The defense lawyers had asked the court to get in touch with Juin, who had been mysteriously sent by de Gaulle on a mission abroad—a mission, apparently, due to last the same length of time as Pétain's trial. Contact was duly made, and Juin's reply was read out to the court on the morning of 10 August. Juin was categorical. "On the 13th or the 14th [of November 1942], I cannot remember which, Admiral Darlan, who had taken charge, told me of another telegram from Admiral Auphan speaking of a 'close agreement of the Marshal'. . . . I can state that these two telegrams from Admiral Auphan were of great help to us. They allowed us to calm down a number of consciences tormented by the oath [they had made to Pétain] and still hesitant."[31] Juin's written evidence, coming from a former Vichy general who had switched sides to de Gaulle, showed beyond doubt, at least in the view of the judges and the remaining impartial observers, that Pétain had been ready and willing to support Darlan in the deal he had done with the Americans.

It was time for the final speeches. On the afternoon of Saturday, 11 August, Mornet started his summing up. The court settled down to hear what was obviously going to be a long speech. It was hard to believe the argument, supported by numerous quotations of doubtful force, that Pétain had hatched a plot while he was ambassador in Madrid and then refused to join Daladier's council of ministers. It was even harder to believe that Pétain and Weygand together had planned the armistice with the deliberate purpose of overthrowing the government. After two and a quarter hours, during which the court listened with a mixture of boredom and incredulity, Mongibeaux gave the court a merciful 50-minute break.

Mornet had thus far failed to make much of an impact. But after the break he found a second wind. He threw all the most powerful accusations at Pétain: acceptance of defeat amounting to capitulation; humiliation of France; devious war against the Allies; the provision to Germany of men to work and to fight for the Germans; in short, treason under the definition of Article 75 of the Penal Code. With a final flourish he concluded "not without profound emotion but in the knowledge that a stern duty is accomplished . . . it is the penalty of death which I demand this High Court of justice to pronounce against he who was Marshal Pétain."[32]

It was then Payen's turn. After a long recital of Pétain's life history, he attacked the indictment on the grounds that most of it was speculation. He took the witnesses for the prosecution to task for defending themselves and, in doing so, trying to throw blame onto Pétain. But his delivery was not good, and, like Mornet, in many parts of the chamber he could not be heard. Some jurors started to fall asleep. Pétain himself had already dozed off. They only woke up because Payen had finished and had abruptly sat down.

Lemaire then stood up, and immediately started to pick a quarrel with Mornet. Payen tried to stop him, but Lemaire was determined. Mongibeaux succeeded in defusing what threatened to become an unpleasant personal dispute. Lemaire went on to attack the indictment, but the most effective part of his speech was his destruction of the evidence for a plot. He was able to show that the much-touted memorandum reporting a conversation with Alibert was no more than tittle-tattle. In fact, the author of the memorandum had confessed that the subject matter was simply no more than rumors which were running around the Resistance at the time.

Payen spoke again. First of all he summarized the views of Laval and his colleagues. Britain in 1940 was doomed. Germany was going to dominate Europe. Pétain, on the other hand, believed in an ultimate British victory. For the time being there was no question of resisting the occupying power. The only sensible policy was to give as little as possible to the Germans. He had therefore refused to give them the fleet, the bases they asked for in North Africa, refused to go to Berlin, refused to approve the Paris Protocols and refused to declare war on Britain. And then, Payen went on, age had taken its toll. He started to explain in the quietest possible tones that Pétain was senile. As though by way of agreement, Pétain had fallen asleep, but then so had a number of jurors.

The stage was now set for Isorni. He made full use of it. Tall and thin, with a high forehead, he loomed over Pétain, as the most hostile journalist of all, Madeleine Jacob of the *Franc-Tireur*, wrote, "like an archangel."[33] Isorni did his best with Riom, the racial laws and deportation of the Jews, the Milice and forced labor—the matters which had been in everybody's mind but had hardly been mentioned in the previous evidence. It was skilful enough, although he begged too many questions for it to be entirely convincing. It was when he started his long peroration that his speech caught fire. He moved into the middle of the court and addressed himself directly to the "Gentlemen of the Resistance." "For half an hour everyone believed that Pétain was in truth the saint and martyr described by the lawyer, the leader of the French Resistance admired by men of integrity."[34] As an orator, Isorni was in those moments almost irresistible. "Judges of the High Court, listen to me, hear my plea. You are only judges. You are only judging a man. But you hold in your hands the destiny of France."[35]

It was Madeleine Jacob who wrote "it seems to me that when, in years to come, people talk about the Pétain trial, it is the name of Maître Isorni that will dominate the whole story."[36] Even Mornet rushed across to congratulate him. In his room Pétain embraced him. But when the court reconvened after a short break, Payen rose to speak yet again. He spoke for three hours. After Isorni's fireworks Payen seemed dull and flat- an anti-climax. When Payen had finished, Mongibeaux asked Pétain whether he had anything to say. Pétain made a short and dignified speech. "Deal with me according to your consciences," he said. "Mine brings me no reproach, since during a life that has already been long, and having arrived at the threshold of death, I affirm that I have had no other ambition than to serve France."[37] With that, the court adjourned to arrive at a verdict. It was five past nine in the evening.

The jurors sat down in front of two narrow tables covered in green cloth. Once they were comfortable, Mongibeaux addressed them. "Gentlemen," he said, "my colleagues and I wish to ask you whether you would agree to a sentence of five years' exile."[38] In other words, he was suggesting what was tantamount to an acquittal. Picard followed him. He did not believe either in the plot against the republic or in Pétain's guilt, and gave the jurors a long discourse on the meaning of the word "treason." Donat-Guigue also gave his view that treason had not been proved.

All this was too much for the lay jurors to stomach. The leader of the parliamentarian jurors, Gabriel Delattre, himself a trial lawyer, spoke of the importance of the verdict in the public perception. There was a question about the sentences provided for under Article 80 and Articles 75 and 87 of the Penal Code. The answer was that Article 80 entailed a sentence of hard labor for life— but this could not apply to anybody over 70; Articles 75 and 87 entailed the death sentence.

There followed a long debate, at the end of which there was a vote. Jurors were asked to record, in secret ballot, whether they opted for Article 75 or for Article 80. When the result was declared, 18 had voted for Article 75 against 8 for Article 80. Mongibeaux, who had not voted, announced the result but pointed out that the result was only provisional. There would have to be a further vote on whether or not to apply the death penalty. If that vote turned out to be against the death penalty, that was the end of the matter, and a lesser sentence could be passed.

The argument dragged on into the night. At about one o'clock some of the jurors called for the second vote to be taken. In silence the ballot box was passed around the table. Nobody spoke while Mongibeaux counted the votes. All waited tensely for the result. When it came, it was as close as could be: 14 for death, 13 against. It soon appeared that the three judges had voted against the death penalty, that 9 of the Resistance jurors had voted in favor, along with 5 parliamentarians. The vote that tipped the balance was cast by Louis Prot, the communist deputy for the Somme. That done, the penalty of "national indignity" was proposed and carried. Pétain was to lose his rank, his decorations and his property. It was only then that a recommendation was passed that in view of Pétain's great age, the death sentence should not be carried out.

Mongibeaux put away the text he had drafted when he expected an acquittal and drafted the text of condemnation. It was after four o'clock in the morning when the court reassembled. Pétain, who had spent the hours in his room making his confession and hearing Mass, was summoned. He listened in silence while the judgment was read out. It was humiliating. A Marshal of France, the "Victor of Verdun," had been found guilty of treason. But nobody was in any doubt about the seismic shock of the event. It was a shock which would resonate, with all its aftershocks, down the years.

Prison for Life

"Je n'ai jamais accepté ma condemnation."

After the sentence was pronounced, Pétain was taken down and immediately told to put on civilian clothes. Most important, his hat, a dark grey Homburg, was brought to him to stand in for the Marshal's képi which his sentence had taken from him. Then, under the guard of Simon, five soldiers, a doctor and several policemen, he was driven to the military airport of Villacoublay, where de Gaulle's own personal aircraft—a DC-3 Dakota painted with the Cross of Lorraine on its fuselage—was waiting. Nini, much to her disgust, was left behind.

The whole thing had been swift. De Gaulle, reasonably enough, wanted to avoid any possibility of disturbances—even riots—after the sentence was announced. Swift it may have been, but the continuing challenge to an unsatisfactory verdict and a continued fear of ambush from Pétain's supporters dragged out what might have been temporary confinement to prison for the rest of his life.

De Gaulle's aircraft, carrying Pétain and his guards, landed at the airport of Pau, in the deep south of France, at about eight o'clock on the same morning, 15 August. It was met by the local Préfet with suitable support, even at that early hour, from a handful of local dignitaries. Pétain was taken to the fort of Le Portalet, high in the mountains of the Pyrenees and only a few kilometers from the Col du Somport and the Spanish frontier. As the cavalcade passed through the towns and villages, people who were out on the streets to celebrate the annual feast of the Assumption of the Blessed Virgin Mary stopped and stared, and even waved to the well-known figure—who responded, as always, by raising his hat to them.

Pétain, old as he was, had not yet come down from the excitement of his trial. In fact, he was rather enjoying the attention. The cheerfulness vanished, however, when he saw the cell in which he was to be lodged. It was the same cell in which Georges Mandel had been confined by the Vichy government, with Blum, Reynaud, Daladier and Gamelin as neighbors. His cell was on the level of the third basement—the fort itself almost clinging to a cliff. It was damp; there was only one electric fire which had to be kept going night and day; and there was nowhere to walk but a small terrace which could only be reached by a steep and dangerous staircase of 32 steps.

Pétain's hopes for an early change of prison came to nothing. True, de Gaulle had signed on 17 August an order commuting the death sentence to one of life imprisonment, and had in mind, as he later wrote, that Pétain "after having been detained for two years in a fortified place he would go to his home near Antibes to finish his life."[1] But de Gaulle, to say the least, had much to think about during the second half of 1945, and the conditions of Pétain's imprisonment were nowhere near the top of his list. Besides, there were many who thought that Pétain should have a taste of the medicine which he had given others. The fact, as it turned out, that the previous occupants of the fort had a much easier time of it was neither here nor there to those who were looking for revenge. Reynaud spent his days with a 23-year-old secretary ("very pretty, too," Simon was told)[2]; Mandel had regular visits from his mistress and was looked after by his valet; Daladier's sons frequently came to see him; and all of them had their food sent up from the Hôtel des Voyageurs in the valley town of Urdos. Pétain enjoyed no such privileges.

By the end of August Pétain's morale, resilient as it had been up till then, was starting to break. On the 30th he told Simon that he was living on the edge of the grave and that he had nothing more to expect from life. But perhaps more revealing was his remark that "I made the gift of my person, it is said, but in truth it is in words, since one holds on to life."[3] At last, he was admitting that the "gift of his person," proclaimed with great ceremony while he was in power, was little more than a rhetorical gesture. Holding onto life was more—much more—important than rhetorical gestures. But if he had finally come round to admitting that the gift of his person was no more than a gesture, there had been no sign as yet that his morale had sunk into anything near to suicidal desperation.

The sign came two months later, after his lawyers had come and gone—promising repeal of the trial verdict on a rehearing—and Nini had paid her first visit, spending much of her time bickering with her husband and shouting at his jailer, provoking Simon to write in his diary that he would like to "kick her up the backside."[4] On 20 October Simon noted that Pétain was badly depressed.

The prospect of long years in prison and disappointment with his wife led him to burst out: "If there were no bars on the window, I would have thrown myself into the Gave [the river below]."[5]

By that time Simon, who at Montrouge had been openly hostile to his charge, had become sympathetic, indeed almost affectionate. The two had daily conversations about the world in general, Pétain with his customary courtesy and Simon with his Breton bluffness. Simon noted, too, how the doctors who looked after Pétain had become devoted to him, how the local curé who came to say Mass every Sunday enjoyed his visits, and how even the guards were happy to exchange a joke or two with the prisoner on his walks on the terrace. He also noted Pétain's surprisingly good physical health. True, there were times when Pétain's morale was so low that he refused to eat or refused to shave himself, and Simon had to encourage one of the guards to play cards with him. In fact, the only thing that cheered him up at all was a series of letters from Isorni promising favorable—but unspecified—developments in the review of his case on appeal. After reading these he was apt, in his most cheerful mood, to tell Simon about what he knew was to happen—a transfer to the Mediterranean island of Sainte-Marguerite, perhaps, or another equally suitable island.

Another island it was to be, although not any of the ones he had imagined. By the end of October 1945 the magistrate in the Ministry of Justice charged with following the case, Alain Jégou, had come to the conclusion that Pétain should not stay at Le Portalet for the winter. The climate was too harsh and, although the fort itself was secure from possible raids by Pétain's followers to get him out, the Spanish frontier was too close for comfort. There were rumors that groups of Spaniards were preparing to make a marauding raid to whisk him off to Spain and to demand political asylum for him from Franco. Real or imaginary, the threat itself was enough for Paris. The last thing the de Gaulle government wanted was Pétain, as it were, on the loose.

At the beginning of November Simon received instructions from Jégou. The prisoner was to be moved from le Portalet to the island off the western coast of France known as the Île d'Yeu. The move was to be accomplished in the greatest secrecy, yet again to give no opportunity to Pétain's friends to take advantage of the move to mount an ambush. The fear was, perhaps, exaggerated. Simon at least thought so. Nevertheless, at half-past eleven on the night of 14 November a new cavalcade left Le Portalet. It was not until eleven o'clock in the morning of the 15th that the party reached the Atlantic coast. At the little fishing harbor of La Pallice, a corvette was waiting to take them on what should normally be no more than an hour or two's passage to Port-Joinville, the main port and capital of the island.

The Île d'Yeu is not a particularly attractive place. An island 9.5 kilometers long and 4 kilometers wide, it lies some 18 kilometers off the western coast of France. It is an appendage, if that is the right word, of the department of the Vendée. Climatically, it suffers from the Atlantic weather. On its eastern side it is buffeted by the strong currents flowing down from the Brittany peninsula and on its western side by fearsome oceanic waves. The winters are always bleak and unfriendly.

About a kilometer to the west of the capital is La Citadelle, whose main feature is the fort of Pierre-Levée. It is, even for today's visitor, a gloomy place. There is a central building of two stories, in the middle of which is an archway which is the only entrance to the fort. At either end of the building two wings of barracks form an enclosure on three sides of a large courtyard. The entrance is protected by a drawbridge. It is secure—suitably so, since it was a military prison during the Napoleonic wars.

In this depressing establishment Pétain was allocated two rooms above the entrance to the fort, looking inward (insofar as a small barred window allowed him to look) onto the square. In one room there was a metal bed, a small chest of drawers, two upright wooden chairs and a little wood stove; in the second there was a largish table, an armchair and another little stove. There was a small bathroom and lavatory next door. Drinking water had to be fetched by the guards from an outside tap some 250 meters away, and the electricity only functioned in the evenings until eleven o'clock. But such as they were, which is not much, these quarters were to be Pétain's home for the next five and a half years.

Apart from Simon and three attendant guards, the most important figures in Pétain's new life at Pierre-Levée were the doctor, the priest and his wife—possibly in that order. The doctor at Port-Joinville, who was instructed to look after him, Dr. Emmanuel Imbert, was a cheerful enough character. He led what can only be described as a colorful life, and was apt to drink too much. In one of his more lively moments he had led a group of sailors to smash up the main hotel in Port-Joinville on the grounds that the owner had made a fortune during the Occupation by denouncing his fellow citizens to the Gestapo. Abbé Germain Ponthoreau was altogether different. Like many of the clergy of the Vendée he was a Pétain sympathizer, and was very happy to engage every Thursday in long conversations with the prisoner. A gentle man, he was considered by his flock to be "a priest of exceptional qualities, both spiritual and human."[6] He kept detailed notes of his talks with Pétain but thought it better, possibly on the advice of his superior, to destroy his manuscript in case it revealed too much sympathy and admiration for his distinguished interlocutor.

Pétain's marriage had had, to put it mildly, its ups and downs. But in his isolation Pétain became, almost like a child, dependent on his wife. When she was there, she could do no right; when she was not there, she was instantly missed. His letters to her from the island, summoning her back, become more and more alluring as time passes. Pétain was lonely. He spent most of the day alone—at one point he tried to keep himself entertained by improving his poor English. He ate his meals alone—the same food as the guards, including a quarter-bottle of wine. Any company—even his wife's—was better than none.

Old age, loneliness and boredom were starting to take their toll. He was still in good physical health, but periods of depression became more frequent. Furthermore, the world outside the Île d'Yeu was changing, and not changing to his advantage. In January 1946 de Gaulle suddenly resigned and walked off home to Colombey-les-Deux-Églises. With him went the last serious possibility of Pétain's early release. True, the lawyers were doing their best, but Payen had died and neither Isorni nor Lemaire had the political clout. Certainly, Pétain was cheered to learn from his wife, on a visit at the end of June 1946, that President Harry Truman had asked the French government to release him, sending the message that if release was politically embarrassing the United States was ready to grant Pétain asylum. There were committees for his release forming as well, not only in Paris but in Switzerland, Italy, the United States, Brazil—and in Britain. Queen Mary, the Queen Mother, and the Duke of Windsor were particularly active on his behalf.

But it all came to nothing. Life in prison went on as before. Nini asked for another armchair for the prisoner. Simon refused. Pétain was caught in the crossfire between his wife and his surly jailer. "She knows," he explained to Simon, "that without me she is nothing. If she is 'la Maréchale' she owes it to me. But at the moment she is perfect, I would never have believed she could be so nice . . . it's a revelation to me."[7] Simon himself was getting fed up with looking after the old man and made it clear to his superiors.

Nonetheless, 1947 itself began promisingly. Isorni and Lemaire were given permission again to visit the prisoner. The Constitution of the Fourth Republic was in place. Elections had been held and a government, under Pétain's old colleague and opponent Ramadier, had been formed. On 16 January, Vincent Auriol was elected president of the new republic. It was customary, the lawyers told Pétain, for an amnesty to follow the election of a new head of state. They were quick to follow up. On 10 February Isorni and Lemaire went to see Auriol full of high hopes—to be immediately brushed aside. Neither Auriol nor Ramadier had any intention of altering the present state of affairs in any way whatsoever. On the same day, Pétain asked for authorization for Nini to stay near him in La Citadelle when she came to visit. Authorization again was refused.

In the early weeks of 1947, Pétain's health was poor. His legs were swollen (Nini proclaimed loudly that he had been poisoned) and one hip was painful. Mentally, too, he was starting to slip further. The "eclipses" became longer and more frequent, and he would occasionally fall asleep in the middle of a sentence. There was little Dr. Imbert could do. Nini, too, was of little help. Moreover, she treated the inhabitants of Port-Joinville with contempt, and shouted at Pétain's guards—all of whom asked for a transfer in the event of her being allowed to stay in La Citadelle. Islanders and guards alike said that she was only "wanting to show Grandfather's supporters the calvary she had to climb to be near her husband."[8] ("Grandfather" was the name given to Pétain by the islanders.)

Pétain's health recovered in time for a further visit from Isorni and Lemaire on 24 April 1947—his 91st birthday. Their visits always cheered him up, and they found him on his best form. They reported that the Académie Française was recruited to the cause, working for his release. At the same time, he was also cheered to receive a telegram from his great-niece, Yvonne de Morcourt. It was the first time he had heard from any of his family since his arrival in the Île d'Yeu. She wrote that she wanted to come to visit him. The news was more than welcome, and Pétain replied as much, saying that he was sure that she would be allowed to do so if she came with Nini.

Pétain's attitude to Nini remained, as always, ambivalent. By then Nini was spending most of her time at the Hôtel des Voyageurs in Port-Joinville, in a small apartment set up for the purpose. At times he seemed less happy seeing his wife than playing on his daily walks in the courtyard, as a child plays, with a little dog which Simon had found and brought into the fort to catch the rats which infested the place—known as Miquette, or "Mickey" as Pétain called her. Simon summed up the mood in September 1947 after one of Nini's departures: "What calm for everybody when she is not there. If she could never come back, how happy we would be, the prisoner and the personnel."[9]

On 7 June 1947, Isorni wrote to Nini at the Hôtel des Voyageurs that there was to be a visit to the Île d'Yeu by the parliamentary commission set up to inquire into the events in France during the period 1933–1945. Nini tried to block the visit, on the grounds that her husband was not up to it, but, yet again, she protested in vain. On 10 July the commission, 13 of them (and three secretaries), including Blum, Daladier and Gamelin, arrived on a warship at Port-Joinville, and immediately went up to La Citadelle to see Pétain. Nini, however, was not to be denied. She went up to Pierre-Levée a couple of hours before the commission arrived there. Her purpose was plain: "to insist with the prisoner that he say 'no' to every question asked."[10]

It was advice that Pétain would have done well to heed. He tried to make it clear that his memory was not what it was. But it turned out to be worse than that. When questions were put to him he kept on referring back to the First World War. He claimed never to have heard of books to which he had contributed a preface. He could not remember having sent Reynaud, Gamelin, Daladier, Blum and Mandel to prison—above all Blum, for whom he claimed to have the highest regard. In fact, when the commission left him after nearly two hours they were none the wiser. But they were suspicious of his memory lapses—perhaps, they thought, Pétain was up to his old tricks. And yet they were impressed by his bearing, and their initial hostility—some wanted just to call him without ceremony "Pétain"—turned to grudging respect. "Whatever one can think about Vichy," said one deputy on leaving, "he is all the same somebody [of consequence]."[11]

1947 dragged on. On 8 October Simon's wife died. Pétain, Nini and Isorni all wrote letters of condolence. But when Simon returned to duty, quite clearly in grief after his wife's funeral, he found he had a much more difficult prisoner to deal with. On 7 or 8 November—the exact date is uncertain—Pétain refused his daily walk. He did not even recognize Simon. "Who are you?," he asked.[12] When Nini arrived for her daily visit he did not recognize her either. She tried her best to revive his memory, explaining that they had been living together, one way or another, for 28 years and that they had been married. Her promptings went without noticeable response. He was surprised when she told him that she had been at his side in Vichy and had followed him to Sigmaringen. Later in the day he recovered his memory, but Dr. Imbert, after prolonged examination, was obliged on the 9th to report that, although physically he was well, "these break-downs, at the moment not very serious because of their short duration and their rare occurrence, point to an unavoidable state of ageing."[13] When Pétain was brought his morning coffee on the next day, he was in tears and, for the first time, refused to make his bed.

What was then bad became even worse. On 2 December, Pétain denied ever having been married to Nini and demanded a marriage certificate to prove the contrary. On 11 December, he soiled his trousers in front of his guards and a weeping Nini, who was in tears. Again and again he was heard by Simon letting out cries of despair. By the end of 1947 it had become clear that the "eclipses" were becoming more frequent and ever-longer in duration. True, in the inter-vening periods of clarity he was mentally alert, but, as Simon noted, they faded ever-more quickly. As 1947 passed into 1948, in the cold and loneliness of his prison, the old Marshal of France seemed gradually to be slipping into what was to become what Isorni was later to describe as an eternal night.

In the late spring of 1948, however, when the small group of flowers bordering the courtyard of Pierre-Levée were blooming, there was an inci-dent on the island which seemed to bring Pétain back to something near to his old life. On 10 May Dr. Imbert suddenly, and unexpectedly, committed sui-cide. He had, according to Simon's report of the incident, an incurable illness and had wished to die without pain. Pétain was told on the following day when he was having one of his brighter periods. "Poor doctor, how sorry I am for him. He was very charming and competent."[14] But Pétain's brighter mood was yet again no more than temporary. On the day Imbert's replacement arrived from the mainland Pétain was moaning to Simon, helplessly and in tears, that he had had enough, that nobody cared about him and that they all wanted him to die.

Imbert's replacement, the young doctor Jean Jouhier, who had only recently finished his training at the hospital of La-Roche-sur-Yon, knew nothing of the island or its most famous resident. His first examination, to which the patient submitted meekly, showed excellent physical health. "I was surprised," he reported, "by the vitality and musculature of this body of ninety-three years."[15] The patient's mental health was another matter. Isorni and Lemaire came on another visit on 4 June, to talk about the committee which had been set up to promote the cause. On the first day of their talks Pétain was lively and interested. The next day he had forgotten all that had happened the previous day, rambled, and kept asking the same questions over and over again.

The summer of 1948 went by without incident. But even Nini was starting to feel depressed. She had every day to walk up the hill to La Citadelle, cross the drawbridge into the fort and spend an hour and a half with Pétain, repeating the reasons for continued hope without any great conviction. Her life improved, however, in August, when she was presented with a little car by one of Pétain's sympathizers and she found a local driver who could take her to the fort and back. She had developed a painful sciatica in her leg—and she was badly overweight. The car was a great blessing. Pétain, in so far as his attention had not wandered, was glad of her visits. From time to time he spoke to her, but what he said was full of gloom. He no longer, he told her, even made a pretense of believing in his lawyers.

On 4 September 1948 Isorni and Lemaire arrived yet again on the island. "The Marshal," Isorni noted, "is slowly losing his lucidity or, more precisely, the lucid intervals are becoming rarer . . . one whole part of his brain has ceased to function."[16] They tried to explain to him that the government was likely to fall and that they were hoping that Henri Queuille, a doctor by background, would be asked to form the next government. It turned out that they were right, and on 26 September they went to see Queuille. There were, indeed, words of sympathy. Queuille fully understood the problem and thought a transfer to the military hospital of Val-de-Grâce in Paris would be eminently sensible. Unfortunately, given the political circumstances of the day, Queuille was sorry to say that he could not possibly accede to their request.

Early in November 1948, for no immediately apparent reason, the government decided to make a film of Pétain, his wife and those who regularly visited him, including his new doctor, Dr. Jean Potéreau. A naval lieutenant, Ernest Laspougeas, was to be in charge of what turned out to be a very old-fashioned camera. Its purpose was not ever explained to the prison staff, but Simon assumed that it was partly to show that Pétain, contrary to the case put forward by his wife and his lawyers, was kept in reasonably good conditions and partly to demonstrate to the veterans of the Resistance, contrary to their insistent opinion that Pétain was receiving preferential treatment, that the rules governing prisoners were being scrupulously applied.

As it happened, the film was never shown—at least not until 1975. Nevertheless, it was enough to show Isorni that the government was taking an interest. He tried to explain this to Pétain during his New Year visit to the Île d'Yeu on 3 and 4 January 1949. At first he was quite successful. Pétain seemed to be having one of his better days. But the next day it was all lost. He talked about "Napoleon, Verdun, Vichy—mixing them up. . . . He repeated over and over again 'You cannot imagine the complexity of large battles.' "[17] It was enough to move Isorni to ask Nini herself (at his dictation) to write to Queuille explaining her husband's real state and challenging the conclusions of the most recent medical examination.

Nini's letter achieved its intended effect. Queuille made sure that three distinguished doctors were sent from Paris to the island to make a thorough examination of the prisoner. The three duly arrived at Port-Joinville on 25 February, to be met by Simon in his car and driven to La Citadelle. They saw Pétain in his cell late that evening and again the following morning, making meticulous notes on his general state of health, his heart and his mental capacities. Their opinion, signed by all three, was emphatic. Pétain, they reported, was not fit to remain where he was and should be moved forthwith to Paris and the military hospital of Val-de-Grâce.

But it was not to be as easy as that. The Council of Ministers met on 3 March 1949 to discuss the experts' recommendation. There was, by all reports, a violent argument. The former (mostly self-proclaimed) heroes of the Resistance insisted that Pétain stay in prison. Others took a more humane view. The upshot was that no consensus was reached and, therefore, no decision was taken, except one on which they could all agree—to improve the medical facilities available to the prisoner. As a result, yet another young military doctor, Alphonse Zeude, was posted, much against his will, to the Fort Pierre-Levée. His duty was to see Pétain each morning and evening and twice a week to make a full examination of the prisoner, to be reported to Paris. Two nurses were also to be sent in support.

Zeude reported faithfully. But by mid-May he was also requesting more nursing help. The two nurses had arrived, but were refusing to do the menial work which they regarded as being more suitable for a personal maid. Besides, his patient was starting to hallucinate. He had become convinced that he was in the middle of battles, that naked women were dancing around in his room. It was no good appealing to his wife. She had gone back to Paris for treatment on her bad leg, where Pétain had written her a letter, referring to his prison—much to her consternation—as "home."[18] The matter was becoming urgent. Zeude needed help desperately. At the end of May four male nurses arrived; it was by then plain that, whatever might be its official designation, the prison was gradually being turned into a hospital.

In fact, that whole process was completed by the middle of 1949. Simon received his long-awaited posting; the guards were replaced by nurses (Nini was furious that one of the guards had claimed ownership of Miquette, "the little dog who was the only entertainment for the Marshal and who never left him," and had taken her away[19]); Pétain was allowed a battery-powered radio; and a new director, Charles Boulay, previously in charge of the hospital prison at Liancourt, arrived on 1 July.

By then, it seemed that everybody was simply waiting for Pétain to die. In August 1949 instructions were issued to all concerned on how to act when death finally occurred. Elaborate telephone codes were set out for every eventuality;

the procedure for laying out the body by nuns fully specified (the corpse to be dressed in civilian clothes); only the family and the authorities were to be present at the funeral, with the possible exception of a few journalists with special authorization; religious service in the fort's chapel, and so on. That was all very well but, as it turned out, they all had to wait another two years.

In fact, the expectation of Pétain's early death was justified by the marked deterioration in his health toward the end of 1949. Physically, he had developed cardiac arrhythmia, had become incontinent at nights and had low blood pressure; mentally, "[senile] dementia [is] practically complete," the doctors reported on 24 November.[20] The doctors also recorded that Pétain had lost a sense of modesty and was given to exposing himself to the nurses.

It would be otiose (and tasteless) to dwell on Pétain's condition during the last two years of his life. Although physically he seemed to improve during the early months of 1950, mentally he remained where he was. Without him being more than even half-conscious of the attempt, in May 1950 his lawyers submitted a request for the 1945 verdict to be overturned. The Ministry of Justice said it would study the matter—and did nothing. Nor was he aware that on 25 February Franco gave an interview to the newspaper *Arriba* on the 35th anniversary of Verdun. In it he had praised Pétain as "a great soldier and a gentleman." He had gone on to say that he had advised Pétain to stay in Spain in 1939. " 'You are the victor of Verdun. Do not join your name to what others have lost.' 'I know,' Pétain had replied, 'but my country calls me and I owe myself to her.' " When asked by the editor of *Arriba* whether there was anything that Spain could do for Pétain, Franco replied: "Very little, since it is involving the intimate affairs of another country. We can only mourn his distress and, if the occasion arises, offer him the hospitality of our country, where he can pass his remaining years in respect and affection."[21]

On Saturday 7 April 1951, Pétain started struggling for breath. It was the start of the congestive heart failure which was to be the final cause of his death. Yet, once again, Pétain surprised his doctors by making at least some sort of recovery. By 24 April he was able to be propped up in bed for his 95th birthday. As it turned out, the event was not as depressing as those summoned to the feast expected. Nini had supervised the baking of a large cake, and onto its top were crowded 95 candles of red, white and blue. His two lawyers were at the party, as were Yvonne de Moncourt and her children. Franco sent a basket of fruit from Spain, and flowers came from all over France. Moreover, to add to the jollity, Pétain was having one of his best days for a long time. Not only was he able to be propped up, but he seemed fully to realize what was going on. "How pretty it is!" he said of the cake, and with his finger he pointed to one candle that was unlit.[22]

But it was only a temporary remission. On 12 May President Vincent was alerted to the daily medical reports. After much hesitation, he finally agreed that Pétain ought to be moved, and on 8 June signed a decree commuting Pétain's

sentence from prison to a "hospital establishment"[23]—provided he was fit
enough to survive the transfer. The decree was kept secret, for obvious electoral
reasons, until after the general election for the National Assembly due to take
place on 17 June. That done, on 25 June the fort of Pierre-Levée was formally
designated as a military hospital. At that point, however, Pétain could no longer
leave his bed. He slept a great deal, had to be fed by his nurses and, when at all
awake, was either silent or babbled without cease.

Nevertheless, to everyone's astonishment, Pétain suddenly had a period of
days of near total lucidity. He recognized his lawyers, his wife and his doctors. It
seemed that he was perfectly capable of being transferred to the house in Port-
Joinville—no. 27 rue Guist'hau, owned by the lawyer Paul Luco—which, for the
purpose, had been named as an annex to the military hospital at Nantes. In spite
of last-minute official nervousness, at 7 A.M. on the morning of 29 June the rue
Guist'hau was sealed off by police, and Petain was transferred.

For a time, Pétain's condition remained as it had been at the time of his
transfer—sleeping most of the time but with bursts of lucidity in an otherwise
semi-conscious day. By 18 July, however, it was clear that he was moving toward
his death. On 20 July, Queuille summoned Isorni to tell him that there was no
time to waste. There were arrangements to be made. There was no question of
the body being buried at Douaumont alongside the dead of Verdun, as Pétain
had wished. The whole thing was politically far too sensitive. It would have to
stay on the Île d'Yeu. His wife could make what dispositions she liked there as
long as it was a private event and did not cause too much trouble. (By this time,
Nini had moved into the Villa Luco.)

Isorni and Lemaire hurried back to the island, to meet those who were
gathering at Pétain's bedside—Yvonne de Moncourt and her children, as well as
Nini and her son Pierre. The lawyers were nearly too late. During the day of the
21st Pétain had slipped into a coma. In the end, Pétain stayed in a coma
throughout the 22nd and, at 9:22 A.M. on the morning of 23 July 1951, he died.
A nurse held his hand as he went and, when he had gone, gently laid it on his
dead body. Nini leaned over and kissed his forehead. A nun knelt in the corner
saying her rosary. She was praying, as was appropriate, for the repose of the old
man's troubled soul.

The prayers said, the nurses and the nuns then busied themselves with
laying out the body. Contrary to the official instruction at Nini's request, he was
clothed in his military uniform, the Médaille Militaire pinned to his breast. His
bed, which had been brought from Pierre-Levée, was surrounded by flowers—
the pots shrouded in black crêpe—and six large candlesticks. Outside, in the
street, a small crowd gathered, but the police made sure that there was no disturbance. The telephone lines between the island and the mainland were
blocked for an hour while the government was informed. The Council of
Ministers met and decided to take all necessary precautions. Police were
deployed in the streets of Paris. Everybody seemed suddenly to be very nervous.

In fact, so nervous were ministers about the political impact of Pétain's final passing from the scene that they immediately decided that the funeral should be completed with the greatest possible speed. The decision turned out to be amply justified. Pétain's death was not only a major public event but, politically, a highly charged one. There were demonstrations in most French cities. The Veterans of Verdun made sure of that. A number of them wanted to go to the island to pay their last respects. They went; but permission to enter the Villa Luco was refused. Nevertheless, they did obtain one concession: they were allowed to be the main pall-bearers in the funeral procession.

At 10 A.M. on 25 July, an aircraft bearing French military markings flew low over the island and circled over Port-Joinville. As it passed over the cemetery where Pétain was to lie bystanders saw a wreath gently floating to earth. Nobody knew who the pilot was or where the aircraft came from—and nobody was minded to find out. At 10:30 A.M. the ferry docked, bringing Weygand, Héring and Fernet, as well as the bishops of Luçon and Angers. Telegrams were still flooding in from those who could not attend: Franco, Stucki, Cardinals Gerlier and Liénart, Poniatowski, Primo de Rivera's grandson and a number from members of the Académie Française. Even General Juin sent a telegram—much to Auriol's fury—expressing his "profound grief at the loss of the great soldier of Verdun."[24]

At 11 A.M. the passing bell started to sound. Led by a choirboy carrying the processional cross and by the assembled clergy, the coffin was brought into the church of Notre-Dame de Bon-Port and placed on the catafalque. It was draped in the French flag. On top was placed Pétain's Marshal's képi. The sermon reminded the congregation, and those outside who could not get into the church, of Pétain's military achievements. "We will pray," the bishop of Luçon intoned, "that God will forgive the sins and crown the merits of this long and tragic life, and we will pray even with the Marshal himself, since I am sure that he wishes it, for the desire and the dream of his life: the union of all Frenchmen and the greatness of France."[25]

At 12:30 P.M. the procession set off from the church to the cemetery. On its way, in the brilliant sunshine, it passed crowds of islanders and tourists (many of them in their bathing suits). It wound its way up the gentle hill leading out of the town. When they arrived in front of the newly dug grave, the bishops and attendant clergy formed a circle round it. The bishop of Angers blessed the coffin, which was then lowered slowly to its resting place. By one o'clock the last rite had been duly performed.

Pétain's long life had come to its end.

Notes

Introduction: On the Wrong Side of History

Epigraph: "Whatever one may think about Vichy, he is all the same somebody [of consequence]." A Parliamentary Commissioner after a visit to Pétain in prison in 1947. Quoted in J. Isorni, *Souffrance et Mort du Maréchal* (Paris: Flammarion, 1951), p. 198.

One: "The Son of My Sorrow"

Epigraph: "So it is with our past. It is labor in vain if we to look to recapture it, all the efforts of our intellect are useless." M. Proust: *Du Côté de chez Swann* (Paris: Gallimard, 1954), p. 44.

1. *Journal de Genève*, 27 April 1945.
2. *Le Monde*, 28 April 1945.
3. Quoted in L-D. Girard, *Mazinghem, ou la vie secrète de Philippe Pétain 1856–1951*; (Paris: private publication, 1971), p. 59.
4. Karl Marx, Friedrich Engels, *Werke* vol. VIII, p. 198, quoted in G. Wright: *Rural Revolution in France* (Stanford: Stanford University Press, 1964), p. 11.
5. E. Weber, *Peasants into Frenchmen* (London: Chatto & Windus, 1977), p. 167.
6. Letter to L-D. Girard from M. Occre of Cauchy-à-la-Tour, quoted in Girard, p. 63.

Two: Choosing the Saber Over the Book

Epigraph: "Don't doubt the sombre atmosphere in which we grew up in a France humiliated and murdered . . . brought up for a revenge which would be bloody, fatal and perhaps useless." Romain Rolland, quoted in C. Digeon, *La Crise Allemande de la Pensée Française (1870–1914)* (Paris: Presses Universitaires de France, 1959), pp. 519–520.

1. M. Perrot and A. Martin-Fugier, in *A History of Private Life*, Vol. IV (Cambridge, MA: Harvard University Press, 1990), p. 216.
2. *L'Indépendant du Pas-de-Calais* 7 December 1873.
3. T. Zeldin, *France 1848–1945*, Vol. II (London: Oxford University Press, 1977), p. 151.
4. A. Lehembre, *Le Bertinien*, Saint-Omer, April 1931.
5. R. Tombs, *France 1814–1914* (London: Longman, 1996), p. 44.
6. Quoted in M. E. Howard, *The Franco-Prussian War: The German Invasion of France, 1870–1871* (London: Hart-Davis, 1961), p. 208.
7. Archives Nationales, Paris (AN) W 111 277.
8. M. E. Howard, p. 397.
9. M. Ducrocq, *Le Collège Saint-Bertin de 1561 à nos jours* (Collège Saint-Bertin, 1998), p. 124, n. 204.
10. L. Lecuyer, *La Revanche par l'Education* (Paris, 1871), p. 24.

Three: Saint-Cyr: Lessons in War

Epigraph: "Cold. Improves on acquaintance, is perhaps not yet entirely made, will make a good officer." Pétain's report from the Ecole Supérieure de Guerre (Ecole de Guerre), 1890.

1. Extract from the official register of the *mairie* (town hall) of Béthune.
2. Archives Nationales (AN) W 111 277.
3. R. Tombs, *France 1814–1914* (London: Longman, 1996), p. 41.
4. AN W 111 277.
5. P. A. Bourget, *Témoignages Inédits sur le Maréchal Pétain* (Paris: Fayard, 1960), p. 26.
6. AN W 111 277.
7. Letter from Mlle. Henriette Laurent, quoted in Girard, *Mazinghem, ou la vie secrète de Philippe Pétain 1856–1951* (Paris: private publication, 1971), p. 114.
8. AN W 111 277.
9. Individual report of the Ecole Supérieure de Guerre, 1890.
10. AN W 111 277.

Four: The Dreyfus Affair

Epigraph: "And I refused to surrender so as not to owe anything to one of the most open activists in the Dreyfus affair." Pétain, Archives Nationale (AN) W 111 277, 1945.

1. Quoted in H. Amouroux, *Pétain avant Vichy* (Paris: Fayard, 1967), p. 23.
2. Quoted in H. Lottman, *Pétain* (Paris: Seuil, 1984), p. 39.
3. AN W 111 277.
4. Mme. Pétain, as reported in P. Bourget, *Témoignages inédits sur le Maréchal Pétain* (Paris: Fayard, 1960), p. 29.
5. D. Bredin, *The Affair: The Case of Alfred Dreyfus*, quoted in R. Tombs, *France 1814–1914* (London: Longman, 1996), p. 466.
6. AN W 111 277.
7. Capitaine Targe, quoted in D. R. Porch, *The March to the Marne: The French Army 1871–1914* (Cambridge: Cambridge University Press, 1981), p. 92.
8. One of Pétain's pupils, quoted in J-R. Tournoux, *Pétain et de Gaulle* (Paris: Plon, 1964).
9. Pétain, letter to his nephew, quoted in Girard, *Mazinghem, ou La Vie Secrète de Philippe Pétain* (Paris: private publication, 1971), p. 134.
10. Ibid.

Five: Love, Retirement, and a New Beginning

Epigraph: "Truly, the little schoolboy of St. Bertin did not expect to have such a fine career." Pétain, during interrogation, AN W 111 277, 1945.

1. J-R. Tournoux, *Pétain et de Gaulle* (Paris: Plon, 1964), p. 49.
2. Quoted in G. Pedroncini, *Pétain; Le Soldat et La Gloire 1856–1918* (Paris: Perrin, 1989), p. 29.
3. M. Buck, "French Army Notes" (unpublished, 2004), p. 2.
4. De Grandmaison, *Deux Conférences faites aux officiers de l'état majeur de l'armée* (Paris: Berger Levrault, 1911).
5. Author correspondence with M. Buck.
6. Quoted in D. B. Ralston, *The Army of the Republic* (Cambridge, MA: MIT Press, 1967), p. 329.
7. Quoted in J. Pouget, *Un certain Capitaine de Gaulle* (Paris: Fayard, 1973), p. 51.
8. Quoted in Tournoux, p. 54.
9. Pétain to Eugénie Hardon, 12 April 1914, AN 523 Mi.
10. Pétain to Eugénie Hardon, 14 May 1914, AN 523 Mi.
11. Ibid.

Six: The Dogs of War

Epigraph: "It was . . . really the first 'cruel' day of the war." Pétain, quoted in E. Laure, *Pétain* (Paris: Berger-Levrault, 1941), p. 28.

1. E. Laure, p. 25.
2. C. de Gaulle, *Lettres, Notes et Carnets,* Vol. I (Paris: Plon, 1980–86), p. 88.
3. Quoted in L-D. Girard, *Mazinghem, ou La Vie Secrète de Philippe Pétain* (Paris: private publication, 1971), p. 206.
4. Quoted in G. Pedroncini, *Pétain, Le soldat et la gloire, 1856–1918* (Paris. Perrin, 1989), p. 51.
5. E. L. Spears, *Liaison 1914* (London: Eyre & Spottiswoode, 1930), p. 272.
6. E. L. Spears, *Two Men who Saved France* (London: Eyre & Spottiswoode, 1966), p. 12.
7. E. Laure, p. 29.
8. H. Strachan, *The First World War,* Vol. 1 (Oxford: Oxford University Press, 2001), p. 250.
9. E. Laure, p. 31.
10. Ibid., p. 33.

Seven: "The German is the Enemy"

Epigraph: "Good-bye 1914 and long live 1915 which will be the year of victory." E. Fayolle, *Cahiers Secrets de la Grande Guerre* (Paris: Plon, 1964), p. 71.

1. E. L. Spears, *Two Men who Saved France* (London: Eyre & Spottiswoode, 1966), pp. 12–13.
2. M. Egremont, *Under Two Flags; The Life of Major-General Sir Edward Spears* (London: Weidenfeld & Nicolson, 1997), p. 5. Spears diary entries of 16 and 27 November 1914.
3. B. Serrigny, *Trente Ans avec Pétain* (Paris: Plon, 1959), p. 22.
4. Ibid., p. 8.
5. Order of 14 December 1914; Service Historique des Armées de Terre, Vincennes (SHAT) 22 N 1792.
6. Joffre, note of 15 January 1915; SHAT 22 N 1793.
7. Pétain to d'Urbal, 6 May 1915; SHAT 22 N 1794.
8. D'Urbal to Pétain, 25 May 1915; SHAT 22 N 1832.
9. Ibid.
10. E. Laure, *Pétain* (Paris: Berger-Levrault, 1941), p. 49.
11. Ministère de la Guerre, *Les Armées françaises dans la grande guerre* (AFGG), Vol. III (1931), p. 539.
12. Pétain's report of 1 November 1915: SHAT 19 N 427.

Eight: The Battle of Verdun

Epigraph: Gen J. J. Pershing to Pétain in 1929. P. Pétain (tr. MacVeagh), *Verdun* (London: E. Matthews & Elliot, 1930), p. 16.

1. A. Horne, *The Price of Glory, Verdun 1916* (London: Macmillan, 1962), p. 36.
2. Ibid., p. 39.
3. Quoted in I. Ousby, *The Road to Verdun* (London: Jonathan Cape, 2002), p. 43.
4. H. Afflerbach, *Falkenhayn; Politisches Denken und Handeln im Kaiserreich* (Munich: R. Oldenbourg Verlag, 1994), p. 363.
5. Pétain to Eugénie Hardon, 11 January 1916; AN 523 Mi.
6. Oulsby, p. 66.
7. P. Pétain, *Verdun*, p. 76.
8. B. Serrigny, *Trente Ans avec Pétain* (Paris: Plon, 1959), p. 44.
9. Ibid., p. 45.
10. Ibid., p. 46.

11. Serrigny, p. 46.
12. Ibid., p. 48.
13. Ibid., p. 50.
14. Serrigny, p. 83.
15. Quoted in A. Horne, p. 233.
16. Serrigny, p. 95.
17. Pétain, *Verdun*, pp. 134, 139.
18. Quoted in H. R. Lottman, *Pétain*, tr. B. Vierne (*Pétain*; Paris: Seuil, 1984), p. 57.

Nine: Hero of France and Commander-in-Chief

Chapter title: Bertie of Thame to Foreign Office, 29 April 1917; NA (PRO) FO 800/169.

Epigraph: "I am only called in catastrophes." Pétain to Henry Bordeaux, *Images du Maréchal Pétain* (Paris: Sequana, 1941), p. 23.

1. M-E. Fayolle, *Cahiers Secrets de la Grande Guerre*, ed. H. Contamine (Paris: Plon, 1964), p. 197.
2. Pétain to Eugénie Hardon, 25 January 1917; AN 523 Mi.
3. Ibid
4. Fayolle, p. 196.
5. E. L. Spears, *Prelude to Victory* (London: Jonathan Cape, 1939), p. 337.
6. Ibid., p. 364.
7. Ibid., p. 365.
8. G. Pedroncini, *Les Mutineries de 1917* (Paris: Presses Universitaire de France, 1967), p. 58.
9. Pétain to Eugénie Hardon, 28 April 1917, AN 523 Mi.
10. Bertie to Balfour, 30 April 1917; NA (PRO) FO 371/2937.
11. Serrigny, *Trente Ans avec Pétain* (Paris: Plon, 1959), p. 131.
12. Haig diary entry, 4 May 1917, in ed. R. Blake, *The Private Papers of Douglas Haig 1914–1919* (London: Eyre & Spottiswoode, 1952), p. 227.
13. Pétain to Eugénie Hardon, 21 May 1917, AN 523 Mi.
14. J. Pierrefeu, *French Headquarters 1915–1918*, tr. C. J. C. Street (London: G. Bles, undated), p. 163.
15. Haig diary entry, 18 May 1917; in Blake (ed.), p. 232.
16. B. R. Serrigny, p. 145.
17. NA (PRO) WO 158/48/92623.
18. D. French, "Who knew what and when? The French Army Mutinies and the British Decision to launch the Third Battle of Ypres," in L. Freedman, P. Hayes and R. O'Neill, eds., *War, Strategy and International Politics; Essays in honour of Sir Michael Howard* (Oxford: Clarendon Press, 1992), p. 142.
19. R. M. Watt, *Dare Call It Treason* (London: Chatto & Windus, 1964; repr. New York: Dorset Press, 2001), p. 160.
20. Directive 1, GQG, 19 May 1917; SHAT 22N 1832.
21. Pétain to Eugénie Hardon, 23 May 1917, AN 523 Mi.
22. R. M. Watt, p. 170.
23. Ministère de la Guerre, AFGG, Tome V, Vol. II (Paris, 1931), p. 198.
24. J. J. Pershing, *My Experiences in the World War* (London: Hodder and Stoughton, 1931), p. 55.
25. Ibid., p. 68.
26. L. Freedman et al. (eds.), p. 150.
27. Haig memo, 19 October 1917; NA (PRO) WO158/48/92623.
28. Haig diary entry, 16 December 1917; in Blake, p. 274.

Ten: Total War

Epigraph: "The French Army is what it should be, what I wished that it should be."
Pétain, quoted in Henry Bordeaux, *Images du Maréchal Pétain* (Paris: Sequana, 1941),
p. 62.

1. *Journal Officiel*, 20 November 1917, p. 2963.
2. Haig diary entry, 7 January 1918, in R. Blake, *The Private Papers of Douglas Haig 1914–1919* (London: Eyre & Spottiswoode, 1952), p. 278.
3. Haig to Lady Haig, 31 January 1918, in Blake, p. 281.
4. Haig diary entry, 1 February 1918, in Blake, p. 281.
5. NA (PRO) WO 158/48/92623.
6. Haig diary entry, 19 March 1918, in Blake, p. 293.
7. Haig diary entry, 21 March 1918, in Blake, p. 296.
8. Haig diary entry, 25 March 1918, in Blake, p. 297.
9. Haig diary entry 26 March 1918, in Blake, p. 298.
10. F. Foch, *The Memoirs of Marshal Foch, tr.* Bentley Mott (London: Heinemann, 1931), p. 300.
11. Churchill, quoted in M. Gilbert, *Winston S Churchill*, Vol. IV, *1916–1922* (London: Heinemann, 1975), p. 98.
12. Ibid.

Eleven: Pétain, Architect of Victory

Epigraph: "Is it possible that they will refuse me that?" Pétain, quoted in P. A. Bourget,
Témoignages Inédits sur le Maréchal Pétain (Paris: Fayard, 1960), p. 44.

1. Haig diary note, 19 April 18, in Blake, ed., *The Private Papers of Douglas Haig 1914–1919* (London: Eyre & Spottiswoode, 1952), p. 304.
2. G. Pedroncini, *Pétain, Le soldat et la gloire, 1856–1918* (Paris: Perrin, 1989), p. 362.
3. M-E. Fayolle, *Cahiers Secrets de la Grande Guerre*, ed. H. Contamine (Paris: Plon, 1964), p. 277.
4. J. Pierrefeu, *French Headquarters 1915–1918*, tr. C. J. C. Street (London: G. Bles, undated), p. 272.
5. Haig diary note, 4 June 1918, in Blake, pp. 313–14.
6. Pétain to Eugénie Hardon, 28 June 1918, AN 523 Mi.
7. Fayolle, p. 285.
8. AFGG, Tome VI, Vol. 2, p. 468.
9. G. Pedroncini, p. 395.
10. Fayolle, p. 296.
11. J. J. Pershing, *My Experiences in the World War* (London: Hodder and Stoughton, 1931), p. 622. Haig diary note, 9 June 1918.
12. Pershing, p. 670.
13. C. de Gaulle, *Mémoires d'espoir*, Vol. I (Paris: Plon, 1970), p. 173.
14. Fayolle, p. 299.

Twelve: Nini, the Wife Next Door

Epigraph: "I note that I love you deeply." Pétain to Eugénie Hardon, 19 February 1919,
Archives Nationale (AN) 523 Mi.

1. Pétain to Eugénie Hardon, 21 March 1919, AN 523 Mi.
2. Quoted in G. Pedroncini, *Pétain, La Victoire Perdue* (Paris: Perrin, 1995), p. 75.
3. Pétain to Eugénie Hardon, 2 August 1919, AN 523 Mi.
4. Quoted in L-D. Girard, *Mazinghem, ou La Vie Secrète de Philippe Pétain* (Paris: private publication, 1971), p. 245.

5. G. Pedroncini, p. 101.
6. Quoted in R. A. Doughty, *The Seeds of Disaster* (Hamden, CT: Shoe String Press, 1985), p. 9.

Thirteen: Saving the Spanish in Morocco

Epigraph: "The Marshal is a great man who . . . died in 1925." De Gaulle, quoted in J-R. Tournoux, *Pétain et de Gaulle* (Paris: Plon, 1964), p. 356.
1. Pétain to Eugénie Pétain, 22 July 1925, AN 523 Mi.
2. Pétain to Minister of War, 22 July 1925 Service Historique des Armées de Terre, Vincennes 3 H 609.
3. S. Ben-Ami, *Fascism from Above* (Oxford: Clarendon Press, 1983), pp. 165–66.
4. *New York Times*, 10 September 1925.

Fourteen: The Politics of Peace

Epigraph: "I have never been subjected to such an avalanche of questions in three days." Pétain to Eugénie Pétain, 4 September 1927, Archives Nationale (AN) 523 Mi.
1. J-R. Tournoux, *Pétain et de Gaulle* (Paris: Plon, 1964), p. 55.
2. Ibid., p. 58.
3. C. de Gaulle, *The Edge of the Sword*, tr. G. Hopkins (London: Faber and Faber, 1960), dedicatory note.
4. J-R. Tournoux, p. 133.
5. Quoted in P. C. F. Bankwitz, *Maxime Weygand and Civil-Military Relations in Modern France* (Cambridge, MA: Harvard University Press, 1967), p. 14.
6. Harold Macmillan, quoted in A. Horne, *To Lose a Battle* (London: Macmillan, 1969), p. 543.
7. Clemenceau, quoted in Bankwitz, p. 29.
8. *ABC Madrid*, 18 March 1930.
9. J-R. Tournoux, p. 160.
10. Ibid., p. 161.
11. Ibid., p. 162.
12. A. J. Toynbee, *Survey of International Affairs 1931* (London: Royal Institute of International Affairs, 1932), p. 22.

Fifteen: The Hollow Years

Epigraph: "I have never practiced politics and I do not wish to do so." Pétain, quoted in E. Laure, *Pétain* (Paris: Berger-Levrault, 1942), p. 362.
1. Quoted in L-D. Girard, *Mazinghem, ou La Vie Secrète de Philippe Pétain* (Paris: private publication, 1971), p. 333.
2. E. Laure, p. 362.
3. M. S. Alexander, "In Defence of the Maginot Line," in R. Boyce, ed., *French Foreign and Defence Policy 1918–1940* (London: Routledge, 1998), p. 72.
4. Ibid., p. 78.
5. Göring, speech in Essen, 4 December 1934, quoted in *Göring, Reden und Aufsätze* (Munich, 1943).
6. Sir J. Burnett-Stuart, quoted in M. S. Alexander, *The Republic in Danger; General Maurice Gamelin and the Politics of French Defence* (Cambridge: Cambridge University Press, 1992).
7. *La Victoire*, 18 February 1935.
8. *Vu* 30 November 1935.
9. *Le Journal* 30 April 1936.

Sixteen: The Unpopular Front

Epigraph: "If the barometer announces rain, is it the barometer which is wrong?," quoted in A. Conquet, *Auprès du Maréchal Pétain* (Paris: Editions France-Empire, 1970), p. 284.

1. Quoted in Pertinax (pseudonym A. Géraud), *The Gravediggers of France: Gamelin, Daladier, Reynaud and Laval* (New York: Editions de la Maison Française, 1944), p. 342.
2. Quoted in A. Conquet, p. 284.
3. Ibid., p. 283.
4. Quoted in G. Warner, *Pierre Laval and the Eclipse of France* (London: Eyre & Spottiswoode, 1968), p. 164.
5. Ibid.
6. Quoted in A. Conquet, p. 152.
7. Ibid., p. 199.
8. Ibid., p. 151.
9. *Revue Militaire Générale*, 1/37, p. 22.
10. Pétain to Eugénie Pétain, 28 April 1937, Archives Nationale (AN) 523 Mi.
11. H-J. Hansen, ed., *Auf den Spuren des Westwalls* (Aachen: Helios Verlags-und Buchvertriebs-Gesellschaft, 1998), p. 59.
12. Pétain to M-A. Pardee, 10 March 1938, in M-A. Pardee, *Le Maréchal que j'ai connu* (Paris: Editions André Bonne, 1952), p. 14.
13. "Conversazione R Ambasciatore-Maresciallo Pétain," *Affari Politici Francia* 20, Foreign Ministry Archives Rome; quoted in M. Cornick, *Fighting Myth with Reality; The Fall of France, Anglophobia and the BBC*, in V. Holman and D. Kelly, eds., *France at War in the Twentieth Century; Propaganda, Myth and Metaphor* (Oxford & New York: Berghahn Books, 2000), pp. 2–3.
14. Quoted in G. A. Craig, *Germany, 1866–1945* (Oxford: Clarendon Press, 1978), p. 704.
15. Pétain to Eugénie Pétain, 14 September 1938, AN 523 Mi.
16. Quoted in H. Amouroux, *Pétain avant Vichy* (Paris: Fayard, 1967), p. 204.
17. Quoted in A. Conquet, p. 284.

Seventeen: Ambassador to Spain

Epigraph: M. Peterson, *Both Sides of the Curtain* (London: Constable, 1950), p. 179.

1. Pétain to Eugénie Pétain, 1 March 1939, Archives Nationale (AN) 523 Mi.
2. Pétain to Eugénie Pétain, 2 April 1939, AN 523 Mi.
3. A. Gazel, in J-M. Varaut, *Le Procès Pétain, 1945–1995* (Paris: Perrin, 1995), p. 96.
4. Quoted in *New York Herald Tribune* (Paris edition), 25 March 1939, p. 10.
5. M. Peterson, p. 175.
6. Quoted in H. Amouroux, *Pétain avant Vichy; La Guerre et l'Amour* (Paris: Fayard, 1967), p. 213.
7. *Arriba*, 3 August 1939, p. 6.
8. Quoted in E. Laure, *Pétain* (Paris: Berger-Levrault, 1942), p. 427.
9. Pétain to Daladier, 11 September 1939, AN AG 2 11.
10. Quoted in *Le Monde*, 24 January 1953, p. 3.
11. Peterson, p. 179.
12. Quoted in J. Szaluta, *French Historical Studies*, Vol. VIII, Pt. 4 (1974), p. 529.

Eighteen: Defeat

Epigraph: "I make the gift of my person to France to lessen her distress." Quoted in E. Laure, *Pétain* (Paris: Berger-Levrault, 1942), p. 435.

1. Lebrun, in J-M. Varaut, *Le Procès Pétain, 1945–1995* (Paris: Perrin, 1995), p. 64.

2. Quoted in B. Vergez-Chaignon, *Le docteur Ménétrel, Éminence grise et confidant du Maréchal Pétain* (Paris: Perrin, 2001), p. 83.
3. E. Spears, *Assignment to Catastrophe*, Vol. 1 (London: William Heinemann, 1954), p. 183.
4. Campbell to Halifax, NA FO 800/312.
5. W. S. Churchill, *The Second World War* (London: Cassell, 1949), p. 100.
6. Campbell to Halifax, 5 June 1940; Cabinet Papers 65/13, in M. Gilbert, *Churchill War Papers*, Vol. II, *May 1940–December 1940* (London: Heinemann 1994), p. 253.
7. E. Spears, p. 84.
8. The Earl of Avon, *The Eden Memoirs: The Reckoning* (London: Cassell, 1965), p. 115.
9. E. Spears, p. 175.
10. J. Colville diary entry, 12 June 1940, in *The Fringes of Power; Downing Street Diaries 1939–1955* (London: Hodder and Stoughton, 1985), p. 154.
11. Quoted in Laure, p. 433.
12. G. Warner, *Pierre Laval and the Eclipse of France* (London: Eyre & Spottiswoode, 1968), p. 174.
13. E. Spears, p. 292.

Nineteen: The Road to Vichy

Epigraph: "It happens that a peasant at home sees his field laid waste by hail. He does not despair of the next harvest." Pétain, speech of 23 June 1940, in P. Pétain, *Quatre Années au pouvoir* (Paris: La Couronne Littéraire, 1949), p. 50.

1. Minute of meeting between French general Charles Huntziger and General Karl-Heinrich von Stülpnagel, 8 August 1940, Archives Nationale (AN) 3 W 283.
2. Laval, quoted in J-M. Varaut, *Le Procès Pétain, 1945–1995* (Paris: Perrin, 1995), p. 235.
3. Pétain radio broadcast, 17 June 1940.
4. Pétain broadcast, 17 June 1940, as reported in *Quatre Années au Pouvoir*, p. 47.
5. P. Baudouin, *Neuf Mois au Gouvernement* (Paris: La Table Ronde, 1948), p. 227.
6. English text of armistice in "Documents on German Foreign Policy 1918–1945," (London: HMSO, 1957).
7. Quoted in G. Warner, *Pierre Laval and the Eclipse of France* (London: Eyre & Spottiswoode, 1968), p. 199.
8. Flandin, in *Le Procès Flandin devant la Haute Cour de Justice, 23–26 juillet 1946* (Paris: Librairie de Médicis, 1947).
9. B. Serrigny, *Trente Ans avec Pétain* (Paris: Plon, 1959), p. 181.

Twenty: The Royal "We"

Epigraph: "This policy is mine . . . . It is me alone that history will judge." Pétain, in P. Pétain, *Quatre Années au pouvoir* (Paris: La Couronne Littéraire, 1949), p. 71.

1. B. Serrigny, *Trente Ans avec Pétain* (Paris: Plon, 1959), p. 179.
2. Quoted in J. Jackson, *France; The Dark Years* (Oxford: Oxford University Press, 2001), p. 171.
3. Serrigny, p. 186.
4. Pétain, in *Quatre Années*, p. 62.
5. "Documents on German Foreign Policy" (London: HMSO, 1959–61), Series D, Vol. XI, no. 227.
6. NA (PRO) FO 370/2769.
7. NA (PRO) PREM 7/7.
8. Memorandum of E. M. Young, 15 June 1964; NA (PRO) FO 370/2769.

9. Pétain, in *Quatre Années*, p. 69.
10. Ibid., p. 70.
11. J. Colville, *The Fringes of Power; Downing Street Diaries 1939–1955* (London: Hodder and Stoughton, 1985), p. 339.
12. Quoted in M. Gilbert, *Winston S Churchill; Finest Hour* (London: Heinemann, 1983), p. 960.
13. Matthews to Hull, 16 November 1940; *Foreign Relations of the United States*, Vol. 2, p. 411.
14. M. Peyrouton, *Du Service Public à la Prison Commune* (Paris: Plon, 1950), p. 179.
15. Laval, in J-M. Varaut, *Le Procès Pétain, 1945–1995* (Paris: Perrin, 1995), p. 250.
16. H. Du Moulinde Labarthète, *Le Temps des Illusions, Souvenirs (Juillet 1940–Avril 1942)* (Geneva: Les Editions du Cheval Ailé, 1946), p. 80.
17. L. Noguères, *Le véritable Procès du Maréchal Pétain* (Paris: Fayard, 1955), p. 652.
18. Quoted in M. Gilbert, p. 957.
19. Ibid., p. 958.
20. Ibid., p. 959.
21. Ibid., p. 960.
22. Ibid.

Twenty-One: The Germans, Darlan, and the Jewish Question

Epigraph: "The leader is he who knows at the same time how to make himself obeyed and how to make himself loved." Pétain, in *Quatre Années au pouvoir* (Paris: La Couronne Littéraire, 1949), p. 81.

1. Abetz to Foreign Ministry, 26 December 1940; *Documents on German Foreign Policy*, Series D, Vol. XI, no. 569.
2. W. D. Leahy, *I Was There* (London: Victor Gollancz, 1950), p. 12.
3. Ibid., p. 22.
4. Churchill to Chiefs of Staff, 7 January 1941, in M. Gilbert, *Churchill War Papers*, Vol. 3 (London: Heinemann, 2000), p. 42.
5. AN 3 AG 2 318.
6. Leahy, p. 26.
7. Ibid., p. 27.
8. NA (PRO) FO 371/8104.
9. Quoted in J. Jackson, *France; The Dark Years* (Oxford: Oxford University Press, 2001), p. 268.
10. Leahy, p. 28.
11. B. Serrigny, *Trente Ans avec Pétain* (Paris: Plon, 1959), p. 192.
12. Churchill to Foreign Office and Chiefs of Staff Committee, 15 February 1941, quoted in M. Gilbert, p. 220.
13. Quoted in R. O. Paxton, *Vichy France; Old Guard and New Order 1940–1944* (New York: Columbia University Press, 1982), p. 113.
14. Pétain, in *Quatre Années*, p. 89.
15. AN 2 AG 656.
16. J. Berthelot, in J-M. Varaut, *Le Procès Pétain, 1945–1995* (Paris: Perrin, 1995), p. 341.
17. Churchill to Eden, 9 July 1941: *Churchill papers 20/40*, in M. Gilbert, *Churchill War Papers*, Vol. II, p. 919.
18. R. Murphy, *Diplomat among Warriors* (London: Collins, 1964), p. 113.

Twenty-Two: The Specter of Communism

Epigraph: "I have serious things to say to you." Pétain, *Quatre Années au Pouvoir* (Paris: La Couronne Littéraire, 1949), p. 105.

1. Pétain, *Quatre Années*, p. 110.

2. W. D. Leahy, *I Was There* (London: Victor Gollancz, 1950), p. 59.
3. Pétain, *Quatre Années*, p. 110.
4. Ibid.
5. B. Serrigny, *Trente Ans avec Pétain* (Paris: Plon, 1959), p. 195.
6. P. Pétain, *Actes et Ecrits*, ed. J. Isorhi (Paris: Flammarion, 1974), p. 41.
7. Leahy to Roosevelt, 22 Novmeber 1941, Franklin Delano Roosevelt Library, New York.
8. Ibid.
9. Turkish Ambassador at Vichy to Ankara, 29 November 1941; NA (PRO) HW 1/277.
10. Serrigny, p. 200.
11. Leahy, p. 84.
12. Ibid., p. 85.
13. Serrigny, p. 203.
14. Ibid.
15. Ibid., p. 207.
16. Ibid., pp. 209–10.

Twenty-Three: The Trap

Epigraph: "I am going to put so much responsibility on his back that he will collapse." Pétain to Serrigny, in B. Serrigny, *Trente Ans avec Pétain* (Paris: Plon, 1959), p. 212.

1. Ibid.
2. *Le Temps*, 22 April 1942.
3. W. D. Leahy, *I Was There* (London: Victor Gollancz, 1950), p. 114.
4. H-H. Giraud, *Mes Evasions* (Paris: Juillard, 1946), p. 131.
5. P. Boegner, *Carnets du Pasteur Boegner 1940–1945* (Paris: Fayard, 1992), p. 192.
6. Abetz to Auswärtiges Amt, 1 June 1942, quoted in G. Warner, *Pierre Laval and the Eclipse of France* (London: Eyre & Spottiswoode, 1968), p. 312.
7. Reproduced (as telegram) in L. Noguères, *Le Véritable Procès du Maréchal Pétain* (Paris: Fayard, 1955), unnumbered page at end.
8. P. Boegner, p. 195.
9. *Le Temps*, 24 June 1942.
10. Quoted in Noguères, p. 399.
11. Minute of meeting between Pétain and Tuck, 8 November 1942, Service Historique des Armées de Terre, Vincennes (SHAT) 1 P 17.
12. P. Billotte, *Le Temps des Armes* (Paris: Plon, 1972), p. 239.

Twenty-Four: The Collapse of the House of Cards

Epigraph: "The Marshal rests . . . inert in his chair." B. Serrigny, *Trente Ans avec Pétain* (Paris: Plon, 1959), p. 225.

1. Tuck to Hull, 8 November 1942, Foreign Relations of the United States (FRUS), 1942, Vol. II, quoted in G. Warner, *Pierre Laval and the Eclipse of France* (London: Eyre & Spottiswoode, 1968), p. 323.
2. Darlan to Admiralty, 8 November 1942, Service Historique des Armées de Terre, Vincennes (SHAT) 1 P 17.
3. Darlan to Pétain, 9 November 1942, SHAT 1 P 17.
4. Noguès to Pétain, 12 November 1942, SHAT 1 P 17.
5. Quoted in L. Noguères, *Le Véritable Procès du Maréchal Pétain* (Paris: Fayard, 1955), p. 449.
6. Ibid., p. 226.
7. Ménétrel's notes as in L. Noguères, p. 508.
8. Serrigny, pp. 227–28.

Twenty-Five: Occupied France

Epigraph: "It is useless now to galvanize this poor old man." B. Serrigny, *Trente Ans avec Pétain* (Paris: Plon, 1959), p. 230.

1. Ibid., p. 225.
2. Ibid., p. 228.
3. A. Conquet, *Auprès du Maréchal Pétain*, p. 385.
4. Paul Dungler, quoted in B. Vergez-Chaignon, *Le docteur Ménétrel, Eminence grise et confidant du maréchal Pétain* (Paris: Perrin, 2001), p. 229.
5. Duncannon note of 8 August 1943, NA (PRO) FO660/149.
6. Duncannon note of 11 October 1943, NA (PRO) FO660/149.
7. Ibid.
8. Noguères, *Le Véritable Procès du Maréchal Pétain* (Paris: Fayard, 1955), p. 568.
9. Serrigny, p. 234.
10. Ibid., p. 235.
11. Ibid., p. 230.

Twenty-Six: Vichy: The Final Act

Epigraph: "There is no salvation for France other than in the reconciliation of Pétain and de Gaulle." Brécard, reported in P. Boegner, *Carnets du Paseur Boegner1940–1945* (Paris: Fayard, 1992), p. 287.

1. Pétain to M-A. Pardee, 11 January 1944, in M-A. Pardee, *Le Maréchal que j'ai connu* (Paris: Editions André Bonne, 1952).
2. Telephone conversation with Frau Cornelia Lutze (Renthe-Fink's daughter), 1 December 2003.
3. Telephone conversation with Frau Gabriele von Heiden (Renthe-Fink's grand-daughter), 1 December 2003.
4. A. Kaspi, *La Libération de la France*, quoted in J. Jackson, *France; The Dark Years* (Oxford University Press, 2001), p. 534.
5. W. D. Hassett, *Off the Record with FDR, 1942–1945* (London: Allen & Unwin, 1949), p. 257.
6. NA (PRO) FO 954/9, Halifax to Foreign Secretary, 3 February 1944.
7. *France Actualités*, quoted in B. Vergez-Chaignon, *Le docteur Ménétrel, Eminence grise et confidant du maréchal Pétain* (Paris: Perrin, 2001), p. 275.
8. Lavagne to Ménétrel, 1 May 1944, AN 2 AG 76, quoted in B. Vergez-Chaignon, p. 275.
9. B. Serrigny, *Trente Ans avec Pétain* (Paris: Plon, 1959), p. 237.
10. French radio, quoted in B. Vergez-Chaignon, p. 277.
11. Serrigny, p. 237.
12. Ibid., p. 238.
13. Quoted in J. Tracou, *Le Maréchal aux Lions* (Paris: André Bonne, 1948), p. 309.
14. L. Noguères, *Le Véritable Procès du Maréchal Pétain* (Paris: Fayard, 1955), pp. 653–55.
15. P. Boegner, p. 287.
16. Letter from a bodyguard to his wife, 20 July 1944, quoted in B. Vergez-Chaignon, p. 297.

Twenty-Seven: Reluctant Flight

Epigraph: "Of the principles which I taught, of all the things which I have freely said, I withdraw nothing." Pétain's message, 20 August 1944, in J-C. Barbas, ed., *Philippe Pétain: Discours aux français, 17 juin–20 août 1944* (Paris: Albin Michel, 1989), p. 340.

1. Ibid.
2. Ibid.

3. Quoted in D. Cook, *Charles de Gaulle* (London: Secker and Warburg, 1984), p. 251.
4. Quoted in J. Lacouture, *De Gaulle: Le rebelle* (Paris: Seuil, 1984), p. 834.
5. Quoted in C. de Gaulle, *Mémoires de guerre*, Vol. III (Paris: Plon, 1954), pp. 222–23.
6. Eugénie Pétain account, Archives Nationale (AN) W 111 288.
7. Ibid.

Twenty-Eight: The Marshal of France Defends His Honor

Epigraph: "The old Marshal could have had no doubt that he was going to be convicted." C. de Gaulle, *Mémoires de Guerre*, Vol. III (Paris: Plon, 1954), p. 112.

1. *Journal Officiel de la République française*, Algiers, 10 August 1944.
2. J. Isorni, *Mémoires*, Vol. 1 (Paris: Robert Laffont, 1984), p. 409.
3. Ibid.
4. Quoted in J-M. Varaut, *Le Procès Pétain, 1945–1995*, pp. 80–81.
5. Quoted in ibid., p. 105.
6. C. de Gaulle, *Mémoires de Guerre*, p. 248.
7. Quoted in J. Roy, *Le Grand Naufrage* (Paris: Julliard, 1966), p. 26.
8. Varaut, *Procès Pétain*, p. 7.
9. Ibid.
10. Ibid., p. 15.
11. Roy, p. 26.
12. Varaut, *Procès Pétain*, p. 13.
13. De Gaulle, *Mémoires de Guerre*, pp. 248–49.
14. Varaut, *Procès Pétain*, pp. 15–16.
15. Ibid., p. 16.
16. Ibid., p. 18.
17. Ibid., p. 19.
18. Quoted in Roy, p. 104.
19. Ibid., p. 107.
20. Varaut, *Procès Pétain*, p. 149.
21. Ibid., p. 158.
22. Ibid., p. 198.
23. Varaut, *Procès Pétain*, p. 240.
24. Ibid., p. 243.
25. Ibid., p. 247.
26. Ibid., pp. 255–56.
27. Quoted in Roy, p. 178.
28. Varaut, *Procès Pétain*, p. 325.
29. Ibid., pp. 344–45.
30. Ibid., pp. 356–57.
31. Ibid., p. 384.
32. Ibid., p. 429.
33. Quoted in Roy, p. 286.
34. Ibid.
35. Varaut, *Procès Pétain*, p. 472.
36. Quoted in Roy, pp. 287–88.
37. Varaut, *Procès Pétain*, p. 490.
38. Quoted in Roy, p. 295.

Twenty-Nine: Prison for Life

Epigraph: "I have never accepted my conviction." Pétain's instruction to his lawyers, 7 September 1946, quoted in J-M. Varaut, *Le Procès Pétain*, p. 395.

1. C. de Gaulle, *Mémoires de Guerre*, Vol. III (Paris: Plon, 1954), p. 250.

2. J. Simon (ed. P. Bourget), *Pétain, mon prisonnier* (Paris: Plon, 1978); (Simon diary entry, 18 August 1945), p. 55.
3. Ibid. (diary entry, 30 August 1945), p. 59.
4. Ibid. (diary entry, 6 October 1945), p. 73.
5. Ibid. (diary entry, 20 October 45), p. 79.
6. Ibid., letter from Mme. Nolleau to P. Bourget, p. 353.
7. Ibid. (diary entry, 10 July 1946), p. 111.
8. Ibid., p. 156n.
9. Pétain to Eugénie Pétain, (diary entry, 22 September 1947), p. 190.
10. Ibid. (diary entry, 9 July 1947), p. 181.
11. Quoted in J. Isorni, *Souffrance et Mort du Maréchal* (Paris: Flammarion, 1951), p. 198.
12. Simon (diary entry, 7 November 1947), p. 194.
13. Ibid. (diary entry, 9 November 1947), p. 196.
14. Ibid. (diary entry 2 May 1948), p. 230.
15. Report of Dr. Jouhier, ibid., p. 233.
16. Ibid., p. 216.
17. J. Isorni, *Le condamné de la Citadelle* (Paris: Flammarion, 1982), p. 257.
18. Pétain to Eugénie Pétain, 16 May 49, Archives Nationale (AN) 415 AP 2 Mi.
19. Eugénie Pétain to J. Isorni, quoted in Simon, p. 287.
20. Simon (diary entry, 24 November 1948), p. 301.
21. British Ambassador to Madrid, report to Foreign Secretary, 25 February 1951, NA (PRO) FO 371/9617.
22. J. Isorni, *Le condamné*, p. 347.
23. Decree, 9 June 1951, quoted in ibid., p. 424.
24. J. Isorni, *Le condamné*, p. 380.
25. Quoted ibid., pp. 378–79.

Bibliography

There are many thousands of books and articles relevant to Pétain's life and times. There is no point in compiling an arbitrary list. I have therefore confined myself to those which I have found particularly useful. An excellent bibliographical essay on Pétain can be found in Professor Atkin's book (listed below), and further bibliographical information can be found in those books I have labelled "General." The bibliography which follows below is therefore selective and, I imagine, regrettably incomplete. Where direct quotations have been used, they are acknowledged in the notes, as are references to some other specialist works, as well as magazines and newspapers not listed here. Archives which I and those who helped me have consulted are not listed either, but are referred to in the notes. On the first occasion it appears the full name of the archival source is given, together with the abbreviation or acronym subsequently used.

Translations are always a problem, as are names. In general, I have translated French quotations myself, but where a translation has been made by an authoritative source I have used it. As far as names are concerned, I have used what I believe to be common sense even at the expense of consistency. Thus, where there is a French or German spelling of a place where the English have a variant (Reims or Rheims, for instance) I have tended to use the French or German version unless the context seemed to require otherwise. There is a further complication. Spears only anglicized his name from Spiers in September 1918. Throughout the First World War he was known, rightly, as Spiers. I have taken the feeble way out to avoid being accused of pedantry. Even more difficult is the matter of Eugénie Hardon. Known as Nini in her youth and beauty, she has seemed to me to have a suitable nickname to be preserved in her less than attractive old age. Pétain in his later, and less passionate, letters addressed her as "Annie." I have stuck with "Nini," if only for the sake of avoiding confusion.

General

Abetz, O. *Das öffene Problem: ein Rückblick auf zwei Jahrzehnte deutscher Frankreichpolitik*. Cologne: Greven Verlag, 1951.

Adler, J. *The Jews and Vichy: Reflections on French Historiography*. Cambridge: Cambridge University Press, 2001.

Alexander, M. S. *The Republic in Danger; General Maurice Gamelin and the Politics of French Defence*. Cambridge: Cambridge University Press, 1992.

Argenson, Marquis de. *Pétain et le Pétinisme*. Paris: Editions Créator, 1953.

Aron, R. *Histoire de Vichy*. Paris: Fayard, 1954.

Atkin, N., and F. Tallett. *The Right in France 1789–1997*. London and New York: Tauris, 1997.

Auphan, G. *Histoire élémentaire de Vichy*. Paris: Editions France-Empire, 1971.

Azéma, J-P. *From Munich to the Liberation 1938–1944*. Cambridge: Cambridge University Press, 1979.

Azéma, J-P., and F. Bédarida, eds. *La France des années noires*. Paris: Seuil, 2000.

Barbas, J-C. *Philippe Pétain. Discours aux français, 17 juin 1940–20 août 1940*. Paris: Albin Michel, 1989.

Barreau, J-M. *Vichy contre l'école de la République*. Paris: Flammarion, 2001.

Barthélemy, J. *Le ministre de la justice. Mémoires, Vichy 1941–1943*. Paris: Pygmalion, 1989.

Bell, P. M. H. *A Certain Eventuality*. London: Saxon House, 1974.

Ben-Ami, S. *Fascism from Above*. Oxford: Clarendon Press, 1983.

Bessborough, E. *Return to the Forest*. London: Weidenfeld and Nicolson, 1962.

Blake, R. *The Private Papers of Douglas Haig 1914–1919*. London: Eyre & Spottiswoode, 1952.

Boegner, P. *Carnets du Pasteur Boegner 1940–1945*. Paris: Fayard, 1992.

Bourget, P. *Témoignages inédits sur le Maréchal Pétain*. Paris: Fayard, 1960.

Boyce, R., ed. *French Foreign and Defence Policy 1918–1940*. London: Routledge, 1998.

Brinon, F. de. *Mémoires*. Paris, La Page Internationale, 1959.

Brissaud, A. *Pétain à Sigmaringen. De Vichy à la Haute Cour*. Paris: Perrin, 1966.

Buck, M. "French Army Notes." Unpublished paper, 2004.

Burrin, P. *La France a l'heure allemande, 1940–1944*. Paris: Seuil, 1995.

Burton, R. D. E. *Blood in the City; Violence and Revolution in Paris, 1789–1945*. Ithaca: Cornell University Press, 2003.

Carcopino, J. *Souvenirs de sept ans, 1937–1944*. Paris: Flammarion, 1953.

Carré, H. *Les grandes heures du général Pétain; 1917 et la Crise du Moral*. Paris: Editions du Conquistador, 1952.

Churchill, W. S. *The World Crisis*. London: Cassell, 1931.

Clayton, A. *Paths of Glory; The French Army 1914–18*. London: Cassell, 2003.

Cointet, J-P. *Pierre Laval*. Paris: Fayard, 1993.

Cointet, M. *Pétain et les Français 1940–1951*. Paris: Perrin, 2002.

Cointet-Labrousse, M. *Vichy Capitale*. Paris: Perrin, 1993.

Colville, J. *The Fringes of Power: Downing Street Diaries 1939–1955*. London: Hodder and Stoughton, 1985.

Conquet, A. *Auprès du Maréchal Pétain*. Paris: Editions France-Empire, 1970.

Coutau-Bégarie, H., and C. Huan. *Darlan*. Paris: Fayard, 1989.

Craig, G. A. *Germany 1866–1945*. Oxford: Clarendon Press, 1978.

Dallas, G. *At the Heart of a Tiger, Clemenceau and his world 1841–1929*. London: Macmillan, 1993.

Darlan, A. *L'Amiral Darlan Parle*. Paris: Amiot-Dumont, 1952.

De Gaulle, C. *Lettres, Notes et Carnets*. Vol. I. Paris: Plon, 1980–86.

——. *Mémoires d'espoir*. Vol. I. Paris: Plon, 1970.

——. *The Edge of the Sword*. Tr. G. Hopkins. London: Faber and Faber, 1960.

——. *Mémoires de Guerre*, Vol. III. Paris: Plon, 1954.

De Wailly, H. *L'Effondrement*. Paris: Perrin, 2000.

Digeon, C. *La crise allemande de la pensée française 1870–1914*. Paris: Presses Universitaires de France, 1959.

Discours de M. le Maréchal Pétain à l'Académie Française et Réponse de M Paul Valéry. Paris: Plon, 1931.

Doise, J., and M. Vaïsse. *Diplomatie et Outil Militaire 1871–1969*. Paris: Imprimerie National, 1987.

Ducrocq, M. *Le Collège Saint-Bertin de 1561 à nos jours*. Arras: Société des Antiquaires de la Morinie, 1998.

Duroselle, J-B. *Clemenceau*. Paris: Fayard, 1988.

Duroselle, J-B. *L'abîme. Politique étrangère de la France, 1939–1944*. Paris: Imprimérie Nationale, 1982.

Duroselle, J-B. *La France et les Français*. Paris: Editions Richelieu, 1972.

Egremont, M. *Under Two Flags, the Life of Major-General Sir Edward Spears*. London: Weidenfeld & Nicolson, 1997.

Fayolle, M-E. *Cahiers Secrets de la Grande Guerre*, ed. H. Contamine. Paris: Plon, 1964.

Fernet, J. *Aux Côtés du Maréchal Pétain*. Paris: Plon, 1953.

Fischer, D. *Le mythe Pétain*. Paris: Flammarion, 2002.

Foch, F. *The Memoirs of Marshal Foch*. Tr. Bentley Mott. London: Heinemann, 1931.

Frankenstein, R. *Le prix du réarmament français 1935–1939*. Paris: Publications de la Sorbonne, 1982.

Freedman, L., Hayes, P., and R. O'Neill, eds. *War, Strategy, and International Politics: Essays in Honour of Sir Michael Howard*. Oxford: Clarendon Press, 1992.

French, D. "Who knew what and when? The French Army Mutinies and the British Decision to launch the Third Battle of Ypres." In Freedman, et al., as above.

Gaulle, C. de. *Vers l'armée de métier*. Paris: Berger-Levrault, 1934.

Gerbod, P. *La vie quotidienne dans les lycées et collèges au XIX siècle*. Paris: Hachette, 1968.

Gervereau, L., and D. Peschanski, eds. *La propagande de Vichy, 1940–1944*. Paris: Collections des Publications de la BDIC, 1990.

Gilbert, M. *Winston S Churchill; Companion Volumes to; Churchill War Papers*. Published seriatim by Heinemann, London.

Gillouin, R. *J'étais l'ami du maréchal Pétain*. Paris: Plon,1996.

Girard, L-D. *Montoire; Victoire Diplomatique*. Paris: André Bonne, 1948.

Girardet, R. *Mythes et Mythologies politiques*. Paris: Seuil, 1986.

Gorce, P-M., de la. *The French Army; A Military-Political History*. London: Weidenfeld and Nicolson, 1963.

Griffiths, R. *The Intelligent Person's Guide to Fascism*. London: Duckworth, 2000.

Guiral, P., and G. Thuillier. *La vie quotidienne des professeurs de 1870 à 1940*. Paris: Hachette, 1982.

Horne, A. *The Price of Glory, Verdun 1916*. London: Macmillan, 1962.

Hubscher, R. H. *L'Agriculture et la Société rurale dans le Pas-de-Calais du milieu du XIXe siècle à 1914*. 2 vols. Arras: Mémoires de la Commission Départmentale des Monuments Historiques du Pas-de-Calais, 1979.

Hughes, J. M. *To the Maginot Line; The Politics of French Military Preparation in the 1920s*. Cambridge, Mass.: Harvard University Press, 1971.

Isorni, J. *Mémoires*. 3 vols. Paris: Robert Laffont, 1984–1988.

——. *Le condamné de la Citadelle*. Paris: Flammarion, 1982.

——. *Philippe Pétain*. 2 vols. Paris: La Table Ronde, 1972.

——. *La correspondance de l'Ile d'Yeu*. Paris: Flammarion, 1966.

——. *C'est un Péché de la France*. Paris: Flammarion, 1962.

——. *Souffrance et Mort du Maréchal*. Paris: Flammarion, 1961.

Jäckel, E. *Frankreich in Hitlers Europa*. Stuttgart: Deutsche Verlags-Anstalt, 1966.

Jackson, J. *The Fall of France; The Nazi Invasion of 1940*. Oxford: Oxford University Press, 2003.

——. *France; The Dark Years*. Oxford: Oxford University Press, 2001.

Jaray, G. L., ed. *Le Maréchal Pétain; Paroles aux Français; Messages et Ecrits 1934–1941*. Lyon: H. Lardanchet, 1941.

Jeantet, G. *Pétain contre Hitler*. Paris: La Table Ronde, 1966.

Joll, J. *The Origins of the First World War*. London: Longman, 1984.

Kaspi, A. *Le Temps des Américains; Le Concours Américain à la France en 1917–1918*. Paris: Publications de la Sorbonne, 1976.

Kedward, H. R. *In Search of the Maquis. Rural Resistance in Southern France, 1942–1944*. Oxford: Oxford University Press, 1993.

——. *Occupied France. Collaboration and Resistance*. Oxford: Basil Blackwell, 1985.

Keegan, J. *The First World War*. London: Hutchinson, 1998.

Keiger, J. F. V. *France and the World since 1870*. London: Arnold, 2001.

Kessel, J. *Jugement dernier*. Courtry: Editions Christian de Bartillat, 1995.

Leahy, W. D. *I Was There*. London: Victor Gollancz, 1950.

Lehideux, F. *De Renault à Pétain—Mémoires*. Paris: Pygmalion, 2001.

MacMillan, M. *Peacemakers; The Paris Conference of 1919 and Its Attempt to End War*. London: John Murray, 2001.

Mangin, C. *Lettres de Guerre 1914–1918*. Paris: Fayard, 1950.

Marrus, M. R., and R. O. Paxton. *Vichy France and the Jews*. New York: Basic Books, 1981.

Maurois, A., *Marshal Lyautey*. Tr. H. Miles. London: Bodley Head, 1931.

May, E. R. *Strange Victory; Hitler's Conquest of France*. London: I.B. Tauris, 2000.

Michel, H. *Le procès de Riom*. Paris: Albin Michel, 1979.

Miller, G. *Le pousse-au-jouir du maréchal Pétain*. Paris: Seuil, 1975.

Ministère de la Guerre. *Les Armées françaises dans la grand Guerre* (AFGG). Paris: 1931.

Mosse, G. *Fallen Soldiers; Reshaping the Memory of World Wars*. Oxford: Oxford University Press, 1990.

Moulin, A. *Les paysans dans la société française de la Révolution à nos jours*. Paris: Seuil, 1992.

Moulin de Labarthète, H. du. *Le Temps des illusions*. Geneva: A l'enseigne du cheval ailé, 1946.

Murphy, R. *Diplomat Among Warriors*. London: Collins, 1964.

Newhall, D. S. *Clemenceau, A Life at War*. Lewiston, N.Y.: The Edwin Mellen Press, 1991.

Noguères, L. *La Dernière Étape*. Sigmaringen. Paris: Fayard, 1956.

——. *Le Véritable Procès du Maréchal Pétain*. Paris: Fayard, 1955.

Oulsby, I. *The Road to Verdun*. London: Jonathan Cape, 2002.

Painlevé, P. *Comment j'ai nommé Foch et Pétain*. Paris: Librairie Félix Alcan, 1932.

Pardee, M. A. *Le maréchal que j'ai connu*. Paris: Editions André Bonne, 1952.

Paxton, R. O. *The Anatomy of Fascism*. London: Allen Lane, 2004.

Paxton, R. O. *Vichy France; Old Guard and New Order, 1940–1944*. New York: Columbia University Press, 1982.

Perrier, G. *Rémy, l'agent Secret no.1 de la France libre*. Paris: Perrin, 2001.

Perrot, M., ed. *A History of Private Life*, vol. 4, *From the Fires of Revolution to the Great War*. Cambridge, Mass.: Harvard University Press, 1990.

Pershing, J. J. *My Experiences in the World War*. London: Hodder and Stoughton, 1931.

Pétain, P. *Actes et Ecrits.*, ed. J. Isorhi. Paris: Flammarion, 1974.

Quatre Années au pouvoir. Paris: La Couronne Littéraire, 1949.

——. *Verdun*. Tr. L. MacVeagh. London: E. Matthews & Elliot, 1930.

Philpott, W. J. *Anglo-French Relations and Strategy on the Western Front, 1914–1918*. London: Macmillan, 1996.

Pierrefeu, J. *French Headquarters 1915–1918*. Tr. C. J. C. Street. London: G. Bles, n.b.

Porch, D. *The March to the Marne: The French Army 1871–1914*. Cambridge: Cambridge University Press, 1981.

Price, R. *A Social History of Nineteenth-Century France*. London: Hutchinson, 1987.

Procès du Maréchal Pétain; Compte Rendu Officiel in extenso des Audiences de la Haute Cour de Justice. Paris: Editions Louis Pariente, 1976.

Prost, A. *Histoire de l'enseignment en France 1800–1967*. Paris: Librairie Armand Colin, 1968.

Pryce-Jones, D. *Paris in the Third Reich, a History of the German Occupation*. London: HarperCollins, 1983.

Ralston, D. B. *The Army of the Republic; The Place of the Military in the Political Evolution of France, 1871–1914*. Cambridge, Mass.: MIT Press, 1967.

Robbins, K. *The First World War*. Oxford University Press, 1985.

Rossignol, D. *Vichy et les Franc-maçons, La Liquidations des sociétés secrètes 1940–1944*. Paris: J.C. Lattès, 1981.

Rothschild, M. de. *Si j'ai bonne mémoire*. Paris: Editions Monelle Hayot, 2001.

Rougier, L. *Mission secrète a Londres; Les accords Pétain-Churchill*. Paris: La Diffusion du Livre, 1946.

Rousso, H. *Vichy: Un passé qui ne passe pas*. Paris: Fayard, 1994.

——. *Le syndrome de Vichy, 1944–198* . . . Paris: Seuil, 1987.

——. *Un château en Allemagne, Sigmaringen*. Paris: Ramsay, 1980.

Roy, J. *The Trial of Marshal Pétain*. London: Faber & Faber, 1968.

——. *Le Grand Naufrage*. Paris: Perrin, 1966.

Smith, G. *Until the Last Trumpet Sounds: The Life of General of the Armies John J. Pershing*. New York: John Wiley, 1998.

Simon, J. *Pétain, mon prisonnier; presentation, notes et commentaires de Pierre Bourget*. Paris: Plon, 1978.

Spears, E. L. *Two Men who Saved France*. London: Eyre & Spottiswoode, 1966.

——. *Assignment to Catastrophe*, 2 vols. London: William Heinemann, 1954.

——. *Prelude to Victory*. London: Jonathan Cape, 1939.

——. *Liaison 1914; a narrative of the Great Retreat*. London: Eyre & Spottiswoode, 1930.

Stevenson, D. *French War Aims against Germany, 1914–1919*. Oxford: Clarendon Press, 1982.

Strachan, H. *The First World War*, vol. 1, "To Arms." Oxford: Oxford University Press, 2001.

Stucki, W. *La fin du régime de Vichy*. Neuchatel: Editions de la Baconniere, 1947.

——. *Von Pétain zur Vierten Republik*. Bern: Verlag Herbert Lang, 1947.

Tombs, R. *France 1814–1914*. London: Longman, 1996.

Tracou, J. *Le Maréchal aux liens*. Paris: André Bonne, 1948.

Turpin, M., and A. Maloire. *Le 24e Bataillon de chasseurs*. Paris: Editions Berger-Levrault, 1959.

Usborne, C. V. *The Conquest of Morocco*. London: Stanley Paul & Co, 1936.

Varaut, J-M. *Le Procès Pétain*. Paris: Perrin, 1995.

Vergez-Chaignon, B. *Le docteur Ménétrel, Eminence grise et confidant du maréchal Pétain*. Paris: Perrin, 2001.

Warner, G. *Pierre Laval and the Eclipse of France*. London: Eyre & Spottiswoode, 1968.

Watt, R. M. *Dare call it treason*. London: Chatto & Windus, 1964, repr. New York: Dorset Press, 2001.

Weber, E. *My France: Politics, Culture, Myth*. Cambridge, Mass.: Harvard University Press, 1991.

Weber, E. *Peasants into Frenchmen*. London: Chatto & Windus, 1977.

——. *Varieties of Fascism*. New York: Van Nostrand, 1964.

——. *Action Française*. Stanford: Stanford University Press, 1962.

Webster, P. *Pétain's Crime*. London: Papermac, 1991.

Werth, L. *Impressions d' audience—Le procès Pétain*, ed. C. Kantcheff, Mayenne: Editions Viviane Hamy, 1995.

Wilhelm, Crown Prince of Germany. *My War Experiences*. London: Hurst and Blackett, 1922.

——. *The memoirs of the Crown Prince of Germany*. London: T. Butterworth, 1922.

Woolman, D. S. *Rebels in the Rif; Abd El Krim and the Rif Rebellion*. Oxford: Oxford University Press, 1969.

Wright, G. *Rural Revolution in France*. Stanford: Stanford University Press, 1964.

Zeldin, T. *France 1848–1945*. Oxford: Oxford University Press, 1977.

Biographies and Part Biographies

Alméras, P. *Un français nommé Pétain*. Paris: Laffont, 1995.

Amouroux, H. *Pétain avant Vichy; La Guerre et l'Amour*. Paris: Fayard, 1967.

Atkin, N. *Pétain*. London: Longman, 1998.

Ferro, M. *Pétain*. Paris: Fayard, 1987.

Girard, L-D. *Mazinghem, ou La Vie Secrète de Philippe Pétain*. Paris: private publication, 1971.

Laure, E. *Pétain*. Paris: Berger-Levrault, 1941.

Lottman, H. R. *Pétain, Hero or Traitor?* New York: Viking, 1984.

Lottman, H. R. *Pétain*. Tr. B. Vierne. Paris: Seuil, 1984.

Pedroncini G. *Pétain: La Victoire Perdue, 1918–1940*. Paris: Perrin, 1995.

——. *Pétain: Le soldat et la gloire, 1856–1918*. Paris: Perrin, 1989.

——. *Pétain: Général en chef*. Paris: Presses Universitaires de la France, 1974.

Planells, A. J. *Pétain, Mariscal de Francia*. Madrid: Viena, 2000.

Ryan, S. *Pétain the Soldier*. New York: A.S Barnes & Co, 1969.

Index

Abd el Krim, Mohamed and Mhamed, 117–120
Abetz, Otto, 206, 208, 231, 239–240, 256
    Darlan and, 192, 194
    Déat and, 229–230
    demands for Laval's reinstatement, 182–183, 184–185, 189–190
    Laval and, 212–213, 226, 234
    plan for France, 175–178, 180
    political pressure on Pétain, 199–200, 202–203, 205
Abyssinia, 135, 137
Action Française, 121, 135–137, 146, 173–174
Affaire des Fiches, 34–35
air defense, 128–129, 136
Alibert, Raphaël, 156, 162, 168–169, 171, 173–175, 181, 190, 257
Alsace, 44, 60, 79, 94, 105, 192, 194, 223
Amiens, 56, 83, 94, 96–98, 103
    Pétain's posting to, 29–31
André, Louis, 33–34, 50
anti-Semitism, 30, 121, 136, 146, 162, 174, 191
Armistice (1918), 105–106, 110, 116, 145
Armistice (1940), 160–162, 164, 166–169, 175, 197–198, 200–201
    and Pétain's trial, 243, 248–254, 256
Army Organization Law, 125
Arras, 8, 39–42, 53, 55–57, 76, 89, 98, 125
Artois, 7–8, 11, 24, 38, 53, 57–58, 60–61
Auphan, Paul, 215–216, 218, 224–225, 227, 234, 256
Auriol, Vincent, 264, 269, 271

Austria-Hungary, 14, 43–44, 89, 107, 144, 254

Barthou, Louis, 132–134
Baudouin, Paul, 153, 157, 165–166, 168, 171, 173–174, 177–178
Belgium, 49, 92, 154
    Armistice (1914) and, 105, 125
    attack through, 26
    importance to WWI German military operations, 44–46
    Maginot Line and, 133
    neutrality, 40, 141–142, 144
Bérard-Jordana agreements, 147–150
Bérard, Léon, 147
Berbers, 117–118
Bergson, Henri, 37
Berthelot, Henri-Mathias, 102, 193–194
Bertie of Thame, Lord, 82
Besançon, 23–26, 28, 32, 110, 114, 177
Bidault, Georges, 189, 238
Blum, Léon, 131, 146, 265
    arrest by Vichy government, 198, 261
    and Pétain's trial, 251
    Popular Front government and, 137–139, 143–144
    and Spanish Civil War, 141
Boegner, Marc, 208, 234
Bonhomme, Léon, 140, 148, 155, 173, 202, 229
Bonnet, Georges, 144–146, 149
Bordeaux, 161–162, 167–168
Bouchardon, Pierre, 244–246
Bousquet, René, 207–208, 229
Bouthillier, Yves, 168, 171, 173, 181, 200, 229
Boy Scouts, 188, 190, 197
    see youth organizations

Brécard, Charles, 173, 190, 230, 234
Briand, Aristide, 71, 75–77, 125, 131
British Expeditionary Force 1914
   (BEF), 45–46, 48, 51, 55, 95

Cagoule, 140, 252
Cangé, 160
Caporetto, Battle of, 87, 96
casualties, 57, 123–124
  at Battle of Artois, 57
  at Battle of Verdun, 73
  at first Battle of the Marne, 51–53
  effect on military strategy, 62, 73, 76
Castelnau, Édouard de, 52, 60–61,
   66–68, 71, 81–82, 104, 106
Catholic Church, 18, 37, 109, 119,
   149, 207–208
  attacks on, 15–16, 33, 35
  influence on Pétain, 7, 9–10, 13,
    190–191
  Pétain's view of, 35, 80–81, 90,
    107, 112–113, 119, 188
  political influence of, 30, 117, 121,
    136, 173–174
Cauchy, 6–9, 12, 17, 19–20, 24
cease-fire, 161, 166, 213–216
censorship, 83, 185, 231
CFLN (Committee for National
   Liberation), 222–224, 229–230,
   243
Chamberlain, Austen, 125, 146
Chantilly, 58, 67, 71
Charleroi, Battle of, 48–49
Charles-Roux, François, 165, 178, 251
Chautemps, Camille, 132, 143–144,
   153, 160, 162–163
Chemin des Dames, 76–77, 79–80,
   83, 85–87, 95, 97–99
Churchill, Winston, 94, 169, 177,
   186, 205, 224
  attempts to prevent 1940 armistice,
    154, 155–160
  Dupuy and, 182–183
  on Mangin, 71
  Pétain and, 97, 190, 194
  reaction to Pétain-Hitler
    handshake, 178–180
civil war, 27, 141, 147–149, 229–230,
   234
Clark, Mark, 213–217

Clemenceau, Georges, 131
  and Dreyfus Affair, 29
  and post-WWI demobilization,
    110–111, 113, 116
  role in WWI, 75, 77, 90, 92–93,
    96–97, 99–100, 105
collaboration, with Germany, 3, 142,
   179, 181, 183, 185, 204–205, 215,
   224–225, 228–229, 233, 239, 244
  military, 192–194, 197, 201, 209
Collège Saint-Bertin, 10–18, 20, 36
Comité de Nîmes, 207
Communards, 15–17
communists, 117–118, 195–199,
   222, 231
  in French politics, 124, 136–137,
    146, 150–151
  opposition to French government,
    140–141, 143, 157
  persecution of, 205, 220
  Pétain's hatred of, 16, 133, 174,
    212, 221
  and Pétain's trial, 246–247, 259
  resistance, 198–199, 208, 224
Compiègne, 3, 82, 86, 93, 96, 101, 106
compromise peace, 221–223
Conseil Supérieur de la Guerre, 115,
   127–128
Conseils de guerre, 85–86
Conquet, Alfred, 221
constitution
  constitutional acts, 171–172, 174,
    189, 203, 218, 224–225,
    243, 254
  new, devised by Pétain, 170,
    222–225
Corvignolles, 140
Cot, Pierre, 136–137
Council of Ministers, 81, 158–160,
   163, 167–169, 171, 178,
   214–215, 218, 226, 252, 268
Council of Political Justice, 198
coup d'état, 139–140, 192
Croix de Feu, 136–137

Daladier, Edouard, 158, 265
  arrest by Vichy government, 198
  and Pétain's trial, 251, 256, 261
  pre-WWII government, 131–133,
    141–142, 144–148, 150–154

Darlan Deal, 217
Darlan, François, 162–163, 168–169,
    173, 181–186, 189–194,
    196–197, 199–203, 206, 209,
    212–219, 256
Darnand, Joseph, 205, 220–221, 228,
    232–233, 237
de Brinon, Fernand, 178, 203–204,
    225, 231, 233, 237–239
de Castelnau, Édouard, 52, 60–61,
    66–68, 71, 81–82, 104, 106
de Gaulle, Charles, 107, 116, 121,
    129, 163, 174, 226, 260–262, 264
    early military career, 47, 107
    at École de Guerre, 125–127
    and Pétain's trial, 247, 250, 256
    post-WWII return to France,
        236–240, 242
    publication of Le Fil de l'Epée, 134,
        145–146, 158
    relationship with Pétain, 40,
        145–146, 158, 165, 183,
        212, 243
    in WWII, 177, 210, 212, 217–218,
        221–224, 230, 234
de Grandmaison, Louis, 38–39
de Langle de Cary, Fernand 61, 71
de Lattre de Tassigny, Jean, 234, 239
Déat, Marcel, 181–182, 188, 205, 217,
    225, 228–230, 232–233, 237
Debeney, Marie-Eugène, 39, 114,
    125, 142, 240
declaration of war, 193, 201–202,
    212
Demarcation Line, 192, 201, 215
demobilization, 110–111, 113, 115
Dentz, Henri-Ferdinand, 192, 194
Directives, issued by Pétain, 84, 92,
    99, 102–103
Douaumont, 3, 64, 68, 72, 123, 270
Doumer, Paul, 131, 172
Doumergue, Gaston, 131, 132,
    134–135, 139, 151
Dreyfus Affair, 24, 27–30, 32–34, 36,
    39, 85
du Moulin de Labarthète, Henri, 148,
    173–174, 178, 199, 204
Duncannon, Lord Eric, 223
Dupuy, Pierre, 180, 182–183
d'Urbal, Victor, 58–59

École de Guerre, 26–27, 32, 34,
    36–40, 123, 125, 142
Eisenhower, Dwight, 213, 217,
    237
Esterhazy, Ferdinand, 29–30

Falange, 149, 152
Falkenhayn, Erich von, 64–65, 73
Falloux Law, 18
Fayolle, Emile, 55–56, 75–76, 95–97,
    99–101, 103, 107, 112, 128
Fighting France, 2, 224
Flandin, Pierre-Etienne, 134, 136,
    169–170, 179, 185–186,
    189–190
Foch, Ferdinand, 2, 71, 127–128, 157
    De la Conduite de la Guerre, 38
    influence on Pétain, 39, 71, 82, 133
    as postwar hero, 109–111,
        113–114, 116, 124
    wartime strategy, 98–107
    in WWI, 51, 53, 59–60, 91–93,
        95–97
Fonck, René, 176–177
Fourth Republic, 264
France, German occupation of, 192,
    199–200, 203, 213, 215–216,
    220–221, 263
    organized resistance of, 208,
        223–225, 231, 233, 236, 239,
        246–247, 257–259, 267–268
    requests to defend her own
        borders, 208–209
Franchet d'Esperey, Louis, 46, 48–51,
    81, 84, 99, 140
Franco, Francisco, 141, 145,
    148–149, 152, 177, 269
Freemasons, 4, 33–34, 164, 174–175,
    188, 197, 220
French Army, 201, 251, 253
    pre-WWI, 39–40
    reduction of between wars, 114,
        124–125, 131, 133
    in WWI, 50, 57, 62, 77–79, 81, 102,
        105–106, 110
French fleet, 162–163, 167, 169, 179,
    201, 215–216, 219
French, John, 45–46, 51, 95
Frente Popular, 141
Friedensturm, 101

Gamelin, Maurice, 128, 131, 134, 141–142, 150–151, 153–154, 156, 198, 261, 265
gas attacks, 58, 61, 72
Gauleiter, 202, 226–227
Gerlier, Pierre Cardinal, 188, 208, 271
German Army, 65, 87, 161
  and Battle of the Marne, 51–52
  breaking of front line by French, 58–59, 76–77
  invasion of Russia, 196
  Operation "Alberich," 77
  rebuilding of by Hitler, 135
  WWI defeat of, 103–104
  WWI offensive, 93–94, 97
  WWII offensive, 156, 158–159
Girard, Louis-Dominique, 229
Giraud, Henri Honoré, 205–206, 212–214, 216–217, 219, 222–224, 243
Göring, Hermann, 134, 176, 180, 200–202
Gort, Lord John, 156–157
Gough, Hubert, 94–95, 98
Gouraud, Henri, 68, 100–102, 104
Graux, Abbé, 10
Guide, Alphonse, 20–21, 23, 36, 110–111

Haig, Douglas, 77, 81–83, 85, 87–88, 90–97, 99–101, 103, 105–107, 145
Halifax, Lord Edward, 177, 183
Henriot, Philippe, 228, 231, 233
Herriot, Édouard, 134, 151, 163, 166, 168, 170, 234, 252
Hervé, Gustav, 135–136
Hitler, Adolf, 146, 215, 217–219, 226, 240, 254
  and building of *Westwall,* 136, 144
  and Darlan, 192–194
  diplomatic relations with France, 175–178, 181–182, 206, 208
  and Disarmament Conference, 131
  and Laval, 184, 189, 212, 213, 215, 237
  and Pétain, 180, 197, 198–200, 221, 222, 233, 236, 238
  and "Saturday Surprises," 135, 137

Huntziger, Charles, 167, 175, 181–183, 185, 193, 199

Île d'Yeu, Pétain's exile to, 3–4, 262, 264–265, 270
infantry tactics, 32, 34–37, 39–40
Isorni, Jacques, 244–246, 250, 252–253, 257–258, 262, 264–267, 270
Italy, 10, 60, 149, 158, 175, 187, 225, 264
  British sanctions against, 137
  relations with France, 132, 134, 135, 151, 170, 254
  signing of armistice (1940), 167–168
  in WWI, 89, 92

Japan, 197, 201, 209
Jardel, Jean, 212, 218, 222–223, 225–226, 229
Jews, 24, 188
  anti-Jewish legislation, 175, 191, 196
  and anti-Semitism, 30, 162, 164, 174
  deportation of, 3, 207–208, 220, 237, 246, 249, 257
  persecution of, 4, 220, 233
Joffre, Joseph, 45–46, 48–53, 55, 57–62, 65–73, 76, 92, 95, 102, 111, 113–114, 116, 127–128, 172
Juin, Alphonse, 213, 216, 256, 271

King Alfonso XIII, 117, 141
King George V, 77, 86, 103, 145, 163, 180
Koenig, Pierre, 5
Krug von, Nidda, Roland, 200, 202, 205, 212, 225–226

Lanrezac, Charles, 45–46, 48–51
Laure, Emile, 128, 132, 193, 199, 204
Laval, Pierre, 129, 131, 145, 156, 173, 190, 232–234, 237
  and armistice, 153
  and changing of constitution, 167–171
  collaboration with Germans, 164, 178, 209, 224–226, 228–230

dismissal from Pétain's government, 181–182, 184–186, 189
as foreign minister, 134–135, 165, 175, 211–218
and Pétain, 161, 167, 175–179,
and Pétain's trial, 245, 247, 251, 253–257
as Pétain's successor, 218, 220–222
and Popular Front, 136, 139–140
return to Pétain's government, 202–209
League of Nations, 125, 131
Leahy, William D., 186–187, 189, 195–196, 200–203, 205, 230, 246, 253
Lebrun, Albert, 132, 134, 144–145, 149, 153, 155, 157, 160–163, 165–170, 190, 251, 253
Lefebvre, Abbé Philippe-Michel, 10, 12
Légion des Anciens Combattants, 200
Legrand, Abbé Jean-Baptiste, 10, 12, 16, 25–26, 31, 263
Lehideux, François, 190, 200
Lemaire, Jean, 246–247, 250–251, 257, 264–267, 270
Lémery, Henry, 130, 145, 148, 151
Lequerica, José Felix, 166
LeRoy-Lewis, Herman, 82
Liberation, 220, 222–223
Ligues, 136, 139
Lloyd George, David, 76–77, 81, 93–94, 97, 99, 105, 111
Lorraine, 44, 94, 105–106, 110, 114, 194, 219, 260
Lubin, Germaine, 109, 112
Ludendorff, Erich, 94, 98–103, 105
Lyautey, Hubert, 118–120, 172

Macmillan, Harold, 223–224
Maginot Line, 127, 133, 136, 142–143, 205, 252
Makins, Roger, 223–224
Mandel, Georges, 163, 166, 233, 261, 265
Mangin, Charles, 71–73, 79–80, 92, 101–102, 111
Maquis, 229–230, 232–234
Marion, Paul, 188, 190, 200, 204, 228, 237

Marne, Battles of
First, 51, 53, 55, 59–60, 64
Second, 100, 102–103
Marquet, Adrien, 167–168, 171
Maud'huy, Louis Ernest, 25, 32, 39, 53, 55–58
Maunoury, Joseph, 36, 49, 51
Maurras, Charles, 173–174, 236
Ménétrel, Bernard, 151, 162, 165, 174, 178, 196, 221, 223, 226, 231–232
final days of, 238–239
medical practices of, 143, 187
as Pétain's aide, 197, 199, 211, 214–215, 216, 225, 234–235,
relationship with Pétain, 139, 155–156, 160, 165, 173, 180, 182, 205
role in Pétain's abdication, 218
Mers el-Kébir, 169
Micheler, Alfred, 76, 79–81, 92
Milice, 3, 220–222, 229–230, 233, 247, 249–250, 257
Milner, Lord Alfred, 95–96, 99
Ministry of War, 21, 29–30, 32, 34, 39–41, 64, 132
Moltke, Helmuth von, 44, 51, 64
Mongibeaux, Paul, 247–251, 253–254, 256–259
Mons, 49, 95
Montoire, 177–180, 184–185, 192, 198, 201, 254
Mordacq, Henri, 96
Mornet, André, 247–248, 250–251, 256–258
Morocco, 58–59, 115–121, 124, 148, 212–215, 217, 253
Mouvement Social d'Action Révolutionnaire, 140
Munich agreement, 146, 153
Murphy, Robert, 194, 206, 213, 216
Mussolini, Benito, 127, 132, 134–135, 145–146, 158, 187, 191, 212, 223

National Assembly, 33–34, 65, 113, 124, 170, 222, 225–226, 234, 238, 254, 270
National Revolution, 3, 174, 188, 190–191, 201–202, 205

Nivelle, Robert, 71–73, 76–84, 87, 92
Noguès, Auguste, 167, 214–217
North Africa, 253, 256–257
  Allied invasion of (Torch), 208–209
  joining of French and Allied troops
    in, 212–217
  Pétain's possible flight to, 217–218,
    223, 224
  plans to transfer government to,
    158, 160, 163, 167, 179,
    182–183
  strategic importance of, 193–194,
    200–202

Occupied Zone, 168, 181
Ossuaire at Douaumont, 123
outbreak of war, 43, 133, 150, 192

Painlevé, Paul, 77–78, 80–81, 85,
    119–120, 131
Paris Commune, 15, 132
Paris Protocols, 193, 257
parliamentary commission, 265
Parti Social Français, 143
Patton, George S., 238
Payen, Fernand, 244–246, 248,
    250–251, 253–254, 257–258, 264
peace treaties
  see treaties
Pearl Harbor, 201
peasants, 1, 6–10, 12, 14, 18, 20–21,
    24–25, 27, 30–31, 38, 42, 46, 57,
    82, 107, 112, 117, 123, 173, 221
Percin, Alexandre, 34, 36
Pershing, John J., 86–88, 99,
    103–106, 111
Pétain, Eugénie (Nini), 75–76,
    108–112
  affair with Pétain, 39, 41–42,
    66–68, 108–109
  correspondence with, 148–149
  early relationship with Pétain, 23,
    31–32
  marriage to Pétain, 112–113,
    190–191
  and Pétain's imprisonment,
    260–261, 264–270
  and son Pierre, 109, 111, 130, 270
  support for Pétain, 218–219, 231,
    241–242

Pétain family
  Adélaïde (sister), 9, 111
  Clotilde (mother), 6, 9–10
  Cyrille (uncle), 7
  history, 7–9
  Omer-Venant (father), 6–7, 9, 25
  Sara (sister), 111–112
Pétain, Philippe
  filming of, 267
  handshake with Hitler, 152, 178,
    180, 217
  health, 139, 149, 156, 165, 187,
    196, 218, 262, 264–266,
    268–269
  lectures on military strategy, 32,
    34–41, 125–126
  old age's effects on, 35, 128, 143,
    155, 161, 165, 187, 203,
    221–222, 264, 267
  political blunders, 4, 14, 165–166,
    178, 183, 191
  promotions, 20–21, 26, 28, 30–31,
    34–36, 41, 49, 53, 60, 62, 66,
    72–73, 123, 204
  relinquishing of executive powers,
    218–219
  seen as senile, 127, 129, 245, 257
  self-importance of, 6, 132, 221
  as *sous-lieutenant,* 22–23, 31, 40
  trial of, 198, 244, 247–251, 261
  as "Victor of Verdun," 1, 73–74, 109,
    116, 123, 154, 189, 197, 259
Peterson, Maurice, 149, 152
Peyrouton, Marcel, 181, 190
Plan XVII, 44–45
  Plan XVII(b), 45
Plevna, 20–21
Poniatowski, André, 223, 271
Popular Front, 137–139, 142–143,
    154, 233, 249
Primo de Rivera, Miguel, 128, 149,
    271
  influence on Pétain, 124, 137, 139,
    164, 187
  relationship with Pétain, 117–122,
    127
Prussia, 14, 16, 19, 22, 24, 26, 37,
    64, 228, 238, 253
Pucheu, Pierre, 190, 199–200, 202,
    204, 243

Rapallo, conference at, 91
Redressement français, 124
Regad, Marie-Louise, 25, 110, 112
Reinebeck, Otto, 240–241
Renthe-Fink, Cecil von, 180, 226,
    228–229, 231–234, 240–241
Reynaud, Paul, 144–145, 151,
    153–163, 251, 253, 261, 265
Ribbentrop, Joachim von, 175–177,
    189, 218, 225–226, 237
Ribot, Alexandre, 77–78, 80–81
Riffians, 118, 120–121, 124
Rochat, Charles, 209, 214, 255
Rommel, Erwin, 193, 202, 209
Roosevelt, Franklin, 3, 160–161, 163,
    186–187, 194, 200–202, 206,
    210, 224, 230, 237
Rougier Affair, 177–180
Russia, 14, 20–21, 43–44, 81–82,
    87–91, 107, 131, 194, 196–197,
    209

Saint-Cyr military academy, 16–22
Saint-Omer, 8, 10–12, 15–16,
    41–42
"Saturday Surprises," 135, 137
Sauckel, Fritz, 207, 220–222, 229
Saussier, Félix, 30
Scheurer-Kestner, Auguste, 29
Schlieffen, Graf Alfred von, 44, 51
Serrigny, Bernard
    on compromise peace, 221
    on France's status in WWII, 171,
        176, 190, 201, 203, 219
    and Pétain's stay in Voisins,
        231–232
    relationship with Pétain, 55–56, 76,
        173–174, 198, 217–218,
        226–227
    in WWI, 67–68
Service d'Ordre Légionaire, 220
    see also Milice
Service du Travail Obligatoire,
    221–222
Sigmaringen, 238–240, 266
Simon, Joseph, 244–245, 260–268
Souilly, 60, 68–69, 72–73, 78
Soviet Union, 133, 142, 194, 197
Spain, 262, 269
    civil war in, 141, 145, 175

involvement in Morocco, 117–118,
    121–122
Laval in, 245, 253
Pétain's ambassadorship to,
    147–152, 154
relations with France, 121–122
Spears, Edward Louis, 54–55, 82, 85,
    91, 127, 155, 158–159
SS (Schutzstaffel), 182, 207, 220, 228,
    239, 252
Statut des juifs, 175
    see also anti-Semitism
Stavisky, Serge, 132
Stohrer, Eberhard von, 152
Stresemann, Gustav, 125
Stucki, Walter, 229–230, 246, 271
Supreme War Council, 92–93,
    99–100, 105
Switzerland, 6, 24, 142, 206,
    241–242, 264

Teitgen, Pierre-Henri, 189, 247
Toulon
    see French fleet
Tracou, Jean, 229, 231–232
treaties
    Frankfurt treaty, 24
    French expectation of during WWII,
        164–165, 173, 175
    Treaty of Locarno, 125
    Treaty of Fez, 117–119
    Treaty of Versailles, 111, 125, 135
Tuck, Pinkney, 210–212

United States, 78, 81, 89, 140, 158,
    160, 162, 186, 197, 201, 203,
    212–213, 217, 221, 230, 237,
    251, 264

Vallat, Xavier, 191, 196
Vauthier, Paul, 128–129, 148
Verdun, 1–4, 80, 87–88, 90, 93,
    104–105, 107–109, 125, 139,
    146, 151, 164, 167, 211, 252,
    267, 269–271
    Battle of, 63–75
Versailles, 15, 19–20, 92–93, 100,
    111, 114, 116, 125, 135, 171,
    181–183, 185
Veterans Association, 124

Vichy
  description of town, 168
  government at, 168–175, 179, 196,
    213, 219–223, 225–239,
    253–256, 265–267
Villenueve-Loubet (L'Ermitage),
    111–112, 127–128, 150, 152, 221
von Bülow, Karl, 48–49, 51
von Hausen, Baron Max, 48
von Kluck, Alexander, 48, 51
von Rundstedt, Gerd, 232
von Tannstein, Kurt, 240–241

Westwall, 136, 143–144, 239
Weygand, Maxime, 202, 212, 214–216,
    218, 225, 252–253, 256, 271
  in North Africa, 176, 179, 186–187
  role in Conseil Supérieur de la
    Guerre, 91, 127–128

and Reynaud's War Committee,
    154, 156–162
in Vichy government, 165,
    167–168, 170–171, 173, 183,
    193–194, 199–200
warnings regarding French Army's
    post-WWI strength, 131–132,
    134–135
Wilson, Henry, 80, 95–96, 100, 105,
    111, 161
Wilhelm (Crown Prince),
    65, 69
Wilhelm (Kaiser), 69

youth organizations, 175, 188
  see also Boy Scouts

Zeude, Alphonse, 268
Zurlinden, Emile, 30